The African American Odyssey of John Kizell

The AFRICAN AMERICAN ODYSSEY *of* JOHN KIZELL

A South Carolina Slave Returns to
Fight the Slave Trade in His African Homeland

KEVIN G. LOWTHER

The University of South Carolina Press

© 2011 University of South Carolina

Cloth edition published by the University of South Carolina Press, 2011
Paperback edition published by the University of South Carolina Press, 2012
Ebook edition published in Columbia, South Carolina,
by the University of South Carolina Press, 2012

www.sc.edu/uscpress

Manufactured in the United States of America

21 20 19 18 17 16 15 14 13 12   10 9 8 7 6 5 4 3 2 1

The Library of Congress has cataloged the cloth edition as follows:

Lowther, Kevin.
   The African American odyssey of John Kizell : a South Carolina slave returns to fight the
slave trade in his African homeland / by Kevin G. Lowther ; foreword by Joseph Opala.
       p. cm.
   Includes bibliographical references and index.
   ISBN 978-1-57003-960-7 (cloth : alk. paper)
   1. Kizell, John, ca. 1760–ca. 1830. 2. African Americans—Colonization—Sierra Leone.
3. Sierra Leone—History—To 1896. 4. Slave trade—Sierra Leone—History. 5. African
American loyalists—Biography. 6. Slaves—South Carolina—Biography. 7. Sierra
Leone Company. I. Title.
   DT516.72.K49L68 2011
   306.3'62092–dc22
   [B]

                                                                          2011005929

ISBN 978-1-61117-133-4 (ebook)
ISBN 978-1-61117-141-9 (pbk)

To Christopher Fyfe and to the ancestors

CONTENTS

ILLUSTRATIONS

FOREWORD

John Kizell's life was filled with danger and determination. Born in the Sierra Leone region of West Africa about 1760, he was torn from his family as a boy and taken on the Middle Passage to slavery in South Carolina. When the American Revolutionary War erupted, he took his chance, like many other slaves, and served in the British army, hoping that his new masters would reward his military service with freedom. When the British lost the war, Kizell was lucky to be among the three thousand "black loyalist" soldiers and dependents the British evacuated to Nova Scotia in 1783.

But his struggles had only just begun. The white loyalists taking refuge in Canada at the same time did their best to maintain the racial hierarchy that had served them so well in America, and Kizell and his fellow former slaves had new battles to fight. Canada's climate was bitter for them in more ways than one—having fought a hot war in America to gain their freedom, they now had to fight a cold war in Nova Scotia just to retain it.

By the time John Kizell was just thirty years old, he had already survived four episodes brimming with danger—the slave trade in Africa, bondage in America, the battlefields of the American Revolution, and the continuing struggle for freedom in Canada. These experiences alone would have made his life a remarkable saga, but his story does not end there. In 1792 Kizell joined the nearly twelve hundred black loyalists—or "Nova Scotians"—who left Canada for Sierra Leone. By a strange twist of fate, he was returning to his home region in Africa to help found the colony of Freetown on the site of an earlier settlement for freed slaves that was destroyed just three years before. Kizell and his fellow settlers had to contend with the African king who burned the first colony and with the British merchants at the Bance Island slave castle just seventeen miles upriver. For decades their colony of freed slaves had to coexist with the Atlantic slave trade still going on around their frail settlement in every direction.

Kizell and the other Nova Scotian settlers also had to contend with the British "philanthropists" of the Sierra Leone Company who sponsored their colony. Their benefactors were well-meaning but also painfully paternalistic; and some of the white merchants they sent out from England to help promote the colony's development were openly resentful of the settlers' economic ambitions. The British officials who ran the colony were also hostile to the settlers' American-style individualism. These former slaves may have fought for the British to gain their freedom, but their political instincts, it seems, were still American, and they bristled when their British benefactors made laws for them without their consent. Kizell's response was to leave

Freetown and spend much of his time trading and farming south of the colony in the Sherbro area, where he originally came from. He became a man of two worlds and not fully comfortable in either. He resented the white man's paternalism, but he also raged at his own people's participation in the slave trade. He confronted the African kings repeatedly and sent detailed reports on their slaving activities back to the British governor in Freetown.

Yet Kizell's success as a merchant and farmer—and the respect he gained from both British officials and local African rulers—put him at the center of some important developments of his time. Kizell befriended Paul Cuffe when he sailed his ship *Traveller* from Philadelphia to Freetown in 1811, bringing black settlers from the United States and trying to establish commercial opportunities for his people on both sides of the Atlantic. And later, when the American Colonization Society sent its first settlers to West Africa in 1820 to establish the Liberia colony, the society turned to Kizell to find the right spot for the settlement. He took these black American pilgrims to his own home area in the Sherbro country, which turned out in the end to be a disastrous mistake that plunged him into bitter controversy. But when Liberia emerged a few years later, it was located not far south of the place Kizell had first recommended.

Kevin Lowther brings John Kizell's tumultuous story back to life. This is no small feat given that the records of Kizell's existence are sparse, to say the least, and scattered across three continents. But Lowther scoured libraries and archives for official documents, newspaper accounts, and Kizell's few remaining letters and dispatches; and he visited the sites of his subject's exploits, including his former haunts in Nova Scotia. Lowther also has the advantage of having served as a Peace Corps volunteer in Sierra Leone during the 1960s, so he knows the language, culture, and character of the people in the place Kizell came from before he was enslaved—and the place he returned to after he gained his freedom. But Lowther's greatest accomplishment with this book is the way he weaves the scattered sources on Kizell together with the myriad details of time and place to produce a seamless narrative that vividly reflects all the danger, passion, turmoil, and commitment of John Kizell's long and eventful life.

Many Americans are only now learning about the black loyalists and their own struggle for independence during the American Revolutionary War and afterward in Canada and Sierra Leone. Two excellent books on this subject appeared in 2005—Adam Hochschild's *Bury the Chains* and Simon Schama's *Rough Crossings*. Both these works allow the Africans—and not just the British and Americans—to speak for themselves, but like so many earlier retellings of this tale, they present the black loyalist saga from a group perspective. The advantage of Lowther's narrative is that it tells the story through the eyes of just *one* interesting and determined man. Looking through John Kizell's eyes, we can see the many complex calculations the black loyalists had to make when dealing with their slave masters in the North American colonies, British officers in the Revolutionary War, white loyalist refugees in Canada, company officials in Freetown, and African chiefs in Sierra Leone. Seeing these situations through Kizell's eyes helps to clarify the politics of the time and brings into sharp focus the many difficult challenges the black loyalists faced in their long journey to freedom.

Lowther's book offers other valuable insights as well. As amazing as it may seem, most readers already familiar with the black loyalist story know little or nothing about John Kizell. Historians have written Freetown's history mostly from the point of view of the British records, and Kizell does not appear there as often as some other prominent "Nova Scotians," such as Thomas Peters. Other settlers, such as Boston King and David George, also left us more autobiographical writings. But Kizell stands out for the fact that he retained his ties to African Americans long after he arrived in Sierra Leone and, believing that black people would never be free and prosperous in America, he was always keen to help other former American slaves return to Africa to rebuild their lives. Lowther has not just given us the first full-length biography of John Kizell; he has also rescued Kizell from obscurity and provided a useful counterpoint to the established literature, which assumes in most cases that, once the Nova Scotians landed in Freetown, they entered a British-dominated world and never looked back to America again.

This book also provides some new insights on a subject of great interest to me personally—the Sierra Leone–Gullah connection, the strong historical ties between Sierra Leoneans and the Gullah people of coastal South Carolina and Georgia. Many South Carolinians were fascinated to learn of this link when it was first brought to public attention in 1990 by the SCETV video documentary *Family across the Sea*. The documentary, for which I was the main historical consultant, covers the eighteenth-century slave-trade links between Bance Island and Charleston and the Sierra Leonean influences that are still evident today in Gullah language and culture. John Kizell's story throws new light on this connection by showing that the Sierra Leone–South Carolina link runs in *two* directions. While many Africans were taken from Sierra Leone to South Carolina, some South Carolina slaves also returned with the black loyalist settlers in 1792, and some of those settlers—like Kizell—had actually been born in Sierra Leone.

Kevin Lowther contacted me when he was first thinking of writing this book, and I put him in contact with Christopher Fyfe, the great old man of Sierra Leone history, knowing that Fyfe would be a font of historical wisdom. Lowther's biography of Kizell is every bit as well written as it is well researched. He gives us a lively, fast-paced narrative worthy in every detail of John Kizell's long and fascinating life.

Joseph Opala

PREFACE

When we met at his London home in 2007, Christopher Fyfe—the late doyen of Sierra Leone historiography—urged me to write about the life and times of John Kizell. He had already gone to the trouble of preparing nine pages of handwritten notes on all the references to Kizell he had found during twelve years of research for *A History of Sierra Leone*, published in 1962. Fyfe was not pleased that I proposed wasting Kizell's story in a historical novel on the colonization movement. Kizell—and history—deserved better, he implied politely but firmly.

Fyfe saw in Kizell an opportunity to begin explaining Sierra Leone's early colonial era through African eyes. There are no serious biographical studies of African figures from this period in Sierra Leonean history. The historical void proved much broader than either Fyfe or I realized. This book, therefore, is as much about the evolution of the African-Atlantic diaspora during the late 1700s and early 1800s as it is about John Kizell. It also is about the forces linking South Carolina and Sierra Leone.

Kizell was born about 1760 near the southeastern coast of present-day Sierra Leone. He was carried to Charleston, South Carolina, shortly before the outbreak of the Revolution. When the city fell to the British in 1780, Kizell reclaimed his freedom and served with English and loyalist forces. At war's end he was evacuated to Nova Scotia with thousands of refugee whites and blacks.

The so-called black loyalists found life in Nova Scotia harsh and not far removed from slavery. Kizell and his young family were among nearly 1,200 people who immigrated in 1792 to Sierra Leone, where British philanthropists hoped to establish a settlement for free blacks. Kizell and his fellow "Nova Scotians" were among the first Africans and African Americans to return to their motherland. He became a trader, peacemaker, and crusader against the slave trade. He also played a seminal role in the colonization movement, which led to the creation of Liberia in 1822.

Kizell's life is accessible largely because he was literate and left behind a body of correspondence and other writing. His reports to British governors at Sierra Leone in 1807–11 are the most detailed firsthand descriptions by an African of the slave trade and its impact on local societies. Although these were published in London in 1812 and again in 1824, historians have largely overlooked them.

The river of Kizell's long life—he lived at least until 1830—was fed by several tributaries. He experienced the age of revolution in America and Europe; he knew the slave trade intimately during its peak decades; having seen more of the "known" world than most of his contemporaries, he probably understood the nature of man as well as many of the great thinkers of his time; he was a critical observer of the political and economic exploitation that animated colonialism; and he was a Pan-Africanist a century before the term was conceived. He also became a devout Christian and accomplished preacher.

Kizell's odyssey allows us to consider several historical themes. His was a distinctly African and American journey. It reveals how West Africans shaped and informed their new world, especially in South Carolina. In Charleston Kizell found a strong sense of community within the city's black majority. Slaves controlled much of Charleston's economic life, exercised a considerable degree of de facto independence, and contributed substantively to the creation of an urbanized nexus that linked Europe, Africa, the Caribbean, the diverse American provinces to the north, and indigenous nations to the immediate west.

Studies of the slave trade have focused on the obvious horrors of its logistics and economics. Less attention has been given to its impact on African communities. Even less has been devoted to the cultural-religious context of a world tangibly shared with ancestors and spirits, both beneficent and evil. Because Kizell's life enables us to examine how the trade developed and flourished in this context and in a specific part of the West African coast, it is possible to discern why this happened with African complicity. It also is possible to consider how the slave trade and the colonial experience may still haunt Sierra Leone in real and troubling ways.

Sierra Leone was the first colony consciously developed by Europeans in Africa. Almost from its inception in 1787, it prefigured Europeans' arrogation of a "civilizing" mission during the next two centuries. Kizell and his fellow pilgrims had been promised that they would effectively govern themselves in Sierra Leone. Their English benefactors, thinking twice of such a radical notion, reneged.

Kizell was a "race" man. Nothing in his seven years as someone's property in South Carolina, or in Nova Scotia's inhospitable exile, prompted him to believe that black people had a tenable future in America. Blacks belonged in Africa, he said, and Africa belonged to black people. He was convinced that blacks, in effect trapped in America, would willingly return to their homeland if given the chance. His involvement in receiving the first African American colonists in 1820 proved abortive, but he was nonetheless a godfather of the free black settlement of Liberia.

Researching and writing this book has brought me full circle to September 1963, when I arrived in Sierra Leone as a Peace Corps volunteer to teach history at a Freetown secondary school. I had been a history major in college but knew nothing of Africa, not to mention African American history. I owe my subsequent reeducation to many: my former students in Sierra Leone, Africans from all parts of the continent, and African Americans too numerous to name. I owe a special debt to John Kizell and to the remarkable life he lived.

Without John Kizell's assistance, particularly the letters and reports he sent to British governors Ludlam and Columbine in the early 1800s, this book would not have been possible. Kizell provided just enough information about his origins and enslavement to reconstruct a plausible account of his youth and his years in South Carolina. Although much else must be inferred, he left a visible trail in a variety of sources throughout his long life. Sadly efforts to uncover oral and family history in Sierra Leone were unproductive. The Kizell name today apparently is unknown in Freetown and the Sherbro region.

Given Kizell's ability to write observantly and at length, his detailed reports on the slave trade and life in the Sherbro suggest that there may be additional written works awaiting discovery. The documents published in London are referred to as "extracts," and the originals appear to have been lost. So, apparently, were documents Kizell prepared for the abolitionists Thomas Clarkson and William Allen. Historians and archivists should be alert for other Kizell manuscripts and correspondence.

History is inherently evanescent. The leather-bound volume containing 225 pages of William Allen's African correspondence, discovered a generation ago in a London warehouse, has again gone missing. Thankfully someone at GlaxoSmithKline, the company that descends from Allen's pharmaceutical firm, thought to photocopy this essential material. It includes, among other things, the only known evidence that Kizell was reunited with his blood relations. Although rebels vandalized the Sierra Leone National Archives in 1999, archivist Albert Moore was able to locate records to corroborate Christopher Fyfe's exhaustive research notes from the 1950s. Otherwise we would not know that Kizell was holding a slave trader—and fellow Nova Scotian— at his village in 1830.

The mosaics of any historical narrative are scattered among dozens of locations— in this instance across half the globe. The most essential for this work have been the South Carolina Department of Archives and History, the South Carolina Historical Society, and the National Archives of the United Kingdom at Kew. Yet virtually every library and archive consulted, from the Library of Congress and the British Library to the Shelburne County Museum in Nova Scotia, the Warren M. Robbins Library in Washington, D.C., the Tompkins Library in Edgefield, South Carolina, and the Massachusetts Historical Society, provided invaluable contributions to a fuller understanding of Kizell's life and times.

ACKNOWLEDGMENTS

John Kizell's life was linked—like any life—to people he knew and many whom he did not. Similarly the exploration and telling of his life's story has connected me with dozens of people, most of them complete strangers, who made this book possible. Their willingness to respond and share at key moments was beyond all expectation. As a nonacademic, I owe special gratitude to the several historians and scholars who have treated this work with unstinting professional courtesy and respect.

In the beginning three people were critical to launching this project. Joe Opala, who had documented ties between the Gullah-speaking peoples and the Mende of Sierra Leone, was the first to suggest that I write about Kizell's life. He also helped me to begin networking with persons with specialized knowledge of Sierra Leone, the slave trade, and colonial South Carolina. The contributions of the late Christopher Fyfe are described in the preface. I can only hope that I have adequately repaid his friendship and faith. Finally Alexander Moore, an acquisitions editor at the University of South Carolina Press, supported the project throughout its genesis.

Special thanks go to Jane Aldrich of the South Carolina Historical Society; William Armstrong, longtime friend and experienced biographer; Margaret Bowen, who made possible my research in London; Finn Bower, curator of the Shelburne County Museum in Nova Scotia; Tonya Browder, of the Old Edgefield (S.C.) District Genealogical Society; Christopher X. Campbell of GlaxoSmithKline in London, who ensured my access to William Allen's African correspondence; Beverly Cox, of the Black Loyalist Heritage Society in Birchtown, Nova Scotia; David Eltis of Emory University, who helped me to navigate the slave-ship database; Adam Jones of the University of Leipzig in Germany, who shared his expertise on Kizell's homeland in the Gallinas region of Sierra Leone; Mary Robertson of the Huntington Library, who was especially helpful in accessing Zachary Macaulay's journals; Lamont D. Thomas, who shared research material from his own biography of Paul Cuffe; Peter L. Tucker, chairman of the Law Reform Commission in Sierra Leone, who was extraordinarily forthcoming in discussing the history of his forebears and their connection to the slave trade; and Ruth Holmes Whitehead, a transplanted South Carolina historian based at the Nova Scotia Museum in Halifax.

Carl Borick, Nicholas Butler, and Harlan M. Greene helped to answer questions about Charleston's colonial history; Robert Dunkerly, Michael Scoggins, and Bobby Gilmer Moss aided my understanding of the battle of Kings Mountain and its aftermath; staff of the South Carolina Department of Archives and History in Columbia and the Library of Congress provided assistance during my several visits; Arthur Abraham, Mac Dixon-Fyle, Tucker Childs, Philip Misevich, and Konrad Tuchsherer offered valuable insights to aspects of Sierra Leonean cultures; and Toni Carrier of the Africana Heritage Project at the University of South Florida was helpful in the early stages of research.

Several librarians and archivists went to special lengths. They include Albert Moore of the Sierra Leone National Archives, Roberta (Robin) Copp of the South Caroliniana Library, Valerie Harris of the University of Illinois at Chicago Library, Janet Stanley of the Warren M. Robbins Library of the National Museum of African Art in Washington, D.C., Marion Wallace of the British Library, and Mary O. Klein of the Maryland Episcopal Diocesan Archives.

Many others have helped in ways whose importance they cannot fully appreciate. They include Danna Van Brandt of the United States Embassy in Freetown; the Honorable Walter C. Carrington, former U.S. ambassador to Senegal and Nigeria; Gary Walker; Helene Cooper of the *New York Times*; Paul Cyr of the New Bedford (Mass.) Free Public Library; Rosemary Franklin of the University of Cincinnati Library; Michael Finley; Phedson Mwambete and Umaru Fofana in Freetown; Niko Pfund, of the Oxford University Press; Bill Nelson, cartographer; Eve Sullivan; Caitlin Corless of the Massachusetts Historical Society; and David Cole of Westport, Massachusetts. Finally my friend and mentor C. Payne Lucas has guided me down many paths, which ultimately led to the writing of this story.

Much of the original research for this book was conducted at the University of Michigan in 1976–77, under a grant for working journalists funded by the National Endowment for the Humanities. Two professors then at the university, Dr. Ali Mazrui and Harold Cruse, enriched my understanding of African history and African contributions to American society and culture.

Every acknowledgment ends, as it should, with family. Without the encouragement and sensitivities of my South Carolinian spouse, Patricia, I could never have begun to appreciate the state's history and culture, particularly as it touches the African American experience. Our daughters, Allison and Andrea, helped me through occasional computer glitches and serendipitously found an unexpected trove of source material.

CHRONOLOGY OF
JOHN KIZELL'S LIFE

1760 | Born in the Gallinas region of modern-day Sierra Leone

1773 | Captured in an attack on his uncle's village; subsequently accused of witchcraft, sold to a slave trader in the Gallinas, and shipped to Charleston, South Carolina

1780 | Joins the British military in a noncombat role following the American surrender of Charleston in May; taken prisoner by the Americans on October 7 at the battle of Kings Mountain; apparently escapes and returns to Charleston

1782 | Evacuated by British to New York with other loyalists and English soldiers

1783 | As a so-called black loyalist, evacuated in April to Nova Scotia and settled near Shelburne

1792 | With his young family, joins nearly 1,200 other black loyalists in an exodus to the new English colony of Sierra Leone

1794 | Travels to London as witness against alleged Nova Scotian dissidents

1796 | With two friends launches a small sloop and begins trading in the Sherbro; participates in the first Baptist mission in Africa in nearby Port Logo

1799 | Sends nine-year-old son, George, to school in England

1805 | Having settled in the Sherbro, negotiates a cease-fire in a widespread and long-standing local war

1810 | On behalf of the British governor, undertakes mission to persuade chiefs and people throughout the Sherbro to stop trading in slaves; his detailed reports and letters are published in London in 1812 by the African Institution

1811 | Meets African American shipowner Paul Cuffe on Cuffe's visit to Freetown and establishes the Friendly Society to promote trade between settlers in Sierra Leone and black communities in the United States

1813 | Reunited with his father's brother and his mother's people

1816–18 | Encourages Cuffe and colonization supporters in America to consider the Sherbro to settle free blacks

1820 | Receives, at his village on Sherbro Island, the first black settlers sent by the American Colonization Society

1821 | Defends his role in the abortive settlement at Sherbro, which leads in the following year to the establishment of the African American colony of Liberia

1825 | Delivers to James Tucker, a powerful chief in the Sherbro, the governor's threat of death if he does not cease trading in slaves

1826 | Testifies to a British commission inquiring into the history and status of the colony at Sierra Leone

1830 | Detains a fellow Nova Scotian for allegedly kidnapping five liberated African boys

The date and circumstances of Kizell's death are unknown.

The African American Odyssey of John Kizell

1

CHAINED TOGETHER

"If you love your children, if you love your country, if you love the God of love, clear your land of slaves; burden not your hearts nor your country with them."

Bishop Richard Allen, to slave owners, 1794

"If I was concerned in the African Trade," Henry Laurens had written from London that March, "I would be cautious this Year of sending many Negroes to Carolina."

The year was 1773. Laurens—once the leading slave merchant in Charleston—worried that South Carolina's planters risked being "overstocked" with slaves and burdened with debt made all the riskier in the province's "present relaxed State of Government."

Laurens had abjured selling slaves years earlier, but his instincts for the business remained honed. The rice and indigo crops had been bountiful in 1772. He feared that his fellow planters would now overexpand production and import more slaves than they could afford.[1]

Laurens's concern seemed misplaced. Supply was failing to meet demand. On May 31, 1773, the *South Carolina Gazette and Country Journal* reported that the large number of slave ships arriving in Charleston belied the number of Africans actually on board. "Although there are now no less than Twelve Cargoes of Negroes for Sale here," the *Gazette* noted, "yet the Number . . . does not exceed 1900; most of the vessels having come off the coast with less than Half the Quantity of Slaves they were sent to purchase."[2]

The African Trade

Laurens had predicted—with some accuracy—that at least eight thousand Africans would be imported into South Carolina in 1773.[3] One of them, in all likelihood, was a spindly thirteen-year-old boy who would be known most of his life as John Kizell. Someone—possibly his African owner—had accused him of being a witch. It was a common pretext for disposing of surplus labor in West Africa.

The boy had been sold to a slave dealer along one of the mangrove-lined creeks feeding the Gallinas River in today's southeastern Sierra Leone. There he would have been confined in a rough stockade, along with those taken in some conflict far from the coast, men falsely accused of "damaging" one of a chief's several wives, and other hapless witches. And there he would have remained until a slave ship captain arrived to negotiate for whatever slaves might be available.

2

The *Blossom*, captained by William Briggs, arrived in Charleston on May 24. It had left Cape Mount, just southeast of the Gallinas, with 336 slaves. When it landed—its cargo to be quarantined for several days on Sullivan's Island—274 were still alive. Mortality on the so-called Middle Passage had been substantially higher than normal. About one in seven slaves died on voyages from West Africa to Charleston in the early 1770s. One in five had died aboard the *Blossom*. Whether it was this ship that had carried him, or some other vessel "concerned in the African Trade," John Kizell had survived the first of many trials to come.[4]

Slave ships represented both the physical and psychological extremes of human degradation. Captains and crews shared a living—and dying—hell with their captives. In percentage terms, crew mortality often exceeded that of the enslaved cargo. A day seldom passed during the several weeks at sea when someone did not die. There was filth and feces. There was fever and dysentery. There was a stench that suffused every nook and cranny. And there was fear—among the crew, especially when Africa remained near, and among the humans stored below.

The boy and the others chained to one another knew what was happening. They understood that they were being separated from family, friends, and—equally important—from their ancestors. They understood that they would never again know their world. They probably had at least anecdotal awareness of where they were being taken and the alien experience in store.

Many may have shared the long-standing belief that they were to be consumed by the white men, which was not altogether illogical in the context of West African history. But it was their sense of loss—not of liberty per se but of their ties to kinship networks, to the land, and to their place in the African continuum of existence—that most frightened them.

An experienced slave ship captain knew this. He knew that, given the chance, many among his cargo would hurl themselves into the sea—to die and join their ancestors. He knew that many would be depressed or suicidal. He also knew that they had every reason—and the capability—to seize the ship and sail back toward the rising sun. It had happened often enough.

So it is no surprise that a woman aboard John Kizell's ship refused to eat, intending to die and return home. Nor was it surprising that the captain had her tied on deck, with Kizell and others brought up to witness her flogged—deliberately—to death. Better to let this one woman "go home" on his terms—terms that would dissuade others from starving themselves to death and depriving him and the vessel's owners of their profit.[5]

It would have meant nothing to the boy that the rice and indigo harvests had been bountiful in South Carolina the year before.[6] If he was not helping his father in their own field, he might have been hunting birds with a slingshot or catching fish in a nearby stream. He might have been sitting with his age-mates beneath a majestic cotton silk tree, talking in hushed tones about their approaching initiation into Poro, into manhood.

In the evening, seated with the other children as the village gathered to be entertained, he might have listened raptly to an old man recite fables and fearsome stories about animals behaving like humans and devils living in the bush. Of such nights, a Sherbro remembered of his youth, "we trembled in the darkness and avoided the loneliest places" for days to come.[7]

The rice and indigo harvests in a place called South Carolina would have been far beyond their ken or caring. They knew about slaves, however. Many of the people in the village were bound to others, who "owned" them and their families, within a traditional framework of mutual obligations. They knew as well about people—even some who lived among them—who were sold to the white men, in their large ships draped with billowing cloth.

They were aware that the white men wanted slaves of their own and were willing to trade rum, muskets, gunpowder, tobacco, and other goods to which their people had become accustomed. But they would not have known about the large crops of rice and indigo that the white men's slaves had grown in the South Carolina lowcountry in 1772. Nor would they have known that the people to whom these slaves were bound planned to clear and drain swaths of new land to grow even more rice and indigo; and that to do so they would need to send more ships to buy more of their people than ever before in a single year.

The importation of slaves into South Carolina over the preceding decade had been extremely volatile—but not entirely unpredictable. Henry Laurens was prescient in 1773. As many as 9,000 Africans may have arrived in Charleston that year—nearly twice the 4,800 in 1772. A mere 2,500 had been imported in 1764, but nearly three times as many in the following year as planters expanded in the lowcountry. Then no slaves were brought in during four of the next five years. In 1766–68 high customs duties virtually shut down the trade in slaves, as did South Carolina's agreement in 1769 to ban importation of British goods.[8]

The legislature, subscribing to the nonimportation strategy taking hold among the colonies, promised that South Carolinians would adopt the "utmost economy in our persons, houses, and furniture, particularly that we will give no mourning, or gloves or scarves at funerals." They would also forgo wine and one other form of consumption: fresh slaves.[9]

Abstinence lasted for a year. While some British manufactures slipped through the colonies' boycott, England in 1770 repealed some of the despised imposts on paper, glass, and painter's pigments. Tacitly conceding Americans' right to refuse to pay taxes without representation, Parliament stubbornly left one duty standing: on tea.[10]

The economy immediately bloomed in Charleston and South Carolina, at least for the merchants and planters. But it was a false prosperity. In her classic analysis of Charleston's business climate in the years leading to the Revolution, Leila Sellers recalls what seemed a bounteous era. "From the spring of 1771 until the fall of 1774," she writes, "was a time of great business activity. Great quantities of East India tea were being imported despite the non-importation agreement, great numbers of slaves were being brought in and sold at fancy prices, and bills of exchange were selling at a premium, a sure sign that the planter was in debt to the merchant."[11]

The dozen or more recently arrived cargoes of slaves prompted mixed reactions in Charleston in mid-1773. Artisans and mechanics already regarded the city's abundant pool of skilled slaves as direct competition. Nor were they benefiting from the reopening of trade with England. Peter Timothy, the publisher of the *South Carolina Gazette and Country Journal*, championed the artisan class. Though a slave owner himself, he was dubious that importing large numbers of slaves was in everyone's best interest.[12]

"Nothing," the *Gazette* warned on June 7, "could have happened more injurious to the British merchants concerned in the Slave Trade, than the recent Stop put to granting of Lands, at the same Time that the First Cutting of Indico is lost: But for these Events, the Cargoes of Negroes now here . . . would have been sold at considerably higher Prices than they are now likely to be."[13]

Merchants and planters—dependent respectively on the trade in slaves and on slave labor—were vulnerable to the crosscurrents of revolutionary ferment and a mercantile system controlled by the mother country. The slave trade, which operated like any other business—on credit—was becoming a financial burden to its principals as the numbers increased dramatically. By late 1773 hard money and bills of exchange had become "very scarce" in Charleston, according to one merchant. "All the Dollars and Heavy Gold has been sent to Great Britain for Remittance."[14] Some of it had paid for a thirteen-year-old boy accused of witchcraft.

Cautious businessman and plantation owner that he was, Laurens had looked beyond planters' unbridled enthusiasm for more land and thus for more slaves. He may not have been alone. While he remained in London, his fellow planters and merchants in the provincial congress never mentioned the slave trade when debating a renewed nonimportation association to take effect on December 1, 1774. By now many may have doubted its benefits.[15] They would import less than half the slaves in 1774 that they had the previous year. They would boycott the trade altogether in 1775. None could know that it would be eight years before another slave ship came up from Rebellion Road.

Charleston and its lowcountry hinterland were the wealthiest—and yet the most dangerous—places in colonial North America. Wealth was measured in land, rice, indigo, and slaves. Danger was measured in violence and disease. Laurens not only feared that the "vast importation of Negroes" would lead to greater indebtedness; he believed it would "greatly expose the capital to Infectious Distempers, Smallpox or Fevers," which in turn would further degrade the sale price of new slaves.[16]

Although slave ships were required to quarantine their human cargoes for ten days, the pesthouse on Sullivan's Island could not effectively handle the thousands of Africans arriving during the peak months. Judging from the arrival and auction dates in newspaper advertisements for large slave shipments in mid-1773, the quarantine process often was cut short.

Like many such announcements, the notice in the May 25 *Gazette* assured the public that the "NEGROES" aboard the *Blossom* were "prime and healthy" and "directly from . . . Africa." Slave merchants and planters could only be certain that the new arrivals were indeed straight from Africa—and thus not "contaminated" by exposure to West Indies slavery. They could not be sure that they were "prime and healthy." What counted was that they were survivors.[17] 5

Survival preoccupied whites. "It was the violence of eighteenth-century life that kept Charleston society fluid," writes historian George C. Rogers Jr. "Disease, fire, hurricanes, and wars kept the people from settling down to a long-term routine. Life was short." Malaria was omnipresent; yellow fever was a periodic reaper; but smallpox was the most dreaded.[18]

Whites internalized what many perceived every day as the greatest threat: a black population that outnumbered them and that—in spite of its enslavement—exerted considerable control over white people's lives and over the economy of the town. When Peter A. Coclanis, in his history of the lowcountry economy, refers to the "spirit and soul" of Charleston on the eve of the Revolution, he is alluding to its embodiment of the area's burgeoning wealth and the white society that fed upon it.[19] Charleston's spirit and soul, however, reflected the vibrancy of its African and African American majority as much as—if not more than—the planter-merchant aristocracy or the white artisans and mechanics. When John Kizell was led in chains onto a Cooper River wharf, he joined the second largest urban black community in the world. Only London's was greater.

Not far to the west of that wharf—somewhere on King Street—the widow of a German innkeeper, Conrad Kysell, was still sorting out his affairs. As his executrix Esther Kysell had already auctioned Lucca and Nancy, their two "negro wenches," as Kysell described them in his will.[20] He had bequeathed to his brother-in-law, George Fulker, most of his other possessions—his land, horses, a watch, and silver buckles, as well as his "artillery regimentals and accoutrements." The latter bespoke a former life in the Palatine.

Esther had the tavern to run and money—perhaps from the sale of Lucca and Nancy—to invest in land. While the *Blossom*'s "New Negroes" were being dispersed, Esther was about to purchase two and a half acres in Charleston, originally part of the "general plan of George Anson, Esquire."[21] Lucca and Nancy each would have been worth the land's price of three hundred pounds.

"New Negroes" in South Carolina would soon detect the tension brewing among whites. The genie of rebellion was out of the bottle. One of the first things a young arrival from Africa learned was that the white people were divided over their loyalty to a king who ruled from a great distance. He would also hear rumors that Africans who lived under that king, in his own country, had recently been restored their freedom. In Africa a good king protected his people—even his slaves. The "New Negroes" from the *Blossom* would begin to form their own opinions about the white people's king and listen closely to what was said about him and his policies.

6   Blacks throughout the American colonies, and especially in Charleston, were at least vaguely aware that a judge in England had recently "freed" the slaves there. Slavery remained legal, but the decision effectively meant that one could not be a slave in England. If the nuances of Chief Justice Lord Mansfield's decision were lost among most in America, slave and free, there was a general apprehension that something important had occurred and that it threatened the basis of slavery. Laurens's servant—"my foolish Rascally Robert"—had followed the Somerset case, as it was known, and fraternized with London's black community. He came and went more or less as he pleased and had begun acting as though he were a free man.[22]

There was much to whisper about, discuss, and ponder in the Charleston that the thirteen-year-old African boy encountered in the bewildering first days ashore. He may not have appreciated the import of the news that the British Parliament had just passed something called the Tea Act, but he could not fail to notice that it agitated the whites.

He would have listened with greater comprehension to those countrymen who understood the white man's language, as they passed along published news reverberating throughout the city: Slaves on the *New Britannia* had seized the ship in the Gambia River. While the crew struggled to restore control, the ship had exploded, killing everyone aboard—including more than two hundred slaves.[23]

To whites this was further evidence that blacks were inherently rebellious and not to be trusted. To blacks—certainly the many who were African born—the demise of the *New Britannia* indicated the agency of powerful spirits. They knew that in Africa all events—as well as one's fate—were linked to forces that the white people did not, and perhaps never would, understand.

"My scruples are vanished"

From shore the vessel anchored in midriver looked like any other seagoing ship. The nearly naked boy and his fellow captives could perhaps glimpse her through the stockade of tree trunks and bamboo poles. They would have seen a few bearded white men, stripped to the waist, lowering boxes to the glistening black Krumen in a large dugout canoe. They might have noticed, near the ship's bow, the swivel gun. Only a slaver, which carried no cannons, mounted a swivel gun, to train on the deck to quell a slave uprising.[24]

They might also have noticed strange gold squiggles painted on the ship's stern, not unlike the Arabic script that some understood or had seen used by itinerant Mandingo merchants. They were unaware that these represented the names given by the white men to each of their vessels—in this case, the *Blossom*, of Liverpool. If they turned their attention from the ship, they might have missed two white sailors dropping the limp body of a black man over the side, and the brief thrashing of the crocodile that had been waiting expectantly.

Such scenes were common along the coast, which Captain Briggs and the *Blossom* had been combing for months to fill his ship to capacity. John Kizell left no account of his Middle Passage—apart from the exemplary execution of the woman bent upon starving herself. Henry Smeathman, however, left little to the imagination when he wrote in July 1773 of what he witnessed aboard the *Africa* as it took on slaves at the Isles de Los, two hundred miles northwest of the Gallinas.

Smeathman had come out from England in 1771 to gather botanical specimens in Sierra Leone for London collectors. Unschooled as a botanist, he soon acquired expertise in another trade: slaving. In May 1773 he could write that "my scruples . . . are vanished" respecting the business. But that did not prevent him from documenting its horrors. The *Africa* had just returned to the coast after delivering 185 slaves in Charleston at the end of May. The rains had begun their almost daily deluge. Smeathman, who had seen slaves awaiting shipment near Sierra Leone, had no scruples about revealing the squalor and human degradation endemic to the trade.

"Alas!" he began. "What a scene of misery and distress. . . . The clanking of chains, the groans of the sick and the stench of the whole is scarce supportable. . . . There was . . . two or three slaves thrown overboard every day dying of fever, flux, measles, worms all together. All the day the chains rattling or the sound of the armourer riveting some poor devil just arrived in . . . irons. The WOEMEN slaves in one part beating rice. . . . Here the doctor dressing sores . . . or cramming the men with medicines and another standing over them with a cat to make them swallow . . . their rice."[25]

The same *Africa*, which disgorged survivors of this nightmare in Charleston, may also have carried five men consigned to Henry Laurens by his friend John Holman, an English slave trader based in the Isles de Los. Holman had also sent five leopard skins and a pair of African earrings. Writing on June 9 to Laurens in London, his brother James said he would give the five male slaves to John Lewis Gervais, a prominent Charleston slave dealer, "to sell as he did the former Parcel." Henry Laurens had not entirely abandoned the African trade.[26]

John Kizell, awaiting his fate in an open stockade, was about to become a "parcel," which would be carefully examined by the ship's captain before he negotiated a price. Captains of slavers had to have a keen eye to distinguish the healthy and robust from the weak or sick. The latter would not endure the hellish voyage to come, much less attract a decent price at market.

Still they died in droves—before the journey, during it, and at journey's end. To Alexander Garden, the port physician in Charleston in the 1750s and 1760s, it was "a wonder any escape with life." They continued dying—in quarantine on Sullivan's Island, if not dumped into the harbor soon after arrival. As many as a third consigned to working in the lowcountry could expect to die within their first year.[27]

Sullivan's Island, a few miles east of Charleston proper, was a holding pen where newly arrived slaves could be sorted out in a macabre death watch. Described by a northern visitor as "very sandy, hot, and barren," it was where more than two hundred slaves waited to see who lived and who died. The quarantine also discouraged ships from dumping dead and dying slaves into the harbor. As the governor warned in 1769, dead Africans were polluting the marshes facing the city. "The noisome smell arising from their putrefaction may become dangerous to the health of the inhabitants." He offered a reward to anyone identifying those responsible.[28]

8

The unprecedented numbers of slaves brought into Charleston in the spring and summer of 1773—and the frequent advertisements of slave auctions closely following arrivals—suggests that many ships were permitted to abbreviate or bypass the quarantine.[29] There are no records of the Sullivan's Island operation in this period, so it is impossible to know which ships might have been waived past, the number of slaves actually held for observation, or the death rate among them.

Whether Kizell was compelled to endure the heat and pestilence on Sullivan's Island is problematic. All that mattered, when he stepped onto a Charleston wharf, was that he was alive and marketable. Where he was destined—to a lowcountry plantation or an urban household—was yet to be decided by the whims of those with the cash or credit to buy him.

Plantation owners' collective appetite for slaves—mainly to produce rice—remained voracious. The cultivation of rice had been expanding in South Carolina since the 1720s. This accounted for increasing slave imports, especially in the early 1760s and 1770s, as more planters adopted Africans' well-developed dike technology to control water levels and harness tidal marshes for rice production. In the meantime the market for rice in Britain, Europe, the West Indies, and the northern colonies was brisk.[30]

Cultivating rice was not just labor-intensive; it was labor-destructive. Digging and maintaining canals for irrigation and drainage was hard work. It wore slaves down. So did the slow mortar-and-pestle processing.

Planters knew this, although few may have been as solicitous as Henry Laurens. Concerned that slaves were being misused in the colony's rice plantations, he wrote a long letter to his partner in April 1773 urging that his slaves not be sacrificed "for the sake of a few barrels of Rice." He did not want them "cruelly treated, & driven by severity to such practices, as were never before known among them."[31]

Laurens knew that many of his slaves were African-born and brought with them substantial knowledge of rice cultivation. Using them wisely made considerable sense. Daniel C. Littlefield, in his 1981 study of rice and slavery in colonial South Carolina, points to obvious links between the growth of the rice industry and the importation of slaves skilled in rice cultivation. However, he is unwilling to attribute the crop's development in South Carolina to the conscious recruitment of experienced African rice farmers.[32]

Building on Littlefield's work and Peter Wood's 1974 *Black Majority*, geographer Judith A. Carney directly credits West Africans' expertise in rice cultivation for its success in the lowcountry. Carney uses "a geographical perspective focused on culture, technology, and environment to support the contention that the origin of rice cultivation in South Carolina is indeed African, and that slaves from West Africa's rice region tutored planters in growing the crop."[33]

In earlier decades slaveholders in South Carolina had flattered themselves that they could discriminate among African-born slaves in terms of their origins and their skills. In stereotyping Gambians, who were expert in rice cultivation, versus Calabars and others who were not, they believed they could isolate desirable traits such as strength, endurance, and obedience.

As the proportion of Africans declined vis-à-vis "country-born," or American-born, slaves, planters gradually lost interest in their home regions. They had effectively adapted African rice technology and no longer placed a premium on importing slaves from major rice-growing areas. By the early 1770s, arriving shiploads of slaves were more often advertised simply as from "the coast of Africa." Small lots of slaves were frequently tagged "unknown origin"—a generic term for African.[34]

Kizell could have fallen into either category. Having been purchased at a relatively minor slave factory, probably as part of an odd lot of captives, he would have found himself aboard ship among people from locales scattered over hundreds of miles. Twenty or thirty years earlier, it might have mattered that he did not come from the Gambia, Gold Coast, or some other area fancied in South Carolina. But in 1773 low-country planters and backcountry settlers alike were concerned only with buying as many slaves as they could.

Never had the colony seen such growth or accumulation of wealth. Josiah Quincy Jr., visiting that year from Massachusetts, marveled at "the number of shipping" in Charleston, which "far surpassed all I had ever seen in Boston."[35] Kizell and his fellow Africans would have been equally amazed, if not more so, at the sheer bustle of the harbor and the city beyond.

The boy's youth likely served him well in his transition from African to African American. He may have been physically and mentally more resilient than his elders in the face of their sudden uprooting and the harrowing voyage. Described in adulthood as short, he would have been noticeably small as a boy. Planters looking for tall men, who were most sought, would have ignored him. They wanted young adults who could become productive immediately and quickly amortize their investment.[36]

Even in Charleston whites preferred young slaves who were fit for hard work, if not for the harsher conditions on the plantations. At thirteen the diminutive Kizell would have been desirable mainly to a household or business establishment in need of a servant or messenger.

No documentation or firsthand accounts of Charleston slave sales and auctions in this period have ever been found. The Africans delivered in the *Blossom* were consigned to the firm of Robert, John and James Smith. Their sale was advertised on May 25. There the trail ends. Nonetheless enough is known generally of the selling of slaves in Charleston to provide a telling portrait of the business that governed the immediate destiny of John Kizell.

In polite society the marketing of slaves was not a sordid profession. It attracted some of the most respected white men in the town—Henry Laurens foremost among them—and occupied a public place in day-to-day life and commerce. Laurens and other slave merchants were general importers. They would not have deigned to sell common trade goods, such as clothing and hardware. But "to deal in slaves and indentured white servants was a highly honorable employment," at least according to Sellers.[37]

The buying, transporting, and selling of slaves was not only complex and risky; it also required enormous capital, collateral, and credit. Slave merchants—or factors, as they were known—frequently were planters as well. Some of the most successful— Laurens and his partner, John Lewis Gervais, included—parlayed plantation profits into equally rewarding slave-trading ventures. "The prosperous planter," Sellers writes, "invested his money in a mercantile establishment so that he might service himself, establish direct relations with merchant firms in England and thus free himself from excessive charges of the Charleston merchants."[38]

It also helped to have a financial godfather, as John Hopton well knew. Hopton had learned the business during five years as Laurens's clerk. In April 1771 Laurens and another merchant provided the young Hopton with sureties worth ten thousand pounds sterling to begin trading in slaves. Hopton became one of the most active and successful slave factors in Charleston during the four golden years before the trade was suspended. He and a partner handled at least twenty-four ships, which brought more than 4,600 slaves into Charleston during this frenetic period. One was the *Africa*.[39]

Colonies were dependent on having enough settlers and adequate labor, so it is hardly surprising that what Sellers calls "the most lucrative . . . branch of commerce in the country" was the provision of people—not just African slaves, but thousands of Europeans as well. Dealing "in immigrants and indentured servants was profitable," Sellers writes, "at a time when there was in Great Britain a class of abject, rootless, landless persons. . . . The most valuable part of the import business of Charleston in the eighteenth century was the traffic in white and black people."[40]

The industrial-scale marketing of slaves was highly organized. Importers carefully monitored conditions such as the weather that could affect demand. They provided detailed instructions and market intelligence to the captains who went to Africa on their behalf, often in ships partially owned by the merchant. They advertised sales widely and maintained a network of fellow merchants in Georgia and East Florida to whom they supplied slaves. Profit depended on keeping inventory low and selling slaves as quickly as possible, often on short- or long-term credit.

Large sales of New Negroes usually were held at "public vendues" on the Cooper River wharves, but the selling of country-born slaves was common throughout the town. They could be found for sale almost anywhere, Sellers relates: "the grocery store, the shoemaker's . . . at the race course between the heats of the races, in the public Negro yard, . . . at the retail stores, and at the wholesale warehouses of the big importing merchant."[41]

Although advertisements of slaves direct from Africa appeared regularly in the newspapers, merchants often dispatched messengers and handbills to notify potential buyers in Georgia and North Carolina.[42] This ensured that buyers far from Charleston would be at the auction to bid up prices.

"One of the marked characteristics of the Carolina trade," notes Elizabeth Donnan, an early student of the slave trade, "was the dispatch with which large cargoes were marketed. . . . To a promising sale planters came from one hundred miles, the length of the journey helping to quicken the bidding, since would-be purchasers from remote plantations were reluctant to return empty-handed, and could not easily linger . . . waiting for later vessels." As the backcountry began to fill with settlers, Henry Laurens and other Charleston merchants observed that "planters from the frontier districts typically paid high prices for slaves and met their financial obligations."[43]

Buyers who paid cash could anticipate a 10 percent discount, but merchants had to exercise their business acumen in managing credit extended to many clients. They received credit themselves from slave traders based in Liverpool, Bristol, and London, who underwrote all or most of a voyage's costs. If the harvests were good and planters were able to pay debts incurred for fresh slaves, the Charleston factors did well. In bad crop years, they and the planters paid the consequences.

If a slave merchant "used good judgment in disposing of his slaves," Sellers explains, "and was a good debt collector [he] could gain in good crop years from twelve to seventeen percent upon the sum he remitted to England. . . . But an element of speculation had entered the business. In poor years the planters could not meet their obligations and the factor who was under contract to remit stood a very good chance of losing."[44]

In warning of the risks posed by ambitious slave imports in 1773, Laurens also sensed that deteriorating political relations with England threatened what was a risky proposition even in the best of times. Writing from London that January, Laurens confided to Gervais that Richard Oswald, their former English partner, was planning to withdraw from dealing in slaves. "Mr. Oswald is endeavoring to sell out his interest" in Sierra Leone, Laurens wrote, "but he does not yet speak it publicly." Oswald had long sold large numbers of slaves, through Bance Island (also known as Bunce Island), into South Carolina. Laurens had handled many of the sales in Charleston. Now, for whatever reason, Oswald wished to be done with the African trade.[45]

Laurens and Oswald must have realized—and discussed—the impact that disruption of the slave trade would have in many quarters. They would have appreciated the financial exposure of slave dealers in England and slave factors in Charleston if the American colonies—as appeared likely—persisted in demanding greater autonomy. Many of Oswald's fellow English slave traders did indeed go bankrupt during the rebellion to come.

The world was changing for Laurens and Oswald as thoroughly, if not as traumatically, as it had for John Kizell. Regardless of their political tendencies, they were men of business who wished only to maintain themselves much as they always had. But

African-born slaves such as Kizell had already endured existential change so extreme that they could only dream of returning to the world that they and their ancestors had known.

The Tolling Bells

Africans arriving in Charleston heard an ominous, surreal, and—until now—unknown sound. The pealing of bells, especially in the night, haunted their confinement on Sullivan's Island. In Africa drums often spoke in the darkness. What strange and terrible things might this unseen signal portend?[46]

What awaited them in the spring of 1773 would have overwhelmed the senses of young men, women, and children who weeks before had known very different sights and sounds in Africa: women singing as they rhythmically pounded rice, men patiently hewing a canoe from a tree trunk, the chattering of monkeys and other forest voices, a python slithering across a path between high grass, the mingled aromas of cooking fires, drying fish, and flowering bushes.

Some would have heard anecdotal, almost mythical, tales of a place where the water ends. There was nothing in nature, however, or in their personal experience to prepare them for the tolling of bells from St. Michael's and St. Philip's. The church steeples would have been the first objects to arrest their gaze upon approaching the city. Next they might have noticed structures unlike anything they had ever seen: a massive building fronting the Cooper River—the merchants' Exchange House, which had been completed the year before—flanked by fine homes, warehouses, and stores.

Having been born into a materially primitive society, they were about to step ashore into what may have been the world's wealthiest. Charleston and its lowcountry hinterland exceeded any other part of North America in economic dynamism, income, and consumption of worldly goods.[47] Its fine buildings were one indication. So was a harbor crowded with shipping. But it would have been the trappings, finery, and bustle of such a large town that mesmerized newcomers abruptly transported from a huddle of thatched huts.

The number of people—black and white—alone would have been incomprehensible. Chiefs at home wore country-cloth robes of woven strips, but so many white men in Charleston paraded in such finery, it would have been difficult to discern who were the chiefs and headmen. Even blacks wore clothes, many of them cutting a fine figure.

The opulence was visible in the way people hid their bodies. Women wore tight-bodiced dresses. Men of prominence were attired in coats of brocaded silk or satin and fine buckled shoes. Tradesmen, on the other hand, were distinguished by their green coats and shoes with plain silver buckles. Craftsmen wore leather aprons. The many sailors in port were obvious in their blue jackets. Calico and poplin dresses betrayed the shopgirls and seamstresses, who often went barefoot in summer.[48]

As alien as this new world was, Africans deposited in Charleston would have quickly discovered one thread common to their former and future lives: wealth and influence were measured in the number of slaves one owned. Coming from a society where as many as half the people were locked into some form of domestic servitude, Africans would have no difficulty in perceiving a social and economic hierarchy defined by slaveholding. It was clear enough in the manner of dress and, by extension, in the manner of work that whites performed.

Africans' first instinct would have been to identify those at the lower echelons—those closest to their own station—who obviously owned no slaves: sailors, sewing girls, apprentices, and indentured servants. Not far above them were the mechanics. These were the carpenters, tanners, blacksmiths, wheelwrights, cabinetmakers, and artisans employed in Charleston's largest industry: shipping.[49]

South Carolina in 1768 had stopped paying bounties to encourage Protestant immigrants from Europe, mainly Irish and German, to settle in the colony. But free land remained on offer, and they continued to arrive in numbers. The last major influx before the Revolution—more than one thousand Scots-Irish—disembarked in late 1772 and early 1773. Irish emigrants were still coming in 1774 and receiving assistance to occupy land grants in the backcountry.[50] Nonetheless they were poor and, for the moment, slaveless. They thus swelled the lower classes, who dwelled in socioeconomic proximity not far removed from blacks.

Henry Laurens believed that the "cruelty exercised upon those poor Irish" exceeded that typically imposed on the slaves. "Self-interest," he wrote to a friend in 1768, "prompted the baptized heathen to take some care of their wretched slaves for a market, but no other care was taken of those poor Protestant Christians from Ireland but to deliver as many as possible alive on shore upon the cheapest terms."[51] Blacks would also have seen what Laurens observed and drawn their own conclusions.

With African slaves and destitute European migrants pouring into Charleston, mechanics began drawing conclusions of their own. Free labor was scarce, leading many artisans to acquire slaves. Others, however, in effect were displaced by skilled and semiskilled slaves.

"The mechanics," according to Sellers, "had a real grievance against the British merchants and their Charleston factors, who were allowed by the British government, almost without let or hindrance, to import vast numbers of slaves. . . . The competition of slave with free labor caused great numbers of mechanics to emigrate to the northern colonies, where wages were lower but where they could count on employment."[52]

If shipbuilding was the city's principal industry, taverns were the most ubiquitous business establishments. By one estimate liquor was sold in at least one of every ten buildings—making for more than one hundred taverns in Charleston. Many doubled as inns.[53]

These were family enterprises, which widows often managed if the husband died.[54] Conrad and Esther Kysell fit this profile. Esther's parents, the Fulkers, may have been among the German and French-speaking Swiss who were lured in the early 1730s to settle in Purrysburg, on the northern bank of the Savannah River. By the mid-1750s, disease, mismanagement, and homesickness had decimated the settlement. But the Fulkers remained to welcome a fresh wave of Palatine immigrants in the mid-1760s.

Conrad had arrived in Charleston in early 1764, carrying his military gear and little else. In March he and several other "Poor Protestants" petitioned the South Carolina Council for land. They were granted one hundred acres each in Belfast, a wilderness tract near present-day Due West, which the Cherokees had ceded in 1755. When whites were slow to apply for grants in what became Ninety Six District, the general assembly offered passage to German and English Protestants to fill the void.[55]

Kysell was one of hundreds who answered the call. He swore an oath that he indeed was a Protestant but then failed to occupy the land. Two years later he successfully petitioned for another one hundred acres, closer to hand in Purrysburg, but he appears to have let this lie dormant as well. In the meantime he married Esther in October 1769 in St. Philip's Church and added his name to the lengthening list of tavern keepers.[56]

The Kysells had become members of Charleston's growing German community; they had joined the middling class of mechanics and small business people; and Conrad had become owner of two slaves, Lucca and Nancy, who probably cooked, served, and cleaned for clientele of the tavern-cum-inn.

In a city distinctly English and a colony ruled by England, the Germans felt vulnerable. Largely artisans and laborers, they clung uncertainly to the lower and middle rungs of Charleston's social and economic ladders. The German community's de facto leader, Michael Kalteisen, was widely respected, but he was still a drayman. His stature may have reassured those Anglo-Americans who, according to A. G. Roeber in *Palatines, Liberty and Property*, "entertained serious reservations" about their German neighbors. But the Germans stubbornly "remained largely isolated, retaining their speech and habits even after years in the colony."[57]

By the 1760s the German community had retreated in the face of commercial expansion and high rents in central Charleston into their own district north and west along King Street. Under Kalteisen's leadership they had established their own church—St. John's Lutheran—and the German Friendly Society. The motivation was not separatist, but to provide mutual aid and defend their cultural traditions against prejudicial attitudes toward the "Dutch," as they were derisively called.[58]

The Germans in Charleston had their own divisions, often played out within St. John's. When it came to the colonies' dispute with the English Crown, however, they were conspicuously united in the patriot cause. Kalteisen again took the lead, helping to establish the German Fusiliers Military Company in 1775, when he also was elected to the provincial congress.[59] The Friendly Society itself was strongly supportive of the rebellion.[60]

Conrad Kysell played an unexceptional role in the life of Teutonic Charleston. He and Esther had chosen to marry in the Anglican Church but later joined the Lutheran parish of St. John's. The Friendly Society marked its fifth anniversary before Kysell was accepted belatedly as its sixty-ninth member in April 1771. He had just been tried for perjury and found innocent. In December he was fined by his new Friendly Society colleagues "for taking God's name in vain." His next mention in the society's minutes, on December 30, 1772, was his last: a fellow member was fined ten shillings for missing Kysell's funeral.[61]

Kysell died three days before Christmas. He had faithfully attended the Friendly Society's weekly meetings until the end of October, when his illness apparently took firmer grip. Esther was prepared to manage. Anticipating his demise, Conrad had dictated his will in late September. As did many German husbands in Charleston, he made his wife executrix.[62] To sustain family control of property, South Carolinians in general extended substantial responsibility to women. "In perhaps no other mainland British colony," Roeber writes, "did married women exercise as much control over . . . both land and slaves."[63]

Conrad did not leave everything "unto my Dear and Loving wife." Although colonial land records do not reveal all that Kysell owned, he held acreage in Berkeley Parish and may have retained title to his original grants in Purrysburg and Belfast. These he apparently bequeathed to George Fulker, along with his horses and cattle. But his lot in Charleston went to Esther, as did Lucca and Nancy, "with their future issue and increase."[64]

Lucca and Nancy knew that the demise of their owner foreshadowed a change in their circumstances, and not necessarily for the better. Within weeks Esther Kysell was advertising their sale, along with her husband's "personal estate of sundry household goods."[65]

Given the complicated dynamics of slavery, race, and gender in the confined quarters of a Charleston household, there are several plausible explanations for the apparent departure of Lucca and Nancy from beneath Esther Kysell's roof. One is that she was uncomfortable owning another human being. Roeber found that "ownership of slaves presented . . . no profound moral dilemmas" to Palatines. "Adapting to the prevailing mode of owning property in human chattels, German speakers . . . apparently had few scruples about the practice."[66] The Fulkers, however, may have been among those who did. The family retained its land and roots in Purrysburg, which in the years immediately following the Revolution began to enjoy plantation-based prosperity. Several families quickly became large slaveholders, according to the federal census in 1790. Only two Purrysburg families owned no slaves. The Fulkers were one.[67]

To infer that Esther had been raised in a family opposed to slavery is speculation. However, the available evidence indicates that neither she nor her relations in Purrysburg depended on slave labor for their livelihood. Only a single piece of evidence connects Esther to slavery: the teenaged African boy who adopted her surname and carried it for more than half a century.

There are no family journals, business ledgers, or bill of sale to reveal when and how the boy became part of Esther's household, or at least close enough to the widowed tavern keeper to assume her surname. The Kysell name—and Esther with it—soon vanished from the public record in South Carolina.

Ironically the Anglicized "Kizell" would be known widely for decades to come— from loyalist encampments during the Revolution to the granite shores of Nova Scotia; from the drawing rooms of English abolitionists to the visionary black American shipowner Paul Cuffe; from a succession of British governors in Africa to antislavery publications and Baptist circles in England; from a Supreme Court justice to other prominent Americans bent upon sending free blacks to Africa; and to African and European slave traders who resented John Kizell's persistent attempts to block their trafficking in humans.

As an adult Kizell recorded virtually no details about his years as a slave in South Carolina. Had he been severely mistreated, he might have been expected to mention such abuse, if only to underscore the violence and exploitation at the core of slavery. No one who knew Kizell in later life referred to his having suffered physically. This includes Cuffe and an American cleric, both viscerally opposed to slavery, who had ample motive to publicize any brutality and hardship Kizell may have endured. Nor did Kizell hint that he was treated humanely or allowed a degree of freedom by his mistress. Had this been the case, he might have been reluctant to acknowledge that— truth be told—his experience as a slave had been relatively benign.

One factor above all supports the assumption that Kizell's slave experience was not altogether oppressive: his literacy. Kizell not only learned to read English, which was uncommon enough among slaves; he became a competent writer. He corresponded at length with members of the British elite and produced vivid descriptions of the slave trade, which would be published in London.

Kizell did not enjoy the celebrity of Olaudah Equiano, a former slave whose auto- biography captivated English readers in the late 1780s.[68] However, his known work— a substantial body of letters and reports to British governors and others, confined largely to a single decade (1806–1815)—made him the leading black writer of his time *in* Africa. They excel the short memoirs of Boston King and David George pub- lished in religious magazines in Britain in the late 1790s.

Unlike Kizell, his two contemporaries wrote mainly about their hard lives as slaves prior to the Revolution and their escape to freedom under the British.[69] Their mem- oirs have been quoted frequently by historians. Kizell's work focused entirely on the slave trade itself, as well as its physical and cultural backdrop in West Africa. It has been largely overlooked by historians.

How Kizell became functionally literate is unknown. He spent his formative years in Charleston. As a bright and evidently observant youth, living in a society where the printed word was available in newspapers, pamphlets, and books, he probably had achieved basic literacy by the time he joined the British military, following the fall of Charleston in May 1780.

He would have needed the indulgence of his owner and someone to teach him at least the alphabet and rudiments of grammar. Did he find a tutor within the black community? The only school for blacks in Charleston had closed in 1764.[70] Was he self-taught? Or was Esther Kysell his teacher? We know only that John Kizell—legibly, and no doubt proudly—signed his name throughout his long life.

Charleston's Black Curtain

The boy who would become John Kizell arrived in Charleston with his birth name. Had he been his mother's first son, born among a Sherbro-speaking people, he would have been called Cho; if the second son, T'ong. Or he might have been San or Barky. Whatever name he carried, it was his umbilical link to the motherland. It is how he might have been known initially among his peers in the city's African community. But it would fall away, like the skin of a molting snake, when he took the name John in his owner's household.[71]

A young African, newly come to this alien place, confronted a complicated acculturation. He first had to assimilate a new identity. In Africa he had been part of a well-defined extended family; in Charleston he was an "African." As two British scholars have suggested, however, the idea of *being* African "did not become commonplace among slaves and former slaves in the Americas until the late eighteenth century. Even then it was clearly adopted from the European habit of using that generic term."[72]

Learning the strange ways and languages of white people—of their masters, in particular—was the most immediate challenge. In terms of survival, it was essential. But slaves' broader socialization occurred within the black community, composed of African- and country-born people, including the Gullah, as well as many from the Caribbean. In the early 1770s, Africans still accounted for about half of all slaves in South Carolina. Many country-born blacks were only a generation removed from the Africa their parents had known. "Coming from highly diverse societies," Philip D. Morgan writes, "African newcomers shared some cultural principles and assumptions—about how the world worked, how people interacted, and how to express themselves aesthetically. This normative bedrock . . . provided . . . a scaffolding on which a whole new culture could arise."[73]

It helped that Charleston was predominantly black. The 5,833 slaves and 24 free blacks in 1770 outnumbered the 5,030 resident whites. But at any given moment, Morgan estimates, there would have been as many as 1,500 transient slaves and perhaps 200 runaways. Because many whites retreated to healthier, cooler climes during the summer, blacks at times could have enjoyed a three-to-one majority. This provided them with an enormous opportunity.

"The invisibility accorded slaves," Morgan explains, "was one of the few advantages they possessed as they attempted to order their lives. They could develop social ties to some extent apart from, and largely unknown to, their owners. . . . Slaves did not arrive in the New World as communities of people; they had to *create* communities."[74]

Charleston, in a real sense, was more African than it was English or German. Morgan's "invisibility," however, applies aptly to published histories of the city's colonial era. Blacks—their society and hybrid African culture, infused by developing lowcountry Gullah traditions—generally are treated as a shadow of the dominant European minority. This is only partly the result of white ethnocentricity; it is the direct consequence of blacks' success in concealing—in ways only Africans could appreciate—the communal life they had constructed.

Whites flattered themselves that they understood blacks. In fact it was the latter who, if only as a survival tactic, closely studied the master class. They perhaps knew whites better than whites knew themselves. Fear and ignorance governed white attitudes toward blacks and contributed unwittingly to the latter's invisibility.

A good example was the conviction, widespread among whites, that masters were at the mercy of those slaves presumed to possess knowledge of poisonous plants. Tea was thought to be the principal medium used. Alexander Garden, Charleston's leading physician in the late colonial years, concluded that the fear was baseless. It was easier for whites to blame their slaves for lingering illness, he believed, than the incompetence of their doctors.[75]

Although conceding that there were "many authenticated" cases of whites poisoned by slaves, Sylvia R. Frey and Betty Wood also believe that the "growing obsession with such a possibility meant that many unexpected deaths were mistakenly attributed" to a slave's malevolence.[76] Ironically this was consistent with Africans' belief that no death—except among the very old—was natural. The fears of poisoning and of witchcraft were far more palpable within the black community, where traditional healers commonly dispensed herbal medicines based on centuries of practice in Africa.

Lowcountry planters and their backcountry brethren would have seen little immediate value in the runty African boy presented for inspection and sale on a Cooper River wharf. Where and when Esther Kysell first saw him is conjectural. He could have come to her secondhand—rejected by the planters and thus purchased cheaply by a merchant who needed an extra pair of hands in his storeroom or to deliver parcels and messages. If he lived and filled out his slight frame, he would be a profitable investment.

Perhaps he had been bought initially by a German tradesman. Perhaps Frau Kysell had prevailed upon him to part with the boy. She had sold Nancy and Lucca (and their issue), but managing the tavern was challenging without someone who could do general chores and safely run errands in streets filled with danger and distractions.

Regardless of how the boy's relationship to Kysell transpired, there can be little doubt that within months of his enslavement in Africa, he had been reborn into the milieu of Charleston's street-savvy young blacks. They were the property of others, as many of them had been in Africa, but in the urban terrain of crowded streets and secluded alleys, they were largely in control of their lives.[77]

The young Cho (or T'ong) quite possibly was enjoying greater freedom than he could have imagined in Africa. He found himself, indeed, in a wonderland of opulence, materialism, excess, choice, and opportunity. He would soon become aware, if only subliminally, that Charleston's slaves were masters of much of the city's life. They dominated the marketing of produce and fish. They operated the small schooners and other craft that connected Charleston to inland and coastal areas. They sustained a vibrant cultural life that remained largely ignored or denigrated by whites. They maintained a communications network that kept them well-informed regarding affairs in the city as well as the lowcountry. And increasingly as they observed colonials' disenchantment with British policies, blacks began developing a political consciousness.

"Slaves conducted their collective activities on several levels," David M. Zornow writes in one of the first serious assessments of black communal life in pre-Revolutionary Charleston. These ranged "from informal to organized. . . . The former were social and the latter religious, and both attracted a large proportion of the community. By themselves, group endeavors of this kind formed a type of covert resistance to the demands of the masters; but they also laid the groundwork for the transformation of collective political demonstrations overtly challenging the ruling order."[78]

One of the first things a newly arrived African would have noticed in Charleston was blacks' self-respect. A visiting Frenchman in 1777, walking the same streets as young Kizell, was struck by "a peculiar kind of pride and bearing" among blacks, which he contrasted with the subservience he found in French West Indian slaves. "Without degenerating into insolence, it at least gives the impression that they regard a man who is not their master simply as a man, not a tyrant."[79]

Charleston slaves "did not act like slaves," Morgan agrees. "They were not servile; they were proud, haughty, self-confident. Perhaps urban life served to undermine the traditional disciplines of slavery. Perhaps urbanization loosened the restraints of bondage to the point where the sense of racial order was in peril."[80]

Slaves' sense of independence was apparent in their freedom of movement, their ability to fashion lives at least partially separate from their owners, and their assumption of unslavish prerogatives. Some "lived apart from their masters and rented houses on their own," Ira Berlin writes of the evolution of African American societies in the colonial era. They would share their earnings with their owners "in return for *de facto* freedom. . . . The small black communities that developed . . . in Charles Town's Neck confirm the growing independence of urban creoles."[81]

Whites acknowledged the reality of slaves' independence in various and subtle ways. The city's grand jury expressed white frustration in early 1772 when it conceded that blacks had a "general disregard" for the law requiring that they have a "ticket" from their master to be abroad at night. Two years later the grand jury continued to be agitated by "Negroes in Charles-town [who] are become so obscene in their language, so irregular and disorderly in their conduct and so superfluous in their Numbers," that yet another law was urgently needed to regulate their behavior.[82]

Masters could also publicly betray the limits of their power in humbling terms. In the spring of 1773, one owner advertised for two runaway men, adding, "If the said Negroes will return of their own Accord, they shall be forgiven." Another wished to sell his "excellent cook" and her three children. "The mother," he stated, was not "contented with her present situation [and] obliges the owner to part with her."[83]

Whites' grudging accommodation of blacks' initiative was most evident in the economy. Whites had been complaining for decades that blacks exploited their control of several economic levers in Charleston.[84] Although the law enjoined slaves from trading, it was seldom enforced.

In his analysis of eighteenth-century slave society in South Carolina, Robert Olwell describes the city's lower market as "the only official institution in the colony where slaves predominated not only in numbers but in power." Slaves "daily acted in ways that defied their proscribed subordination. . . . The activities and relations that 'governed' the marketplace stood in stark contrast to the social order that prevailed in the remainder of the colonial slave society. . . . It was the place where the town met the country and where news and gossip were exchanged. . . . In trade, town and country slaves could cooperate to their mutual advantage."[85]

Black women dominated the market, often with the collusion of their masters. The latter were content to allow their slaves to sell their own produce as long as they profitably sold the owner's. This in turn empowered the market women to acquire capital with which to buy and sell other goods. An anonymous individual expressed whites' alarm in September 1772, writing to the *Gazette* about the "great numbers of loose, idle and disorderly negro women, who are seated [at the market] . . . from morn till night, and *buy* and *sell* on *their own account*, what they please."[86]

The implied freedom of these "huckster wenches," as whites called them, defied white authority and created space, at the very heart of slave owners' power, where blacks openly controlled events. It would have been one of the earliest lessons learned by an impressionable African youth sent by his mistress to purchase food for that evening's table at her King Street inn.

Fishmongering and butchering also rested largely in black hands. Black peddlers could be found throughout the city, selling virtually anything edible, from oysters and tarts to milk, fruit, and cooked rice. In late 1770 the city commissioners expressed concern over the "riotous and disorderly" behavior at the new fish market near Queen Street—code words, among whites, for any black congregation. The marketplace was inherently "boisterous." Blacks were free to socialize, joke, bargain, and "palaver"—a West African "pidgin" term Kizell would have known, derived from the Portuguese *palavra* (or "word"), for animated discussion and argument.[87]

In addition to misapprehending the hullabaloo of a typically African marketplace, whites were bedeviled by many other real and imagined fears of the overwhelming black presence. They complained that blacks were keeping horses—a valuable commodity—and dressing in "excessive and costly apparel." Both were violations of laws collectively known as the Negro Acts.[88] They were especially concerned with the authorities' laissez-faire tolerance of blacks' moving about at all hours without tickets and their consumption of liquor.

West Indian rum, Portuguese wine, and distilled spirits were considered essential commodities in the colony. "It was an age when drunkenness seems to have been expected of gentlemen in Europe and America," Sellers relates, ". . . and when quantities of liquor were used on the plantations as medicine for the slaves."[89] In Charleston itself it was the rare retail shop that did not keep rum and the rare block that did not have at least one drinking place.

Although the law prohibited tavern keepers and retailers from selling liquor to a slave without permission of his owner, "Stranger" wrote in the *South Carolina Gazette* in September 1772 that by noon "the dram shops are crowded with negroes." Three years later, as fear of black insurrection flared, the grand jury recommended that liquor be sold to blacks during daylight only. Because they could buy liquor at almost any hour, "Negroes have their opportunity of getting intoxicated before their owners can employ them or of their being hired as Porters." It also resulted in "their rioting through the streets in Evenings."[90]

Some white citizens suggested taking matters into their own hands. Melchior Werly, a butcher and prominent member of the German Friendly Society, was one of five men who published a warning in October 1772: "We the Subscribers, living on Charles Town Neck, having been much injured by the great Number of NEGROES who are continually passing and repassing, selling Vegetables, &c without Tickets, so that we cannot distinguish Run-Aways or others that rob us, Do give this public Notice, That we have determined forthwith to put a stop to this pilfering Trade by Seizing whatever we shall find in the Possession of any Slaves, not having Tickets . . . and by executing the other Powers wherewith we are invested by the Negro Act."[91]

Perhaps goaded by the prospect of vigilante justice, the grand jury proposed several months later "the erecting of Public Stocks in every cross street . . . with power to be lodged in every white person to put offenders there as the only means to . . . check the intolerable insolence of Negroes and other Slaves in Blaspheming, talking obscenely and gaming in the public streets as they daily do, but particularly on Sunday" when the town watch house was shut.[92]

There is no evidence that either of these expressions of white angst and frustration was acted upon. Young Africans soon learned yet another lesson: white people liked making laws better than they did enforcing them. Charleston abounded with streetwise boys and adolescents who understood white ways and how to turn them to their advantage. Kizell was now one of them.[93]

Blacks were alert to any opportunity to assert a degree of independence from white surveillance and control. What whites regarded as insolence often was nothing more than blacks' mimicking their masters' mores and lifestyle. That could embrace wearing stylish clothes in defiance of the coarse garb prescribed by law;[94] speaking good English and displaying "white" manners; or owning property, even slaves.

Time and circumstance provided urban blacks with frequent cover to engage in "communal" activities beyond the pale of white oversight. Sundays afforded the chance to gather outside town with plantation friends and runaways while their masters spent long hours at church. At night, meanwhile, the black community pulsated.[95]

It was in the workplace where blacks truly challenged whites on their own ground. Skilled slaves undercut the economic power of white mechanics and displaced many; the unskilled monopolized the market for casual labor. The grand jury conceded the point in 1771 when it proposed "to empower the Commissioners of the Streets to punish such Negroes as refuse to work unless it be agreeable to themselves and such pay as they may require."[96]

Slave owners profited by hiring out their slaves, skilled and otherwise, or by allowing them to sell their own services. Morgan estimates that 10 percent of Savannah's blacks were living on their own and paying their masters a fixed amount by the mid-1770s; in Charleston, he believes, the practice was even more widespread because of the higher level of development. "Slaves who 'hired their own time,'" Morgan writes, "had a considerable measure of independence. . . . In addition, masters were not too particular about how their slaves acquired their wages."[97]

Skilled slaves were in great demand and could earn their owner 15 to 20 percent of their value annually. This was further incentive to the slave to freelance his talents and pocket the full proceeds. Masters and employers could be fined if a hired-out slave had no badge, but like many laws in Charleston, this one may have been observed more in the breach. Thus one owner felt compelled to advertise in 1772: "WHEREAS sundry Persons have made a practice of employing my Negro Man Stepney 'without my knowledge or consent,'" the public was warned not to pay him without her permission.[98]

Charleston whites regarded slave society as largely monolithic. In fact it was "deeply fragmented," Morgan suggests, along both ethnic and occupational lines. Inevitably there were cultural divisions, especially among the recently arrived African-born and between them and their country-born cousins. There was still a tendency to identify with one's ethnic group, but not necessarily as "African" or even as "black."[99]

By the time Kizell was becoming acculturated to life in Charleston, the social and economic hierarchy among blacks was well-defined. There were the house servants and liverymen; the carpenters, masons, and other skilled workers; the market women; and the legion of porters, wharf men, and menial workers. There were at least three additional classes of blacks, occupying relatively privileged positions, that whites regarded warily.

The most important men were connected to the water: pilots, fishermen, boatmen, and seagoing mariners. The latter were already "creating a black Atlantic maritime tradition" according to W. Jeffrey Bolster in *Black Jacks: African American Seamen in the Age of Sail*. They were fashioning "a new cultural self-consciousness that linked meaning and experience in ways foreign to whites, and that reflected Africans' fusion of the sacred and the secular. . . . Across West Africa, the surface of the water served variously in myth and ritual as the boundary through which spiritual communications occurred."[100]

Water was a medium that allowed slaves to escape white vigilance, to control a significant part of their lives, and to link urban, coastal, and plantation blacks. They were the pilots who intimately knew Charleston's treacherous bars and currents; they were the fishermen who supplied the city's seafood and enjoyed the collateral right to own their vessels; and they navigated the harbor boats and the schooners that conveyed produce, supplies, mail, newspapers, and gossip up and down the coast and to the waterside plantations.[101] They were an important conduit for communication and intelligence among slave communities throughout the lowcountry and the coast.

Another identifiable class of blacks was the women with whom "respectable" white men openly consorted. South Carolina seems to have been unique in this respect among the southern colonies. Given that black and mixed-race women vastly outnumbered black men in Charleston, it is not surprising that white men exploited their availability. What is notable is that interracial liaisons were conducted in plain view and generally accepted within white society.

Visitors to Charleston often remarked upon the phenomenon. Josiah Quincy Jr. confided in his journal in 1773 that the "enjoyment of a negro mulatto woman is spoken of as quite a common thing: no reluctance, delicacy or shame is made about the matter."[102] Another itinerant diarist, Ebenezer Hazard, in 1778 recorded "a peculiarity which I did not hear of in any other state. I mean the 'black dances' . . . which are balls given by Negro and Mulatto women, to which they invite the white gentlemen, and it is said that many of the first gentlemen (so called) attend at them. These women, it is said, are generally in keeping, dress elegantly, and have no small acquaintance with polite behavior."[103]

Local commentators were not shy about the matter. One writer in the *Gazette* wondered in August 1772 that white men could "cohabit, as Husband, with Negro Women, treating them as Wives even in public, and do not blush to own the Mongrel Breed . . . which is thus begotten."[104]

Whites do not appear to have bothered themselves with how *blacks* perceived the sexual license on display or the implicit exploitation. However, at least one young African—whose puberty coincided with his early days in Charleston—was shaping his opinion. As an adult Kizell exhibited a strong animus toward an anomalous class who represented, to him, the worst in each race. He probably had already inherited in Africa his people's antipathy toward those of mixed race. They were, after all, the principal slave traders. Indeed one could have been the middle man who sold him to the captain of the *Blossom*. His distrust of mulattoes would only have deepened during his formative years in Charleston.

Finally there was the tiny population of free blacks—another anomalous presence—who numbered just two dozen in 1770 in a city of nearly eleven thousand souls. Several were women and mixed-race individuals who had purchased their freedom.[105] A few had been manumitted by their owners.

Some were freeborn. George Harris's father had captained a slave ship and left his son five slaves. William Snow was born free in Charleston, cultivated a plantation on the Cooper River, and operated a tailor shop. A mulatto, he married a servant of James Simpson, the last royal attorney general in the colony. He forfeited his property when he refused to join the rebels, then served General Cornwallis after the fall of Charleston. He left with the British evacuation in late 1782 to settle in England.

24   Yet another free black landowner, Lazarus Jones, lost his possessions through loyalty to the king. He served in the Little River Loyalist Militia Regiment during the latter stages of the war before leaving for exile in Nova Scotia.[106]

Such then was the diversity of Charleston's African American community on the threshold of the Revolution. The operative word is *community*. If black society appeared opaque, cacophonous, and threatening to most whites, to blacks it provided a means to assimilate newcomers, to exercise remarkable control over their lives, to assert identities that contradicted their enslavement, and to sustain the essentially spiritual-magical coherence of their African cultures. Kizell's transformation into an African American had begun.

2

THE UPROOTING

"The invisible world presses hard upon the visible."
John S. Mbiti, African theologian, 1969

John Kizell was born into a watery world. His people may have been Sherbro or Bom. More likely they were Kim, whose language was mutually intelligible and who inhabited the same waterlogged West African coast. Theirs was a domain of mangroves and alluvial mud, innumerable creeks and languid rivers, which merged in brackish union with the nearby Atlantic. There were (mostly small) islands, swamps, and lagoons. People communicated and traveled largely by canoe. They lived by the cycle of tropical rains, which deluged them from April to September. They fished and farmed—mainly cassava, and also rice, which like everything else in their world depended on water.[1]

Strangers from the Sea

Water had also brought them strangers from the sea. These were the Portuguese, Dutch, English, and other white-skinned peoples who began to visit the coast in the 1400s, three centuries before John Kizell fed at his mother's breast and slept securely wrapped against her strong back. First they came as explorers, looking for a route to the spice-producing regions of Asia, but soon enough it was the quest for trade, resources, and wealth that drew them to Africa. Now their primary desires were gold, ivory, and camwood, a source of red dye. The quest for slaves came later.

A Portuguese expedition led by Álvaro Fernandes in 1446 provided Europeans with their first glimpse of the forested mountains guarding a magnificent river mouth. To the Portuguese the hills may have resembled a lion reclining by the sea. The inhabitants had their own names and traditions for this place, but for Portuguese cartographers it was now *Serra Lyoa,* or "leonine mountain."

It was another sixteen years before Pedro da Sintra, a former page to Henry the Navigator, returned in two armed ships to map the area. Presaging European rivalries along the coast, which would endure almost to the twentieth century, the Portuguese regarded their maps as state secrets. So would every nation and most ship captains who followed in their wake.[2] The expansion of the known world—known, that is, among Europeans—was becoming a driving economic and political force.

"Somewhere in the heart of Africa," writes the historian A. P. Kup, "were supposed to lie huge quantities of gold; the king of the ancient state of Ghana was said to own a nugget so vast that he used it to tether his horse. Mansa Musa, king of the Mali, added to this legend when, setting out for Mecca in 1324, with the accumulated wealth of years, he arrived in Cairo with one-hundred camel-loads of gold which he proceeded lightheartedly to spend."[3]

Among the Africans who greeted the increasing visitation of white-skinned strangers, the known world stretched in the opposite direction—inland toward the forest belt; the hills and mountains of the Futa Jallon; the vast savannah extending beyond one's imagination; the legendary centers of learning and trade such as Timbuktu; great rivers and the enormous camel caravans that had long before brought tales of the white tribes to the north. The Temne, Bullom, and other peoples encountered by these questing, curious, itinerant Europeans were at least vaguely aware that they existed in a larger physical universe. But it was only their immediate surroundings—and their metaphysical world—that were tangibly real.

Their history, encoded in oral tradition and dense lineages, does not begin with the arrival of Fernandes, Sintra, or the many freebooters and European traders to follow. To comprehend the bare outlines of the cultural microcosm into which John Kizell was born, it is important to recognize that his world was not an unchanging backwater suspended in time. African society was constantly attuned and adaptive to new circumstances: declining soil fertility, climatic changes, the encroachment of people speaking a different language, the rise and fall of regional political alliances, and the dynamics of trade controlled by distant groups.

African history is no less complex than Europe's. As early as the thirteenth century, the Soso in present-day Guinea were displacing the Temne, Limba, and others living in the fertile inland valleys of the Futa Jallon. The latter, driven toward the coast, established the Sapi confederation, a loose alliance of several linguistic groups. In the sixteenth century, the Sapi would have to cope with Mane warriors sweeping northward up the coast, intermarrying with ruling families among the resident peoples.

The confederation had dissolved by the seventeenth century in the face of Mane pressure. But like the original Mane leaders, who paid allegiance to a distant overlord, the Temne, Bullom, Kim, and others whom they had subjugated were now subject to an emperor south of Cape Mount in present-day Liberia.[4]

Between 1600 and 1725, Kizell's home region experienced sustained instability as waves of immigrants washed over the disintegrating Sapi confederation.[5] The details of the ensuing conflicts and population movements are incidental. What is key is that life in precolonial coastal Sierra Leone—well before the onset of large-scale selling of people into foreign bondage—was neither static nor idyllic. It was filled with uncertainty and danger.

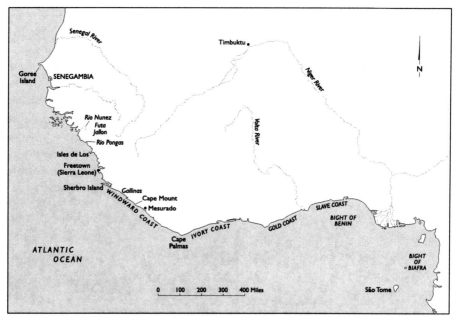

Major slave-trading centers along the West African
coast from the early 1700s to the mid-1800s

During the century prior to Kizell's birth in about 1760, two forces began to intrude upon the southern Bullom and Kim peoples. These profoundly affected them. They also helped to spawn slave-based societies throughout a "new world" far to the west, beyond the "big water."

The most important of these forces initially was the penetration of Islam into the Futa Jallon and the establishment of an Islamic state among the Fulani. The second was the growing presence of European traders and the heightened demand for slave labor in Brazil, the Caribbean, and ultimately in the plantation economies of the new mainland American colonies.

In 1497 Askia Mohamed, the leader of the inland empire of Songhai, returned from Mecca and embarked on jihad among the Mandingo, Fulani, and other "pagan" peoples to the southwest, forcibly converting them to Islam. Over the next century, the Islamized Fulani and Mandingo achieved dominance in the Futa Jallon highlands. By 1725 the Fulani were waging their own jihad against neighboring peoples toward the coastal region. By 1776 they had established an Islamic state. The Fulani and Mandingos now exercised the political, military, and economic might to exploit and control the burgeoning trade in slaves.[6]

This ultimately resulted in a more efficient trade in slaves, conducted at major transshipment points, or factories, along the West African coast. The Fulani and Mandingos, while generally refusing to sell their own people into foreign slavery, nonetheless ensured that supply would meet demand in America in the decades immediately before and after the Revolution. The slave trade would have prospered in the absence of organized Fulani-Mandingo involvement, but its scale would have been diminished and the price of slaves in American ports such as Charleston made more dear.

The Fulani jihad did not penetrate the thick forest belt extending well inland from much of the coast. However, it triggered a prolonged period of localized conflict. Groups fled from danger, jostled for secure living space, and competed for access to European traders who had established a foothold wherever a river entered the sea and fresh water could be obtained. These "wars"—largely raids involving relatively little bloodshed—also generated slaves who could be sold to the European traders and ship captains.

The white men were no longer strangers. Indeed many of them married into chiefly families and founded lineages that endure to this day in Sierra Leone. Prominent among them were the Tuckers, Caulkers, and Rogerses—families that Kizell came to know well in later life. It is not inconceivable that a Tucker or Rogers might have been complicit, at least indirectly, in his being sold abroad. All were engaged in the slave trade.

Although the Sierra Leone River estuary was an important watering and trading outpost for the early Portuguese and other European visitors, the Sherbro and Gallinas regions one hundred miles and more to the southeast soon attracted attention as well. Several rivers, including the Deong, Sewa, Waanje, Kerefe, and Moa, filtered down to the coast, where ships could shelter and trading companies could erect their factories. The rivers and their tributaries provided access to a roadless interior.

Chiefs and headmen were quick to appreciate the advantage of moving their towns and villages closer to the traders. These brought a steady supply of rum, guns and powder, clothing, pewter, kettles, brassware, snuff, and other European goods to exchange for abundant ivory and hardwood. The modest amounts of gold available never matched the imagination spurred centuries before by Mansa Musa's legendary shopping spree in Cairo. The occasional slave was sold, but this perishable commodity remained a sideline until well into the seventeenth century.

The origins of the Afro-European families who came to dominate trade along the coast are dimly remembered. The Rogers family in the Gallinas may have descended from Zachary Rogers, who served as chief agent of the British-chartered Royal African Company in the Sherbro in 1677–81. Thomas Corker arrived in Sherbro from London in the mid-1680s, married into local royalty, and fathered two sons to begin an enduring line of Caulkers. Corker's descendants inherited control of the shoreline between the Sierra Leone peninsula and the Sherbro and extended their domain to the Banana Islands and Plantain Islands.

William Cleveland, a young Englishman shipwrecked in the Banana Islands in the late 1730s, settled there and added his bloodline to the family. He began trading in slaves, married a Caulker chief's daughter, and fathered a girl in 1741. Elizabeth

Clevland (as she spelled her name) was educated in England before coming to South Carolina in 1764 to purchase two plantations on behalf of a brother. Meanwhile her half-brother James, schooled in Liverpool, returned to rule the Bananas, where he joined the powerful Poro society. He later dethroned—and beheaded—the Caulker chief in the nearby Plantain Islands.[7]

It is the Tuckers, however, who exerted the most influence in the Sherbro and Gallinas regions from the mid-1700s into the early 1800s. Kizell as a boy would have been aware, if only vaguely, of their power; he became all too well acquainted with the Tuckers when he confronted them and their slave dealing decades later.

The first Tucker probably arrived on the coast in the mid-1660s in the employ of the Company of Royal Adventurers Trading into Africa. While managing the company store in the Sherbro, he fathered a son, Peter, with an African woman from the Kittam peninsula, near the Gallinas. In 1672, about the time the son was born, King Charles II in England chartered a new firm to take over from the Royal Adventurers. As part of its charter, the new Royal African Company was obliged to provide three thousand slaves to English colonies.[8]

Young Peter was sent off to England for schooling. Returning in the 1680s, he eventually settled near his mother, in Kittam, and began trading in the usual European goods, camwood and ivory. His ambition and business sense became apparent in the lands he acquired in the Gallinas and elsewhere on the coast. Peter Tucker's Town, as it was known, became an important port of call for the slaving ships, which began to frequent West Africa in greater numbers. By 1699 Tucker also had become the Royal African Company's agent in the Sherbro.[9]

As the trade in slaves gradually eclipsed "legitimate" commerce, succeeding generations of Tuckers prospered. An Irish slave trader living just a few miles from Henry Tucker in the Sherbro, in 1757, left a portrait of a man "who has acquired a great fortune by his skill . . . in the way of trade." Tucker had traveled to England, Spain, and Portugal. He spoke excellent English and had numerous wives and children. "His strength consists of his own slaves and their children," wrote an envious Nicholas Owen. "His riches sets him above the Kings. . . . almost all the Blacks owes [sic] him money, which brings a dread of being stopt [sold into slavery]. . . . He is a fat man . . . and lives after the manner of the English, having his house well-furnished with English goods."[10]

That Englishmen named Corker, Rogers, and Tucker could assimilate themselves into coastal society is hardly surprising. Their control of European trade goods was an obvious advantage. But to achieve and sustain social and political position depended largely on what historian Lynda Rose Day calls "an intriguing pattern of integration characteristic of Sherbro society."

Owen's Eurocentric reference to kings implied the existence of powerful monarchies, but Day describes "a largely de-centralized political structure with the main focus of political loyalty as the village," which "facilitated the assimilation of stranger elements into the region."[11] Other factors that enabled integration of European "strangers" and their male progeny were what Day terms the "matrilineal bias" of Sherbro society and the nonexclusivity of Poro, the primary male secret society.

30   In the Sherbro, Day writes, "property rights, group identity, and social rights are transmittable through women . . . [who] can legitimize the position of the in-marrying foreigner."[12] Meanwhile initiation into Poro was not restricted on tribal or racial terms. Because Poro served important political, judicial, and other functions, its members had good reason to incorporate Euro-Africans whose wealth and ties to the white world endowed them with substantial influence in local affairs.[13]

Europeans who married into local families did so for practical, political, and mercenary purposes. Their motives were hardly egalitarian, civilizing, or religious. William Cleveland's mixed-race son, James, may have been schooled in Liverpool and regarded highly by European traders, but he was a ruthless seller of slaves. He was feared by the common people and probably responsible for depopulating a swath of coastal territory to the north of the Sherbro.[14]

Where they could, whites on the coast lived with other Europeans in trading centers, such as Bance Island in the Sierra Leone River and York Island in the Sherbro. "The relations of the York settlement with their neighbours," Kup says, "were seldom amicable." He quotes William Smith, who visited the several whites living on the island in 1726, that there was a "Law at Sherbro that whosoever struck a White Man, should, if he was merchantable, be sold for a Slave, but if old, or unmerchantable, that he should be put to Death."[15]

Even those whites who lived alone kept their distance. "To keep as far from these people as we can," said Owen, "we seldom get so far engaged with any black as to envolve ourselves into quarrels."[16] Owen was obliged, through liquor and other presents,

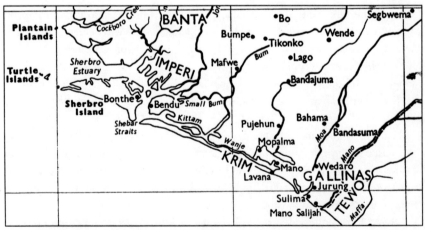

Coastal regions of present-day Sierra Leone. John Kizell was probably born and raised near the modern town of Pujehun. Map reproduced from A History of Sierra Leone, *by Christopher Fyfe, courtesy of Oxford University Press*

to maintain his tenuous status with a local "landlord" who in turn accepted responsibility for the "stranger."

The inherently disputatious nature of local human relations inevitably led to frequent "palavers" to settle petty and large affairs alike. It was virtually impossible not to become embroiled in indigenous matters. Owen, who regarded the buying and selling of slaves as "very troublesome,"[17] is described by one historian as a "pathetic, lonely figure, struggling to stay alive and purchase perhaps two or three dozen slaves . . . a year."[18] He operated in the shadow of the Tuckers' prosperous operation.

Thanks to malaria, yellow fever, and other tropical diseases, West Africans never had to deal with large-scale European settlement or with the alienation of their lands. But any stranger arriving in an African community typically was welcomed, watched for his character and true intentions, and, if appropriate, incorporated into its social structure. This vetting process made the newcomer feel less cautious and more likely to reveal himself.

Kizell appreciated the essential hospitality of African culture. "If strangers come to them," he told a governor of Sierra Leone decades later, "they will give them water to wash, and oil to anoint their skin, and give them victuals for nothing; they will go out of their beds that the strangers may sleep in them."[19]

How coastal peoples perceived the white-skinned outsiders who insisted on living near them can only be surmised. The complexity of their reactions is suggested by the insights of Malidoma Patrice Somé, who was born in a remote village in French colonial West Africa in the 1950s. In the remarkable story of his youth, *Of Water and the Spirit*, Somé tells how the Dagara, a few hundred miles inland from Sierra Leone, regarded the European missionaries, soldiers, and administrators who had come among them: "For some of my people, befriending the white man was the best way they could find to fight back. By doing this, they hoped to get to know how the white man's mind worked and what they thought they were accomplishing by invading another people's ancestral lands. . . . Some village people . . . believed that to have become so spiritually sick, the white man must have done something terrible to his own ancestors."[20]

Europeans dismissed Africans' spiritual world in the midst of what they perceived as primeval poverty devoid of cultural worth. More than half a century after Owen described the Sherbro people's mud-and-thatch huts, furnished with a few stools and earthen pots, Kizell himself pictured an identical scene.[21] Kizell went deeper, however, revealing that "the great and the poor" lived much alike. "You cannot tell the master from the servant at first," he wrote Sierra Leone's governor, Edward Columbine, in 1810. "The servant has as much to say as his master in any common discourse. . . . The king is poorer than any of his subjects."[22]

Kizell, who eventually advocated mass migration of African Americans to Africa, observed that there was "a great deal of land on which no people live. There are, in my opinion, millions of acres that never were cultivated. The people ought to be taught to work the ground." Otherwise, he lamented, "they will always have the foolish notion, that all riches must come from Europe." Yet Kizell lauded his people's subsistence philosophy. "Sometimes I am astonished to see how contented they are with so little; I consider that happiness does not consist in plenty of goods."[23]

32

Although Kizell, in his later years, criticized the Sherbro-Gallinas peoples as sometimes lazy and wicked, he more often praised their simplicity, honesty, and hard work. He recognized that they were able to grow large quantities of rice on small plots, rely on abundant fish and wild animals, and raise sheep, goats, and fowl aplenty. The women produced salt to trade in the interior for woven "country cloth" and slaves. And the men, when not clearing land to plant rice, made canoes and cut camwood. But he reserved his highest regard for the women. "*They* have the hardest lot; they do all the drudgery; they beat the rice, fetch wood, make salt, plaster the houses, go fishing with hand nets, make oil from the palm nuts which the men bring home."[24]

Significantly Kizell explained more about the visible environment—people's homes, their subsistence economy, burial practices, and social and political structures—than he did of the invisible world. Although he devoted considerable attention to witchcraft, he revealed nothing of the people's understanding of their cosmos. This may reflect his ambivalence, as a westernized Christian adult, toward a dimension of African life and culture that remains mysterious, unsettling, and denied among Africans and non-Africans alike.

For Africans, the theologian John Mbiti writes, "the whole of existence is a religious phenomenon; man is a deeply religious being living in a religious universe." Somé explains that, in Western reality, "there is a clear split between the spiritual and the material, between religious life and secular life. This concept is alien to [my people]. . . . For us . . . the supernatural is part of our everyday lives. . . . The material is just the spiritual taking form."[25]

In the Africa that Kizell knew, especially as a child, the spiritual side of life manifested itself in ways that non-Africans cannot properly comprehend. Kizell was born into a world, in Mbiti's words, "densely populated with spiritual beings, spirits and the living dead"—those who have died but are remembered by those still living.[26] To begin understanding how an African, transported to an alien place, might react to new surroundings and circumstances, it is essential to acknowledge his or her perception of the spirit world.

"The religious worldview of early American slaves was primarily magical," Morgan writes in his study of South Carolina lowcountry and Virginia tidewater slave cultures in the eighteenth century. Morgan suggests that the "unpredictability of the slave world may . . . explain why Christianity had little appeal for most eighteenth-century slaves" until they discerned that the white people's religion "could serve as an expansion of their . . . hope for the future."[27]

Mbiti may have come closer to the truth, however, at least for the African-born, who still made up a large proportion of slaves in South Carolina in the early 1770s. "The notion of a messianic hope . . . has no place in [an African's] traditional concept of history," he writes. "So African peoples have no 'belief in progress.'"[28]

The Sherbro and their coastal kin recognized the existence of an omniscient deity, but his role in their lives was passive. "Being the essence of goodness itself," a Sherbro divinity student in America observed in 1886, "and not disposed to harm his creatures, the pagan does not realize any necessity to worship Him. The devil is supposed to possess supreme power . . . and is concerned with the affairs of men, and his demands are many."[29]

In the African cosmos, god is more overseer than overlord.[30] One does not appeal to a god to intervene in earthly matters; one appeals to ubiquitous spirits through offerings—often quite modest—to acknowledge their existence and their power for good and ill. Having been raised in such an en-spirited environment, and having experienced events that defied conventional explanation, an African had every reason to accept the overriding influence of spirits in his or her daily existence.

"African peoples know that the universe has a power, force or whatever else one may call it," Mbiti concludes. "It is difficult to know exactly what it is or how it functions."[31] The force was real enough. It deprived Africans of free agency, of the concept of materially changing what was and what was to come. This sense of fatalism, a direct consequence of the demonstrated efficacy of spirits and other mystical forces, existed among the men, women, and children who found themselves chained together with John Kizell, marching toward the coast and an unavoidable future.

"Surprising Things"

Land is sacred in Africa. It provides the people "with the roots of existence," Mbiti writes, "as well as binding them mystically to their departed. People walk on the graves of their forefathers, and it is feared that anything separating them from these ties will bring disaster to family and community life. To remove Africans by force from their land is an act of such great injustice that no foreigner can fathom it."[32]

John Kizell certainly understood the mystical links between the land and its people. When he sat down at the end of 1810 to describe the Sherbro and Gallinas regions to Governor Edward Columbine, he promised "to place the country in the truest light that I can."[33] But the fifty-year-old Kizell, entrusted by a European with a delicate mission, restricted himself to the material world. He knew from long experience that no foreigner was likely to appreciate Africans' sacred attachment to the land or mumbo-jumbo about a hidden spirit world.

Kizell had become a devout Christian. As someone who had been victimized by popular belief in witchcraft, he was prepared to reflect critically on Africans' "superstitious" nature. He was not inclined to explain to a colonial official that Africans resided among their living dead and unseen spirits. This was not something the governor or his European colleagues wanted to hear.

Also to be considered is that Kizell probably had become a member of Poro, which enforces a rigid code of secrecy. To have written, even tangentially, of Poro or occult matters could have had consequences. His opposition to trading in slaves already had made him controversial in the Sherbro. To discuss the spirit world openly could have made it difficult or impossible to continue residing in the area and jeopardized his livelihood as a trader.

34   Kizell did not necessarily reject the concept of a spirit world. In almost fairy-tale language, he recounted for Columbine "a very beautiful island" in the middle of a lake in the Boom country. He had not seen it, but the "natives speak much of a cave not far from this island, which is inhabited by spirits and of which they relate many surprising things." He said no more.[34]

Kizell was content to satisfy Columbine's curiosity, as well as indulge his own biases, by ridiculing the "Mandingo-men"—Muslims from the interior who traveled about selling charms. "They do not like to work," Kizell wrote. "They go from place to place; and when they find any chiefs or people whom they think they can make any thing of, they take up their abode for a time with them, and make greegrees [charms], and sometimes cast sand for them, for which they make them pay." A man of strong opinions, Kizell made clear that he "could say much" about the Mandingo-men, Muslim diviners believed to have supernatural powers. Instead he quickly moved to safer ground by describing the physical attributes of the Sherbro and Gallinas regions.[35]

He began with the large island of Sherbro, about twenty miles wide—a sandy, "swampy ground" that guards the mouth of the Sherbro River. The land was good only for growing abundant palm trees and bamboo, from which the people nonetheless provided many of their basic needs: palm oil for cooking, palm wine for refreshment, fibers to make rope and baskets, material for weaving mats (much in demand in Europe), and poles to build their houses.

The people lived in scattered family groups, fished, boiled seawater to produce salt, and traded for rice and cloth. They were superstitious, Kizell conceded, but "they do not want sense in other things: they . . . talk a palaver well, but then they make use of it to enslave and sell each other."[36]

The nearby mainland was fertile because of the alluvial soil deposited annually by rain-swollen rivers. Kizell grazed his own bullocks there and depicted a land of plenty. "Whatever is planted will come to the greatest perfection," especially rice. There were ducks and geese, freshwater fish, sheep, and goats. The people's "wants were few, and they are content with what they have," Kizell wrote. "I say they might [be] happy, if it was not for the Slave Trade."[37]

Kizell regarded the Shebar peninsula at the western point of a sandy strip extending toward the Gallinas as "a very good harbour," which sadly also provided shelter for slavers. The Shebar probably had been shaped by the Boom and Kittam rivers. The latter drained grassy lowlands. Rice grew well in the flood plains; camwood trees thrived in the sandy higher ground.

There were many lakes and "very beautiful views." Of one lake, he wrote Columbine, "if a gentleman had it in England, he would not take" a fortune for it. However, "a mortal poisonous tree" grew by the lake. "The natives will not shew it to any man; although they love me, and would do much for me, yet I could never get them to shew it to me."[38]

It was the Boom country, where the people spoke of cave spirits and of "surprising things," that most impressed Kizell. "The plantain grows wild. . . . The cassada (cassava, or manioc) is the best I have seen. . . . Rice is plenty. Of this country I cannot speak too well." Wild buffaloes roamed "in droves." Vast numbers of birds, large and small, filled the air. Many nested in the looming cotton silk trees.

"I am much taken up with this country," he wrote enthusiastically. "Only it is too far from Sierra Leone [meaning the colony at Freetown]. It is a good country; the people however are lazy; but this is no wonder: . . . they feel no need of riches. . . . all things are free: articles of food grow wild in the woods. . . . They live content . . . and if it was not for the cursed Slave Trade, I think that they would be the happiest people in the world."[39]

Kizell's narrative tells much about the Sherbro region and the Boom and Kittam districts. He does not refer to the Gallinas, however, where he was marched into bondage thirty-seven years earlier, and it is unclear that he was able to travel that far to the southeast on this mission. Nowhere in his reports does he mention an area that might have been familiar in his youth. Nor does he disclose that any of the peoples he describes might be his own.

Columbine had dispatched Kizell with a letter introducing him to the chiefs as "one of yourselves," but he was almost certainly referring generically to his emissary's being an African. Kizell had told Columbine that he came originally "some leagues" from the Sherbro. Historians have long inferred that he was *from* the Sherbro, but as a later incident strongly suggests, he actually came from the western verges of the Gallinas.

Kizell's vague reference to "some leagues" could have placed his home terrain anywhere well to the south and east of the Sherbro—in Kim country, for instance, south of the modern-day town of Pujehun. This would explain why, in what later ran to more than thirty printed pages, Kizell documented life in the entire Sherbro region and in the numerous communities he addressed without once betraying that he was on or near the sacred land of his forefathers.

To have disclosed Sherbro ancestry openly would have enhanced his credibility with the people and their leaders, as well as with the British authorities. But Kizell already had told Columbine that, as a boy, he had been taken to the Gallinas, not to the Sherbro, and been "carried as one of a cargo of slaves to Charlestown."[40]

Whether he was Kim, Sherbro, Vai, or even Mende—the warrior people who were beginning to penetrate the nearby interior in the mid-1700s—is less important than *who* and *what* he was. In a biographical note that accompanied Kizell's report, Columbine asserted in early 1811 that Kizell's father had been "a chief of some consequence, and so was his uncle."

Columbine also relates Kizell's dramatic tale of his enslavement: how the boy "was sent by his father on a visit to the uncle, who was desirous to have him with him. On the very night of his arrival, the town was attacked; a bloody battle ensued, in which his uncle and most of his people were killed. Some escaped; the rest were taken prisoners, and amongst those was Kizell. His father, as soon as he heard of his son's disaster, made every effort to relieve him, offering three slaves and some goods for him; but his enemies declared they would not give him up for any price, and that they would rather put him to death."[41]

The heart-wrenching story passed along by Columbine is curious. It appears to contradict a very different account, which Kizell had shared many years earlier with another British governor. It also suggests improbably that most in the town died.

People in the coastal Sherbro and Gallinas region lived in small, dispersed, kin-based villages. It is unlikely that Kizell's uncle lived in a large town. It is even less likely that the attackers would have slaughtered the majority of the people. This was atypical in localized African conflict and extremely wasteful if the objective was to capture slaves. Most telling is Kizell's revelation that his father owned slaves.

How and why Kizell actually was sold into slavery probably was complicated. His enslavement may have had some connection to cultural norms and to institutionalized domestic servitude in particular. It is necessary to look closely at how society in the Sherbro-Gallinas region was organized and why it was easily exploited by strangers seeking to meet the inflated demand for cheap labor in the Americas.

Early European visitors, as noted, were struck by the thinly scattered "towns" and villages—and the equally diffused political authority—along this part of the West African coast. This remained the pattern in the mid-1700s when the slave trader John Newton, years before he repented his sins and wrote the hymn "Amazing Grace," operated in the Sherbro. Newton and other outsiders soon learned that real power resided in Poro and not in individuals. Every village had its headman, who normally was the eldest Poro member, but it was the society that silently, secretly, and, if necessary, violently maintained order and decorum.

An appreciation of Poro is essential to understanding the sociopolitical environment in the Sherbro-Gallinas region during Kizell's lifetime. To "understand" Poro, however, is not to know its secrets or how it functions. Only its adepts possess such knowledge. Many African peoples have secret societies that, to non-Africans, often appear sinister. But secret societies are guardians of arcane knowledge critical to preserving the people's harmony with both their physical and spiritual surroundings.

"To be literate in an esoteric practice," Malidoma Patrice Somé writes, "one must belong to the school that teaches it and have the ability to keep silent about the school's secret practices." To an African, "the esoteric is a technology that is surrounded by secrecy. Those who know about it can own it only if they don't disclose it, for disclosure takes the power away. . . . If you cannot keep secrets, everyone in the tribe will soon know about it, because in a self-contained community there is no anonymity. . . . The number of secret societies is proportional to the number of technologies that must be kept alive to make the tribe what it is."[42]

The Poro society's Gorboi spirit, cloaked in raffia and charms, appears with its attendants on festive occasions in villages of the Sherbro region. Author's photograph (1963)

Newton could not have appreciated the interior functions and "esoteric" responsibilities of Poro, but he recognized its impact on daily life. In his *Thoughts upon the African Slave Trade*, published in 1788, he credited Poro with providing the Sherbro people with "regularity" in their government. In spite of their widely dispersed settlements, the people were integrated "by means of an institution which pervades them all."

Poro had legislative, executive, and policing authority. "Every thing belonging to the Purrow," Newton suggested, "is mysterious and severe, but, on the whole, it has very good effects; and as any man, whether bond or free, who will submit to be initiated into their mysteries, may be admitted of the order, it is a kind of commonwealth. And, perhaps, few people enjoy more, simple, political freedom, than the inhabitants of Sherbro."[43]

Another English slave trader in the Sherbro during this period stressed Poro's role as an arbiter and terrifying enforcer of peace. John Matthews, also writing in 1788, explained how Poro reduced the level of bloody conflict that Kizell claimed had led to his enslavement. When contending peoples wished to resolve potentially violent enmity, they could ask a "neighbouring state" to mediate. "If they do not agree to terminate their differences amicably," Matthews wrote, "they will send for the purrah.

Should they . . . prove refractory, the purrah is ordered out; and the grand fundamental article of the purrah law is, that no blood shall be shed while it is in force; so the late contending parties follow their several occupations without fear."

If someone violated the Poro injunction, Matthews continued, the latter "come down in a body of forty or fifty men armed and disguised . . . [and] dispose of [the transgressors] in such a manner that they are never more heard of. . . . It is impossible to describe the dread and terror this institution strikes into the common people."[44]

Newton and Matthews focused on Poro in eighteenth-century Sherbro. It also operated among the Gallinas peoples. Adam Jones, who has written extensively on the Gallinas, describes Poro "as a semi-religious constitutional watchdog, obliging kings and commoners alike to conform to certain established laws. . . . The Poro exercised control by terrorising those who had been initiated and, more particularly, nonmembers." Revealing Poro secrets was punishable by death.[45]

Although young boys were obliged at puberty to begin initiation, the process could extend over some years. It is questionable that Kizell would have been fully initiated when he was shipped to Charleston at age thirteen. It is likely, however, that he became a full member of Poro as an adult, after returning to Sierra Leone and settling in the Sherbro. Initiation would have been essential to live and function as he did, but he would have been proscribed from telling Governor Columbine or any noninitiate of his Poro connection.

Many, if not most, of the adult Sherbro and Gallinas men arriving as slaves in colonial America belonged to Poro. They brought with them—as did enslaved men from elsewhere in Africa—secret knowledge and experience of "surprising things." How this was assimilated into evolving African American societies, urban and plantation alike, will never be known. But there can be no doubt: the knowledge preserved and used by Poro was present in colonial South Carolina.

The ubiquitous spirits and Poro were accepted by all Sherbro-Gallinas peoples as an integral part of their existence. So was indigenous servitude. The institution survived in Sierra Leone well into the twentieth century, until banned in 1928 by the colonial government nearly a century after chattel slavery was made illegal in the British Empire. As many as half of the Mende people may have been domestic "slaves," tied to a master in a form of mutual dependency, in the latter part of the nineteenth century.[46]

There is ample testimony that "benign" forms of domestic servitude were common in the Sherbro-Gallinas region more than a century earlier, when Kizell was enslaved. "There are Free people and Slaves," the Swedish botanist Adam Afzelius wrote in his journal for March 29, 1796. He was a keen observer of life and nature during his two extended stays in Sierra Leone. Afzelius described how the free people employed slaves in rice farming. But they seldom sold any unless they had committed a serious crime. "They are commonly settled in separated towns. . . . Their children are born Slaves and continue so during their lifetime."[47]

Scholars disagree on the origin of domestic slavery in West Africa. Walter Rodney argued that it evolved and expanded in response to foreign demand for slaves. John Grace, however, believes there were "social institutions akin to slavery" well established in what is now Sierra Leone before the arrival of Mane invaders. Grace contends that the Mane imposed "the harsher form" of servitude and that the external slave trade merely distorted, rather than energized, the indigenous form.[48]

Afzelius and other visitors to the coastal region in the middle and late 1700s found the practice widespread. According to Grace, most of these slaves would have been controlled by the relatively limited number of influential people found in a typical village. The sparse population in the Sherbro-Gallinas meant that labor to cultivate rice and produce salt would have been in great demand. Carol MacCormack, who recorded oral traditions in the Sherbro in the 1970s, found painful memories of the wars and slave raiding of generations past, "but domestic slavery as productive labor is not remembered as harsh."[49]

Slave status was not merely the result of war or misfortune; it frequently was inherited. "Slave children were usually taken from their parents between the ages of seven and ten," Grace adds. "The boys went to work for their masters." In the Sherbro, MacCormack says, "children were purposely trained for their subordinate role."[50]

If Kizell, as he claimed, was the son of a chief, then he had not been born into domestic servitude.[51] His father owned slaves; his uncle probably did as well. From an early age, Kizell was conscious of the divide between the "free" and the "unfree." He understood that one day he would inherit his father's slaves.

White Slaves or Black?

The Europeans who began appearing along the West African coast in the fifteenth and sixteenth centuries understandably had no appreciation for the history, cultures, and politics of the people they encountered. Apart from a few notional maps and rumored kingdoms far across the Sahara, Africa was both terra incognita and a tabula rasa.

The Portuguese were the first to use improved seafaring technology to probe African shores. In 1444 Senegalese fishermen and coast dwellers found themselves seized unexpectedly by Portuguese raiders and sent back to Europe as slaves. The Senegalese effectively fought off subsequent forays, deflecting the Portuguese toward pursuit of commercial arrangements and diplomatic treaties with African states where they could find them.[52] As they pushed farther south, seeking the "spice route" to the East Indies, they discovered polities worthy of king-to-king relations.

Although the Portuguese and, eventually, other Europeans periodically visited what became known as the Windward Coast, they perceived it as an economic and political backwater in comparison to the strong, well-organized kingdoms in the Congo-Angola region. Europeans were left to construct a self-serving image of West Africa that invited exploitation. They found no robust political structures, no visibly organized religions, and no formal institutions to manage trade. They found no written records.

40 Europeans were blind to the larger physical world to which coastal peoples had belonged for centuries. What they knew of the spirit world, witchcraft, and secret societies, however, confirmed their assumption that Africans were legitimate objects of economic gratification. What they knew of Africa beyond the coast and the forest belt was limited and misapprehended. Coastal societies existed in an ahistorical void. West Africans were seemingly stranded in a state of nature and vulnerable to the external forces lapping at their shores.

The peoples of the Sherbro-Gallinas region were anything but disconnected from the world at large. As Walter Rodney, Rosalind Shaw, and other scholars have pointed out, they had long been integrated economically, if not politically, with the trade-based empires of the interior.

"Well before the coming of Europeans [to Sierra Leone] in the fifteenth century," Shaw writes, "the peoples of the region were organized into trade networks that connected different parts of the coast and rivers of upper Guinea and linked them to long-distance trade routes controlled by Mande-speaking peoples to the northeast. . . . At the other end of these Mande trade routes, in the urban centers of the Mali Empire and its satellite states, there was considerable demand for the salt that the coastal communities . . . produced. There was also demand for forest commodities such as cola nuts and malaguetta pepper, for which Mande elites had developed a taste."[53]

West Africa remained relatively untouched by European influence for the next two centuries. European interest was drawn primarily to the more accessible—and exploitable—New World. The sixteenth and seventeenth centuries were periods of extensive penetration of the Americas by Europeans drawn to a more clement environment and to empires, such as Mexico's, rich in silver and gold. Along the West African coast there were no empires or El Dorados.[54]

The Portuguese, English, Dutch, and other Europeans continued to trade on the coast throughout this period, but their interest in slaves was marginal. There was neither demand nor a substantial supply. Africans were loath to sell their people to the whites, who were widely reputed to be cannibals.[55] They preferred to meet Europeans' appetite for gold, ivory, and camwood. English traders such as William Hawkins were welcomed at first because, unlike the Portuguese, they did not seek to trade for—or seize—people.

This changed soon enough. With the support of Queen Elizabeth I, who had taken a personal stake in trading opportunities, Sir John Hawkins, William's son, obtained three hundred slaves on the coast in 1562. Two years later the queen supported a second slaving expedition. These voyages "had the most adverse effects upon the hitherto joyful relations of English seamen and the Africans on the coast," Kup writes. "English ships were no longer welcome after they had begun to obtain slaves 'partly by the sword, partly by other means.' . . . The Africans now regarded the English as no better than the Portuguese."[56]

The trade in slaves nonetheless remained modest for another century. Gold and ivory continued to drive European interest in Africa until the late 1600s. When King Charles II of England granted a new charter to the Royal Adventurers Trading into Africa in 1663, it was the first time that a European company had been officially mandated to secure slaves. But it was not until the 1680s that the trade gained the impetus that eventually transformed it into the largest forced human migration ever known. The Royal African Company, which succeeded the Royal Adventurers, had already been obliged by its patrons in 1672 to supply three thousand slaves annually. By the mid-1680s the company had a contract to supply slaves to Spanish plantations, mainly in Jamaica. Many of these were shipped from the Sherbro.[57]

The Gallinas remained peripheral in terms of Europeans' interest in trade and in slaves. In the 1680s the Royal African Company finally posted a lone Englishman to represent its interests in the Gallinas. Complaining of "abuses by the natives," he soon expired and was not replaced.[58]

The Dutch, much earlier in the century, had established a factory in the Gallinas as part of their attempt to seize control of the trade in slaves to Brazil, principally from the Congo-Angola region. Their grander scheme failed, but Dutch traders continued to loiter in the Gallinas. As late as 1682, chiefs in the Sherbro were threatening to shift their business from the English to the Dutch.[59]

English interest in the slave trade heightened in the mid and late 1600s as Britain took control of Barbados and Jamaica. Development of the islands' sugar plantations required cheap and easily replenished labor. Given the near-total demise of the native Carib peoples through disease and conquest, English planters had to look elsewhere for strong arms and backs.

Peoples from Senegambia to the Bight of Benin had no way to know that they were about to be incorporated into a massive uprooting that would last for nearly two centuries. David Eltis, whose documentation of the slave trade sheds fresh light on this tragedy, suggests several factors that led to reliance on African slave labor to develop English colonies in the Caribbean and America. This was not inevitable, he maintains: "The tightening labour market in Britain after 1650 is an argument for more coercion, but not for more Africans."[60]

Conventional analyses link expansion of the slave trade to the mounting European desire for sugar and tobacco and to the consequent demand for labor to cultivate more and more plantations. Eltis argues that this ignores coincidental population dynamics in England, Ireland, and the colonies.

More than one hundred thousand English emigrants left for Barbados and other colonies in the 1640s. Emigration increased in the 1650s. But by then, Eltis asserts, "there was much stronger competition for migrants from elsewhere in the British Empire, noticeably Ireland." At the same time, natural population growth in England was slowing sharply. Having achieved control of most of Ireland in 1651, England now faced the challenge of colonizing it at the same time that opportunity beckoned in the colonies to expand settlement and agricultural production. "It is striking," Eltis says, "that these developments coincided with the most enduring check to English population growth in four centuries. . . . There were thus new pressures on both colonial and domestic labour markets after 1650."[61]

Rising prices for indentured servants and declining prices for sugar underscored the need for alternative sources of affordable labor. One option considered and rejected was to exile Irish children to work in England and the colonies. Another was to send convicts—and there were many—directly to the New World plantations at considerably less cost than expanding the nascent trade in African slaves. This option also went begging. Yet, as Eltis writes, there was "no purely economic explanation as to why European prisoners were never sentenced to a lifetime of servitude in the plantations."[62]

The cost of labor in England naturally rose in response to the nearly stagnant population growth after 1650. This helped to brake immigration to the colonies, but the wealthy were still compelled to seek affordable workers in other ways. "The second half of the seventeenth century saw not only a larger slave trade to the colonies," Eltis notes, "but also an increased interest in obtaining labour through coercion within England. The rapid expansion of slavery in the English colonies . . . coincided with revisions of the Poor Laws at home" in the late 1600s. These shifted the emphasis of the poorhouse as a social welfare institution to one focused "on using the poor as an economic resource."[63]

Eltis does not shy from concluding that, without a conscious English "aversion to enslaving Europeans, it is hard to see how there would have been any Africans in the New World before the twentieth century." More than three hundred thousand English left for America and the Caribbean between 1650 and 1700. A similar number could have been sent to the colonies without materially affecting labor costs in England—that is, if government and business leaders had drawn upon the ample white-skinned manpower available among Irish children, the poor, convicts, and prisoners of war.[64]

Simply put, in Eltis's view African slaves were not needed to develop the plantation economies in England's New World colonies. Although the free white labor market was tight, there was no lack of coercible and inexpensive whites. Nonetheless the British, in what Philip D. Curtin terms an "overwhelmingly racial" policy, began consciously to substitute Africans in large numbers. "Europeans in tropical America," Curtin writes, "believed that Negroes were peculiarly immune to the effects of a hot climate, just as Europeans seemed peculiarly liable to death in the climate of the West Indies. . . . The general conclusion, that certain races had inborn qualities of strength and weakness fitting them for specific 'climates,' became an accepted 'fact' and a cornerstone of pseudo-scientific racism."[65]

The English economy depended heavily on the sale of textiles and other manufactures to Europe in this period. This required maintaining low wages to compete with equally depressed labor costs in continental Europe. But, Eltis believes, "the strong growth of the slave-based Atlantic system . . . removed some of the urgent need to keep domestic wages as low as those in mainland Europe." England thus was able to sustain higher wages for its own workers, still compete with European manufactures, and avoid sending impoverished kith and kin to toil in the colonies.[66]

Complex as these economic circumstances may have been, they do not obscure a hard truth. For Eltis "the most important implication of the race-based slave system on seventeenth-century England may not have been economic at all . . . but rather ideological. In effect, the growth of the slave system . . . allowed the full celebration of English liberties. English ideologues did not have to cope with the dilemma of free labour in land-abundant environments until the nineteenth century."

This, Eltis contends, is "why the ideological tensions between slavery and freedom in Revolutionary America have received more attention than the same phenomenon in late seventeenth-century England. The oft-cited case of John Locke writing a constitution for the Carolinas that incorporated a slave code, while at the same time laying out the theoretical basis for the Glorious Revolution in England, is nevertheless striking."[67]

In the ongoing academic debate over the root causes of the African slave trade, Patrick Manning and many scholars reject pure racism as an animating factor. "There is no way," Manning writes, "a simple European prejudice against Africans could have constructed a system so vast and so iniquitous." Rather "slavery and racism reinforced each other through an intricate dialectic."[68]

Manning endorses the long-held proposition that Africans' relative resistance to tropical diseases made them more suited than Europeans to the hard work in the Hades-like clime of the Caribbean. He also emphasizes the underlying low productivity of Africans' hoe-based agriculture, which cheapened the value of African labor.

"If African agricultural productivity had been as high as that in the Occident," Manning writes, "prices for African labor would have been bid up until only a trickling stream of laborers flowed across the Atlantic, rather than the great rush . . . who crossed . . . in the holds of slave ships."[69] In other words had African agriculture been substantially more productive and the market value of African labor high enough to make European labor economically competitive, it is possible to imagine the slave trade playing a marginal role in developing Britain's colonies in the Caribbean and North America.

The "political fragmentation" of West Africa, as Manning terms it, compounded the coastal region's low agricultural productivity. At the turn of the eighteenth century, therefore, West Africans thus found themselves drawn increasingly into a British mercantilist system whose ethos only later became increasingly racial and cultural. But for the moment it appeared to Africans in the Sherbro-Gallinas region as nothing more than a convenient means to dispose of criminals, debtors, war prisoners, and domestic slaves, even the occasional witch.

The Windward Coast still lagged well behind the Gold Coast and the Bights of Benin and Biafra farther to the east as sources of slaves. British-based ships concentrated on Biafra and the Gold Coast. The French and the Brazil-based Portuguese dominated the trade in Benin. Slave exports from the latter rose sharply in the late 1600s and peaked at more than two hundred thousand in 1700. Comparable figures for England's sphere of interest in Biafra and the Gold Coast totaled perhaps a third of this. It was not until the 1720s and 1730s that slave exports in English vessels increased dramatically from these regions.[70]

By the early 1700s, the transatlantic slave trade was maturing as a business enterprise and as an institutionalized component of colonial expansion. The process was rapid and traumatic between the Gold Coast and Angola. In the Sherbro-Gallinas, however, it evolved slowly. The small numbers of slaves usually available for sale could not compete with the considerable bodies of captive Africans marketed to the east and south.

As late as 1728, a British slave captain calling at Bance Island for fresh water and food expected to find few, if any, slaves to be purchased there. He was "bound down the Coast for 300 Slaves," he said. By 1750, however, another English captain was

Ruins of Bance Island slave "factory," through which thousands of South Carolina–bound slaves passed in the mid-1700s. Author's photograph (1964)

reporting "a prodigious Trade for Slaves" at Bance.[71] Slaves also had become an important commodity for trade in the Sherbro and Gallinas.[72]

Increased demand accounts only in part for slavers' relatively sudden interest in the Windward Coast. Events deep inland had coincided with the growth of the slave trade. Ships arriving at Bance and the Sherbro-Gallinas during the midcentury decades began finding more slaves on offer. For this they could thank Fulani Muslims in the Futa Jallon for renewing jihad against their animist neighbors.

Commencing in about 1725 and extending into the 1740s, this final phase in more than a century of Muslim expansion displaced people toward the coast. It destabilized much of the region and generated a steady supply of war prisoners and other unfortunates. European slave traders were attracted like vultures—a common sight in West Africa—to fresh carrion.

Although slaves had replaced ivory and camwood—which were playing out—as the leading exports in the Sherbro and Gallinas, the trade remained relatively modest compared with Bance Island to the north. Nicholas Owen's journal makes this clear for the Sherbro. In the Gallinas evidence also suggests that large numbers of slaves were not to be expected.

In the slave trade's peak years in the early 1770s, individual ports of call in the Gallinas and its environs supplied no more than five hundred slaves annually. The Vai, who lived on the eastern side of the Gallinas watershed, would sell a few slaves when they were available. But according to Svend E. Holsoe, "the Vai country and surrounding regions remained an area of relatively low slave yield. . . . Slave traders' account books . . . indicate that they never obtained . . . more . . . than ten to fifteen [slaves] at any one stop."[73]

The outbreak in 1754 of armed confrontation in America between England and France, and the wider Seven Years' War (1756–63) that ensued, effectively halted slave trading throughout West Africa. The conflict revealed just how modest the slave trade was along the Sierra Leone coast even in times of peace. The struggle had barely started when Owen complained of the "great decay of trade . . . occasioned by the French war and scarcety of English shipping." The British navy, which normally cruised the coast, had been deployed to protect more profitable parts of the empire. By the end of the war, John Newton observed, only a few European traders survived where many had once prospered.[74]

Such was the world into which John Kizell was born—while the English and French contended across faraway expanses of ocean and land; while the Fulani consolidated power in the Futa Jallon; while Euro-African traders named Tucker, Rogers, and Caulker accumulated wealth and influence in their coastal fiefdoms; and while life in his parents' village went on as it had for as long as anyone, including the ancestors, could remember.

His village was somewhere in the Gallinas watershed and not more than ten or twenty miles from the Atlantic coast. His precise origin and social status are clouded by divergent versions of his enslavement. The one passed down by historians is what he related to Governor Columbine during that officer's blighted tenure in Sierra Leone in 1810–11. Kizell told essentially the same story in 1818 to two visiting Americans, Samuel Mills and Ebenezer Burgess. However, while he repeated that most of his uncle's family had been killed, this time he said nothing of the uncle's death.[75]

The story of the attack and Kizell's being carried into bondage excited sympathy with English and Americans, whose governments in 1808 had finally made the slave trade illegal for their subjects. It would also have enhanced his moral stature in the Sherbro vis-à-vis those engaged in the slave trade. However, in early 1798, before he had settled permanently in the Sherbro or achieved prominence as an active opponent of the slave trade, Kizell had divulged a very different account of his enslavement to the young Englishman then serving as governor for the Sierra Leone Company.

Zachary Macaulay disdained African superstitions. He was especially concerned that many of the so-called Nova Scotian settlers—African Americans who were supposed to be building a new society based on Christian principles—had not completely abandoned the "idolatrous practices of their fathers."

When he learned that some of the black settlers were planning to try two local African men accused of theft by forcing them to drink the feared "red water," Macaulay was outraged. He was impressed that Kizell had tried to intervene. "Some of the more thinking Settlers," Macaulay wrote in his journal, "had got an intimation of what was going forward [and] . . . interrupted for the present such disgraceful proceedings. One of them"—Kizell—"spoke with much feeling."

"When I saw what was going on," Macaulay quoted him the next day, "my Spirit was too much moved, but really Sir I was not Master of myself at the moment. I am a Native of this Country. At the age of Thirteen I was accused of witchcraft, found guilty by some such trial & sold into slavery. I have blessed God a thousand times for having placed me and my children where we run no risk of the like injustice."[76]

Kizell had no motive in 1798 to hide the accusation of witchcraft that had condemned him to slavery in America. Such charges were a common device to brand individuals for sale to the nearest slave trader. Confiding that he had been victimized in this fashion played to Macaulay's biases. It also confirmed the latter's growing regard for Kizell as one of the worthier Nova Scotians.

Kizell's accounts of his enslavement may not have been as contradictory as they appear. Both stories, one involving witchcraft and the other an attack on his uncle's village, are plausible by themselves; they also can be plausibly linked.

Kizell probably *was* taken in an attack on his uncle's village, which in effect made him someone's domestic slave. His master may then have decided later to dispose of him to the foreign slave trade. Under local customs the master would have had to charge the boy with some nominal offense, witchcraft being expedient, without having to prove it by subjecting him to a potentially fatal dose of the "red water."[77]

The nature and context of domestic slavery are important to understanding how Europeans and Euro-Africans were able to expand their profitable trade in human chattel along this part of the West African coast. Domestic slavery in its several forms was common throughout the Sherbro and the Gallinas.

The Vai, living just to the east of the Kim, distinguished among indentured labor- **47** ers, pawns, and absolute slaves. Indentured servants either owed debts they could not pay or were compensating a husband with whose wife they had engaged in sex. Pawns worked for a relative, without compensation, to satisfy debts incurred by another family member. However, indentured servants and pawns were not slaves; they were collateral, bound to a master and his family through debt.[78]

Vai slaves might be war captives or criminals, those born of slaves or at least of a slave woman, and people bought from outside the tribe. Slaves belonged to the family head and were seldom sold. Their treatment, as Holsoe writes, "varied depending upon the character and social position of their master. . . . Some Vai felt complete contempt for slaves and treated them accordingly. They thought of them as unclean and had no more contact with them than was necessary. Harshness sometimes occurred on the institutional level: slaves were often buried alive at the funeral of an important master, and slave babies were sacrificed in ceremonies when crocodiles, who were believed to be the embodiments of ancestors, were honored."[79]

Whether Kizell was Sherbro, Kim, or even Vai, he was raised in a society where large numbers of people belonged to individual masters and their extended families. Their labor and offspring also belonged to others, but they existed in a socioeconomic environment knit together by a matrix of mutual obligations. Domestic servitude was a means to settle debts and thus to reduce disharmony in the village. It also enabled groups to strengthen economically through increased food production (principally of rice and salt) and to defend against aggressors. Having slaves meant having labor to cultivate new land and warriors to respond to incursions.

The advent of the export trade in slaves gradually distorted traditional forms of domestic servitude. An accepted aspect of indigenous life metamorphosed into a convenient mechanism to dispose of surplus labor, undesirables such as thieves and witches, war captives, and the unwary kidnapped along forest paths.

By the time of Kizell's birth, the foreign slave trade had become the commanding reality for coastal peoples. It would shape the boy's understanding of a dangerously uncertain habitat, shared with invisible spirits, all manner of wild beasts, and the white men—and partially white men—who "swallowed" their people at the edge of the great water. Two and a half centuries later, the few remaining Kim speakers told how their ancestors vanished quickly into nearby swamps whenever slavers appeared.[80]

Kizell's revelation to Macaulay that he had been charged with witchcraft fits contemporary accounts of both domestic slavery and the slave trade. Matthews, testifying in London before the Privy Council, described in 1789 how masters in the Sherbro condemned their own slaves as witches in order to sell them abroad. The village elders, many of them also slave owners, would hear the "evidence" and accept their neighbor's judgment. There was no need to administer the fatal "red water" and lose the slave's value in cash or kind. Case closed.[81]

48   A troubling irony might have occurred to Kizell the putative witch as he trudged toward a rendezvous with the ship that would carry him to Charleston. Or perhaps it came while he lay, parched and chained, in the heaving darkness and stench of the slave deck. He would have reflected that the Africans, Europeans, and mulattoes profiting from the slave trade were said to be the greatest witches of all.[82]

3

THE OVERTURNING

"No persons would have seen the Civil War with more surprise and horror than the Revolutionists of 1776; yet from the small and apparently dying institution of their day arose the walled and castled Slave-Power."

W. E. B. DuBois, The Suppression of the African Slave Trade, *1896*

In Westminster Henry Laurens continued reading the political tea leaves with deepening concern. By early 1774 he had concluded that there would be "trouble and Confusion in America" and that "Carolina will partake of the Evil." Where a year earlier he had warned against importing slaves into an overheated market, now he feared that volatile relations with England made the slave trade even riskier. "If I was an Owner of African Vessels on this Side," he wrote to a friend, "I would not trust a Congo there; if a Merchant there, I would not wish to receive a Congo." [1]

Laurens had recently alerted John Lewis Gervais that accepting further slave consignments "would be injurious to your Interest." He admitted to being "pressed by Some friends on this Side" to arrange them. "I will do a great deal to Serve you," Laurens added, "but Entring into the African Trade is So repugnant to my disposition & my plan for future Life that . . . nothing but dire necessity could drive me to it." [2]

"Notions of Liberty"

A few weeks later, Laurens asked Gervais for a favor for his old London associate, Richard Oswald. Once a major supplier of slaves from Sierra Leone to South Carolina, Oswald was disengaging from the business. He felt responsible, however, for about a hundred *grumettas*—de facto slaves—who worked at his factory on Bance Island. If Oswald simply dismissed the men, they would be seized by neighboring chiefs and sold to the first slaver that appeared.

Oswald "is under a promise to those Negroes not to expose them to public sale," Laurens explained. But he hoped it would be possible "with their liking & good behaviour to keep them together to work on his plantation" in South Carolina. They were slaves "to all intents & purposes," Laurens conceded, but they also were "free"— up to a point. Some were water men, who might prefer settling in Charleston. [3] Would Gervais oversee their placement in South Carolina?

Gervais received just one consignment of slaves in 1774. The sloop *Amelia*, Captain McNeill, arrived from Bance on September 12 with about 150 people. Oswald's *grumettas* may have been among them, some of the last Africans to arrive in Charleston before the colonies suspended trade with Great Britain. Nine ships, carrying close to 2,000 slaves, were recorded by the Charleston customhouse on the same day. Three more ships, from Senegal and Gambia, slipped into Charleston in late September and early October, disembarking another 500 slaves into South Carolina's very uncertain economic and political arena.[4]

50

On October 20 the topic of conversation among black Charlestonians—along the wharfs, in the tippling houses, in the lower market—was a verbatim announcement in that day's *Gazette* of a resolution recently adopted by the Continental Congress: "We will neither import nor purchase, any slave imported after the first day of December next, after which time, we will wholly discontinue the slave trade, and will neither be concerned in it ourselves, nor will we hire our vessels, nor sell our commodities or manufactures to those who are concerned in it."[5]

Four days later the sloop *Maria*—with just fifty-two slaves consigned to Powell and Hopton—arrived from the Isles de Los. It was the last permitted to land slaves in Charleston. The following March the ship *Katharine* anchored with three hundred Angolans consigned to another Charleston merchant. With provisions and water almost gone, it was resupplied and quickly sent on its way to the West Indies.[6]

With the departure of the *Katharine*, white *and* black Charlestonians might have pondered when if ever the African slave trade would resume. By December it was clear that South Carolina would abide fully with the ban on English trade,[7] but this was by definition a temporary measure until the dispute with Great Britain was resolved. Whites were prepared to do without molasses, sugar, tea, and other items for the time being. Whether they were prepared to do without a reliable supply of slaves was less certain.

There had been vocal opposition in South Carolina during the debate over the proposed nonimportation policy in general. When it came to the slave trade, however, those who profited most from slavery clearly anticipated its timely revival. In the meantime its suspension might actually benefit planters and merchants alike. Laurens had correctly foreseen both the glut of slaves and the market's dislocation.[8]

If there were any doubt where South Carolina's elite stood vis-à-vis the future of slavery and the slave trade, it was dispelled when the Continental Congress considered Thomas Jefferson's initial draft of a Declaration of Independence. Jefferson had charged King George III with waging a "cruel war against human nature itself, violating its most sacred rights of life and liberty in the persons of a distant people who never offended him, captivating and carrying them into slavery in another hemisphere, or to incur miserable death in their transportation thither."[9]

Hypocritical as these words were, coming from a slave owner who depended throughout his life on slave labor, Jefferson's was the severest indictment framed up to that time. As he confided in his notes, it was deleted "in complaisance to South

Carolina and Georgia, who had never attempted to restrain the importation of slaves, and who on the contrary still wished to continue it."[10]

Blacks in Charleston and elsewhere in the southern colonies could not be insulated from the mounting political agitation. Many would have heard reports in 1773, carried by black sailors and in newspapers, that slaves in Boston had petitioned for freedom. James Madison and others in Virginia tried to hide discovery of a slave plot to assist British troops, but this incendiary news eventually seeped southward. As Frey notes, Madison understood "the dilemma of a slaveholding society about to embark on a war against tyranny: how to prevent their slaves from imbibing the heady notions of liberty and equality . . . [and] how to exploit white fears of a slave rebellion to unite the white population behind the patriot cause."[11]

Whites in Charleston were aware as early as 1772 that blacks were meeting frequently and in large numbers. Initially whites seemed to have had little concrete knowledge of what actually was being discussed by their slaves. However, a report in the *Gazette* of September 17, 1772, suggested the worst. The anonymous "Stranger," who often wrote knowingly about the black community, was "informed, that such assemblies have been very common, and that the company has sometimes amounted to 200 persons, even within one mile's distance of this place. Nay he has been told, that intriguing meetings of this sort are frequently held even in Town, either at the houses of free negroes, apartments hired to slaves, or the kitchens of such Gentlemen as frequently retire, with their families into the country, for a few days. . . . Wherever and whenever such nocturnal rendezvouses are made, may it not be concluded, that their deliberations are never intended for the advantage of white people."[12]

The provincial assembly's committee of intelligence, according to one member, knew by 1774 that slaves in the colony "entertained ideas that the present contest was for obliging us to give them their liberty."[13] If they needed confirmation, the English House of Commons provided it by considering in late 1774 a proposal to humble the colonies by freeing all slaves. The measure failed, but blacks were left to draw their own conclusions when word reached them in early 1775.[14]

This coincided with the near lynching of a black, British-trained Methodist preacher. He had been invited by a prominent white boot maker to address blacks at his home. The pastor reminded them that "the Jews of old treated the Gentiles as Dogs & I am informed the people of this Country use those of my Complection as such. . . . but let them remember that the Children of Israel were delivered out of the hands of Pharo and he and all his Host were drowned in the Red Sea, and God will deliver his own People from Slavery." The preacher was hustled to Georgia and put on an England-bound ship before any harm came to him.[15] But his message must have reached the ears of most black Charlestonians, including John Kizell.

Whites also got the message and tried to prevent clerics' access to the black communities in Charleston and on plantations. "War was coming on," wrote David George, who had run away from his Virginian owner and come to Silver Bluff, near Augusta. "Ministers were not allowed to come amongst us lest they should furnish us with too much knowledge."[16] Under the influence of George Liele, another Virginia slave whose master had brought him south, George became a Baptist and began preaching to fellow slaves. George and Kizell met after the war, in Nova Scotia. George may have baptized Kizell and perhaps given his name to Kizell's son George. The two men remained close in Sierra Leone.

Kizell, now fifteen, would not soon forget the year 1775. In the swirl of rumor and uncertainty, blacks throughout the American colonies were watching whites—*their* whites, in particular—and taking the measure of their fears, self-interest, and political loyalties. Slaves by nature developed coping mechanisms and survival skills. These would be fully deployed as whites debated, resolved, and ultimately acted upon measures that could only bring down the might of England upon their heads. In their own debates and discussion, blacks would have focused on one question: Who was strongest? Most whites would have agreed with blacks' obvious conclusion: the king.

No one in the early spring of 1775 could have imagined what was about to happen in America or how it would affect their lives. Henry Laurens had already predicted "trouble and Confusion." Slaves were thought to cherish liberty, prompting the provincial assembly to begin probing possible slave insurrection.[17] In late March Lieutenant Governor William Bull wrote to London that "the Men of Property begin at length to see that the many headed power the People . . . have discovered their own strength & importance, and are not now so easily governed by their former leaders."[18] Another genie was out of the bottle.

Laurens, Esther Kysell, who was buying land that April, and whites in general clearly hoped that, come what may, they would continue life much as they had known it once the storm had passed. Endowed with the authority and power of the king, colonial officials assumed they would prevail.

Blacks had the most to gain by any upheaval of the status quo. Frey believes that "a black liberation movement was central to the revolutionary struggle in the South."[19] Whether a "movement" existed in South Carolina is problematic. Black "liberation" proceeded during the Revolutionary era largely on the basis of individuals' assessment of risk and opportunity, not through any organized attempt by blacks to overthrow the slave power. Randall M. Miller argues that "South Carolina blacks . . . did not take advantage of their owners' predicament, nor did lowcountry planters exhibit the anxiety about their slaves' loyalty manifested by Maryland and Virginia slaveholders." As one South Carolina patriot believed, slaves would be guided by their "opinion . . . of our superiority or inferiority."[20]

Premonitions of slave violence were not groundless. At least one "plot" was discovered among slaves and a free black who allegedly planned to time their rising with the imminent arrival of the new governor. Lord William Campbell was widely rumored to be bringing troops and a large supply of weapons and ammunition to suppress dissidence and to reopen trade. News had arrived in early May 1775 that the British government had considered encouraging insurrection among "loyal" slaves in exchange for freedom. Then came word that British redcoats had been defeated by

Massachusetts minutemen at Lexington and Concord. White fears rose with the tide of rumor and fact.[21] Militia companies were soon patrolling Charleston night and day, creating what one person described as a "garrison town" atmosphere.[22]

Kizell would have known, at least by name, the accused ringleader of the supposed plot. Thomas Jeremiah (sometimes recorded as Jeremiah Thomas) was a wealthy free black, skilled harbor pilot, fisherman, and slave owner. Just how serious the plot was is conjectural. Two slaves, including his brother-in-law, testified that Jeremiah had been recruiting blacks to help the British take control of the harbor. Only a few others were implicated and sentenced merely to be whipped.

Laurens, who had recently returned from London and been elected president of the provincial congress, regarded Jeremiah as "puffed up by prosperity, ruined by Luxury and debauchery and grown to an amazing pitch of vanity and ambition." Although he presumed Jeremiah guilty, he questioned how evolved the plot actually was. "One or two Negroes are to be Severely flogged & banished," he wrote to his son John in England. "I ask for what? If they deserve any punishment nothing less than Death Should be the Sentence."[23]

Jeremiah may have been guilty of nothing more than incautious bravado. Charleston whites, however, were convinced of blacks' malevolence; the charge against Jeremiah provided an opportunity to vent their fears. The committee sitting in judgment obliged by sentencing him to death. Lord Campbell, who had arrived without troops or arms, protested and was warned that the execution would be held at his front door if he continued to remonstrate.

On August 18 Jeremiah, professing innocence and refusing to implicate white loyalists to save his life, went to the gallows with dignity. A mob then burned his body. "They have now dipt their hands in Blood," Campbell announced to London. "God Almighty knows where it will end."[24]

Blacks did not need the example of Jeremiah's execution to warn them of white alarm and the advent of the "mob." Two white men had been tarred, feathered, and carted through the streets in June for boasting that the British were arming slaves, Indians, and Catholics. The provincial congress meanwhile had required whites to swear fealty and to defend against any British assault. Harassment of royal officials increased, forcing some to leave. Dissent retreated behind people's front doors.[25]

Whites either were galvanized by the news from Lexington and Concord or compelled to keep their own counsel. Blacks watched and waited. Laurens gathered his Charleston slaves together in early June and "admonished them to behave with great circumspection in this dangerous times [*sic*] [and] set before them the great risque of exposing themselves to the treachery of pretended friends."[26]

Many slave owners probably did likewise, some blustering and threatening, others pleading and cajoling. A few perhaps promised an indefinite freedom. Laurens believed that "my Negroes . . . are strongly attached to me."[27] It was only natural and self-congratulatory to trust one's own slaves; it was the mass of faceless, unknown blacks who were most to be feared.

Although a very real and potentially bloody plot was discovered among plantation slaves in the Cheraw District, the summer passed without overt signs of organized black resistance in Charleston. That changed when Governor Campbell, humiliated by the execution of Jeremiah and lacking the arms to enforce royal authority, dissolved the colony's assembly and withdrew to HMS *Tamar* in the harbor. Charleston and South Carolina were now in de facto rebellion. With the line drawn vividly between colonials and king, blacks could better choose which side served their best interest.

Several hundred Charleston blacks decided in the fall that a better future lay with the king. Some sought refuge on Sullivan's Island, where they hoped to be protected by the three British ships anchored in Rebellion Road. Angolan-born Isaac Anderson, a young carpenter, and other blacks claiming to be free managed to reach safety aboard the ships. Many others appear to have been turned away.[28]

The provincial council of safety considered Sullivan's Island, no longer needed to quarantine newly arrived Africans, a nest of white and black banditti. On December 16 it resolved "to apprehend and disperse the runaway slaves . . . who have lately, in armed parties, committed several robberies and depredations" along the coast. The council believed that they were being supported by the British. Two days later Laurens wrote to the captain of the *Tamar* that permission to obtain supplies in the city was being withdrawn until the black refugees aboard were returned. They were not.[29]

In the meantime a company of rangers had raided the island, killed three or four blacks, and taken five others.[30] Militia also arrested a free black fisherman for allegedly carrying messages for the British and intercepted several slaves who were trying to escape in canoes.[31] For blacks water remained the boundary between good and evil.

Having waited in vain for reinforcement, Lord Campbell and his small fleet withdrew to the open sea on January 6, 1776. They headed north to join a strong British naval force preparing to attack Wilmington and the Cape Fear region of North Carolina. Fifty blacks sailed with him, including Anderson, who would serve the British cause through the long war years to come. A quarter century later, the British governor of Sierra Leone would hang him for leading a "rebellion" against colonial authority.[32]

Word had reached Charleston before Campbell's withdrawal that blacks in Virginia were being enlisted into British military units. Lord Dunmore, the royal governor, also had retreated aboard ship in the Chesapeake Bay. There he published a newspaper and organized Tory support in the Norfolk area. On November 7, alerted that patriot militia were assembling at Williamsburg, Dunmore imposed martial law. He pledged freedom to slaves who left their owners for the king's standard and formed an "Ethiopian" regiment. Eight days later white and black Tories marched with Dunmore and his regulars to hold the patriots at Great Bridge and then occupy Norfolk.[33]

Their success was short-lived. By mid-December Dunmore had retreated once more to his fleet, and the patriots had reoccupied Norfolk. When Dunmore bombarded the town on New Year's Day, the patriots began looting and set fire to Tory homes. One belonged to John Lowndes, a prominent merchant. His path crossed Kizell's during the loyalists' final days in America and later on the granite shores of Nova Scotia.

The flames that consumed Norfolk were felt throughout the colonies. Charlestonians lived in daily fear of fire. When they learned of Norfolk's fate, they could only wonder when they would be visited with similar devastation. The firing of Virginia's port was a political tipping point.

The sympathies of blacks were increasingly important but difficult to gauge. One of the patriot stalwarts who drove Dunmore's forces from Norfolk was a free black from Portsmouth. His heroism was celebrated publicly for decades.[34] But slaves had not been slow to answer Dunmore's call for volunteers. Virginians offered pardons to those who returned to their masters within ten days.[35] Gen. George Washington, however, had little doubt where slave loyalty lay. "If . . . [Dunmore] is not crushed before spring," he wrote to a fellow Virginian, "he will become the most formidable enemy America has . . . if some expedient cannot be hit upon to convince the slaves and servants of the impotency of his designs."[36]

The obvious expedient, freedom, proved beyond whites' imagination. When South Carolina's council of safety resolved in January 1776 to enroll "able-bodied negro men . . . without arms" to service artillery batteries in and around Charleston, it promised only "suitable rewards" for those "who behave well in time of action."[37] Freedom was not on offer in the southern colonies. Laurens made this clear to his abolition-minded son, John, during the war's bleakest days.

Why did William Flora, the free Portsmouth black, help break the British charge across Great Bridge, while Thomas Jeremiah apparently lost his life for siding with the colonial power? Why did hundreds of Virginia slaves and hundreds more in Charleston try to reach Lord Dunmore and Lord Campbell? And why did thousands of slaves, including Laurens's at Mepkin plantation near Charleston, stay rooted where they were? Why did Isaac Anderson run and Kizell—for the moment—not?

Decades later Kizell told two white American visitors at his home in the Sherbro that he believed all blacks would gladly trade life in America for life in Africa.[38] He had left the United States thirty-five years earlier, but his guests made no pretense that things had materially improved for blacks in America. Slavery was wrong and certainly doomed. But they agreed with Kizell: no black could be truly free in America.

Anderson had understood this and had taken his opportunity to run. Did this mean he valued freedom more than Kizell and the majority of slaves who awaited events and the war's outcome? Or did it have something to do with how blacks interpreted concepts such as freedom and liberty in a world where there was little of either?

Neither Anderson nor the younger Kizell was far removed from his African roots. Each would have defined freedom to some degree in the context of his cultural origins and the political organization he had experienced in Africa. Anderson had been born and raised in a region of Central Africa where coherent, often powerful, political entities had existed for centuries and where Christianity was well established and

Africanized by the mid-1700s.[39] Kizell came from a society characterized by weak political authority, where secret societies enforced behavioral norms and governed human relations and where people's essentially fatalistic worldview gave little scope to improving the human condition.

Perceptions of freedom and slaves' decisions to pursue it were necessarily based on a complex of factors. Cultural conditioning was one. Opportunity was another. Motive, however, was the key determinant. To run or not depended on a careful weighing of family ties and friendships; security versus fear of the unknown; the desire to escape hard labor, brutal overseers, and bad masters; a sense of responsibility to one's fellow slaves; and even loyalty to a humane owner.

Whites faced much the same anguishing calculation: to rebel or not against *their* master. Whether one chose to be a patriot or a loyalist was no less difficult or intimidating than for a slave in Charleston to seek something as elusive and ill defined as liberty.

The prospect of whites' rebelling against an overwhelming power and a figure of authority in the king must have seemed as quixotic to blacks as their own fantasies of freedom. They knew slaves who had successfully vanished or brazenly took extended leave from their masters.[40] They knew of maroon communities of escaped slaves who sustained themselves in the swamps. They knew the runaways who lived among them.

They also had before them the anomaly of "free" blacks, whose position did not always advertise the advantages of freedom. They were free perhaps to keep all that they might earn, free to own slaves. But they were still social pariahs to whites, resented especially by those who fell beneath them economically.

To many slaves the predominantly mulatto free blacks would have been objects of jealousy, envy, and worse. In Africa to acquire wealth and enjoy prosperity greater than your neighbor was antisocial at best and suggestive of witchcraft. To be free *and* black in colonial South Carolina was not necessarily to be a role model for the vast majority of slaves. If anything Thomas Jeremiah's trial and execution had underscored free blacks' ambiguous and vulnerable status.

Anderson and about fifty other blacks made their decision and decamped with the British fleet. Kizell and more than five thousand other slaves in Charleston considered the pros and cons of making their own break and exercised that singularly African virtue: patience.

White Chess, Black Pawns

The American Revolution plowed under England's colonial vanities. But it also sowed South Carolina, in particular, with hardy seeds of violence and oppression. They sprouted quickly in a blood-soaked terrain, where rebellion soon degenerated into vicious civil war.

The Revolution failed to plow slavery under free soil. Thomas Jefferson was not alone in believing that slavery deserved to die—and *would* die when the English yoke was struck. In the meantime, like many of his generation, he internalized slavery as a blemish of nature on the white face of American democracy.

Henry Laurens epitomized the dichotomy posed to the Revolution's elite. He was a practical and successful man of business. He could abhor slavery intellectually and even morally; he could express a paternalistic concern for his slaves' welfare; and he could foresee that slavery and freedom could not coexist indefinitely. But for the moment he had plantations to run.

Laurens's "only strategy to end slavery," writes Gregory D. Massey, biographer of his son John, "was to watch and wait. . . . Because slaves were a majority of South Carolina's population and formed the bedrock of the economy, the proper conditions for emancipation did not exist. Thus, once Laurens recovered from the shock of independence and the initial threat of slave insurrections, antislavery sentiments disappeared from his correspondence."[41]

S. Max Edelson is less subtle. "Laurens," he remarks in a study of South Carolina's plantation economy, "claimed to have ended his career as a slave trader on ethical grounds. He meditated on his slaves' well-being to other elites with a language of tender regard. . . . Yet he brooked no dissent from field slaves. . . . When his strategy of catering to material desires left slaves dissatisfied, he responded with violent discipline."[42]

In the wake of a failed British attempt in June 1776 to retake Charleston, Laurens claimed to be planning a revolution of his own: to liberate his slaves, albeit at some distant time, presumably when peace had been restored. Whether he had shared his intent with fellow plantation owners is unclear, but for the president of the provincial assembly to put such thoughts to paper suggests the degree to which the sudden reality of rebellion—of treason—was forcing at least some influential whites to imagine the brave new world they might inherit.

Laurens wrote proudly on August 14 to John in London that his slaves "all to a Man are strongly attached to me." Professing his horror of slavery, Laurens endorsed the Jeffersonian indictment and declared that the British bore full responsibility for establishing slavery "before my existence."

Laurens paused briefly to assess the auction value of his slaves—twenty thousand pounds sterling—and then protested disingenuously that "I am not the Man who enslaved them." His slaves, he wrote, were "indebted to Englishmen for that favour"—excluding, one assumes, his old friend Oswald. "Nevertheless, I am devising means for manumitting many of them & for cutting off the entail of Slavery." He acknowledged that "great powers oppose me, the Laws & Customs of my Country. . . . What will my children say if I deprive them of so much Estate? These are difficulties but not insuperable. . . . I perceive the work before me is great. I shall appear to many as a promoter not only of strange but dangerous doctrines, it will therefore be necessary to proceed with caution."[43]

Within a few weeks, Laurens was no longer boasting of the loyalty of "my Negroes." Nor was he expanding on plans for manumission. One of his overseers had just "seduced & carried off" several slaves from one of his five plantations. Another slave had tried to manumit himself by fleeing to the British. "I would not have him Succeed . . . for twice his value," Laurens complained to a friend. The slave was now in irons.[44]

Responding to his father's extraordinary announcement in his August letter that he proposed to free many, if not most, of his family's three-hundred-plus slaves, John wrote on October 26 to applaud the "equitable Conduct which you have resolved upon with respect to your Negroes." He agreed that this would "undoubtedly meet with great Opposition from interested Men. . . . Without Slaves how is it possible for us to be rich."

John conceded that "advancing" slaves to freedom "too suddenly" was fraught with danger. But this was the same John Laurens who less than two years later would be urging—much against his father's opposition—the *arming* of slaves and their subsequent liberation. If Henry Laurens had been prepared to flirt with ending slavery, the son seemed ready to take concrete steps. Referring to "the complete Mischief occasioned by our continued Usurpation" of blacks, he told his father bluntly that "we have sunk the Africans & their descendants below the Standard of Humanity, and almost rendered them incapable of that Blessing which equal Heaven bestowed upon us all."[45]

The war, if war it was, had started well for South Carolinian patriots. They had driven the royal governor from their midst and cowed the loyal and irresolute among them. Martial preparations had commenced in the fall of 1775 with the collection of arms, gunpowder, and ammunition. A fort of palmetto logs had been partially erected on the southern end of Sullivan's Island, with cannons to deter British ships from returning. But return they did, on June 4, precipitating panic among whites, who began searching frantically for horses, carriages, and boats to carry them away to the country.[46]

The British tarried for weeks outside the harbor before attempting a combined sea-land assault on Sullivan's Island on June 28. Whites and blacks watched anxiously along the waterfront as more than forty warships and transports descended on the unfinished fort. The attack failed dismally, at the cost of more than two hundred dead and wounded sailors and a frigate.[47]

Charleston's slaves would not have shared the joy of this unexpected victory. They may have helped their masters escape the city; they may have been enlisted to erect shoreline defenses and build the fortress on Sullivan's Island; but all the while they would have been watching, waiting, and calculating what they would do if the British force stormed back into Charleston. As many as five hundred had avoided militia patrols several months earlier in a vain but daring attempt to seek safe haven on British cruisers in the harbor.

In September 1776, not far to the south, large numbers of slaves, believing they would be freed, flocked to English ships occupying the Savannah River. The British reluctantly took them on board, then had to leave the river entrance to replenish provisions consumed by the refugee slaves. "The rebels immediately fortified it," one officer grumbled, "so that it could not be regained."[48] But blacks had again sent a clear signal, as they had to Lord Dunmore in the Chesapeake and in Charleston the year before: many would join the British if given the chance.

Henry Laurens was determined not to afford them that chance. The British foray into the Savannah River prompted him to transfer a quarter of his slaves from a nearby plantation to Santee, closer to Charleston.[49] But increasingly blacks sensed that they could move more freely and seize greater advantages in an unsettled environment. Slaves from Laurens's Mepkin plantation began venturing into Charleston almost as they pleased. "Another negro came to me from Mepkin," Gervais reported in mid-1777 to Laurens, now presiding over the Continental Congress in Philadelphia. "As I am afraid too many of them might take it into their heads to come to Town, I have kept my promise & ordered him a Gentle Whipping at the Workhouse."[50]

Slaves were doing what slaves inherently do: testing the limits of their master's power, vigilance, and good will. Laurens lost a fourth of his slaves during the Revolution. Some ran away or simply vanished in the maelstrom. Many succumbed to disease and destitution.[51] But most remained steadfastly where they were—as did slaves generally in the province. Slaves often refused to abandon their homes and meager property, even in the face of danger from marauding armies.[52]

Slaves resident in Charleston probably had less incentive or reason to roam unless it was on an errand for their owners or because of the desire to see friends and relatives. Although opportunity to venture into the interior would have increased with general insecurity, so would have the dangers. In effect blacks were trapped in Charleston—some resigned to their status, others less so.

Among the former were twenty-five fishermen caught outside the harbor entrance by a British cruiser in early June 1777 and later sold at St. Augustine in East Florida.[53] What is notable is that they still enjoyed the privilege of fishing in waters where they could easily have defected. Another slave, who was captured absconding to an English man-of-war, was sentenced to hang during the same period.[54]

The British made several critical miscalculations during the early years of the Revolution. Two seriously weakened them in South Carolina. One was to overestimate the depth of loyalist sentiment among whites. The second was to assume that blacks would rise against their masters.

William Henry Lyttelton, who was governor of South Carolina in 1755–60 and then of Jamaica for another six years, proposed in the House of Commons in October 1775 that inciting slave uprisings would end rebellion in the southern colonies. His fellow parliamentarians were scandalized and voted the motion down overwhelmingly.[55] However, Lyttelton's proposal anticipated Lord Dunmore's proclamation two weeks later in the Chesapeake and similar initiatives to come.

While many blacks willingly took up the arms offered to them, there was no widespread bloodletting by blacks of whites. The colonists' fear of insurrection, fueled by isolated plots real and imagined, proved largely groundless. Given the chance, many blacks did cross to the British, but there is no evidence that they were prepared to engage in wholesale slaughter of their masters and other whites. Sensitive to loyalist qualms, the British remained reluctant to deploy significant numbers of armed black troops. The military potential of the black majority was lost.[56]

Whether blacks would have engaged in indiscriminate killing of whites is highly questionable. Lyttelton was not the first white to assume that blacks would happily do to them what they had long been doing to blacks. African cultures emphasize forgiveness and communal harmony. The British might have crushed the rebellion by freeing the slaves and organizing black military units, as the United States government did to end the Civil War, but they would have found little stomach among blacks for sanguinary revenge.

Slaves resisted their masters in other ways: stealing supplies, providing intelligence, pretending illness, or simply running away. Their primary objective was to survive amid confusing and dangerous shifts in fortune and loyalties. "The surpassing cruelty that was the hallmark of the war in South Carolina," Frey suggests, "constituted a compelling reason why many slaves viewed the British offer of freedom with caution."[57]

Because many loyalists owned slaves, the British faced an obvious dilemma. Unless they were prepared—and they were not—to emancipate all slaves (not to mention arming large numbers of them), the British were forced to defend slavery. This would not have gone unremarked in the black community. Nor would the abandonment and poor treatment of refugee blacks by British forces while retreating in 1779 through coastal areas south of Charleston.[58]

If the British sent mixed signals to blacks, they did as well to whites. On the one hand, they falsely assumed that the great majority of whites were loyal at heart. On the other they often alienated their supposed adherents. During the same retreat from Charleston, Gen. Augustine Prevost's troops plundered the property and slaves of loyalists and patriots alike. Loyalists were furious that Prevost would permit such gratuitous harm to Britain's friends.

The British were beginning to doubt their ability to suppress American independence, in which case opportunistic plundering became the order of the day. Asked by Lord George Germain, the secretary of state for America, to assess loyalist sympathies in South Carolina, James Simpson, the former royal attorney general in the province, reported frankly that Prevost's indiscriminate raiding "is likely to prove fatal to our interests."[59]

As John Kizell would discover, after joining the British the following year in Charleston, whites weighed their political allegiance as carefully as slaves calculated their best interests in South Carolina's increasingly volatile environment. Men switched sides frequently to protect their families and property. Murder and retribution were common. Destruction was widespread.

Loyalist sentiment was strong initially but gradually waned. In *Three Peoples, One King*, Jim Piecuch reminds that early British and American assessments of southerners' allegiance agreed that loyalists predominated. However, the rebels "relentlessly murdered, imprisoned, abused, and intimidated those who supported the king's government."[60] By the summer of 1780, a British officer in Cheraw was disabusing Cornwallis, in occupied Charleston, of loyalist hopes. "It is impossible for me to give Your Lordship an idea of the disaffection of this country," he wrote. "Every inhabitant has been or is concerned in the Rebellion & most of them very deeply."[61]

Blacks must have pondered the violence and vitriol that whites inflicted upon one another. Nothing in their experience, in America or in Africa, would have prepared them for such a phenomenon. They were accustomed to the violence committed by whites upon their slaves. That was in the nature of things. But what whites were doing to each other, and the vengeance they exhibited, seemed to defy nature. It raised new questions about the humanity of their masters and about a country dominated by such a violent and unruly race of men.

Charleston became a cockpit of animosity and division. Backcountry representatives to the provincial congresses changed the political dynamic. Merchants and planters now found themselves dealing as equals with a "lesser" class of men from the interior. They pressed for more radical reforms, including the "disestablishment" of the Anglican Church, and forced adoption of a revised constitution in 1778. It was, according to George C. Rogers Jr., "the price that the merchant oligarchy paid for the help of the new men and an extension of Carolina solidarity to the upcountry."[62]

In early 1777 seventy-five citizens were given a year to wind up their affairs, sell their property, and leave the province for refusing to acknowledge its independent sovereignty.[63] When the Continental Congress recommended in April 1778 that the states pardon loyalists who presented themselves to a civil or military officer, South Carolina Whigs threatened violence if the state's own "act of fidelity" was not enforced. Nonetheless Christopher Gadsden, the state vice president, pardoned more than thirty Tories.

Gervais wrote urgently to Henry Laurens in Philadelphia that pardoning Tories, while it "might be politic to the Northward . . . [is] very unpopular here. The Tories will have no place in this Quarter, indeed experience teaches us, they will never be our friend longer than we are successful. . . . Witness so many . . . that took the Oath when they were released from Gaol, who nevertheless are gone over to the Enemy after doing a great deal of mischief . . . by carrying away with them horses & negroes. Several of them were taken in arms."[64] Gervais later informed Laurens that Tories continued to be "very troublesome in the backcountry—they have cut of[f] several peoples ears."[65]

Whites' emotions were rubbed raw by the strain of the war's uncertain course, the fear of slave insurrections, and the precipitous decline of the economy and living standards. The rapid depreciation of both local and Continental currency "brought economic chaos to Charleston," Richard Walsh writes in his study of the city's artisan class. "After January, 1777, speculation was rampant. Fortunes fell or were made overnight. Prices soared to unbelievable heights. Real estate traded hands like poker chips."[66]

The feared apocalypse of fire finally visited Charleston on January 15, 1778. Starting that night near Queen and Church streets, it destroyed nearly a sixth of the city—250 buildings. A New England merchant, Elkanah Watson, vividly recorded the catastrophe: "Every vessel, shallop, and negro-boat was crowded with the distressed inhabitants. Many who, a few hours before, retired to their beds in affluence, were now reduced . . . to indigence. . . . The fire had extended far and wide. . . . half dressed matrons, delicate young ladies and children, wandering about unprotected and in despair." The next morning there remained only "the smoking ruins, and the constant falling of walls and chimneys."[67]

Kizell would have heard the ugly rumors that the fire had been set by slaves or Tories. Watson chose to say nothing in his journal, however, about the civil and political tensions that were beginning to drag South Carolinians into the abyss. Charleston's "splendor and style" had impressed him; the planters "live in almost Asiatic luxury . . . all produced by the sweat and blood of the slave."[68] In the midst of revolution, he found the state's slaveholding aristocracy clinging firmly to their prewar lifestyle.

Nothing had visibly changed for their slaves, as he made clear on his way back north in March. "I witnessed a heart-rending spectacle," he wrote of the sale of a black family in Wilmington. "They were driven in from the country, like swine for market. A wench clung to a little daughter, and implored . . . that they not separated."[69]

Thomas Peters knew Wilmington well. Born in Yoruba country, about the same time as Kizell more than a thousand miles to the west, he had been enslaved as a child in French Louisiana. By the early 1770s, he was the property of an ardent Wilmington patriot. When the British fleet appeared off Cape Fear in 1776, Peters reached one of the ships and joined the black guides and pioneers. Several weeks later he watched, from the deck of an English ship, the futile bombardment of Sullivan's Island. He served in the British cause for the full course of the struggle. Wounded twice and evacuated at war's end to Nova Scotia, he considered himself as much a loyalist as the thousands of whites who also migrated to Canada.[70]

Peters was to play a central role in the eventual exodus of black Nova Scotians to Sierra Leone. He and Kizell were part of an African diaspora, which was given shape and identity, in part, by the American Revolution. The conflict enabled many slaves *and* free blacks to reconsider who and what they were in the context of a novel political ideology and of the violent dispute between members of the "master" race. Slaves already had developed a sense of self within their plantations and town-based communities, but the Revolution presented opportunities to *choose* their own path, to define themselves as something other than slaves.

The Revolution dispersed tens of thousands of slaves. Many died of disease and privation. Many remained slaves after the war. But Thomas Peters, Isaac Anderson, and John Kizell were among several thousand who risked life for liberation and established free black settlements in Nova Scotia and, paradoxically, in Africa.

The Revolution also energized abolition movements in England and America. It led to a brief postwar spate of manumissions in the mid-Atlantic states and the sudden expansion of free black populations in northern cities. Americans—blacks *and* whites— were compelled to reassess their relationship to one another and, ultimately, the true nature and complexion of American democracy.

None of this could have been anticipated. In the first years of the rebellion, whites took sides—or tried to *avoid* taking sides—over issues that had nothing to do directly with race and color. Blacks took sides, when they could, according to self-interest and sheer survival, not overtly in terms of racial solidarity. They sought to escape slavery for objective reasons.

As the free black community expanded in the late 1700s and early 1800s, African Americans began developing a stronger sense of racial consciousness. American-born free blacks largely opposed back-to-Africa schemes. The African-born, such as Peters, Kizell, and Anderson, retained spiritual and cultural affinity to their homelands. Their indigenous traditions gradually shaped an *African* identity where none had existed.

"Africa is the land of black men,"[71] Kizell said much later. Such a thought would not have been obvious to a teenaged slave trying to survive from day to day in wartime Charleston.

Choosing Sides

The Revolution was not only a white man's war; it was also a black man's war. John Kizell knew this. So did John Laurens. They were on opposing sides but would have found much in common had they met: a shared conviction that slavery was wrong and a belief that black men were prepared to fight for their freedom. The war made soldiers of them both. They served in contending armies, yet shared a cause: to end slavery and, by extension, the slave trade.

Laurens went to his premature death in a pointless skirmish at war's end, intending no doubt to pursue this purpose when peace was restored. Kizell, with a slave's-eye view of the institution's deep-rooted nature, would have had no illusions. Laurens could afford to indulge his idealism. Kizell could not afford to dream. He understood that he would remain a slave unless he left South Carolina. That meant joining the British if the chance offered and becoming a "soldier." This is how he would identify himself when answering a muster of black loyalists in Nova Scotia in the summer of 1784.[72]

Had the impetuous Laurens realized his vision of forming and leading a regiment of South Carolina blacks, Kizell might have become one of his recruits. He would have been aware in early 1779 that the provincial assembly was considering the recommendation of Congress that Georgia and South Carolina mobilize two battalions of armed blacks. They would be rewarded with freedom for their service, and their owners compensated.[73]

Laurens certainly appreciated the implications. He had long nursed revolutionary thoughts on slavery and had witnessed the bravery and fighting ability of soldier-slaves at the battle of Rhode Island in August 1778.[74] A black regiment held the critical right flank for four hours against experienced redcoats and Hessians. It was a costly lesson for European troops who had openly ridiculed their sable opponents before the battle.[75]

64   Free blacks had fought in militia units at the early battles of Lexington, Concord, and Bunker Hill. It was clear that slaves as well as their free brethren were more than willing to risk their lives for what they hoped would be an all-inclusive liberty. The Congress and Continental army officers decided in November 1775 to limit the fight to white men. Not even free men of color were to be enlisted. The policy, writes David Brion Davis, arose not only from the opposition of southerners but also "from a fear of British retaliation, and from a desire to make the rebellious forces as 're-spectable' as possible."[76]

While the Revolution's leaders were trying to remain "respectable," Laurens was completing legal studies in London. He was also pondering the incompatibility of liberty and slavery. An English friend who sympathized with the American cause expressed deep concern that slavery fatally compromised patriots' ideals. He scoffed at American claims that slavery was the result of colluding African chiefs and English slave merchants.

"If there be an object truly ridiculous in nature," the friend wrote, "it is an American . . . signing resolutions of independency with one hand, and with the other brandishing a whip over his affrighted slaves." Laurens made no attempt to defend the indefensible. To another colleague in London, he confessed that "we Americans, at least in the Southern Colonies, cannot contend with *a good grace*, for Liberty, until we shall have enfranchised our Slaves." If his people could not sustain life in America without slaves, Laurens said candidly, "Let us fly it."[77]

By the time Laurens returned to America, the difficulty of filling the ranks of the Continental army and local militia in the north had forced de facto acceptance of blacks' enlistment. Several states allowed slaves to exchange military service for freedom. Many blacks were paid by whites to substitute for them. Others served on American warships and privateers. Over the course of the war, up to one in four regular army soldiers may have been black.[78] It had indeed become a black man's war.

Now serving as an adjutant to General Washington, Laurens was camped at Valley Forge during the killing winter of 1777–78. He was acutely aware of the army's manpower deficit, which persisted in spite of enlisting blacks. Death, disease, and desertion threatened the army's survival. What would eventually be seen as the decisive and improbable American victory at Yorktown was nearly four years in the future. The Americans needed to use every advantage available. To Laurens that meant only one thing.

On January 14, 1778, he wrote the president of the Continental Congress—his father—to propose formation of a black regiment under his command. "Cede me a number of your able bodied Slaves, instead of leaving me a fortune," he suggested. "I would bring about a two-fold good, first I would advance those who are unjustly deprived of the Rights of Mankind to a State which would be a proper Gradation between abject Slavery and perfect Liberty—and besides I would reinforce the

Defenders of Liberty with a number of gallant Soldiers—Men who have the habit of Subordination almost indelibly impressed on them, would have a very essential qualification of Soldiers."[79]

Henry Laurens replied warily. He would think about his son's proposal. On January 28, having apparently sounded out a few congressional colleagues, he asked John whether he had sought General Washington's counsel. "I have been cautious of speaking openly of the project, but hitherto I have not heard one person approbate the idea from hints I have dropped."

Henry cloaked his apprehension of arming large numbers of slaves with solicitous concern for their well-being. "Have you considered," he asked, "that your kind intentions towards your Negroes would be deemed by them the highest cruelty, & that to escape from it they would flee into the Woods—that they would interpret your humanity to be an Exchange of Slavery, a State & circumstance not only tolerable but comfortable from habit, for an intolerable—taken from their Wives & Children . . . to the Field of Battle. . . ."[80]

John responded spiritedly. Without revealing whether he had consulted his general, he underscored the military urgency of "completing our Continental Regiments." John was no longer thinking modestly of leading a band of the family's slaves. Now he was proposing "a well chosen body of 5,000 black men properly officer'd" who "might give us decisive Success in the next Campaign."

Laurens was convinced that blacks would willingly trade the supposed comforts of enslavement to fight for their freedom. He was "tempted to believe that this trampled people have so much human left in them, as to be capable of aspiring to the rights of men by noble exertions"—by dying, if necessary—"if some friend to mankind would point the Road." But the son left his father in no doubt of his real concerns: "I have long deplored the wretched State of these men and considered their history, the bloody wars excited in Africa to furnish America with Slaves."[81]

To Henry his son's "Negro scheme" had become an obsession. "I will undertake to say," he wrote John on February 6, "there is not a Man in America of your opinion." If John wanted a regiment to lead, "go to Carolina & I'll warrant you will soon get one" and have no difficulty "in raising a Regiment of White Men."[82]

John Laurens was not alone, however. Within weeks, Gervais was writing Henry from Charleston that turning slaves into soldiers had merit. "I think we might . . . form a very good Regiment without danger of our Slaves—promise them freedom if they behave well & pay a Value to the Owner."[83] By early 1779 the idea was attracting even more adherents. The British had seized Savannah and obviously planned to take Charleston as part of Gen. Henry Clinton's new "southern strategy." This opened minds to fresh consideration of means to resist an alarming turn in the war.

In mid-March Henry Laurens urged Congress to defend against the British thrust into the south. Laurens was appointed to a committee of three southerners and two northern delegates. The committee recommended several measures, including the mobilization of two battalions of black soldiers in South Carolina and Georgia.

Congress would fully fund the initiative, including the slaves' emancipation, by compensating the owners. Gen. Benjamin Lincoln, a northerner commanding Continental troops in the South, strongly approved. So did another general, Nathanael Greene, who had witnessed the gallantry of black troops in Rhode Island.[84]

Laurens would not have been surprised—or disappointed—when the South Carolina and Georgia legislatures rejected Congress's offer in spite of his son's eloquent advocacy. Blacks in Charleston would not have been privy to the actual debate, but they would have known the essentials. Blacks' "loyalty" was still available to the most credible bidder. With the war now directly threatening the slave states, whites faced a moment of truth. So, in a sense, did the British. Was either side prepared to engage large numbers of armed blacks in a dispute between white people? And who had the most to gain by doing so?

Parliament had already decisively rejected any massive employment of armed black soldiers. Thousands of Hessian mercenaries were hired instead. Apart from Lord Dunmore's brief use of blacks in combat early in the conflict and the ad hoc deployment of a few hundred refugee slaves in Savannah, British commanders—proud and professional soldiers—seemed even more disdainful of blacks' fighting abilities than their American counterparts. Nonetheless the British had to take note of the telling role played by the Americans' black regiment in Rhode Island and the substantial number of blacks appearing in the front lines of the Continental army.

The British did not need to issue proclamations or entice slaves to follow their banner. No official encouragement was needed in late 1778 when the British arrived in the Savannah River to launch their southern invasion. Thousands of slaves deserted plantations in Georgia. But the British had no plan or intent to enlist them as soldiers.

How many were actually seeking British protection or simply fleeing danger is unclear. William Moultrie, commanding South Carolina troops at Purrysburg, reported in early January that the countryside was inundated by thousands of "poor (white) women and children and Negroes of Georgia . . . traveling to they knew not where." It was, he wrote a friend, "a spectacle that even moved the hearts of the soldiers."[85]

The exodus of slaves in Georgia was unprecedented in scale, but the British failed to take any real advantage.[86] As in 1776 they were again logistically burdened by the influx of destitute black and white refugees. Had the British brought the necessary arms and supplies to equip a large black legion of Georgia slaves, they might have marched successfully into Charleston within a few weeks and struck a fatal blow to the American cause in the south. Unless, that is, South Carolina had accepted Congress's invitation to form its own black counterforce. Had both sides chosen to arm and commit slave regiments to battle in the South, an even bloodier fratricidal conflict would have ensued. The choice for blacks would have been agonizing.

The British never came genuinely to grips with the racial dynamic of the rebellion or strategically analyzed how to exploit the black presence militarily. Framing another halfway measure, General Clinton on June 30, 1779, issued a proclamation from Philipsburg, New York, to trump the Continental army's "enrolling Negroes among their Troops."[87] While threatening to confiscate and sell any blacks captured in rebel service, Clinton offered those who crossed to the British a vaguely worded promise of protection and an opportunity "to follow . . . any Occupation" they "shall think proper."

This was hardly a clarion call to blacks to shoulder arms in the front ranks. Nor did it trumpet opposition to slavery. As Frey states, it was devoid of "moral or philosophical convictions." It succeeded only in infuriating slaveholders (including many loyalists) "who saw the . . . proclamation as an attack on property . . . and an invitation to anarchy." Frey points out that "the proclamation . . . in many cases, created pro-rebel sympathies. In South Carolina it prompted a successful insurgency that turned the state into a battleground and plunged it into the most savage war fought in America during the Revolution."[88] Within a year Kizell was a participant in this bloody saga.

South Carolina, meanwhile, had not entirely foreclosed blacks' participation in the patriot military. As early as November 1775, the provincial congress had authorized militia officers to use slaves "as pioneers and laborers." Free blacks also were permitted to serve under arms.[89] Ironically a free black was among two militiamen killed in early May 1779 at the Coosawhatchie River because of John Laurens's disregard of Moultrie's order to retreat.[90]

Moultrie and General Lincoln had been maneuvering to recover Georgia and to block British designs on Charleston. They ultimately saved Charleston but not Georgia. In the process Lincoln had left the city exposed to British attack. Although he managed to return with his force in time to defend the provincial capital, several influential Carolinians blamed Lincoln and the Continental Congress for endangering the city and their property. The crisis passed when the British withdrew in mid-May rather than assault the city's well-manned defenses.[91]

With Charleston reprieved, General Lincoln—despite his declamations of ill health—agreed to remain in charge of the southern department. But a die had been cast. When a stronger British force appeared early the following year, Lincoln bowed to civilian pressure and defended the city against overwhelming odds. This time there were to be no abject offers of neutrality—and no reprieve.

The military utility of blacks remained a matter of public debate. In late August the legislature renewed consideration of a "Bill for the More Effectual Defence of This State." Once again Charleston's blacks listened, watched, and waited while Whig leaders confronted the obvious means to shore up gaping holes in the ranks of the militia and the Continental army: arm "well chosen" slaves. And once more in spite of John Laurens's ardent support, only one in six legislators had the nerve to endorse the enlisting of blacks. Even its few adherents may have had misgivings.

Dr. David Ramsay, a transplanted Pennsylvanian, was typical. He believed blacks had been so degraded by slavery that they could not possibly perform capably as soldiers.[92] But consciously or otherwise, many informed whites may have feared just the opposite. They knew about blacks' combat experience in Rhode Island and Savannah; they knew about the tough maroons operating in the swamps and deep forests; and they knew about warrior traditions in Africa. They knew that armed slaves might indeed make very good soldiers. And then what?

When Henry Laurens, in Philadelphia, received word that black recruitment in South Carolina had been defeated decisively, he could not resist gently mocking his son's naïveté. "I learn that your black Air Castle is blown up, with contemptuous huzzas," he wrote John on September 27.[93]

Still the concept refused to die. Although Lincoln was under no illusion that the state's slaveholders would reconsider their opposition, he felt obliged in early 1780 to revive the option of forming black fighting units. As he advised Governor John Rutledge, the British were committed to seizing all of South Carolina. There was "little prospect of an early reinforcement from the North" to counter a much-strengthened opponent.[94]

The legislature immediately appointed a committee of five, including Henry Laurens and Ramsay, to review Lincoln's request to arm a black regiment or at least create a corps of unarmed slaves to serve in the artillery and perform "fatigue" duties. The committee shrank from arming blacks but proposed that there was "publick utility" in acquiring one thousand "able bodied Negro men" through private contributions, hire, or purchase to work in support roles—*not* in the artillery. Owners were to be amply compensated for any slaves lost or injured. The slaves, however, were not to be rewarded with freedom, no matter how nobly they served.[95]

Blacks in Charleston would draw their own conclusions regarding slave owners' motives and intent. They would take note that emancipation, in exchange for serving the patriot cause, was no longer on the table, as it had been the previous year. They would also have been assessing their readiness and ability to carry arms. They knew that liberated slaves would fight if given the chance. Sixty armed blacks had just been reported killed by South Carolina militia near Savannah.[96]

John Laurens never had the chance to lead black men in battle. Nor would he have the opportunity to test his abhorrence of slavery when the war was done and his father had abandoned the idea of freeing his slaves. Like most whites Laurens had not known any black, slave or free, well enough to pretend that he knew them genuinely as human beings. As his biographer Massey concedes, "his concerns about slavery and its effects on individuals, albeit sincere, focused on slaves in the abstract."[97]

Whether his pointless death deprived the South of a leader who could have steered the region away from slavery is intellectually intriguing but moot. In Charleston Laurens was mourned even by the British and loyalists. The *Royal Gazette*, Massey notes, eulogized him. It "could identify only one blemish on Laurens's character—his decision to rebel against his king."[98] Blacks would have remembered him for a different sort of rebellion.

Freedom—of a Sort

The siege and seizure of Charleston in May 1780 deluded General Clinton and his commanders into believing they would soon detach the tail and stinger of the rebellion; that they indeed had struck the fatal blow to American independence. The spring tide in March, lifting English warships over the bar guarding Charleston's harbor, had enabled Clinton to establish a stranglehold. But the taking of the South's commercial and maritime center was itself the high-water mark of Britain's counter-revolution.[99]

By nature the siege was slow and laborious. Carl P. Borick, in *A Gallant Defense*, provides the most thorough account of what was in terms of men and logistics the largest and most complex military operation during the Revolution. There was the huge fleet that sailed south from New York in the closing days of 1779; there was General Lincoln's decision to defend the city and risk losing his army; there were the carefully constructed defenses erected across the neck and the parallel trenching that night by night brought British soldiers closer to striking distance; there were the Virginia and North Carolina regiments slogging through hundreds of miles of mud to join the defenders; and there was the pounding roar of guns from both sides. Those barrages were a lasting memory for all who lived through them.

The stakes were enormous for the British, for loyalists, for patriots, and for the slaves who still outnumbered Charleston's whites.[100] Blacks inside Charleston knew that a British victory presumably would make them free. But they could not be entirely certain what that might mean. Would the British feed them? Give them work? Weapons?

Blacks knew what to expect from the Americans and from those owners who had not fled. Able-bodied men such as twenty-year-old John Kizell were dragooned into building the defensive line and carting supplies to the troops manning it. Some must have grumbled—or laughed—that they were helping to defend their own servitude.

What they were hearing from the other side of the barrier was not altogether assuring. Information sifted through the siege lines. A Hessian captain warned Lord Cornwallis "that it was very easy, especially for Negroes, to pass between our picket and the 2nd battalion of light infantry, since everyone was granted free passage."[101]

Blacks carried intelligence to the British. One reported on American troop strength and food supplies.[102] But others may have informed the black community that British treatment of runaway slaves could be exploitive. Although the British might feed and clothe them, runaway slaves learned soon enough that life in the British army was problematic.

The British faced serious labor constraints in sustaining the massive siege. Using runaways was an obvious expedient. "That many African Americans," says Borick, "found conditions with the British no better than on the plantations is suggested by their attempts to flee the British. . . . The slaves were caught in the middle of the conflict, and for many the choice of participation was not theirs to make." Many died or suffered, laboring on military works on both sides. "They may be the most tragic civilian casualties of the operations around Charleston," Borick writes.[103]

For slaves, Frey explains, the war was "a paradox." The British seemed to offer freedom of a kind, but they gave no sign that they would tamper with an economic structure that depended on slave labor. "Ironically," Frey continues, "although the British army's invitation to slaves and its wholesale appropriation of them seemed to foretell the destruction of the plantation regime, in fact emancipation as practiced by the army kept alive the plantation economy . . . and was a major factor in preventing the outbreak of a slave rebellion."

Frey argues that Clinton's Philipsburg Proclamation and the army's subsequent actions sent slaves a dangerously mixed message. The proclamation offered them "the luminous hope of freedom, but time and events made it clear that the British war aim was not directed at the overthrow of the slave regime. Indeed the moral hypocrisy of the military command gave slaves good reason to doubt that the British offer of freedom could be counted upon at all."[104]

Regardless of which side of the siege line they were, slaves had good reason to consider their actions and "loyalty" with caution. The closer the war came to home, the more violent it became for whites and blacks, especially for those who declared themselves. Runaways who volunteered or were conscripted as guides by either side risked death. Patriots executed one near Moncks Corner in mid-April and stuck his head on a pole.[105]

Another black messenger-spy, this one serving the patriots, was intercepted in the same area by Lt. Col. Banastre Tarleton's advance guard. The letter he was carrying to General Lincoln revealed that Brig. Gen. Isaac Huger's cavalry was positioned eighteen miles away at Biggin's Bridge. Tarleton and Major Patrick Ferguson, commanding an American loyalist infantry regiment, marched through the night of April 13 and launched a predawn attack, completely surprising Huger.[106] The rout cleared the main road to Charleston.

The twenty-six-year-old Tarleton was the Oxford-educated scion of a Liverpool family whose wealth derived from the slave trade.[107] He was one of the aggressive young officers whom Cornwallis relied upon for counsel. He is generally remembered for the near annihilation of a three-hundred-man patriot contingent at the Waxhaws, in present-day Lancaster County, South Carolina. The battle, on May 29, 1780, was part of Cornwallis's effort to pacify the province following the surrender of Charleston. The Waxhaws slaughter, which local patriots blamed on Tarleton's alleged refusal to grant quarter, sent precisely the wrong signal to the backcountry populace. Where Cornwallis hoped to establish a sense of security and normalcy, the Waxhaws conveyed the very opposite.[108]

The war to be fought for southern sympathies was now destined to be nasty and internecine, sundering families and communities alike. One of its victims was Ferguson, a professional soldier and Tarleton's junior, although a decade older. A soldier since youth, Ferguson had commanded troops sent to suppress slave uprisings in the West Indies just prior to the Revolution.[109] Impressed early in the war by American marksmanship, he invented a breech-loading rifle in 1776 whose rapid-fire capability would have provided the army with an overwhelming advantage.

The following year, at the battle of Brandywine in Pennsylvania, Ferguson had an opportunity to use his own excellent aim to shoot an American officer—believed, in some accounts, to have been George Washington. He refused to do so, in deference to the code that British officers did not kill their enemy counterparts. Later in the battle, Ferguson was shot in the right elbow. By the time he recovered, the rifle unit he commanded had been disbanded. Jealous superiors mothballed his invention.[110]

Ferguson now led the American Volunteers, a loyalist regiment mostly from New York and New Jersey. He seemed to relish the war's increasingly brutish character. Although he acknowledged the fighting quality of his loyalist troops, he was still an English—albeit Scottish—gentleman who habitually underestimated backwoods Americans. He and his men had swept easily through the countryside between Georgia and Charleston, seizing rebels, cattle, and other supplies and destroying what they could not carry. They also seized slaves and put them to work driving cattle and transporting goods. A loyalist officer remarked approvingly of the wanton destruction left in their wake.[111] The lack of any real resistance was further evidence that the rebels were a distinct minority who would submit soon to the threat of fire and sword.

With Charleston about to fall, General Clinton knew that he lacked enough troops to police the city *and* subdue the rest of the province. Ferguson soon had a new assignment: to organize and train an expanded loyalist militia. On May 22, 1780, ten days into the occupation of Charleston and a week before the blood-spilling at the Waxhaws, Clinton gave Ferguson responsibility for creating a more effective loyalist force.

Clinton appreciated how difficult this might be. Ferguson was to establish among loyalist units "a certain degree of order, regularity and discipline, which, however, must be done with great caution, so as not to disgust the men or mortify unnecessarily their love of Freedom."[112] He was to supply them with arms "when practicable"— a possible reference to the substantial store of ordnance lost when a transport sank in a storm.[113]

Clinton regarded the independent-minded Ferguson as the best-suited officer available to make the most militarily of an undisciplined rabble. However, as events showed in the coming months, his professional training and experience in suppressing inferior opponents—slaves in Tobago and rebellious backwoodsmen—contributed to the failure of British strategy in South Carolina and the South.

Through April and into May, the British cordon tightened around Charleston. Men and supplies continued to reach the city until the British closed the last access across the Cooper River. Both sides sustained a shuddering cannon fire, often day and night. Food supplies diminished. Lincoln and his officers considered how long they should hold out, while Governor Rutledge and government officials left before the last exit closed. Meanwhile British and loyalist soldiers, along with runaway slaves, inched their trenches closer.

Several thousand townspeople shared an urgent wish: to see the siege ended. General Lincoln and his men knew that the city would fall. To resist meant suffering death and widespread damage for no credible purpose. The fighting spirit remained strong almost to the end, but Lincoln capitulated on May 12 to save lives and to save Charleston.

White and black civilians would have regarded the British victory almost a blessing. Many of the more committed Whigs had departed, leaving behind a white populace whose political sentiments were adaptable. Hundreds of people swore allegiance to the Crown in the weeks following surrender. This was in spite of the rebels' having—they thought—culled all hardcore loyalists during the previous four years.

"The people who ran occupied Charleston," Robert S. Lambert writes, "were . . . the loyalists and the protectionists." The latter included "reluctant rebels, persons whose sympathies probably had lain with the British but who had . . . been able to remain in the state during the American Period." And there were the "reluctant Tories, persons who were rebels at heart but who figured after Lincoln's surrender that their cause was lost. . . . These distinctions . . . were very real to their rebel and loyalist contemporaries."[114]

Blacks were well aware of the loyalties of their owners and of whites in general. They would have been considering *their* loyalties in the event of British success. As General Clinton and his men rode triumphantly into the city, blacks in the crowd could have had little doubt concerning the ultimate course of the rebellion. But what did this mean in their individual circumstances? If his or her owner was an unrepentant rebel, was a slave now free? If a white nominally professed loyalty to the king, did this protect all his property, including his slaves?

The British were preoccupied with military contingencies and the logistics of dealing with conquered territory, a disrupted economy (especially food production), and the needs of displaced people and runaway slaves. They viewed blacks either as a pool of labor, an inconvenient burden, or—in the case of those infected with smallpox—a danger to be isolated and left to their fate. Emancipation was not the order of the day nor an objective of the war.

It was difficult nonetheless to ignore the many blacks who had joined the British and served loyally. The men who had laid siege to Charleston included black pioneers—men such as General Washington's African-born Harry and at least one Charleston native, Samuel Burke.[115] While General Clinton had no compunction about protecting the property of loyalists, including plantation owners, he recognized the need to reward loyal blacks and to provide an appropriate postwar dispensation.

Few senior British officers gave much thought to the broader consequences of the Philipsburg Proclamation. Its author, however, made clear to subordinates that blacks serving in their ranks were not mere pawns. Before returning to New York, Clinton issued explicit instructions regarding their status. Writing on June 3 to Cornwallis, who was assuming command in the South, Clinton recognized blacks' extreme vulnerability in the turmoil that had been unleashed in the region.

Historian Simon Schama summarizes Clinton's strictures: "Slaves who had run away from *loyalist* plantations . . . should be returned to their masters *only* after the latter had given a formal undertaking 'in the presence of the Negro' not to punish runaways for 'past offenses.' Should loyalist slaveowners be proved to have inflicted punishment notwithstanding this order, 'he or she shall consent to forfeit their claim to the Negro.'" Schama believes that Clinton may have doubted Cornwallis's own views toward the blacks. He took care to remind Cornwallis that blacks who had fled rebel masters and served the British faithfully "are entitled to their freedom." They also were to be properly paid and clothed and to be "under the care and protection of some humane person."[116]

Clinton already was thinking ahead to the war's conclusion. There would be serious political challenges. How to punish the most treasonable and unreconstructed rebels? How to reconcile the reestablishment of royal sovereignty with the rebels' leveling instincts? How to prevent the colonies from again finding common complaint, to keep them divided by self-interest?

Clinton may have been the only English official who was pondering a social and humanitarian conundrum: the fate of several thousand slaves who had thrown themselves upon British mercy. Those whom loyalists could justly claim would have to be returned. The vast majority, however, expected—and deserved—to be rewarded for services rendered and pain suffered in supporting "their" king.

"Why not settle the Negroes on forfeited land after the war?" Clinton asked in his orders to Cornwallis.[117] The remark sounded rhetorical, but its premise was blunt. Patriots would lose their plantations. Allowing former slaves to occupy and work them would be inherently just. Clinton did not reveal how deeply he had examined the practicality of this idea, but blacks themselves, given the chance, would have raised awkward matters of detail—concerns of control, security, and economics. These bedeviled black resettlement schemes for decades to come.

There was little time, however, for the British *or* blacks to indulge in postwar imagining in May 1780. The future came at them fast. A powder magazine in the town center accidentally detonated soon after the surrender, killing several British soldiers and blacks, as well as destroying a large number of weapons that could have been issued to loyalist recruits. "It was a terrible sight," a Hessian officer recalled. "Some were blown to bits, others thrown two hundred paces against walls and doors."[118]

The occupation unleashed fresh dangers and opportunities. With the injection of British expenditures for housing, storage, and supplies and the reopening of the port, there was a rush of commercial activity. Retailers were quick to take advantage of consumer demand to soak up the freshet of cash.[119]

Along with the freer movement of people and goods came the dreaded smallpox. Fear of the contagion, which had broken out before the siege, had deterred many backcountry militia from joining the city's defense. Now the flood of loyalists and run-away slaves renewed the epidemic. The British had inoculated their troops and could safely ignore the disease as it scythed through the populace. Infected blacks were quar-antined outside the city—essentially abandoned to succumb in unrecorded droves.[120]

Charleston's fair-weather loyalists were joined by their more hardened brethren from the backcountry. "Inflamed loyalists," wrote one diarist, " . . . were already col-lected in great numbers at Charleston, determined to seize the first occasion of retal-iating on the rebels [for] the many murders committed upon their relations by their mock courts."[121]

The British also were not shy about evening accounts. They moved quickly to sequester estates—more than one hundred, along with more than five thousand slaves—to produce food and supplies for the Charleston garrison. One month after the capitulation, Samuel Massey, Henry Laurens's most valued slave, was writing to him that "the king troopes have been to mepkin twise in a plundering manner."[122]

The plantations proved unproductive. Many were in disrepair, and large numbers of slaves either withdrew their labor or absconded. "The blacks' deliberate departure from the fields" in 1780, writes Robert Olwell, "forced many masters to realize that in the absence of civil government they . . . lacked the coercive power."[123]

Whites in Charleston who refused to take the oath of allegiance suffered British plundering as well. The German community, patriot to its core, did not remember the British fondly. A committee of the German Friendly Society reported in early 1783, less than a month after the British evacuated Charleston, that "Britons antiently Re-nowned for Honour [and] Humanity . . . had outdone the very Vandals . . . by the most wanton Depredations on Property."[124]

From the outset of the occupation, the British disabused blacks that they had come to free them. As a matter of honor and equity, Clinton was committed to reward-ing those who abandoned masters and served the war effort. But slaves who tried to escape from loyalist owners and whose numbers threatened to hamper military oper-ations were another matter.

The British had begun to realize as well that many of the runaway slaves serving as pioneers and drovers and in other support roles belonged to loyalists—or at least to those who *claimed* to be loyal. Clinton ordered Cornwallis "to make such arrange-ments" that would discourage slaves from fleeing loyalists and thus alienating their owners' support. He also recommended restocking derelict plantations with the excess runaways. There they could subsist without burdening the army.[125]

Clinton had more serious concerns than feeding a footloose slave population. "Wartime destruction," Frey observes, "and the desertion of slaves from almost all of the plantations within eight miles of Charleston threatened the economic system and imperiled the traditional social order. . . . Many slaves took advantage of the confusion endemic to war to run away to their own people or to flee to . . . Charleston, where they tried to pass as free blacks. Living 'in a state of idleness,' as the *Royal Gazette* char-acterized slaves' unaccustomed leisure, they congregated in punch houses and dram shops that sprang up to serve the soldiers and the influx of 'disorderly Persons and Negroes.'"[126]

The city was suddenly awash with humanity. Most were black and, it seemed to whites, idle and dangerous. Charleston was still a majority black city. "I am almost pestered to Death with Vexatious Complaints about the Negroes," complained James Simpson, the former provincial attorney general. Clinton had given Simpson special responsibility to handle the issue of slaves.[127] With the army's help, the police board tried to control blacks' mobility by requiring them to carry tickets from their owners. Taverns were closed to prevent blacks from congregating.[128]

If Charleston's white citizens were increasingly agitated by the presence of anonymous and self-liberated slaves, blacks had very real problems of their own. The most fortunate, in a sense, belonged to loyalist owners who could maintain and protect them. Those who could attach themselves to the British military also were relatively safe. But the rest were subject to mercenary instincts, which Clinton surely would have decried had he remained in direct control. Runaway slaves, as well as those taken from sequestered patriot estates, soon found themselves in extremely vulnerable circumstances. They had misread English motives.

"Whatever the blacks . . . might have believed," writes James W. St. G. Walker, "the British government and army were definitely not committed to the abolition of slavery or to the equality of black citizens." Walker, a Canadian scholar who has studied the black loyalists, describes the fate that awaited thousands of slaves who thought they were running to freedom:

> Those slaves who belonged to Loyalists were never offered their freedom, and indeed steps were taken to ensure that Loyalist-owned slaves were protected or retrieved if strayed or stolen. Slaves who were captured from the rebels or removed from sequestered estates were often allocated as bonuses to reward Loyalists for a job well done or to compensate for losses at the hands of rebel raiding parties. There were even instances of voluntary runaways being sold back into slavery—especially by provincial officers not unaware of their value—either to Loyalist planters or into the West Indies. Others were simply kept as "servants" by officers; and despite their promised freedom they were treated as property and prevented from leaving the service of their liberators. For those black Loyalists who survived such threats to their freedom, conditions in the British camps often meant death.[129]

John Kizell had an easy decision to make. Although Esther Kysell vanishes from the public record in April 1775, he presumably remained connected to her household and/or business in the intervening years. He was tied to a German community that was conspicuously Whig. That left Kizell one option in May 1780: to join the British military. Otherwise he risked being swept into the labor pool of sequestered plantation and urban slaves.[130] He was by now probably semiliterate and well-spoken. A British officer would have considered him a choice servant.[131]

Kizell had another incentive to join the British: they were winning. Not only had they taken Charleston, but their loyalist allies in the countryside also appeared to be gaining strength. Kizell was aware, for instance, that the many Germans settled in Orangeburg District, including Esther Kysell's brother, were staunch loyalists. George Fulker, perhaps donning some of his late in-law's military regalia, had become a lieutenant in the local militia. How this influenced Kizell's decision is impossible to know. But any political cleavage within the family would have underscored the uncertainty of his circumstances. Joining the British was his safest gambit.[132]

Kizell became a free man the moment he presented himself at a British barracks. If an orderly recorded Kizell's liberation, however, the ledger is long lost. Among surviving military records and other sources, where a trace of Kizell's service might be found, there is nothing on paper to document his crossing over from slavery to freedom.

A Summer of Soldiering

While Kizell was about to become a soldier and a free man, General Clinton was forming his strategy to wrest the entire state from patriot control. Clinton believed that the majority of South Carolinians remained loyal. He had captured the main Continental force in the South. His task thus seemed self-evident and attainable: rally and strengthen loyalist militia, suppress pockets of Whig opposition, and restore a semblance of law and order.

The southern strategy had accomplished its primary objective. The governors and lieutenant governors of South Carolina and Georgia had proposed in August 1777 that the economic wealth of the South was indispensable to the American cause. Depriving the rebellion of the South's production of tobacco, rice, indigo, and deerskins would be fatal, they argued. "Royal officials," Borick writes, "persuaded British leaders that operations in the south would not only bring loyalists to the fore, but would also injure the northern colonies by cutting off the rebels' source of economic power." Clinton had concurred.[133]

Patrick Ferguson was the logical choice to mobilize loyalist militia. He commanded several hundred Americans and had operated effectively in the backcountry between Charleston and the Savannah River. He seemed to have earned the respect of his troops. Only Lt. Col. Francis (Lord) Rawdon, among Cornwallis's senior officers, could say the same.[134]

Clinton was well aware of loyalists' difficult circumstances and their concern for leaving their families exposed. Ferguson was instructed to recruit "young and unmarried men" in Georgia and the two Carolinas. He was to impose discipline, which "must be done with great caution so as not to disgust the men." They were to be limited to six months' service in the next twelve and given written assurance that they would "not be obliged under any Pretense to march beyond North Carolina and Georgia." Finally those "averse to serve on foot may be allowed to serve on horse back at their own expense."[135]

The immediate response was encouraging. "Most of the people round Charlestown came in," a British officer recalled after the war, "and . . . not a few actually took up arms . . . under the direction of major Ferguson."[136] Reports from the backcountry also were reassuring. On the march by late May, Ferguson wrote Cornwallis to relay intelligence that "the Commander in Chief has no reason to doubt that the inhabitants are very well disposed to take an active part" in restoring royal authority.[137]

Ferguson and his American Volunteers had left the city four days before under the command of Lt. Col. Nisbet Balfour. For the moment Balfour had preempted Ferguson's responsibility for mobilizing loyalist militia. Balfour regarded the Scot "as capricious, whimsical, and dangerously independent-minded."[138] One historian has described him as "proud and arrogant."[139]

Kizell came to form his own opinion of the officer whom he was to serve during the violent summer ahead. He later told British listeners that he had been near Major Ferguson when he was killed that October at Kings Mountain. Although there is no supporting documentation that he was ever attached to Ferguson, Kizell's reference to a specific battle and commander argues that both were genuine landmarks in his first months of freedom. Kizell, it must be assumed, marched with the American Volunteers and Patrick Ferguson.

Their first destination was Orangeburg, where Ferguson—and Kizell—may have encountered George Fulker. Balfour and Ferguson added 240 men before pushing on to Ninety Six, a trading and military outpost south of the Saluda River. They arrived on June 22 to establish a base for training recruits and supporting raids into the state's north and west.[140]

Ferguson, his militia role restored, had already sent Cornwallis a recruiting strategy consistent with Clinton's admonition not to ask more sacrifice than necessary from loyalists. It divided men into those older than forty or with four or more children, on the one hand, and others eighteen and over, who would serve actively for six months in the year. The latter would form the core of loyalist power. The former would "not be called out . . . except in case of an insurrection [meaning of slaves] or invasion of the Province."[141]

Although the number of men coming forward was encouraging, the farther the British penetrated the backcountry, the less certain they became of loyalist sentiment. As early as July 13, Cornwallis was warning Lord Rawdon, based in Camden, to conserve his forces and "keep everything as compact as possible." As Michael Scoggins suggests in *The Day It Rained Militia*, Cornwallis "knew the danger of sending small groups of British soldiers into the hostile settlements of the upper districts."[142]

As Ferguson got to know his men, he would also have developed an understanding of their varied backgrounds and motives. Robert Stansbury Lambert, in *South Carolina Loyalists in the American Revolution*, writes that "his zeal and apparent interest in his men seemed to inspire a degree of mutual respect and admiration."[143] But their lack of military discipline was frustrating.

Ferguson was bound, as well, to question the fervency of some recruits. *Tory* and *Whig* often were situational terms. Each could be found in several guises, and it was common for people to switch allegiance as much for reasons of sheer survival as for political beliefs.

Two backcountry "camps" opposed the Revolution in its early years, according to Lambert. Some were "deeply loyal to the Crown on principle" but were "overcome by the coercive tactics of the [provincial] congress. . . . They simply waited in exile or quietly at home in the hopes that British arms would ultimately release them from Whig control."

There were also "men with no particularly deep commitment to the Crown." They resented "being pressured to give lip service to a cause they vaguely understood and whose implications for the security of their persons and property were equally unclear." They viewed the rebellion as "the immediate threat to whatever tranquility they had hoped for in the hard life of their isolated farms and settlements." But these same people, Lambert argues, "might find a degree of security under American rule that they could live with."[144]

Clinton's intelligence squared with what he had heard from Simpson, who reported that upcountry loyalism was more promising than that among lowcountry planters. The backcountry poor had every reason to resent wealthy lowlanders. "Through intimidation," writes George S. McCowen Jr., ". . . and lack of support from the British authorities, they had been forced into the rebel camp. . . . Nevertheless, Simpson did not believe the support of the king to be irretrievably lost. . . . He advocated stricter methods of ascertaining allegiance and more stringent punishment of those disloyal to the Crown."[145]

Possibly on the strength of Simpson's recommendations, Clinton on June 3 issued a proclamation requiring an oath of allegiance. As Cornwallis later admitted, the move backfired. It fed "the flames of the Loyalists' desire for vengeance," McCowen explains, "but also it forced men to declare their loyalty . . . under false pretenses or else to flee to the partisan bands of patriots just beginning to form."[146]

Kizell's understanding of the American character was evolving through daily contact with the rough-hewn and largely illiterate backcountry men. He knew that they and he were not fighting for precisely the same objective. White loyalists wished to be free to make a life for themselves and their families, away from the influence of officialdom. They wanted to be left alone. Kizell wanted simply to be free and remain free. That was problematic in a society where being black equated to being a slave.

Necessarily a close observer of whites, Kizell would have discerned that the men claiming to be loyalists were essentially the same men he had seen on the patriot side during the siege of Charleston. They were largely poor and uneducated. Few were slave owners. Some were landless and hardly better off than slaves.

If they desired material benefit from their militia service, it was more land. That would raise them in South Carolina's property-based pecking order. It would make them better off, no matter which side prevailed in the war. It would strengthen their

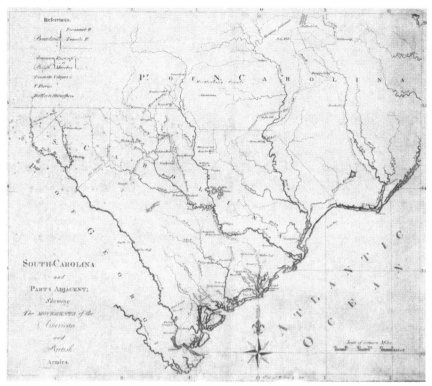

South Carolina during the Revolution. Map, circa 1785, courtesy of the South Caroliniana Library, University of South Carolina

sense of liberty, for a man could not be truly free without land. Kizell would have pondered this as he tried to determine the bounds of his freedom.

It is not hard to imagine Kizell, as he became better acquainted with the British officers, asking about the Somerset case and the status he would be accorded under English rule. It is also not hard to imagine his experiencing mixed loyalist attitudes toward an intelligent young black man who had been discovered, more than once, reading dog-eared newspapers or a borrowed Bible.

In spite of his slight stature, Kizell would have stood out among other blacks in Ferguson's growing force. The only blacks known among loyalist units gathering at Ninety Six were slaves accompanying their owners. Although there was no rule to prevent free men of color bearing arms in loyalist militia, only a few had done so, mainly in the first years of the rebellion. Several mulattoes had been captured in the backcountry with other loyalists and brought to Charleston in the winter of 1776. Another may have served as an officer in a loyalist group operating near the Saluda River.[147]

Free blacks did enlist in patriot ranks. One had died in John Laurens's escapade early in the year. Kizell may have known of Isom Carter, a free black from Beaufort, who served in a South Carolina artillery regiment. Carter was imprisoned in

Charleston after the surrender. Other black combatants detained included Isaac Perkins and Joel Taburn, who had marched to Charleston with their North Carolina unit. Thomas Buckner and Ephraim Hearn had come south with fellow Virginians.[148] These men, Kizell understood, had their reasons for aiding the rebellion.

Ninety Six lay on the path leading northwest toward the Cherokee lands. Ferguson and his men had forded rivers and passed through deep woods to reach it. In a sense Kizell was returning to terrain he had known as a child, mystical places where spirits lived. Even if he had been exposed in Charleston to the white religion, Kizell would have retained vestiges of his African worldview, in which the visible surroundings hid "surprising things." If there was a spirit world in Africa, there must be one in the wild vastness of America. The whites were oblivious to this. But the blacks were not, and neither, certainly, were the indigenous peoples who had lived so long on this land and related to it spiritually as no one else could.

Ferguson was concerned only with a single spirit—that of rebellion. Having reached Ninety Six, he determined to reinforce it by constructing a small fortress.[149] Building blockhouses and defensive works revealed how little the British understood the fluid nature of warfare practiced in the South Carolina interior. Ferguson's military success had come in open battle.[150] He and senior British commanders were unaware of what Scoggins calls the "profound influence" that the Cherokee War in 1760–61 and the Regulator-Moderator civil conflict in the mid-1760s had on militia in the backcountry.

"The unconventional and often brutal nature of this warfare," Scoggins writes, "forced . . . militia to learn new tactics than those practiced by . . . military forces of Europe." South Carolina militia leaders had refined the use of "small troops of mobile rangers . . . on horseback. Backwoods ambushes, surprise attacks and small skirmishes—accompanied by the burning of homes, destruction of crops and looting of property—replaced large-scale, organized battles. . . . The deliberate targeting of officers . . . abhorred on the European battlefield, also became commonplace on the frontier."[151]

The truth of this became increasingly apparent during the bloody summer and early fall of 1780. The British won the most conventional and best-known battle—at Camden—on August 16. But they lost a series of smaller confrontations, starting on June 20 at Ramsour's Mill, three weeks after the Waxhaws.

The most significant Whig victory occurred on July 12 at Williamson's plantation near present-day Rock Hill. Whig militia decimated experienced soldiers in a surprise dawn attack in what also is known as Huck's Defeat. The defenders included the New York Volunteers and elements of Tarleton's British Legion. They had "seemed invincible," Scoggins writes in his history of the summer campaign, but the defeat of this tested corps "demonstrated once and for all that the rebel militia could defeat the Provincial regiments in battle."[152]

Ferguson's lack of respect for rebels' fighting abilities survived the summer intact. With the exception of a day-long battle on August 8 in the vicinity of Wofford's ironworks, Ferguson missed the major encounters with patriot forces. At Wofford's, in Spartan District, militia from Georgia and South Carolina under Col. Isaac Shelby had defeated a strong loyalist contingent led by Ferguson.[153]

Whatever lessons Ferguson took from that battlefield failed to save him. He was preoccupied with keeping together a force that spent much of its time foraging and with trying to improve the military preparedness of his here-today, gone-tomorrow followers. At one point he had only 650 "old and infirm" men. The "younger classes were sent home to draw lots and prepare for the campaign," he reported.[154]

Although news of the British victory at Camden strengthened loyalist morale throughout the state, it could not erase a general sense that the rebels were not fading from the scene. Stories circulated about the depredations of Col. Francis Marion and his men. They were known to live in swamps and thick forest, moving only under the cover of darkness.[155] Kizell would have recalled that warriors in his homeland often used "darkness"—magically induced invisibility—to hide from enemies.

There may also have been gnawing doubt among loyalist combatants that they were a match for the rebels. Operating from fixed bases such as Ninety Six and Camden, they were tethered to these for support. They were led largely by English officers who neither knew the terrain nor the temperament of their opponents. Where Ferguson was burdened with recruiting and training inexperienced soldiers, the rebels serving under American command were prepared for the contest at hand. As Scoggins writes, "the Whig militia generally outperformed the Tory militia in battle, due partly to greater resolve and partly to more military experience and better leaders."[156]

Conscious that the British were failing to attract greater loyalty among backcountry folk, Cornwallis alerted Clinton that they had yet another problem. There were "reports industriously propagated in this province of a large army coming from the northward [which] had very much intimidated our friends, encouraged our enemies, and determined the wavering against us."[157]

Soldiers' scuttlebutt, if not his own intuition, would have warned Kizell that all was not going well. Kizell had a vested interest in an English victory. What he was hearing in various quarters could not have been reassuring. Nor was what he was learning of British handling of slaves. Although there is no evidence that Ferguson was involved, British practice in South Carolina was to treat captured slaves as a means to reward loyalists. Instead of liberating them, the British shared them out to their civilian supporters, as well as to officers. One of the first British actions at Ninety Six had been to round up slaves belonging to rebels and share them among local loyalists. Colonel Balfour informed Cornwallis that he had required the loyalists to accept responsibility for the slaves "when called for."[158]

This implied that there was no intent to free the slaves when the war was finished. As Frey writes, the British were "anxious to placate loyal whites . . . [and] assigned much of the property in land and slaves seized by the army to loyalist families for their use. . . . The rest were sent to labor on public works. Other captured blacks were given to loyalist militia officers as a reward for extraordinary service. . . . The final irony . . .

is that when the imperatives of war seemed to require it, the army openly abandoned its pose as liberator by selling some of its captives and using the proceeds to buy supplies for the army."

A dozen black soldiers had been captured in the Whig ranks at Camden. "Will it not be worthwhile," Balfour reasoned, "to convince *Blacke* that he must not fight against us—to sell them and buy shoes for your corps?"[159] One of the armed free blacks captured was fifteen-year-old Andrew Ferguson, a Virginia militiaman whose path soon crossed his British namesake's at Kings Mountain.[160]

On Friday, September 1, one of Ferguson's officers, Lt. Anthony Allaire, recorded in his diary "the disagreeable news that we were to be separated from the army, and act on the frontiers with the militia."[161] They were to move northward from Ninety Six into North Carolina, where they would rally loyalists and harass rebel militia. They also would shield the main army, now headquartered under Cornwallis in Charlotte.

Their assignment was indeed disagreeable. Ferguson would have preferred participating directly with Cornwallis in crushing the remnants of the American army in the Carolinas. This would seal British control of the South and all but end the rebellion. As Ferguson led more than eight hundred men into North Carolina's Tryon County, however, they soon realized that they were operating in hostile territory.

Lord Rawdon confided a few weeks later that the British had seriously overestimated loyalist sentiment in both Carolinas. "It was imagined that the Tranquility of South Carolina was assured," he wrote from the backcountry to Maj. Gen. Alexander Leslie in Charleston. The same was presumed in North Carolina. However, the "Approach of General Gates's Army unveiled to us a Fund of Disaffections in the Province, of which we could have formed no idea. . . . To this hour the majority of the inhabitants . . . between the Pedee and the Santee are in arms against us."[162]

Ferguson's arrogance finally got the better of him. After spending a frustrating September among the inhospitable residents of Tryon County, he paused on October 1 at Denard's Ford, on the Broad River, to issue a proclamation intended to rally wavering loyalists to join his ranks. To summon them for king and country was not enough for Ferguson, however. He closed with a sentence that may have cost him his life: "If you choose to be pissed upon forever and ever by a set of mongrels, say so at once and let your women turn their backs upon you, and look out for real men to protect them."[163]

These were fighting words to local patriots as well as to hundreds of mounted North Carolina and Virginia riflemen already riding to intercept Ferguson.[164] Ferguson retreated eastward and might easily have found safety with Cornwallis in nearby Charlotte. Instead, cocksure and complacent, he occupied a flat-topped hill—known locally as Little Kings Mountain—which he was convinced he could easily defend.[165]

The men tracking Ferguson included a few free blacks and slaves whose names and background have been combed from pension records, diaries, and other sources by Bobby Gilmer Moss. He and others, who have studied the ensuing battle, have found no documentation that definitively places even one black among the loyalists camped atop Little Kings Mountain, but they suspect some were there.[166]

Few surviving loyalists wrote accounts of the battle. They also were excluded from submitting pension applications, in which they might have mentioned the presence of blacks. The lack of proof that Kizell or any other black was on the loyalist side is hardly surprising.

Was Kizell at Kings Mountain? The strongest evidence is that he said he was there. There is intriguing anecdotal evidence, as well, in Lyman Draper's classic 1881 narrative, *King's Mountain and Its Heroes.* Two patriot scouts, William Twitty and Lewis Musick, accidentally spotted Ferguson and his force spread for more than a mile along a road near Denard's Ford. It may have been the morning of October 1, the same day Ferguson challenged Americans' manhood. Draper describes the scene: "The Whig scouts had a good view . . . and as [the British] passed David Miller's place one of the enemy and a negro remained behind, the latter going to the spring to catch his horse. The soldier . . . proved to be Ferguson's cook; and, it seems, was completing the preparation of a savory meal to take along for the Colonel's breakfast."

The scouts hid their horses and "secreted themselves, awaiting the advance of the supposed officer and his servant. The negro, in about fifteen minutes, came dashing along some fifty yards in front. Twitty was to rush out and take the negro, while Musick was to prevent the Red Coat in the rear from shooting him; and the colored fellow was seized so suddenly that he made no defense. Musick demanded the Red Coat to surrender. . . . At this moment the negro put spurs to his horse and escaped."

When the scouts discovered that their prisoner—probably Ferguson's orderly, Elias Powell—was the commander's cook, they expropriated the breakfast and then wrote a cheeky message for him to carry to Ferguson. Twitty and Musick said—in Draper's re-creation—that they were returning "so important a personage, and trusting that he [Ferguson] would restore him to his butlership."[167]

The cook's black companion presumably rejoined Ferguson's train on its march toward Kings Mountain. He is one of history's ghosts, but he may well have been John Kizell.

Death on Kings Mountain

Ferguson and his men scrambled up the wooded, boulder-strewn mountain slope on October 6. Elias Powell and his black assistant—arguably Kizell—busily set up Ferguson's tents near the supply wagons on the northeast knoll. Ferguson immediately dispatched a fifth of his force on a foraging mission, then reported confidently to Cornwallis that he planned to stand and fight. "I hold a position on the King's Mountain," he wrote, "that all the rebels out of hell cannot drive me from." But his courier was intercepted, and the provocative words passed among the Whigs.[168]

Ferguson might still have retreated. He was within a day's march of Cornwallis. There were other loyalist units nearby who could have reinforced him. But Ferguson believed that his one hundred elite troops, experienced fighters in the King's American Rangers, the Queen's Rangers, and the New Jersey Volunteers, would steel his green militia. He had chosen virtually impregnable terrain. Let them come, he proclaimed, and so they did.

The Whig army comprised three divisions—angry North Carolinian frontiersmen, several hundred South Carolinians under Col. James Williams, who had arrived the day before, and the Virginia militia commanded by Col. William Campbell, Patrick Henry's brother-in-law. After animated discussion it was agreed the Virginian should lead.[169]

Campbell was accompanied by his mulatto son and servant, John Broddy. At a distance he resembled his tall, well-proportioned father, which had occasioned some good-natured joking during the ride to Kings Mountain. One officer addressed Broddy as Colonel Campbell, to the amusement of several—certainly to Broddy.[170]

There was little cause for humor on the morning of October 7. The Whigs had been soaked by a chill rain during the night. The rain finally gave way to a cool breeze by noon, and as one private recalled, "the roll of the British drums informed us that we had something to do."[171] By midafternoon the rebels were instructed to "tie up overcoats, pick touch-holes, fresh prime, and be ready to fight." Some put four or five rifle balls in their mouths "to prevent thirst, and also be in readiness to reload quick."[172] Then they began ascending the rampartlike hillside, screaming as Campbell had ordered. The loyalists "met us with tremendous fire," one of Campbell's men remembered.[173]

The first men to come within striking distance of the defenders fired from behind trees and rocks. The Virginians and South Carolinians directed withering fire at the center of the British line. Ferguson was quick to appreciate the riflemen's advantage over his muskets and ordered a bayonet charge. The South Carolina men received the full force of the attack. In the words of a survivor, they "obstinately stood until some of them were thrust through the body, and having nothing but their rifles by which to defend themselves, they were forced to retreat."[174]

Given the terrain, no combatant could have understood the battle's ebb and flow.[175] Broddy, tending his father's spooked horse, may have had a relatively panoramic view from below. Andrew Ferguson, the young Virginian black in a late-arriving unit, could hear the earsplitting roar of battle ricocheting through the forest. He later claimed to have seen Major Ferguson riding along the rim of the hill.[176] Kizell, perhaps tending the wounded or distributing powder and shot from the wagons, would have experienced the never-to-be-forgotten sounds and smell of battle, of agony and death. He was now truly a soldier.

Kings Mountain remains shrouded in controversy and conflicting accounts. Ferguson's second-in-command tried to explain to Cornwallis the chaos on the battlefield. Writing four days later as a prisoner near Gilbert Town, in North Carolina, Capt. Abraham DePeyster, a New York loyalist, revealed how suddenly the defenders lost their presumed advantage. The Whigs' numbers "enabled them to surround our post," DePeyster wrote. "Ours was only sufficient to form a simple line on the slope of the hill."

Trouble started on the right flank. Inexperienced North Carolina militia gave ground, demoralizing nearby units. DePeyster's "little detachment of soldiers charged the enemy with success & drove the right of the enemy back in confusion." But Ferguson, concerned that the faltering North Carolinians had exposed the higher ground, signaled retreat.

"The militia," DePeyster reported, "being ignorant of the cause of our retreat, it threw the few that stood their post . . . in disorder, tho the officers cut some of them down. . . . The left on seeing us break gave way, got all in a crowd on the hill. . . . Major Ferguson while the . . . officers were doing their best amongst the crowd . . . I am sorry to say . . . was killed before he advanced 20 yards."[177]

Several Whig marksmen recognized Ferguson as he attempted to charge his mount to safety. They fired almost simultaneously from close range, hitting him with at least seven bullets. One of his boots caught in a stirrup, and the major's disoriented horse dragged the bleeding body across the rocky mountaintop for several horrifying minutes.[178]

DePeyster and a few men took cover behind the wagons and continued fighting until "I thought proper to surrender as the only means of saving the lives of some brave men still left."[179] A Whig officer rode forward, seized the flag of surrender from DePeyster, and raised it for all to see.[180] But the killing continued when a stray bullet mortally wounded Colonel Williams. His men responded by firing into the huddled mass of prisoners.[181] Many of the 157 loyalist dead and 163 badly wounded resulted from the Whigs' retributive frenzy. The "rebels out of hell" lost just 28 killed and 64 wounded.[182]

As dusk fell Ferguson's orderly and others, possibly including Kizell, washed the battered corpse, wrapped it in a hide, and buried it not far from the tents and wagons. Interred with him was Virginia Sal, his presumed mistress. The previous day she had been plaiting his hair.[183] Darkness meanwhile prevented the living from ministering to the scattered casualties and dying men. One Whig remembered "that we had to encamp on the ground with the dead and wounded, and pass the night amid the growns [sic] and lamentations."[184]

Leaving the seriously wounded to be tended at nearby homesteads, the rebels began marching nearly seven hundred captives north early the next morning, a Sunday. They moved rapidly between double lines of mounted Whigs, each man carrying two muskets. Their officers took up the rear.[185] Some of the latter had served on the patriot side at Musgrove's Mill only weeks before but claimed they had since been forced to join Ferguson. Once this was verified, they were treated well.[186]

In spite of the Whigs' haste — in part to avoid retaliation from Cornwallis — it took five days and fifty miles to reach Biggerstaff's plantation near Gilbert Town.[187] The loyalists were ill clothed and stripped of their blankets. Kizell likely marched with Elias Powell and helped serve the officers.

It is reasonable to suppose that Broddy or other free blacks among the victors spoke to Kizell. They would have been curious to know something about any man of color on the loyalist side. Perhaps Kizell conversed with Andrew Ferguson and his father, free men from Virginia's Dinwiddie County. Perhaps Ishmael Titus had a moment to tell Kizell furtively about his own life as a slave in Virginia, how he had secured his freedom by substituting for his owner in the local militia.[188]

Kizell was in real danger. Not only was he a prisoner; he could be requisitioned by the rebels or made a servant to one of the Whig officers. Worst of all he could be sold back into slavery. These more worldly-wise black patriots—all of them American-born—may have urged the runaway African to escape if he could.

Conceivably Kizell could have volunteered to join a patriot regiment, which Broddy, Titus, or the Fergusons might have facilitated. If that was an option, he chose not to take it, either out of loyalty to the British or, more probably, in the somewhat shaken belief that the king's men would triumph in the end. To go over to the Americans had its own risks. To remain their prisoner had potentially more serious consequences.

The prisoners' morale would have been bad enough, but it was about to plummet further. Soon after they arrived at Gilbert Town, word spread that eleven patriots had been hung a few days earlier at Ninety Six. A paroled officer had witnessed the hangings. "In the opinion of the patriots," Robert Dunkerly writes, "it required retaliatory measures to put a stop to these atrocities."[189] Starting at ten the next morning, two Whig magistrates and a jury of twelve officers met throughout the day to try thirty-six loyalists. Two dozen were convicted of capital crimes. Nine were quickly hung in lots of three before a senior officer abruptly ordered the executions stopped.[190]

Fearing that Tarleton was on their trail, the Whigs drove their captives thirty miles the next day in foul weather. A loyalist officer described it as a death march. They "were so wearied that many of them were obliged to give out on the road—they then roll'd them down in the mud and many of them they left there trod to death." Many of the North Carolina militia began taking their leave, enabling about one hundred prisoners to slip away that same day. The rest trudged on to Quaker Meadows and Burke Court House, crossing the Yadkin River to the Moravian settlement at Bethabara.[191]

The last-minute killings at Kings Mountain, the executions at Gilbert Town, and the rough handling of the prisoners soon became grist for acrimony and accusation. In a scathing note to his American counterpart, Cornwallis on December 1 told General Gates that "the officers and men taken at King's Mountain were treated with an inhumanity scarcely credible." He hinted at retaliation "for those unhappy men who were so cruelly and unjustly put to death at Gilbertown."[192]

Having replaced Gates as the southern commander, General Greene refused to answer for militia who were not under formal army discipline. They were merely seeking an eye for an eye. "I leave them to judge," he wrote Cornwallis on December 17, "of the nature and tendency of your Lordship's orders . . . after the action at Camden" and of Tarleton's "conduct in laying waste the country and destroying the inhabitants who were taught to expect protection and security if they observed but a neutrality."[193]

Both sides had agreed in principle to exchange the Kings Mountain prisoners for rebels held in North and South Carolina. The loyalists preempted that plan by escaping with suspicious regularity. "Most of the prisoners taken managed to escape in the weeks after the battle," according to Dunkerly, "and made their way, singly or in groups," to Ninety Six, where they remained through the coming winter.[194]

Greene had his own theory. He suspected that many of the prisoners had been allowed to go free on the pretense of enlisting in patriot regiments. "We have lost by the folly, not to say anything worse . . . upwards of six hundred" prisoners, he wrote General Washington on December 7. By January virtually all who had joined Whig units had deserted. Two hundred were reported under arms with the loyalists.[195]

The two weeks following the battle had been hard. Kizell would have been thinly clothed and poorly shod as winter approached. If he remained a prisoner, the food would have been meager. If he had escaped, he would have survived largely on haws—an almost tasteless cherrylike seed then common in the Carolina forests.[196]

Given his precarious situation, his loyalist inclinations, and the likelihood that he was now the servant of one or more officers, Kizell had both motive and opportunity to escape as soon as possible. Three British lieutenants absconded on November 6. One reached Charleston just nineteen days later.[197]

Kizell may well have left the Moravian settlements, near present-day Winston-Salem, with the officers. They would have provided a degree of protection that he would not have enjoyed if he had escaped with a small group of backcountry men, and certainly not if he had gone alone. In the lawless countryside, a solitary black youth would have faced daunting threats at every turn.

Kizell could also have found his way to Ninety Six. More likely he accompanied one or more officers to Charleston, possibly with the aid of Lieutenant Fulker as they passed through the loyalist stronghold in Orangeburg. To Kizell Charleston and its supportive black community were home. Presumably he was reabsorbed by the military. Given that his name does not appear in surviving British muster rolls and pay lists, he may have continued in the personal service of one or more officers.

Wherever he went, and regardless with whom, Kizell appears to have seen his last fighting. Had he been at Cowpens in January 1781 or at other battles that year in South Carolina, he would have mentioned this along with his account of Major Ferguson's demise.

Kings Mountain was a turning point in the Revolution. The immediate military and political consequences were clear. To General Washington Greene wrote on October 31 that it would "give a severe check to the Tories, and spirit and confidence to the Whigs." Much later Clinton ruefully admitted that Kings Mountain was "the first link in a chain of evils that followed each other in regular succession until they at last ended in the total loss of America."[198]

For Kizell Kings Mountain also represented a turning point. His exposure to backwoods life in the months leading to the battle would have accentuated his antipathy toward a society committed to the exploitation of slave labor. The defeat at Kings Mountain also forced Kizell, perhaps for the first time, to contemplate his options if the British ultimately conceded independence to a nation of slaveholders.

4

EXODUS

"They assured me they were unanimous in the desire for embarking for Africa, telling me their labour was lost upon the land in this country."

John Clarkson, after addressing free blacks
in Birchtown, Nova Scotia, October 26, 1791

The next link in Clinton's chain of evils—forged on January 17, 1781, at Cowpens— effectively ended British hopes of detaching South Carolina from the rebellion. Kings Mountain had been a humiliation; Cowpens was a debacle. Pursued by a roughly equal force under Tarleton, the Americans turned to face their opponents north of present-day Spartanburg. Brig. Gen. Daniel Morgan, a battered veteran aged forty-five, was old enough to be Tarleton's father. He administered nothing short of a whipping.

The early morning contest was over in little more than an hour. Morgan's Maryland and Delaware Continentals, Virginia riflemen, and dragoons killed 100 attackers, including 39 officers, wounded 229, and captured another 600. Among the latter were 60 black batmen—further evidence that some blacks had accompanied loyalists at Kings Mountain. American casualties were just 72, including 12 killed.

Beyond the Americans' Reach

Tarleton escaped with his life, if not with his reputation. His hubris had finally got the better of him. But it was Cornwallis, as Page Smith aptly notes, who had sent a boy to do a man's job.[1] The British were being outgeneraled, as they had been since Gen. John Burgoyne surrendered at Saratoga in 1777. Cornwallis himself ten months later surrendered ignominiously at Yorktown, having been ordered by Clinton to occupy an untenable position in the Virginia tidewater.

While conceding their defeats as well as the disaffection of more and more Americans, the British continued to believe in ultimate triumph. Yorktown was not immediately perceived as a great victory, and the British vowed to hold Charleston.[2] But to what end? After Cowpens the British military presence outside Charleston was restricted largely to the areas around Camden, Ninety Six, Orangeburg, and, for a time, Georgetown.

Raiders under Francis Marion, Elijah Clarke, and others moved at will in the countryside. By spring of 1781, Marion's men were operating near Charleston. A critical line of British posts in the interior had fallen in May, including Orangeburg and Fort Motte, where George Fulker, having surrendered, was executed for an alleged atrocity.[3] By year's end Greene was threatening Charleston but seemed content to confine the British and loyalists in powerless isolation.

Yorktown added to the British and loyalists' beleaguered sense of doubt over what was to come next. Civil administration in Charleston, which Cornwallis had vested in a police board, had proven ineffectual. As if to signal lack of faith in the future, not to mention civilian leadership, the British in January ordered that the board, which served as a court of common pleas, should hear only suits of "pressing and immediate necessity."

In Charleston the English displayed "the same vacillation and failure of communication . . . evident in other aspects of British policy during the Revolution," George Smith McCowen Jr. writes in his history of the Charleston occupation. "The board had been established without any definite conception of its functions. . . . Most of the members . . . had returned to South Carolina with the expectation that royal government would soon be established. . . . Yet the British had no real plan for . . . restoring civil government."[4]

Charleston, no longer a jewel, had become a thorn. With the lowcountry and interior devastated, the city's economic revival in mid-1780 had been abortive. Charleston served no real purpose economically or even militarily. It was a garrison town populated by a mélange of loyalist whites, time-biding rebel sympathizers, prisoners, and blacks. Superintending and sustaining these diverse elements was a daily challenge.

Cornwallis wanted to be rid of the prisoners taken at the city's fall. As early as February 1781, he was again corresponding with General Greene about an exchange.[5] Suspected rebels also were a constant concern to the authorities. To suppress rebellious sentiment altogether, the British abandoned the terms of capitulation and insisted that all whites support the king. Angered by this apparent breach, many militiamen and paroled prisoners left Charleston to fight alongside the Americans rather than against them. The British responded by making this a treasonable act.[6]

In spite of the exodus of exchanged prisoners, rebels, and those alienated by the British decree, Charleston was becoming more congested. Tories from throughout the state crowded into the city along with a steady stream of refugees. Food and other supplies grew scarce, and prices escalated beyond the means of many.[7]

By the time residents learned of the British defeat at Yorktown, Charleston was effectively under siege itself. Greene's December attack at Dorchester, fifteen miles northwest on the headwaters of the Ashley River, underscored the threat. British engineers were already strengthening the barrier across the neck and had requested the inhabitants "to send all the negroes they can spare . . . every morning at Six O'Clock."[8]

Needed as black labor might be, the city was being overwhelmed by unsupervised slaves and runaways. In a proclamation issued the day after Christmas, the army asserted that "numbers of Negroes, the property of the enemy in general, and of the sequestered estates in particular, are held in this town [by those] who have no right or authority to detain them." They were going about "uncontrolled, to the distress of the inhabitants [and] the detriment of Government." The army authorized seizure of these blacks and hiring them out to "publick departments."[9]

British frustration with uncontrolled blacks moving about town "under various pretenses" was a refrain familiar to whites in prewar Charleston. It indicates that the black community remained essentially intact. It certainly remained large. In June 1782 General Leslie reported that four thousand blacks wished to leave with the British. Loyalists had another six thousand slaves whom they wanted to take with them.[10] Charleston's black population had nearly doubled during the war, forcing the British finally to stop receiving slaves from outside the city.[11]

As the military situation deteriorated, the British, fearing an all-out attack by Greene,[12] reconsidered forming armed black units. General Leslie recommended in March 1782 that black soldiers be deployed under command of Col. James Moncrief. Because hundreds of blacks already worked under his supervision of engineers, Moncrief seemed a logical choice—"being well acquainted with their disposition and in the highest estimation amongst them."[13]

Leslie, in fact, had already incorporated a few blacks into combat operations. As many as seven hundred black troops were reported in Charleston by spring of 1782, although their actual number probably was considerably less. They saw little action, if any, and only slightly bolstered a force whose regular ranks had been dangerously depleted. "The dramatic effects of disease," Frey writes, "particularly epidemic yellow fever and malaria among British troops . . . had already seriously compromised Britain's ability to wage war in the South."[14]

In January John Cruden, the British officer responsible for sequestered property and slaves, had proposed arming no fewer than ten thousand blacks to reclaim the entire province. Lord Dunmore, recently arrived in Charleston after the loss of Yorktown, endorsed the idea. It would "open a large door for our friends from North Carolina to join us," he told Clinton, "till such time as . . . we have a sufficient command of the sea to enter Virginia."

The black janissaries would be drawn from slaves seized from rebel estates and those volunteered by their loyalist owners. Cruden recommended they be promised freedom; Dunmore suggested giving each a guinea, as well as their freedom, adding that the blacks must be "fully satisfied that this promise will be held inviolate." Some loyalists in Charleston reportedly planned to enlist armed blacks to help defend the city after the British left.[15]

Cruden and Dunmore were caught up in what Schama calls the "air of defiant unreality" in Charleston.[16] From a purely military standpoint, they would have seen the large numbers of blacks congregated in the provincial capital as a resource to be mobilized. Seven years earlier, when the British thought they could smother the rebellion in its crib, Dunmore had been reluctant to resort to full-fledged militarization of the slave population. Now, in the fog of unreality, anything was possible. Most whites, however, remained viscerally opposed to arming blacks. William Bull referred sarcastically to "our black dragoons"—a small cavalry detachment that had recently shed copious white blood—and said this proved their savagery.[17]

As it was, the British in Charleston were already facing pressure from both loyalists and Whigs. Sensing the war's drift, the opposing camps were focused on postconflict priorities. Respect for property rights became paramount. Loyalists believed that returning Americans' property bettered their chance to be compensated for the land and wealth they could not carry with them, if they were compelled to leave. Loyalists and Whigs remained divided on most things, but not on slavery or the sanctity of property, especially slaves.[18]

Clinton had agreed to study Dunmore's proposal to create a large black strike force under white officers. By March, however, he had resigned, in part over a contentious debate with Cornwallis regarding "who lost Yorktown." More important, a new government in England was committed to negotiating a peace and, if need be, accepting American independence.

When this news reached Charleston, the British commander had to confront a new pressure point. Those blacks who had sided with the king began approaching him for assurance that the British would recognize and protect their freedom. Kizell was an interested party, along with the other four thousand loyal blacks in Charleston.

Leslie determined that runaway blacks "who cited the Philipsburg Proclamation or who had given military service should be considered free." They were to be sent to another British dominion, where, in Leslie's words, "their past services will engage the grateful attention of the Government to which they will continue to be useful." The rest were to be returned to their American owners.[19]

In New York Gen. Guy Carleton, having replaced Clinton, approved Leslie's proposed handling of blacks. He also set in motion the evacuation of Savannah in July, when sufficient transport ships finally were provided. They would carry four thousand Tories and five thousand slaves to East Florida—numbers foreshadowing the evacuation that everyone knew would follow closely in Charleston.

Savannah also foreshadowed for blacks a darker aspect of the British retreat. Leslie had instructed civil departments in Savannah not to evacuate runaways who had been employed by them. "Likewise," Cynthia Pybus writes in *Epic Journeys of Freedom*, "he tried to restrain his officers from taking their black servants." He feared they would be kept, or sold, as slaves. His injunction was largely ignored.[20]

David George, destined to be Kizell's close friend in Nova Scotia and Sierra Leone, decided not to trust his family to chance. Nor did George Liele, the Baptist preacher. Both had found themselves in Savannah under British protection. Liele boarded a transport for Jamaica and survived to establish the first Baptist church in Kingston. George, his wife, Phillis, and their three children decamped by sea for Charleston.[21]

The evacuation of Charleston was traumatic for all concerned, but especially for the several thousand blacks who had either fled rebel owners or who remained the property of loyalists planning to leave with the British. In August nearly seven thousand blacks, most of them loyalists' slaves, were enrolled for departure.[22] Blacks who had been sequestered from rebels accounted for several thousand more. Not included were people, such as Kizell, who had been attached to the British military. There were also the armed dragoons.

As many as twelve thousand blacks expected to leave Charleston. Few knew where they might be going or the circumstances awaiting them. Given the trials that most had endured, in slavery and in war, they could entertain only the barest hope that better times were in store.

It did not help that the blacks were the spoils of war. Loyalist slave owners were focused on holding onto their property; patriots were demanding compensation for slaves who had run away or been sequestered by the British; English officers were conspiring to remove slaves as booty and sell them in the West Indies; even the slave traders continued to ply their business.[23]

Blacks' fates were almost entirely in the hands of whites, whose conflicting interests and motives were largely mercenary. Loyalists were adamant in their demands. On September 8 more than one hundred petitioned the military command to stop officers' trafficking in rebel-owned slaves, which jeopardized loyalists' claims for recompense. The petitioners sympathized nonetheless with blacks' dilemma. "Although reduced to slavery in this country," they said, the blacks were "entitled to humanity, which forbids the separation of them from their kindred, and the dispersion of them in countries where their *Bondage would be more grievous.*'"[24]

With less humanitarian intentions, the new American governor in South Carolina, John Mathews, had informed Leslie in August that the state would block repayment of debts owed to British merchants if the removal of slaves did not halt. He would also make it impossible for loyalists to redeem any claims on property confiscated by the state.[25] This threat led to a negotiated agreement in October. Slaves would be returned to their owners, "except such slaves as may have rendered themselves particularly obnoxious on account of their attachment and services to the British troops, and such as had specific promises of freedom."[26]

The operative word was *obnoxious*. Those who had rendered service to the British (and probably some who had not) quickly stepped forward to be included in that category. Mathews abrogated the agreement, however, when American inspectors discovered 136 slaves hidden on ships about to sail for East Florida. Although this relieved the British of potentially staggering financial liability for compensating American slave owners, Leslie still had to arbitrate competing claims of loyalists and British officers over the disposition of slaves.[27]

The British military had a decided advantage. They also had pecuniary incentive. Gen. William Moultrie, who had been allowed to visit Charleston, wrote in his memoirs that the "prospects of gain, from the sale of plundered negroes, were too seducing to be resisted by the officers, privates and followers of the British army. . . . Upwards of eight hundred slaves, who had been employed in the engineer department, were shipped off to the West Indies. It was said, and believed, that these were . . . sold for the benefit of Lieutenant Colonel Moncrief,"[28] the same officer supposedly held by his black engineers in the "highest estimation."

With the formal agreement abandoned, Leslie persuaded loyalist leaders to participate on a board to consider the status of blacks who claimed to be obnoxious. "A strange scene ensued," Olwell writes. "As hundreds of black refugees lined up in the street outside the Statehouse awaiting their turn to testify, low-country masters who had acquired permission to enter the city sought to persuade them to return to their duty."[29]

The board was quickly at odds. Loyalists objected to the military's dominance. When Moncrief unilaterally designated more than 250 slaves for the military in St. Lucia, the loyalists resigned.[30]

To the loyalists their slaves represented hard cash because they could be sold in East Florida or the West Indies. This would compensate somewhat for property left behind. Each white evacuee was to be allowed one and a half tons of freight and another three quarters of a ton for each slave.[31] Because "obnoxious" and ostensibly free blacks had priority over loyalist slaves for evacuation, some whites tried to pass their slaves off as black loyalists. A few reportedly sought to sell their slaves or allow them to buy their freedom.[32]

Twenty-seven transports had come down from Nova Scotia in late October, only to ride at anchor while the fate of several thousand blacks was decided. Among them were those belonging to John Lewis Gervais. "The British . . . carried all my Negroes to Charles Town," he wrote Henry Laurens—now languishing in the Tower of London—in September. But he reported that most of Laurens's slaves at Mepkin "have behaved very well."[33]

So, evidently, had Moultrie's. Imprisoned in Charleston since its fall, he had been exchanged in 1782 for General Burgoyne. He had been absent for more than two years when, escorted by Colonel Marion's men, he arrived unannounced at his ruined plantation near Santee. His slaves were stunned. "I stood on the piazza to receive them," he wrote years later.

> They gazed at me with astonishment, and every one came and took me by the hand, saying, "God bless you, massa! We glad for see you, massa!" And every now and then someone or other would come out with a "ky!" And the old Africans joined in a war-song in their own language, of "welcome the war[rior] home." It was an affecting meeting between the slaves and the master: the tears stole from my eyes and run [sic] down my cheeks. . . . I then possessed about two hundred slaves, and not one of them left me during the war, although they had had great offers, nay, some were carried down to work on the British lines, yet they always contrived to make their escape and return home.[34]

The British ultimately endorsed for evacuation more than three hundred blacks (their names are unrecorded) who had served them well but who rejected an undefined freedom in East Florida or the Caribbean. One was David George, who was given passage with his family to Halifax in late November, along with about five hundred white loyalists and their servants. Another probably was John Kizell.

Why Moultrie's people chose in effect to remain slaves in South Carolina, when they had stood before liberty's open gate, went with them to their graves—or in the case of his "old Africans," back to the world of their ancestors. What survives from this moment is the deep uncertainty that confronted *all* blacks. Even whites could not know what was truly in store, whether in the new American republic or in some English colony. All that blacks could know for sure was that they would find slavery alive and well.

The mood among evacuees gathered in mid-December 1782 at Gadsden's wharf was sour and subdued. Loyalists were departing with an embittered sense of dispossession, leaving behind a way of life few would be able to replicate. But it was the five thousand blacks who faced the more daunting prospect: even harder working conditions, especially in the killing fields of West Indian sugar plantations, and the separation from family and friends. Whether they were owned by loyalists or in the "care" of British officers, they had no cause to relish their imminent future.

Nor could George, Kizell, and other "obnoxious" blacks have been very sanguine. Having arrived destitute in Halifax, George already was enduring the first days of what would be a hard ten years in the wilderness. Kizell, apparently unattached, probably was among fifty blacks who accompanied General Leslie to New York.[35] They hardly knew what to expect there. They would be strangers again, in a strange land.

One black aboard Leslie's fleet who had much to fear was Harry Washington. He had fled Mount Vernon at the beginning of the war and probably knew that General Washington was headquartered near New York.[36] His former owner would soon note that the peace treaty prohibited the British from "carrying away any Negroes or other property of the American Inhabitants." David George was now beyond the Americans' reach; Washington and Kizell were not.

Many blacks were left behind. In desperation some tried to reach the ships. They clung to the sides of skiffs and harbor boats and had to be clubbed back into the water to prevent capsizing. Soldiers were posted with cutlasses and bayonets to keep them off the wharves. Those who did manage to board a transport—many of them seriously ill—were put off on Otter Island. Hundreds died. Their bones strewed the island for years thereafter.[37]

Carleton's Honor

The forty thousand soldiers, loyalists, slaves, and runaway blacks crowding Manhattan Island's southern extremity in early 1783 presented new arrivals with an intimidating kaleidoscope of humanity. The city's population had doubled during the war. It had become the base for the British army and navy, and since Yorktown it had become the refuge of loyalists driven from their homes and farms.

"In the tedium of confined living," Ellen Gibson Wilson writes, "they gathered in the taverns to read gazettes, exchange rumors or draw up petitions." Military officers and civilian gentry had taken the best houses. Others were converted to barracks and warehouses. In a wide area between the Broad Way and the North River, fired by patriot arsonists in 1776, sailcloth roofed the brick shells of once fine buildings. "Canvas Town" was a teeming home to refugee blacks, camp followers, and what one person described as "very lewd and dissolute persons."[38]

It had been a winter of excruciating uncertainty for Kizell and the three thousand blacks in New York. They assumed, in the absence of documentation, that the British would respect their freedom. When the peace treaty arrived in March 1783, blacks' worst fears were confirmed when they learned of a provision regarding the inviolability of American "property."

Boston King, who had been born into slavery in 1760 near Charleston, poignantly captured blacks' dismay and confusion in a memoir for English readers many years later. He had fled an abusive master and joined the British in Charleston. Several months before the final evacuation, he had come to New York on a British cruiser.

"The horrors and devastation of war" were behind him, he wrote in the *Methodist Magazine* of April 1798, "which diffused universal joy among all parties; except us, who had escaped from slavery." A "dreadful rumor" had begun circulating that "filled us all with inexpressible anguish and terror, especially when we saw our old masters coming from Virginia, North Carolina, and other parts, and seizing upon their slaves in the streets of New-York. . . . For some days we lost our appetite for food, and sleep departed from our eyes."[39]

King's insomnia resulted from an eleventh-hour amendment to the peace treaty, engineered by Richard Oswald and his old friend Henry Laurens. Captured at sea on a diplomatic mission to Holland, Laurens had been released from the infamous Tower of London in late 1782 barely in time to join the American negotiators in Paris.

The draft peace agreement already had been accepted by both sides when Laurens arrived. No one, including John Adams and Benjamin Franklin, objected when he insisted on an addendum to prohibit the British from "carrying away any Negroes or other property of the American Inhabitants." The two delegations signed the treaty, with the handwritten amendment in the margin, at Oswald's residence on November 29, 1782.[40]

General Carleton would have none of it. Sir Guy had been humiliated by his government's decision to sue for peace. Now he was outraged that Oswald and company had dishonored the good-faith pledge of freedom that British commanders had made to blacks serving the Crown. "The treaty in his eyes did not deal with them," Wilson asserts, "since they were no longer 'property.' He had found them free, and they would remain so."[41]

On his own authority, Carleton instructed Brig. Gen. Samuel Birch to begin issuing certificates to blacks to confirm that they had sought British protection and had

Carleton's permission to go to Nova Scotia "or wherever else He/She may think proper."[42] Carleton's refusal to surrender blacks—including many who had not served with the British but simply wished to be free—was a point of honor.

It was also a contentious matter with General Washington, who knew that several of his slaves were sheltered in New York. Although he refused to concede Carleton's prerogative, Washington seemed resigned to the inevitable loss of people who would be difficult to reconcile to reenslavement. "It was Carleton's moment of truth," Schama suggests, "and . . . the vindication of his woeful, defeated kingdom."[43]

Washington had been pressed by fellow Virginians to seek the return of their slaves. He did so vigorously when Carleton and he finally met on May 6, 1783, at American headquarters north of the city. Later, as president, Washington continued seeking the slaves' return. But he appears to have done so for political appearances and without genuine enthusiasm.

Washington's evolving discomfort with slavery led him shortly before he died in 1799 to manumit his slaves once his wife, Martha, joined him in death. He also made clear that they should be allowed to remain in the state as free people. To Henry Wiencek, in his study of Washington's attitude toward blacks and slavery, this was telling. "Virtually every emancipation plan proposed in Washington's time included forced exile for the freed slaves," Wiencek writes. But Washington "insisted that . . . [they] had a right to live on American soil."[44]

Carleton seems to have foreseen, in 1783, what Washington recognized only much later: that blacks not only had a right to be free, they were capable of using that freedom responsibly. Washington had known blacks largely as slaves; Carleton had known them mainly as soldiers, and as free people. In August 1782 he had put the black pioneers on the army's payroll. In effect, as Graham Russell Hodges writes in *The Black Loyalist Directory*, Carleton "granted the Black Loyalists veterans' status, which the African Americans regarded as a key component of their republicanism."

A second aspect of blacks' ideology was economic independence. Carleton, who had been stationed earlier in Canada, proposed that the pioneers each be given twenty acres of land in Nova Scotia. By so doing, Hodges explains, Carleton also ensured that every black would have a berth on the limited shipping available to transport more than thirty thousand loyalists.[45]

Carleton and Washington continued to spar until the last redcoats and loyalists had departed in November 1783. The Englishman was not impressed with the man soon to be "the Protector of America," as he wrote a few weeks before the final withdrawal. Influenced no doubt by loyalist friends, Carleton detected in Washington a "deep endless ambition" and a man "great, not by shining talents, but by . . . an unwearied passive perseverance [and] the mediocrity of all his competitors."[46]

Whether Kizell found accommodation in Canvas Town, in a barracks, or possibly serving in an officer's house, he would have discovered an existing black community in

New York as cohesive as Charleston's. He would also have encountered many free blacks. Although slavery survived in the city and on the farms northward along today's Hudson River Valley, there was no plantation economy linked to the city as the low-country was to Charleston. Slaves enjoyed considerable latitude and were less subject to harsh controls. Free blacks were numerous, living in impoverished areas such as Bancker Street.

New Amsterdam—as it was first known under Dutch dominion—had a pro-nounced black presence as early as 1638, when about one hundred Africans repre-sented a third of the population. Within a few years blacks had settled along a marsh known as Fresh Pond, near what centuries later was the site of the World Trade Center. Drawn principally from Angola and the Bakongo region of Central Africa, the black community, free and slave alike, had "considerable solidarity," according to Linda M. Heywood and John K. Thornton in their history of African creoles' impact on early American settlement.[47]

Blacks still constituted about 20 percent of New York's population in the late colonial period. This *eminence noire* induced endemic fear among whites. Several blacks implicated—falsely, it seems—in an alleged plot to burn the city in 1741 were hanged or banished. Kizell would have heard of this and similar events recounted by black New Yorkers. But he would have heard, as well, about blacks' growing sense of place and possibility; of Peter Williams, a prominent store owner; of plans for an African free school; of white politicians' talk of emancipating slaves under a new state constitution.[48]

There is no evidence that Kizell joined the British payroll in New York, but he likely remained engaged in some way with the military. Through the winter, while pondering his fate and trying to stay warm, he would have socialized with the black community and met others who had cast their lot with the British. He may also have met Phillis, a seventeen-year-old servant in the home of George Patten. The loyalist had left Boston with the British army when it retreated to Halifax in 1776. He later came to New York and was preparing to evacuate yet again—back to Nova Scotia with a group of loyalists calling themselves the Port Roseway Associates.[49]

Phillis's origins are obscure. If she had escaped from slavery, as seems probable, it was most likely from Virginia or the Chesapeake watershed, which would best explain her presence in New York. Unless she had been a favored military servant in Charleston, she would not have obtained passage to the city. If she was African born, there is no indication in the sparse information available. She was young and appar-ently alone.[50] She and Kizell traveled to Nova Scotia in separate loyalist "companies," implying that they were not yet "connected."

Kizell may also have been introduced during the winter to the two white loyalists under whose aegis he went to Nova Scotia. John Lowndes and James Ferguson were members of the Port Roseway Associates. Kizell may have been recommended by a British officer or come to their attention via the loyalist network. He joined Ferguson's company, which fell under Lowndes's overall command. If Kizell was attached to either of their households in New York, it was likely Ferguson's. Lowndes already had several "servants." Ferguson, about whom little is known, had few, if any.[51]

Lowndes had been a general merchant in Norfolk, an important seaport on the mid-Atlantic coast. He stocked earthenware, glass, china, rum, and cordial among other items and traded in local produce such as indigo.[52] He also had shipping interests and owned at least four slaves in Norfolk and Portsmouth.[53]

Lowndes had cast his lot with the king early in the conflict. As he later attested to British claims commissioners, he joined Lord Dunmore's forces at Norfolk and fought at Great Bridge and in other engagements in Virginia.[54] The Norfolk merchant lost all his possessions when the town burned on the first day of 1776.

While they could not have known it at the time, the English and their local allies had lost far more. With the destruction of Norfolk, Virginians now realized that reconciliation was beyond reach. Jefferson cited the town's fate in declaring the colonies' independence.[55]

Kizell and Lowndes would have found something in common in their military experiences. Kizell's presence at Kings Mountain and service with Major Ferguson—regarded now as a tragic hero—gave him a certain cachet among combat-tested loyalists such as Lowndes. The latter had witnessed Lord Dunmore's black troops in action and may have developed grudging respect for them.

Soon after he arrived in New York and learned that he was to superintend an ignominious withdrawal from the rebel provinces, Carleton began encouraging the thousands of loyalists to organize for their inevitable pilgrimage to Nova Scotia. He had already written the acting governor "to reserve as much land as possible in your Province to answer demands which are so likely to press, both on the generosity and good faith of the public."[56] A few days earlier, a Rhode Island shipowner and merchant had sent a letter on behalf of about one hundred loyalist families to inquire about settling near Port Roseway, on Nova Scotia's southwestern coast.[57]

Considering the lateness of the season and the inherent uncertainties of the peace negotiations in France, Carleton discouraged loyalists from venturing to Nova Scotia before the spring of 1783. However, an encouraging official response from Halifax raised interest in Port Roseway. The associates met the previous November to elect officers and approve bylaws. Membership was to be selective and excluded Jews, who were forbidden under English law from owning land. They were to be "chiefly of the number of those, who for their attachment to Government, and after numberless fatigues in supporting the Royal Cause—have been Obliged to quit their All and take refuge within the King's lines."[58]

The Port Roseway Associates were predominantly farmers, merchants, and skilled tradesmen. Most hailed from New York, New Jersey, and New England. But there were southerners such as Lowndes and Alexander Murray, another Virginian, under whose protection Phillis sailed as a member of his company.[59] Murray had emigrated from Scotland in 1762 and become a successful merchant and shipowner in Gosport, near Norfolk.

Murray appears to have avoided becoming directly embroiled in the rebellion until its later stages, when he volunteered to command Lord Cornwallis's dispatch vessel at Yorktown. For his pains the Whigs sold his land, two houses, and a newly built schooner. Rebels burned his other ship in the James River. Following Cornwallis's surrender at Yorktown, Murray, his wife, and their child made their way to New York, where he served as a pilot for the royal navy.[60]

One of the associates' first moves was to send two representatives to Nova Scotia to discuss with Governor John Parr the terms under which they would settle at Port Roseway. They were anxious to reserve the area—then largely uninhabited forest—solely for themselves. They sought various assurances: the right to select their own officials, exclusive fishing and fowling access in the rivers and bays, and military protection. They wanted the province to survey their grants at government expense. And they wished to be relieved of paying a quit rent.[61]

Slavery was legal in Nova Scotia, and many loyalists planned to bring their "servants," as they were euphemistically termed. They had not anticipated that Carleton would ask Parr to accept one thousand free blacks at Port Roseway, but many may have welcomed a pool of cheap labor to help build and tend the settlement. Their main concern was another body of white loyalists who desired to share the wilderness preserve.

As desolate as it might be, Port Roseway was considered a prize. The elected head of the associates, a Connecticut farmer named Joseph Pynchon, reported from Halifax that Governor Parr and others believed it "will be one of the *Capital ports* in America" and serve as "the best landfall in the Province to all European vessels." It would excel "any port of the New England shore."

The provincial surveyor-general assured Pynchon that the associates had chosen well: Port Roseway was "the best situation in the province for Trade, Fishing, and Farming." There was good land behind the port for crops and fruit. But land to the immediate west, where the black loyalists would be settled, was "indifferent."[62]

In the meantime the associates had expanded to about three hundred families—more than 1,500 people, including 420 servants. Their numbers continued to grow, as the sixteen militia captains, including Lowndes and Murray, exercised their prerogative to include other deserving loyalists.[63]

Carleton remained committed to protecting the freedom of virtually all blacks who had found refuge in New York. "Unlike the brutal and chaotic exodus from Charleston," Schama writes, Carleton "took pains . . . to make the ordeal less harrowing." He established a board of inquiry to consider American and loyalist claims to the ownership of specific runaways. The board began meeting in April every Wednesday at a popular tavern operated by "Black Sam" Fraunces.

The American representatives faced Carleton's principled conviction that blacks in New York were de facto and de jure free. British law gave "freedom and protection to all who came within," as he wrote later in the year in a "Precis relative to Negroes in America."[64] Astoundingly to blacks and whites alike, the British-dominated board accepted the word of blacks regarding their personal histories. In the end only a few were restored to American and loyalist petitioners.[65]

The board would not have considered Kizell's status. Had he been pursued by a former owner, he would have shared this dramatic element from his past with sympathetic listeners in later years. He probably had received a certificate from General Birch. No record exists of those issued, however, and only one actual certificate survives.[66] Nonetheless Kizell and many others would have protected their "freedom paper" at all cost during the years to come in Nova Scotia.

Carleton was determined to keep meticulous records of the blacks who departed for Nova Scotia under British protection between April and November 1783 in case of American claims for compensation. The so-called *Book of Negroes* includes the names and physical descriptions of about three thousand former slaves. Also noted are their former owners, the year they fled, and the location they fled from.

Ishmael Warren, age twenty-five, had been the slave of Joseph Warren of Charleston. He was described as "stout" (meaning healthy) and had "left in 1779." James Wright, age twenty-one, was "remarkably stout." He had been owned by Stephen Wright of Norfolk and fled in 1778. Both men served in John Lowndes's company and sailed for Port Roseway aboard the *Apollo*.

American inspectors participated in a dockside verification of the passenger manifests and checked each departing black against the list. Ships' masters, Schama writes, swore "on pain of 'severe penalties'" that they were taking only legitimate passengers and cargo. "In theory blacks could be removed at the very last minute, but in practice this last excruciating denial seems to have happened only very rarely."[67]

Registration of the Port Roseway Associates and their servants had been completed on March 25. Carleton's April 1 deadline for departure proved impossible to meet. But he clearly wanted to expedite this first mass sailing of loyalists. He had yet to meet General Washington or inform him that hundreds of former slaves were about to leave for Nova Scotia. When they finally met, ten days after the Port Roseway fleet had sailed, Washington expressed shock and reminded Carleton of the amendment to the peace treaty.[68] Washington's shock notwithstanding, the Americans must have known what was afoot.

Capt. John Adams of the *Apollo* and all masters in the fleet were given a list certified "to be all the negroes on board" their ships. Each was warned of serious consequences if he allowed any black not on the list to disembark in Nova Scotia. Blacks who were found aboard without authorization were to be returned to New York.[69]

In spite of Carleton's dedication to careful documentation, many of the loyal blacks evacuated are absent from the *Book of Negroes*. The document was prepared by many hands, in varying circumstances, over many months. At least six men who later mustered in Lowndes's company in Nova Scotia, including Kizell, do not appear. Phillis also is missing from Carleton's record of the first exodus.[70]

Kizell, it must be assumed, was aboard the *Apollo*. Ten years earlier almost to the day, he was being shoved chained and virtually naked into the bowels of a slaver. On

April 26, 1783, clothed and free, he stood on the ship's deck, adrenalin flowing and breathing fresh sea air, not the suffocating musk of fear and closely packed bodies. He was about to be reborn.

A King's Bounty

If any of the three thousand refugees who departed in the spring fleet were equipped to survive the rigors of Nova Scotia and to establish a productive settlement, it was the blacks. They had endured hardship beyond most whites' knowing; they had fought and labored for their English liberators; they had broken their chains; and they looked forward to a better life.

Their white compatriots had suffered, but few could have hoped to better their former existence when the ships anchored on May 4 in Port Roseway's northeast harbor. Stepping onto the boulders lining the shore, they did not see a promising land.

Benjamin Marston quickly took their measure. A Massachusetts man who had come years earlier to Nova Scotia, Marston was asked to help survey streets and town lots for the new community, as well as land behind the harbor that could be logged and farmed. Marston was soon writing in his journal that the whites "upon the whole—[were] very unfit for the business they have undertaken. Barbers, Taylors, Shoemakers and all sorts of mechanics, bred and used to live in great towns, they are inured to habits very unfit for undertakings which require hardiness, resolution, industry and patience."

As May gave way to June, Marston's disenchantment took a sharper edge. "These people are like sheep without a shepherd. They have no men of abilities among them. Their captains, chosen out of the body at New York, are the same class as themselves. . . . Sir Guy Carleton did not reflect that putting 16 illiterate men into commission, without subjecting them to a common head, was at best contracting a mob."[71]

These were the war's real losers. They had lost almost everything, had little to fall back upon, and had limited means with which to build a new life. Most were dependent on British largesse in terms of land and provisions and believed they were owed more for their loyalty than was forthcoming. As Schama points out, "those with substantial fortunes had gone back to Britain to try to forget that they had ever been American; or to the West Indies to remake their fortunes with sugar and the slaves they had taken from Georgia, Carolina and East Florida." Most of the white refugees in Nova Scotia, on the other hand, "were middling sorts who had backed the wrong horse—farmers, small merchants, the odd advocate, people accustomed to a decent fashion of life."[72]

Blacks in contrast arrived hardened and resilient, accustomed to physical labor and almost primitive living conditions. They possessed practical skills that enabled them to cope in a frontier environment. They probably also had a more supportive sense of community derived, in part, from the strictures of slave existence. Finally their expectations were modest. They had had few material things to lose or an elevated station in life to lament. They had instead gained something few would have thought possible a few years earlier—their freedom. All that they expected from the British was a plot of land and an opportunity to sustain themselves and their families through honest effort.

Inhospitable as it looked—and turned out to be—Nova Scotia was a logical choice for a loyalist settlement. It was within easy sailing of New York; it had established ties to New England through the fishing and timber trade; and it was largely unsettled. Just ten thousand people (excluding the vanishing Micmac population) lived in a province nearly the size of South Carolina. Officials in London saw in Nova Scotia a "place from which a new British America would be resurrected," Schama writes. Halifax "was the sleeping princess waiting for the kiss of Empire."[73]

With its huge natural and well-defended harbor, Halifax was potentially a world-class port accessible to shipping from Europe, America, the West Indies, and even West Africa. Yet Governor Parr envisioned Port Roseway as the future capital. Indeed within a few years, Shelburne, as Parr renamed the town in July 1783, briefly became the largest town in British North America, far outstripping Halifax and exceeded in the United States only by Philadelphia, New York, and Boston.[74]

The Port Roseway region was virgin territory when John Kizell first glimpsed its desolate coast. The Megumawaach—Micmac to tongue-tied Europeans—had lived for centuries on the seemingly endless tracts, which were now to be carved geometrically into generous land grants for the loyalists. For at least the previous two centuries, as Marion Robertson recounts in *King's Bounty*, the area had been frequented by seafarers from Europe and New England. Basque and Portuguese fishermen, French adventurers and fur traders, and a few English-speaking colonists had gradually "pushed their way along the shores and into the bays and inlets."[75]

The French especially had been drawn to what one of them in 1686 named Port Rasoir, for the razor clam—or *rasair*—that bred in the bay. By the time the English had taken control of Acadia, as the French fancied Nova Scotia, under the Treaty of Utrecht in 1713, the name had been transliterated to Port Roseway.

When England and France again went to war in the mid-1750s, French settlers were forced from their holdings. Twelve hundred were expelled and arrived unannounced in Charleston in 1759. Dr. Alexander Garden, accustomed to tending the maladies of newly arrived slaves, now had a fresh set of equally miserable patients.[76]

Having removed the Catholic French, the British government encouraged Scots-Irish and then New England Protestants to fill the void in the 1760s. These were largely pioneer stock who had chosen consciously to plant themselves some distance from their fellow men. They quickly began imbedding their mores, values, and customs. The loyalists arriving from New York in May 1783 discovered that these predecessors

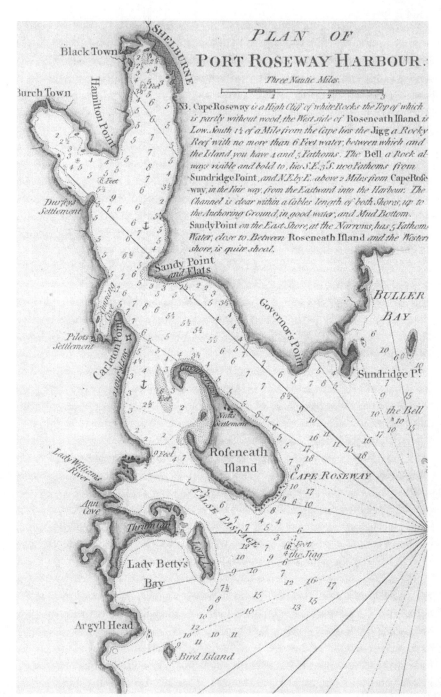

Plan of Port Roseway Harbor in Nova Scotia, published in London in 1798.
Nova Scotia Archives and Records Management

were already shaping a Nova Scotian culture. "Their insistence on religious toleration for all Protestant religions, and on a representative government, laid a solid foundation," Robertson writes.[77]

The racial divide that existed in the American colonies was imported intact to Port Roseway. The immediate priority was to survey the new town and draw lots for the white loyalists. A squatters' camp was designated for the black loyalists pending Governor Parr's receipt of instructions from London.[78] They would have to wait while whites were properly situated—on the best land available—and could begin building shelters.

Marston and his fellow surveyor, William Morris, got promptly to work. They coaxed the Port Roseway Associates to appoint a few members to explore the harbor shore for an amenable location for the town. But when others began coming ashore, they objected to the northeast side of the harbor and demanded that a committee with three representatives from each of the sixteen companies be delegated to find an alternative.

"This cursed republican, town meeting spirit has been the ruin of us already," the former New Englander Marston complained.[79] Nevertheless by May 9 he and Morris had started laying out the town on the original location according to the gridlike plan approved by Carleton and Parr. With a burst of energy, the loyalists cut trees and cleared land sloping up from the shore. Their enthusiasm for this backbreaking task soon waned, but the initial surveying was done in a week with the help of a contingent of engineers.

The Harvard-educated Marston had little patience with the plebeian spirit he detected among the newcomers. Most of the captains were self-centered men "whom mere accident has placed in their present situation." The whites in general were "a set of Licentious villains whose only motive for coming here seems to have been the King's Provisions and a short respite from that Fate which ever must attend men of their character."[80]

Carleton and Marston both had seen enough of rebellion.[81] They believed in the need for a firm hand in all things. Given the times, they were perhaps oversensitive to any hint of democratic subversion of constituted authority, particularly of the royal persuasion. But where Marston saw the loyalists as spoiled, selfish, and disputatious, Carleton saw in them the human material, however flawed, needed to preserve a viable British presence in America. He was sufficiently attuned to loyalists' sense of personal liberty—innately American attributes—to beware the heavy-handedness of imperial policy. This may explain why Carleton was urging London not to impose a quit rent on loyalist land grants.

"I beg leave to observe," he wrote Lord North in October, "that Quit Rents will . . . sooner or later become a source of popular disquiet" among the loyalists in Nova Scotia. They would be regarded "as a proof that they are Tenants only and not Proprietors of the lands they possess."[82]

These words proved prophetic for the black loyalists who later sailed for Sierra Leone with what they believed to be a promise of land without an annual quit rent. Nearly half a century later, Kizell reminded a British commission of inquiry that this promise had never been explicitly honored.

The Port Roseway Associates were reluctant to share their portion of the "king's bounty." However, hundreds more loyalists, most in organized bodies, descended on the town in June and July. Many came up from New York on the *Kingston*, a 338-ton ship that shuttled refugees monthly until November. The largest contingent was from the Carolinas. Variously estimated at between three hundred and five hundred, they had been staying in distressed circumstances in Halifax since the previous winter.

"Those from Charleston are in a much more miserable situation than those from New York," Parr wrote to London, "coming almost naked from the burning sands of South Carolina to the frozen coast of Nova Scotia." Parr had agreed earlier to allow them to settle in Port Roseway if the first-come associates concurred. They did so grudgingly.[83]

Morris and Marston were hard-pressed to survey additional divisions, streets, and town lots to accommodate the unexpected influx. Knowing that the clement season would be short, they were frustrated that their clients often found occasion to waste precious time. Celebrating the king's birthday on June 4 consumed several days; so did Maj. Gen. James Paterson's inspection visit later in the month. Marston recorded the many distractions. There was "dancing and bonfires in the streets at night; a ball somewhere in the town; a proposed duel between two of the captains narrowly averted. . . . The D---l is among these people."

Speculators also were hard at work. Town lots drawn at no cost were selling from 10 to 250 guineas, according to one resentful loyalist. Some speculators, Robertson says, were "adventurers who inveigled the captains into adding their names to the lists prepared for Marston's guidance."[84]

None of these matters plagued Governor Parr's visit in late July, which was replete with cannon salutes and a dignified reception in the town. Armed loyalists flanked King Street as Parr walked from the waterfront to the place of ceremony. There, quite unexpectedly, he proudly announced that Port Roseway was to be rechristened in honor of his benefactor, the Earl of Shelburne.

Loyalists forced themselves to swallow the toast to the former prime minister, whom they blamed for conceding independence to the Americans. Oblivious to their anger, Parr wrote on the same day to the earl that he "had the heart felt satisfaction of shewing a small mark of my gratitude, by naming the first Harbour in the world after Your Lordship, and I flatter myself that the Town will in a very few years, be worthy of so fine a Harbour."[85]

All was not so promising on land. New arrivals continued to add pressure to the surveyors and aggravate the Port Roseway incumbents. They pleaded with Carleton to prevent the town from being inundated with "all sorts and ranks of men." But events in the United States had generated a freshet of new refugees. The states had ignored a recommendation by Congress that they restore Tories' civil rights and possessions. Many who had chosen to remain in their homes were being driven out.[86]

Carleton was preoccupied in New York with arranging the final evacuation in the fall. In Halifax Parr had been waiting vainly for instructions from London on how he was to handle "this vast Emigration." He believed that he was about to confront "a Crisis which never happened to any Governor before." Official guidance never did arrive. The crisis did.

"The coming of the last shiploads of refugees," Robertson writes, "filled the streets of Shelburne with hundreds of people. Men who had fought in the provincial regiments, their wives and children; Loyalists who had tarried in New York hoping the evacuation . . . would be delayed; disbanded soldiers from the British army enticed . . . by the offer of free grants of land; freed slaves for the first time in their lives making homes of their own."[87]

The former slaves were hardly making "homes of their own." None of the white captains sworn by Carleton to look after the welfare of the black loyalists had said or done anything to ensure that they had an equal opportunity to establish their own community. Most of the free blacks who arrived in early May had been forced to camp in the "Black Quarter." Many of the servants who had accompanied their loyalist owners probably were living on their masters' lots. Having indentured himself either to James Ferguson or Lowndes for three years, Kizell may have pitched a tent or built a rudimentary shelter on his employer's property.

Blacks would have been quick to perceive that their fellow white refugees were intent upon restoring the natural order between them. Free or not, blacks were expected to provide labor for the whites. They were essentially at the mercy of people who had exhibited no particular support for their freedom and who regarded them as a potentially dangerous element. For the moment, however, they were a convenient source of labor to perform the hardest tasks of wresting wealth from a wilderness.

Kizell probably regarded indenture for sixty dollars a year as the best means to buy time needed to establish an independent existence. Many blacks (and some whites) did the same. Kizell's arrangement with Ferguson or Lowndes seemed to work well enough. When a muster was taken of the blacks the following year, he could have reported either man's failure to honor their agreement. He did not.

Phillis, who by then had taken Kizell as her surname, had not been so fortunate. She had been promised clothing and provisions by George Patten, but the muster noted that he "never gave her any."[88]

This was not unusual. Several blacks "hired themselves to unscrupulous employers," Robertson observes, "who paid them only in part for their labour or failed to pay them at all; gave them less than their quota of rations and even turned them away without provisions, keeping their rations for their own use."[89]

Their first months in Nova Scotia were anything but reassuring to black loyalists. There were no instructions regarding where they would be given land to settle; many whites were withholding provisions and pay; yet they were expected to serve the needs of the whites, especially for hard physical labor. Blacks soon realized as well that there was no "Somerset" policy in Nova Scotia. Slavery was still legal, which the provincial legislature affirmed in 1781 when it resolved that a baptized slave remained a slave.[90]

The governor could wait no longer for official guidance from London. He was expecting another 1,500 blacks to land in the province. Several hundred who had been living in miserable conditions in Halifax were about to sail for Shelburne. The magistrates were advised by the provincial secretary that the black loyalists "must have an accommodation of land for their habitation and gardens." Meanwhile Parr awaited "the King's pleasure and the determination of the Legislature . . . for their final privileges and settlement."[91]

Accompanied by a frigate, the military transport *L'Abondance* on August 27 delivered 489 free blacks from New York. Among them were Boston King and his family, George Washington's former bondsman Harry, and a Barbados-born mulatto and self-styled colonel named Stephen Blucke. Their coming, as Ellen Gibson Wilson suggests, marked "the real start of a separate black community" in Shelburne.[92]

Blucke is an intriguing figure. His historical debut came in the final years of the Revolution. He served under the infamous "Colonel Tye," commander of an all-black unit that terrorized patriots in New Jersey and Staten Island. When Tye died from an infected wound in late 1780, Blucke, then twenty-eight, assumed command.

Somewhere in life Blucke had acquired education and a degree of worldliness. A British officer who knew him in Shelburne conceded that he was a man "of surprising address, being perfectly polite," as was his wife. Margaret Blucke was about ten years older and had been raised in a well-to-do New York family. Each cut an extraordinarily refined figure amid the humble residents and surroundings of Shelburne. Blucke sported a cockade hat atop his wig and wore fine clothes. A cane enhanced his aura of authority.[93]

Not surprisingly Blucke was the acknowledged leader of the new arrivals, who were organized into six companies. He was eager to inspect the northwest arm of the harbor, which Parr had now designated for the black settlement. Marston, fed up with a long summer of white discontent, was equally anxious to get blacks onto their land. He and Blucke traversed the site—about three miles west of Shelburne—on August 29. To Marston's delight, Blucke was "well satisfied" with the forbidding landscape.

Two days later Marston was busily surveying an area not much more than 1,100 feet on any one side.[94] Someone, conceivably Blucke, suggested naming the spot for General Birch, whose certificates of freedom were squirreled away in blacks' small chests, leather pouches, Bibles, and other hiding places. Birchtown was about to become the first black town in America.

They were not the first to attempt settling there. Irish immigrants had been encouraged by a local land speculator to establish their New Jerusalem in the early 1760s. Within a few years they had drifted away, dissatisfied with trying to cultivate the stony soil.[95] What attracted Blucke could not have been the granite boulders and

*This pit house, re-created by the Black Loyalist Heritage Society Museum,
is the sort of shelter in which free blacks lived during their first year in
Birchtown, Nova Scotia. Author's photograph (2008)*

dense woods, but his people would have their own harbor and access to good fishing. And they would be living apart from overlording whites.

By mid-September, however, white loyalists were casting covetous looks upon a portion of the land already surveyed by Marston. Led by one of the Port Roseway captains, they claimed that Birchtown infringed on an area that was to be divided into fifty-acre farms for whites. They sent their own surveyor to mark out land from the western edge of Marston's Birchtown south toward Cape Negro.

Marston complained that the whites' preemptive survey "utterly" ruined his plan. Although various maps of the period present a confusing picture of Birchtown's actual boundaries, the black loyalists clearly had drawn the short straw. "That the small block of land left to them," Robertson writes, "was far too small to accommodate the number of persons requiring land must have been immediately evident."[96]

Marston managed to protect blacks' interests to some degree. However, whites' greed and bias had effectively limited blacks' access to land for subsistence agriculture, market gardening, and even for housing. None received any of the nearby eighty-one farms, ranging up to 550 acres. All were granted to whites.[97] Some blacks eventually obtained small grants of land a few years later. The ingratiating Blucke secured the largest, a 200-acre farm.[98]

Accustomed to the "normal" living conditions for slaves in the United States, white loyalists would have had few second thoughts about assigning blacks to plots substantially smaller than their lots in Shelburne. Slave families—such as they were in the American colonies—typically lived in a rough, single-room cabin. They did not "need" much space. Nor did black loyalists have the financial means to build larger structures. A bit of ground would suffice for the 1,485 blacks who called Birchtown home by late 1783. Another 1,269 "servants" and free blacks stayed in Shelburne.[99]

Whites had drawn for their spacious town lots as early as May 22; blacks did not begin occupying Birchtown until three months later. Although they received provisions, most were destitute and therefore unable to purchase building materials. With winter approaching they would have to make do.

A Nova Scotian writer in the early 1930s ambled across what had been Birchtown a century and a half before. "I wandered throughout the woods, where the early, pioneer black men had their habitations," Clara Dennis recalled. "'Surely human beings could never have lived in these places,' I said. 'They are only holes in the ground!' 'That's all they ever were,' said the present owner of the land. 'I've heard grandfather tell about them. . . . They just dug a hole in the ground and put a little peaked roof over it. They chose a hill . . . because the ground was drier. . . . And that was the black man's home—a hole in the ground."[100]

A Peculiar Providence

Pioneering and exile were fraught with tension and frustration. There was tinder aplenty awaiting a spark: race, religion, land, poverty, labor, politics. All were potential flash points. One finally ignited in Shelburne on July 26, 1784. Not surprisingly it was directed at blacks.

Again it was Benjamin Marston who recorded the moment. "Great Riot today," he wrote in his journal. "The disbanded soldiers have risen against the Free negroes to drive them out of Town, because they labour cheaper than they—the soldiers." There was more violence to report the following day. "The soldiers force the free negroes to Quit the Town—pulled down about 20 of their houses."[101]

David George was a principal target. George apparently had built a house in Parr's Division, just to the north of the Black Quarter and where a number of demobilized white soldiers had been located. "Several of the Black people had houses upon my lot," the Baptist preacher wrote many years later, "but forty or fifty disbanded soldiers were employed, who came with the tackle of ships, and turned my dwelling house, and everyone of their houses, quite over; and the Meeting house they would have burned down, had not the ringleader of the mob himself prevented it."[102]

Governor Parr sailed immediately for Shelburne to investigate. Although he would have been concerned with the treatment of George, whom he knew and respected, he ultimately focused on whites' agitation over the delayed granting of promised farms. He needed someone to blame, and Marston was a convenient scapegoat. Many whites resented his perceived sympathy for the blacks and his willingness to hire some to assist with surveying. Warned that he was in danger, Marston quickly left for

Halifax. Parr fired him and informed London that the troubles had been the result of Marston's "ill-conduct."[103]

Land certainly had been an underlying cause for mounting anger among whites. **111** The Shelburne magistrates had alerted Parr that "this settlement must fall through" and that "anarchy and confusion" would result if land allocations were not completed expeditiously. This was three days before the demobilized soldiers ran amok. But the riot can be linked to virtually every aspect of life in Shelburne and its Birchtown satellite. Poverty, labor competition, race, and that most divisive of influences, religion, were at the core of the "anarchy and confusion" that threatened.[104]

Undeterred by the initial violence, George continued to preach in the meeting-house to his growing flock of about fifty. But not for long. His persecutors returned "one night and stood before the pulpit and swore how they would treat me if I preached again. But I stayed a preacher and the next day they came and beat me with sticks and drove me into a swamp. I returned in the evening and took my wife and children over the river to Birch Town where the black people were settled and there seemed a greater prospect of doing good than Shelburne."[105]

An uneasy symbiosis was developing between whites and blacks in Shelburne, and between white-dominated Shelburne and its independent-minded black neighbors in Birchtown. Whites needed blacks' array of skills and their labor if they were to develop Shelburne into a thriving agricultural and shipping center. But they did not want blacks' American notions of liberty, which in their view made them a bad example for their servants.

Deprived of land, implements, and cash, blacks were left to bargain their labor and talents to whites accustomed to exploitive relations with slaves and indentured Europeans. Yet whites themselves were ill prepared to develop a strong economy, even with abundant cheap labor. Had Shelburne met Parr's high expectations, blacks would have had an opportunity to leverage their skills and establish sustaining livelihoods in Birchtown. Whites' economic shortcomings condemned the black community, along with many whites, to endemic poverty.

The pool of skilled black labor was impressive. To service the shipping industry, there were boat builders, shipwrights, caulkers, sail and rope makers, and anchor smiths; there were carpenters and painters to build and maintain homes and businesses; there were sawyers and millers, tanners and skinners, blacksmiths and shoemakers; there were sailors and pilots. There was even one doctor.[106] But these skills went begging. Apart from those engaged in fishing, Birchtown residents had few options for regular employment.

An English officer, after visiting the community in March 1789, found most men working as laborers, clearing land, cutting cordwood, and hunting in season. "But there are no farmers," William Booth wrote. "The farmers, who are the men most desirable in every Young Country . . . are off—or at least, very few remaining." Blacks who were experienced farmers "should have been the first People," Booth scolded, "both in respect to choice, and to situation." In other words, he implied, the best farmers should have been settled on the best land, regardless of race, if the region's agricultural potential was to be met.[107]

Having learned in South Carolina and elsewhere in America that ownership of land and property equated with civil liberty, Birchtown's blacks attached considerable importance to receiving their farms. White loyalists, however, had headed the queue to secure the best land. Three farming cycles passed before Birchtown's turn came in November 1787. Black families received forty acres; single persons twenty.

John Kizell, self-described farmer, was duly granted forty remote acres near Beaver Lake Dam. It was not good land, as Booth remarked. And it was encumbered by a quit rent that, in spite of Carleton's advice, had been reinstated by London officials fixated on covering government's costs.[108]

John Lowndes, on the other hand, had been awarded five hundred acres on the banks of the Roseway River for a mill and farm lots. In March 1784 he had received a choice wharf lot. James Ferguson was allocated fifty acres on the eastern side of the harbor.[109]

Although the unfortunate Marston bore public blame for the violence visited upon blacks in Shelburne, Parr knew that whites bore the real responsibility. White captains remained in charge of distributing rations to blacks, as well as to white loyalists. This invited malfeasance, which Parr determined to expose in the immediate wake of the rioting.

On August 1, 1784, a muster was conducted of the Shelburne population and of the blacks in Birchtown. It was then that Phillis Kizell charged George Patten with failing to provide her clothing and food as promised. The muster revealed widespread misconduct toward blacks.[110]

Their lack of bargaining power with white employers or recourse to the courts reminded blacks that they had not entirely distanced themselves from slavery. Slaves had accompanied their masters to Nova Scotia and to neighboring New Brunswick. They were found in many Shelburne homes. Their bondage contrasted awkwardly with the large body of free blacks and led some to run away. As Schama writes, "white loyalists had mixed feelings about so many unpoliced blacks in their very midst. . . . They fumed over the insolence spread by free blacks among their own slaves."[111]

Birchtown's citizenry and the free blacks living in Shelburne could not fail to note that the existence of slavery in Nova Scotia contradicted the Somerset decision in England. How could an English judge proclaim that a man might be a slave in an English colony but not in England itself? They had wondered about this before leaving America; now they had even more reason to be concerned. Were they safe in a country where slaves were openly held and sold? Were they safe from American slave catchers if, as was being bruited, Shelburne were opened to free trade with the United States?[112]

Blacks in Birchtown would have heard reports of slavery elsewhere in Nova Scotia and particularly in St. John, New Brunswick, a port city with an estimated five hundred slaves in 1784. County records reveal widespread slavery in New Brunswick, especially in the late eighteenth century. Slaves often were auctioned along with cattle and household effects.

Living and working conditions were deplorable. Many tried to escape because of inhumane treatment or to secure freedom. Most were recaptured. As one New Brunswick researcher writes, some slave owners had basements "equipped with chains . . . to confine slaves who had attempted to run away. Some slaves made several attempts to escape."

Ship captains kidnapped runaway slaves in St. John. Some worked as sailors, but many were sold in other ports.[113] There is no reason to believe that what prevailed in St. John did not exist to some degree in Shelburne.[114]

Court records "document a fierce struggle between two worlds," according to Schama. Many white loyalists from the South "assumed that the institution [of slavery] would be upheld by the Nova Scotian courts. . . . But the climate of moral and legal opinion was changing, just as it was in England and in the United States north of the Potomac." Senior judicial officers "were beginning an active campaign to outlaw slavery from the province altogether. So the white slaveholding loyalists and those who wanted to convert the impoverished free black labour force into slaves ran into impressively fierce resistance. . . . This first generation of free British African-Americans put up a fight against re-enslavement and especially against their families being divided."[115]

John and Phillis Kizell had to navigate carefully within a society comprising such disparate parts—free blacks and slaves, indentured servants (both white and black), colonial officials, southern slave owners, flinty New England farmers, speculators, disbanded British soldiers, and even a few former Hessian mercenaries. In a hostile social and economic environment, the Kizells and other free blacks faced a grim and murky future.

By the time of the 1784 muster, Phillis Kizell may have been pregnant with the first of three children, two daughters and a son, who were born in Nova Scotia. Although John appears to have been indentured at least until 1787, they probably lived in Birchtown. To judge by her dispute with Patten, Phillis no longer worked for his family, but she might have cooked and washed for other whites in Shelburne.

Living conditions in Birchtown were substantially worse than most of its denizens would have experienced in slavery. The African-born among them might well have thought longingly of the relative comfort of a thatched hut and the abundance of tropical fruits. Kizell's home village may not have been idyllic, but he would have preferred it to what an English visitor pictured in 1788.

Birchtown was "beyond description," wrote William Dyott, a traveling companion to Prince William Henry, the future king. It sat "in the middle of barren rocks. . . . Their huts miserable to guard against the inclemency of a Nova Scotian winter, and their existence almost depending on what they could lay up in summer." Dyott had never seen "such wretchedness and poverty so strongly perceptible in the garb and countenance of the human species as in these miserable outcasts."[116]

Boston King testified to his people's hardships in even more excruciating terms. The winters proved unusually harsh. Many people were without blankets or adequate clothing. Some died in the streets from starvation. Others, King said, "ate their dogs and cats; and poverty and distress prevailed on every side."[117]

These were hardly the circumstances in which John and Phillis could hope to raise their children to self-reliant and self-respecting adulthood. As whites began to abandon Shelburne in despair of their future, blacks could not have been happy with their own prospects. Although many had received land by late 1787, they were no longer receiving rations and therefore had neither time nor means to clear distant plots.

Poverty deepened. In February 1789 Shelburne's overseers of the poor asked the magistrates to assist blacks there and at Birchtown, "who are in the most distressing circumstances." Many would have died during the winter had they not already been helped. "But as the Number of White People whom we have constantly to supply, are very considerable, it is not in our power to afford the Blacks that assistance which their pressing necessities loudly call for."[118] Blacks again stood at the end of the queue.

Birchtown's saving grace was the religious faith of its people. Christianity had not featured prominently in slaves' existence in the southern colonies. Black refugees had arrived in Nova Scotia without an established tradition of organized religion or allegiance to particular denominations. Yet religion soon became the focal point for Birchtown's social cohesiveness, foreshadowing the important role it later played among those who immigrated to Sierra Leone.

Black theology took shape in Birchtown in forced isolation. Blacks internalized Christianity in a deeply personal way. "The test of truth," James W. St. G. Walker explains, "was in the feeling, and every point of doctrine, indeed every preacher, would be judged by the effects produced upon the assembled people. . . . Inevitably this produced a feeling of being closer to God, of being, in fact, a chosen people."[119]

Black Christianity was barely nascent in the pre-Revolutionary American South. Slave owners were wary of the "radicalizing effects of Christianity" on their chattel, as Frey suggests. For their part slaves were wary of missionary attempts to proselytize the white man's god. Those blacks who professed a Christian faith were usually connected to white churches. Most of the forty Baptist congregations in South Carolina had black members on the eve of the Revolution.[120]

Nonetheless black preachers who had the greatest impact on Birchtown's religious fervor came from slave societies in the South. Three later led their people to Sierra Leone, where they continued to struggle against Europeans' disdain for blacks' emotive and personal demonstration of faith. Each was remarkably resilient and provided leadership in the formative years of black settlement in Nova Scotia and Sierra Leone.

David George's zeal and character had impressed British officials and attracted white adherents. He was a missionary at heart and established several Baptist churches in Nova Scotia and New Brunswick. John Clarkson, the English naval officer who led the black exodus to Sierra Leone, regarded George as a gifted exhorter. Shortly before they sailed from Halifax in early 1792, Clarkson slipped into a barracks where George was conducting a service for two hundred people. "I never remembered to have heard the Psalms, sung so charmingly, in my life before," Clarkson wrote in his journal that evening. "The generality of the Blacks . . . seemed to feel more at singing, than they did at Prayers."[121]

The demobilized soldiers who beat and expelled him from Shelburne in 1784 did not share the same high regard for George. But within months—after establishing a Baptist congregation in Birchtown—he returned to revive his flock in Shelburne. George somehow reclaimed his meetinghouse, which had been converted to a tavern. "The old Negro wanted to make a heaven of this place," the proprietor had boasted, "but I'll make a hell of it."

George was not to be intimidated. He later risked his life again when he assisted Clarkson in promoting his people's immigration to Sierra Leone. He also confronted the hostility of white clergy in Sierra Leone who were scandalized by his popularity and what they regarded as a lack of doctrinal substance.

Ellen Gibson Wilson suggests that George retreated from Birchtown because of Blucke's prominence as a community leader and because of competition for souls from Boston King's Methodists and other sects.[122] But nothing in George's life reveals a pattern of surrender to daunting circumstance. He may well have returned to Shelburne not only to save the province's first Baptist congregation, but also to use it as a base to answer calls coming from great distances to preach. In Birchtown he left behind a vigorous core of supporters who later followed him to Africa. One of them was Kizell, whose considerable skills as a preacher in later life probably began to form while listening to his friend George in the pulpit.

The Kizells could have chosen to follow the Methodists, led eventually by Boston King; the Wesleyan Methodists under the blind Moses Wilkinson, who escaped in 1776 from his owner in Nansemond County, Virginia; or the Church of England. Although they ultimately became Baptists, John and Phillis may have been baptized and married in the Anglican Church.

They and other black couples newly arrived in Nova Scotia would have been anxious to celebrate their relationship in an ecclesiastically recognized marriage. The Anglican rector reported on August 1, 1784, the same day as the muster, that he had baptized eighty-one black adults and married forty-four couples in Birchtown and Shelburne during the previous six months. No records exist for other denominations, but the Anglican ceremonies probably accounted for most of the formalized black marriages during this period.[123]

In time blacks perceived that the hierarchical Anglican establishment allowed little if any room for black preachers or for spontaneous and ardent expression of the spirit. The official church, Wilson observes, "rather easily became linked in the eyes of the poor and black with privilege, with discrimination . . . and with 'anti-republicanism' shown by officeholders and influential loyalists."[124] Significantly the only Birchtown communicant at the Anglican church was Stephen Blucke. He could afford the pew fee.[125]

Birchtown was fertile ground for religion, if not for growing food. And religion in turn was fertile ground for division. The novelty of a large, liberated, and independent black community had gained notice in America and as far away as London. It began to attract itinerant preachers such as Freeborn Garrettson, who arrived in 1785 on behalf of Baltimore's white Methodists. Garrettson found "the greater part of [the blacks] . . . willing to be instructed" and asked Bishop Francis Asbury to send an African American exhorter, whom he considered better suited to Birchtown.

When that fell through, Garrettson asked Boston King and the crippled Wilkinson to serve during his frequent absences on mission in the province. But King moved back into Shelburne in a desperate effort to support his family as a carpenter, and Wilkinson's stature declined, in part because the people resented his financial links to an anonymous English gentleman.[126]

When Garrettson returned to Birchtown from mission work in 1786, he found a new black preacher poaching his flock. John Marrant had been converted by no less than Reverend George Whitefield during his last Great Awakening tour of America in 1769. Born free in New York, the well-educated fourteen-year-old was living in Charleston when he was saved by Whitefield. He became "so obsessed with the Bible that people thought him mad," Wilson recounts. "Saintlike, he went off into the woods for long trials of strength." He later committed himself to carrying the word of God into the wilderness. Like Garrettson he was no stranger to the tribulations of trekking about Nova Scotia.

The charismatic Marrant soon had forty followers in Birchtown, but he had been ordained by the Countess of Huntingdon Connexion in England, not Asbury's Wesleyans. Garrettson reported to the bishop that the interloping Marrant had "done much hurt" among Birchtown's Methodists. "I believe Satan sent him."[127]

Undeniably Marrant had found considerable favor in Birchtown. In April 1786 one of the Wesleyans, possibly Wilkinson, started a rumor that Marrant had drowned while crossing a river. When he reappeared, the people "rejoiced" and "would not let [his] feet touch the ground." Marrant felt vindicated. God had "disappointed the devil . . . by restoring me to them in such a wonderful manner."[128]

Marrant endured life-threatening hardship as he ministered to isolated white families and pockets of black pioneers. In Birchtown "he saw a people set apart, chosen to participate in the unfolding of a peculiar providence."[129] What that might be he never knew. Marrant returned to England in 1789 and died the following year, unaware that the people he had left behind in Birchtown were soon to be carried to Africa.

Perhaps some already anticipated their exodus. In 1787, a year of famine and smallpox in Birchtown, Boston King "found my mind drawn out to commiserate my poor brethren in Africa. . . . As I had not the least prospect . . . of ever seeing Africa, I contented myself with pitying and praying for the poor benighted inhabitants of that country which gave birth to my forefathers."[130]

Word had been circulating in Nova Scotia of plans in London to send several hundred destitute blacks to Sierra Leone. Among the many Africans in Birchtown, this was bound to have excited animated discussion. For Kizell and others who had been born near Sierra Leone, it may indeed have seemed a peculiar providence.

Africa Beckons

If Boston King and other blacks were turning their thoughts to Africa, white loyalists were directing theirs to greener pastures. As Benjamin Marston predicted, they had proved ill suited to their calling. Many were pulling up stakes—some to England, some to the West Indies, some to their American roots in the hope, often unfulfilled, that their former neighbors would accept them back into the fold.

Lowndes had returned to Norfolk by 1790 but soon regretted it. "You are a happy people in Shelburne if you can think so," he wrote to a friend who had remained. Evidently not many thought themselves happy: by the turn of the century, Shelburne's white loyalists had dwindled to about three hundred.[131]

Blacks in Birchtown and Shelburne had fewer options than disenchanted whites. Some Birchtown settlers may have moved to New Brunswick to find land.[132] By one estimate Birchtown had lost about a third of its people by 1789.[133] However, unless they wished to chance reenslavement in America or worse in the West Indies, there was no place they might go other than Somerset country in England, where their freedom would be guaranteed under law.

Their deep poverty and the cost of passage compelled most blacks to stay put. There also was a budding sense of community in Birchtown, embodied in their religious life, which became a cohesive force.[134] To separate one's self and family from this supportive structure was not a decision taken lightly.

When newspapers and sailors—black seamen, in particular—began bringing reports of London blacks being resettled in Africa, this was bound to generate conversation in Birchtown and Shelburne. Boston King may have been moved to pray for his benighted kin in Africa. Others would have resurrected tangible memories of their homeland, of *malagueta*—the peppery "grains of paradise" for which early European visitors had named the continent's west coast.[135]

To blacks Africa *was* malagueta. The African-born knew its pleasantly sharp aroma, one of many smells and sensations that came back to them at odd moments. Africa might be distant, but it was real enough in a community where a substantial number of adults were African or had African parents.

The idea of returning to Africa was not new. It had been canvassed before the Revolution by a few visionary whites and free blacks, but the war had intervened. Serious consideration of black emigration in America revived after the war. Among free blacks it was prompted by unmet expectations of civil liberty. Among whites it was a response to a wave of emancipation in Virginia, in particular, and the unwelcome increase in the free black population in northern cities and towns.

It was hardly surprising that the first mass immigration of blacks to Africa originated in London. The city was home to the largest African-descended population outside Africa—an estimated 15,000 of 676,250 Londoners in 1768.[136] It had been augmented at the end of the Revolution by an influx of black refugees—some directly from America, or via East Florida and the Caribbean—and by hundreds of discharged black soldiers and mariners.

As Gretchen Holbrook Gerzina notes in *Black London*, "England felt itself 'overwhelmed' by an influx of black soldiers who had served the loyalist cause and who crossed the Atlantic for their promised freedom and compensation."[137] Although white Londoners had long been accustomed to blacks—servants, musicians, sailors, and liverymen—the latter's presence and their extreme poverty did not reach critical mass until the immediate postwar period. While several hundred black loyalists were being crammed onto the stony ground of Birchtown, many of their brethren were being cast without support upon the mercies of London's unhealthy and unforgiving streets.

"There seemed to be one possible solution to black poverty in England," Gerzina writes, "and oddly enough it was one on which the government, the philanthropists and the poor themselves agreed. They could leave Britain. . . . Black people themselves wanted to find a place where they could establish a working community and support themselves independently."[138]

This prospect was welcomed by a group of bankers and businessmen who had raised funds in 1786 to assist the most destitute blacks. The Committee for the Black Poor had focused initially on alleviating suffering and preventing blacks from dying in stark view of the general public. Then came suggestions that the blacks might prefer to join their fellows in Nova Scotia, or perhaps in the Bahamas. Neither destination was attractive, especially to the blacks consulted. Nova Scotia was too cold, they said, and the Bahamas dangerously proximate to the slave-consuming plantations of the Caribbean.

Henry Smeathman, a witness to the horrors aboard the *Africa*, had a better idea: send them to Sierra Leone. All agreed with the good sense of this proposal, founded as it was on his informed assurance that the environment would be conducive to agriculture and healthy living. This was the news that had reached Boston King, John Kizell, and other blacks in Nova Scotia and New Brunswick.

The reports filtering back from Sierra Leone in late 1787 were not encouraging, however. With government assistance the private Sierra Leone Company had recruited several hundred blacks willing to relocate to Africa's verdant coast. The white wives of a few dozen had accompanied them. They arrived in March, just as the rains were about to commence, and were soon dying of malaria, dysentery, and other maladies. There was little time to build decent shelter or to clear land for cultivation.

The local people treated them cautiously, regarding the unheralded strangers as an unprecedented threat.

One of the more outspoken pilgrims was Abraham Elliott Griffith, of mixed Welsh and African ancestry. His education had been partially underwritten by a British clerk who had helped to form the Committee for the Black Poor. Granville Sharp was de facto godfather of the Sierra Leone initiative. When he opened Griffith's first letter, written in late July, he was dismayed to learn "that this country does not agree with us at all and without a very sudden change, I do not think there will be one of us left at the end of twelve month. Neither can the people be brought to any rule or regulation, they are so very obstinate in their tempers. It was really a very great pity ever we came to this country."[139]

Griffith lived to marry a local princess. He later became adviser and translator for the Temne king who "owned" the land on which the settlers tenuously established their ramshackle Granville Town. Fewer than a third remained alive by late 1789, when the Temne burned the village. Some of the survivors, desperate for any means of support, had begun trading in slaves.[140]

While the ill-prepared black settlers faced annihilation in Sierra Leone, those in Nova Scotia contended with their harsh social and economic environment. Land remained their principal concern, as it did for many whites. Enter Thomas Peters. The former North Carolina slave had joined the British in 1776 and served in black military units throughout the war. Peters and his fellow black pioneers had been among the last to leave New York. Forced by rough seas to winter in Bermuda, they arrived in Nova Scotia in May 1784. Because Birchtown was already overcrowded, they were settled in Annapolis County, about seventy-five miles due north on the Bay of Fundy.

The hundred or so blacks in Digby township had received one-acre lots but no farms. They remained virtual squatters by the late 1780s. Across the bay blacks in New Brunswick chafed under similar disadvantage. To Peters and others, England had breached its promise to blacks who had fought against the rebellious Americans—and Peters and the black pioneers had indeed fought in several engagements.

With funds subscribed by Annapolis and New Brunswick blacks, Peters worked his passage to England to petition the government for redress. Arriving in London in 1791, he was embraced by Sharp and became, as Nova Scotia historian Charles Bruce Fergusson recounts, "something of a celebrity . . . lionized by the fashionable press, and . . . the newest object of philanthropy."[141]

Peters and his cause were a godsend to Sharp and the Sierra Leone Company. In spite of all that had happened to their first settlers, the directors retained unshakable faith in the viability of their great object. But where to find a fresh cadre of willing souls? Few blacks in London were interested in sharing the fate that had befallen their friends and acquaintances. Many distrusted the motives of the Sierra Leone Company and the government.

Even before the first settlers sailed, prominent blacks had suggested that the true purpose was to remove an unwanted portion of London's population. "I do not know how this undertaking will end," wrote Olaudah Equiano, a former slave and abolitionist who had agreed at first to assist the venture. "I wish I had never been involved in it."[142]

Although Peters was not demanding to be resettled, he and his followers were willing to go wherever they could support themselves and enjoy a full measure of freedom. As a people with demonstrated coping skills and an ability to adapt to challenging circumstances, they were seen by Sharp and his colleagues as hardier stock than the demoralized urban blacks who had gone before.

Sharp immediately set to work with the illiterate Peters to present a new plan to the government: invite blacks in Nova Scotia to migrate to Sierra Leone, where they would promote Christianity and legitimate trade. Their memorial left open the option of remaining in Nova Scotia if suitable land was provided.

The government responded with alacrity by asking Governor Parr to verify whether blacks had received the land promised to them. He was to remedy the situation if their claims were just. It was assumed that most would stay, if properly encouraged. Peters announced his readiness to resettle in Sierra Leone, but he and the company were thinking in very modest terms. No more than perhaps one hundred blacks were expected to leave Nova Scotia—enough to revive the embryonic colony in Sierra Leone.

The assumption in Nova Scotia as well was that only a few malcontents would leave. Parr acted smartly to examine blacks' concerns, but he believed Peters's case was a "misrepresentation." Although he officially advertised the company's offer to transport people to Africa and to provide them with land, Parr had little enthusiasm for the scheme. He probably hoped it would fizzle, proving that most blacks were content with their circumstances.[143]

The Sierra Leone Company, meanwhile, had persuaded John Clarkson, a twenty-seven-year-old navy lieutenant, to lead the venture. Having been furloughed by the cost-conscious admiralty, he was available. As the brother of Thomas Clarkson, an ardent abolitionist and director of the company, he was someone known and trusted who could provide the leadership and discipline lacking among the previous settlers. He also, as it turned out, proved deeply committed to the blacks who followed him to Sierra Leone.

Clarkson had no way of knowing that the seemingly routine mission he had undertaken would become both Herculean and emotionally draining. In Nova Scotia he would have to confront the barely concealed opposition of Parr and his government, the overt hostility of white loyalists, and the self-interested animus of Stephen Blucke. Almost as soon as he arrived in Halifax on October 7, Clarkson sensed trouble.

As a naval officer, Clarkson soon made clear who was in command. Meeting with the governor to discuss "the whole of the business," he told Parr that he objected to his using *Guinea* instead of *Africa* in the public notice of the Sierra Leone project. "I was convinced it would be made a handle of by many to frighten [the blacks] from accepting the offers of the Company." Clarkson understood the word's slave-trade connotation. Parr apologized and "promised me it should be erased."[144] The young Clarkson was not to be underestimated.

As soon as he learned of Clarkson's presence in Halifax, Blucke wrote from Birchtown to request more information on the company's offer. Without betraying his own reservations, he revealed that "a number of the inhabitants of this place appear desirous of emigrating" from Nova Scotia and had "applied to me . . . concerning the adopted mode to be pursued for their subsistence" in Africa. He also had questions about passage and the terms under which land would be granted.[145] Clarkson began making plans to visit Shelburne.

Given Blucke's ties to the local elite—Hodges calls him "essentially a client of paternalistic whites"[146]—his real purpose in writing is suspect. Knowing that a majority of Birchtown's residents were seriously considering emigrating, Blucke—possibly with whites' encouragement—may have sought to establish himself as Clarkson's principal liaison with the black community. It was David George, however, whom the people of Birchtown asked to meet Clarkson in Halifax. And it was George whom Clarkson found, standing on the Shelburne dock, at seven o'clock on the morning of October 25.

"Immediately on quitting the vessel," Clarkson wrote in his diary, "[we] were met by a black man of the name David George. . . . He was on the point of embarking for Halifax, having been . . . chosen by his brethren to go there and inform himself from me of the real intentions, both of government and the Company, as they were at a loss to know how to act from the various reports circulated by interested people, some to induce them to stay."

Clarkson went to obtain lodgings at the Merchants Coffee House on Water Street. While he breakfasted George reappeared to warn him to tread carefully. "The same man who addressed us upon landing," Clarkson recalled, "came to inform us that the principal inhabitants and white people of this neighbourhood were averse to any plan that tended to deprive them of the assistance of the Blacks in the cultivation of their lands. . . . He said his companions were kept in the most abject state of servitude and that if it were known in the town that he had conversed with us in private his life would not be safe. He cautioned us from appearing in the town or country after it was dark."[147]

George might have been expected to invite Clarkson to meet the people in Birchtown, but it was a white loyalist who made the suggestion. Clarkson and Maj. Stephen Skinner had met by accident that same day. Skinner was a New Jersey man and had known Blucke during the war. Now he was the governor's agent, appointed to register blacks wishing to go to Sierra Leone and arrange their transport to Halifax. Skinner struck Clarkson as "disinclined to the present undertaking" but willing nonetheless to assemble the Birchtown community.[148] Blucke probably did this on Skinner's behalf. George meanwhile had faded discreetly into the shadows.

Clarkson and Skinner arrived in Birchtown on horseback the following noon. It had been raining, but more than three hundred people by Clarkson's estimate had crowded into the church. John and Phillis Kizell, perhaps cradling their infant boy, watched as the young Englishman mounted the pulpit. Clarkson was acutely aware of "the eyes and attention of every person fixed upon me."

He realized that what he said would for better or worse affect the lives of them all. So he merely recited the facts, including the three choices before them: remain in Nova Scotia, where they would finally receive the land that had been pledged to them; enlist for military service in the West Indies, with the "same privileges as the British Army"; or join the free settlement at Sierra Leone.

His audience had only one question for Clarkson. They had read the company's notice and desired clarity regarding the provision that their land would be "subject to certain charges and obligations." Clarkson tried to reassure them. It was "by no means," he said, "to be considered as an annual rent, which idea had been industriously disseminated amongst them, but as a kind of tax for . . . the maintenance [of] their poor, the care of the sick, and the education of their children." Clarkson "promised to make it my business to see that their proper allotments of land were given them and declared I would never leave them till each individual assured me he was perfectly satisfied."[149]

Clarkson made no effort to hide the dangers that lurked in Africa. Only those prepared to sacrifice and work hard would survive. Having applauded him several times, the people assured Clarkson that "they were unanimous in the desire for embarking for Africa, telling me their labour was lost upon the land in this country . . . that being now sunk to the lowest pitch of wretchedness, their condition could not be otherwise than meliorated."

It seemed to Clarkson that, even before his coming, "they had already made up their minds for quitting this country [and] they would not be diverted from their resolution though disease and even death were the consequence." He then asked all "who after serious reflection were determined to embark for Sierra Leone" to call upon him at his rooms in Shelburne during the next three days.[150]

Clarkson needed a full week to register the 155 families—50 headed by men and women born in Africa—who wished to follow him.[151] They queued patiently to be interviewed by him and Major Skinner, who was developing a healthy respect for Clarkson's integrity. Each had a story to tell. Kizell probably mentioned his service with Patrick Ferguson; others would have briefly shared their life histories; but none was so moving as the plea of a Shelburne slave, not a freeman from Birchtown, that Clarkson should take his wife and children, who were free, to Sierra Leone.

"With tears streaming down his cheeks," Clarkson wrote that evening, "he said, that though this separation would be as death to himself, yet he had come to a resolution of resigning them up for ever, convinced . . . that such a measure would ultimately . . . render their situation more comfortable and happy. Much more he said which is impossible to convey in language adequate to air our feelings on this occasion." Clarkson offered to buy the man's freedom but was informed the next day that legal complications "prevented the master from selling him."[152]

The visit to Shelburne and Birchtown had transformed Clarkson's mission. His chance encounter with the intrepid George, the uplifted faces of hundreds in the church, and now his one-on-one contact with people who regarded him as a latter-day Moses imposed on Clarkson an inescapably deep sense of responsibility.

He was beginning to understand why so many of the free blacks wished to be rid not of Nova Scotia but of the white loyalists and former soldiers who treated them as though they were still slaves. They saw in Clarkson a white man who was prepared to listen to them, to consider their views, and to treat them as human beings. He soon appreciated that, for many, their principal reason for going to a place where they could govern themselves was their children. No matter what happened to them, their progeny would be placed "upon a better foundation."[153]

Blucke and the white loyalists still believed they could prevent the wholesale departure of blacks from Birchtown. On November 1, while Clarkson met with prospective emigrants, Blucke petitioned the governor ostensibly on behalf of the household heads who intended to stay—"His majesty's most dutifull and loyal black servants." But he clearly believed that others could be enticed to stay if the government acted more generously.

Blucke begged to inform Parr "that numbers of our brethren are so infatuated as to embrace the proposals of the Sierra Leone Company which . . . we conceive will be their utter annihilation." Accepting tacitly that some of his black brethren would not be dissuaded from their suicidal intention, Blucke proposed that those remaining be rewarded for their loyalty. They should receive financial assistance comparable "to the vast expence of transporting so many of our fellow Subjects to Africa."[154]

The government chose in the end not to reward Blucke and its "most dutifull" black loyalists. John Wentworth, who assumed the governorship upon Parr's death the following year, told the king that the government had made a serious error. He pointed out that a fraction of the cost to convey more than 1,100 people to Sierra Leone, if invested in strengthening the black communities in Nova Scotia, would have encouraged many to stay. "For government to spend so much to remove laborious people and . . . spend nothing to help those who remain" was irrational.[155]

Wentworth and Blucke had missed the point. Money and material wealth were not the main issues for those who departed. It was the realization that they would always be at the mercy of whites, that Nova Scotia could never truly be for them a free country. Nova Scotia was the devil they knew, but their emerging religious faith girded them to face the unknown in Africa. Virtually all David George's flock, including the Kizells, vowed to leave with their pastor.[156]

If Blucke was resigned to the mass departure of what Captain Booth had called "really spirited people,"[157] whites were not. As Clarkson prepared to return to Halifax in early November, an agitated George came to him. "He appeared to stand in fear of the principal white people of this town," Clarkson wrote in his journal, "who had thrown out several menaces against him, with a view to prevent his taking an active part in this business. . . . Two of the most inveterate against the plan, the one a Magistrate, and the other a gentleman of this place, could scarcely refrain from insulting me."[158]

Whites themselves were abandoning Shelburne and Nova Scotia, and former British and Hessian soldiers were demanding that *their* sad state be addressed. Many white former servicemen, "with tears in their eyes," asked Clarkson to take them to Sierra Leone.[159] Major Skinner, reporting to the colonial department in March 1792 on the high number of blacks who had left, conceded that "numbers of the White inhabitants have suffered . . . but not more than might reasonably be expected, from the hardships and disappointments natural to the settling of all new countries."[160]

Skinner too had missed the point, but not the opportunity to profit. With Clarkson back in Halifax urgently seeking ships and provisions to accommodate nearly 1,200 emigrants, Skinner was avidly buying up forty-five town lots and 480 acres of land from sixteen departing Birchtowners, including Harry Washington and Isaac Anderson, at sacrificial prices. Most landowners either refused Skinner's offer or tried to make other arrangements. Given one man's lament years later that he never received compensation for his Nova Scotian land, it seems likely that Kizell and many others lost whatever value their plots might have had.[161]

Knowing that—against his advice—the people had been prematurely selling off land and possessions, and that shipping was scarce, Clarkson dreaded the possibility that he could take no more than two thirds of the 560 souls registered in Shelburne alone. Writing on November 28 to Henry Thornton, the Sierra Leone Company's president, Clarkson laid bare the burden of responsibility he felt for people who were prepared to follow him on faith. Clarkson described some of the men as "better than any people in the labouring line of life in England: I would match them for strong sense, quick apprehension, clear reasoning, gratitude, affection for their wives & children, and friendship and good will towards their neighbours."[162]

Clarkson's humanity and egalitarianism were evident in his planning for the voyage and the instructions he issued to the ship captains. He mandated adequate space and ventilation of the sleeping areas; the quarters were to be rigorously cleaned; and crew members were to treat the passengers with respect. To the extent possible, there would be nothing, save the sea itself, to remind the African-born of their last voyage across the Atlantic.

By mid-December many of the 1,190 blacks who would sail for Africa sheltered in drafty barracks in Halifax. Ship by ship, Clarkson gradually assembled the tonnage needed. In England his brother Thomas crisscrossed the country to raise additional funds for transport and sustenance of the settlers in the first year. News that more than a thousand Nova Scotian blacks—not just a hardy hundred or so—were prepared to cast their fate with the Sierra Leone Company opened purses and renewed hope that the beleaguered colony would redeem Africa after all.

The adults huddling with their children, awaiting word that the ships were ready to board, had been hardened by years in slavery, in revolutionary turmoil, and in the maritime forests of Nova Scotia. They understood the risks and considered them preferable to what they had learned to expect in Nova Scotia and New Brunswick. They were, in effect, casting their first vote as free people: to stay or to go.

Most of the African-born chose to return to their world. At least one was going only to touch African soil—to smell her dear *malagueta*—one more time. She had lived longer than a century and wished to die in Africa. She would survive the difficult voyage.[163]

Kizell's mind would have been preoccupied with family—the extended kinship network from which he had been stripped nearly twenty years before, and which he had never hoped to know again; and the new branch of that network, which he and Phillis had created within her womb.

Kizell's emotions may have been mixed. He had blood relations in Africa who would remember him. The ancestors would not have forgotten him. Had he dreamed of his people welcoming a long-lost son? Or had he dreamed of their fear that he returned with vengeance in his heart?

Would some wonder whether he was, in fact, a witch? That, after all, would explain how he had found his way back to them.

5

RANSOMED SINNERS

"The dust of Africa lodged on our rigging."
Paul Cuffe, as he approached Sierra Leone,
February 21, 1811

"There was great Joy to see the land," David George remembered of March 6, 1792. "The high mountains, at some distance from Free-Town . . . appeared like a cloud to us."[1]

Clarkson had been the first to catch sight of Cape Sierra Leone, well to the southeast, in the early morning brilliance. He could hear the people giving three cheers aboard the other ships and firing volleys from their muskets. Weakened by illness that should have killed him during the gale-lashed voyage, Clarkson was at a loss "to describe my sensations at this moment."

Return to Malagueta

Far from being elated, Clarkson was worried about the fate of those ships that had been separated from the fleet; he had only a month's provisions and no idea what supplies the company may have sent ahead; and he wondered whether they would be greeted by the same hostile people who had attacked the previous settlement.[2]

Sixty-five had died en route—a third, percentage-wise, of the toll typical on the Middle Passage. Three were elders from George's congregation. One man had been washed overboard in a storm.[3] Of the fifteen ship captains, two had perished shepherding the black pilgrims. But Clarkson was relieved to find a peaceful reception and the supplies in place. The missing ships soon appeared. He believed that they had come through the worst.

The people and the crews had treated one another civilly. The black captains, whom Clarkson had appointed in Halifax, came aboard his ship to convey "the general joy of themselves & comrades. . . . The respect and gratitude expressed in every look, affected me very sensibly, their decent dress, and their becoming behaviour, was noticed by all who were present, for the most perfect peace and harmony reigned on board each Transport." The ships' masters applauded the "regular and orderly" conduct of the settlers; the black captains returned the compliment.[4]

The people and Clarkson had ample reason to exchange congratulations. The storms they had encountered soon after leaving Halifax could have destroyed several of the transports. Clarkson's insistence on hygiene and his designation of his flagship to serve as a hospital probably saved dozens of lives. The discipline and good conduct testified to Clarkson's leadership. He and the settlers could now focus on the urgency of clearing yet another forest and building shelters before the rains began. This time they would not be digging holes in the ground.

Two days before hailing land, Clarkson and the settlers were reminded that they had entered the realm of the slave trade. They had spotted another ship, hoisted the Union Jack, and fired a shot to speak it. The *Mary*, of Bristol, was bound for Annamabo on the Gold Coast. "For slaves," Clarkson noted laconically in his journal.[5]

Fatigued and ill, Clarkson probably lacked the energy to confide his true feelings. He and the settlers knew that the *Mary* would soon be carrying more than two hundred people in the opposite direction. Many of the settlers had survived the "rites" of the Middle Passage. They knew what occurred on a slaver.

For the children the *Mary* looked innocent enough, a welcome diversion on a voyage devoid of any other sail. But for their parents it was a sobering sight. They had heard the rumors spread by whites in Shelburne and Halifax that they would surely be sold back into slavery. There, rolling in the ocean's swell as Clarkson conversed hoarsely with the *Mary*'s captain, was the unavoidable truth. The slave trade still thrived.

Ashore there was no time to reflect grimly on the slave trade. There were trees and bush to be cleared, poles and thatch to cut, sailcloth tents to erect. Clarkson was impressed as the work advanced. So were the resident whites employed by the Sierra Leone Company. "The progress made by the Nova Scotians in clearing the woods is visible every day," Clarkson recorded, "and the Company's officers are continually commending their industry and exemplary behaviour."

A fifteen-year-old Nova Scotian boy, Anthony Elliott, captured the spirit of the settlers' first days. The men had started clearing a wide path from the landing. Pausing from their labors, they "marched towards the thick forest," as Elliott relived the moment, "with the Holy Bible, and their preachers (all coloured men) before them, singing the hymn . . . 'Awake! And sing the song / of Moses and the Lamb, / Wake! Every heart and every tongue [To praise the Saviour's name! . . . Return ye ransomed sinners home.']" "They proceeded immediately to worship Almighty God," continued Elliott, who himself became a preacher, "thanking him for . . . bringing them in safety to the land of their forefathers."[6]

Clarkson assumed that, having escorted the Nova Scotians to Freetown, he would return to England and marry his fiancée. He had asked the Sierra Leone Company to prepare temporary housing and building materials to settle people quickly on their plots and envisioned leaving them under the benign management of Henry Hew Dalrymple. The former army captain had achieved notoriety for describing to the

Privy Council the inhumanity he had witnessed at the slaving factory on Goree Island, off the Senegal coast. He had then freed slaves that he had inherited on Grenada.

While Clarkson had been engaged in Nova Scotia, Dalrymple had been plucked by the company to superintend the resurrection of its fortunes in Sierra Leone. But he soon proved cantankerous and resigned. Clarkson found letters from several directors imploring him to act as interim governor. "My astonishment was beyond measure . . . as I had positively declared before I left England, that nothing should induce me to continue in Africa."[7]

Astonishment rapidly gave way to agitation. As he read through the correspondence waiting for him, Clarkson discovered that the directors were disavowing the promise he had made in Nova Scotia regarding settlers' land grants. Beginning in mid-1792 the Nova Scotians were to pay a quit rent of one shilling per acre annually, and possibly more.[8] Had this decision reached Nova Scotia before the emigrants departed, many would have abandoned the enterprise. All would have questioned the company's motives, not to mention Clarkson's integrity.

Clarkson decided not to inform the colonists. He would try instead to convince the directors that they were misguided. The Nova Scotians, he would explain, were bound to regard the imposition of a quit rent as devaluing their status as free people.

The directors thought they were doing the people a favor. "I trust," Henry Thornton had written to Clarkson, "the Blacks will not consider this a grievance." It would help defray "the necessary expence of government & return to the English Subscribers who have stood forth so liberally to serve them."[9] The directors were businessmen, as well as self-satisfied philanthropists, who had a fiduciary obligation to the company's investors. The Sierra Leone Company had been formed with dual objectives: to make a profit and to promote Christian well-being in Africa. But profit came first.[10]

One loaded die had now been cast against the Nova Scotians. Another would be the form of government. The settlers had assumed that they were to have a prominent role in their governance. If they were free people, they had a right to perform the civic duties that whites had arrogated to themselves in North America. They may have run from American slavery, but they had assimilated American republicanism, which would long grate against Britain's colonial paternalism. They might be black loyalists; they might regard themselves as subjects of King George III; but they were a curious hybrid—African, British, yet stubbornly American.

The "Old Settlers" who had come in 1787 were to have enjoyed a form of self-government conceived by Granville Sharp. There would be "hundredors" and "tythingmen" to represent the people, while the company's employees busied themselves with agricultural production and trade. Sharp's model had succumbed, however, along with the settlers, reduced now to just sixty.

True to its paternal and profit-making instincts, the company had established an executive and administrative structure that precluded black participation. The company's European servants—the engineer, the surveyor, the chaplain, the surgeon, even the gardener—were to make up a council with the governor. Sierra Leone and its black citizenry were to be ruled by whites, elected by no one and responsible only to distant directors who could barely begin to comprehend African realities.

Clarkson was only just beginning himself to comprehend the reality of his situation. Within the first week, the delirium and death of the company's alcoholic doctor exposed his fellow whites' lack of judgment and responsibility. John Bell had been intoxicated since Clarkson's arrival, but council members proposed burying the doctor with military honors—ships' flags flown at half-mast, minute guns saluting the corpse as it was rowed ashore. Clarkson was outraged with the impropriety of honoring a drunkard and with the example it would set for the Nova Scotians.

"I replied," he recounted, "that if I had not heard it from their own mouths I could not have believed it possible, that any set of men situated as they were . . . to form a Colony on virtuous principles could have made so extraordinary a request. . . . I . . . begged them to consider the effect it would have upon the Nova Scotians." The council members, however, wanted their ceremonial funeral. Reminded that he had no authority to override the council, Clarkson attended for harmony's sake.[11]

Clarkson determined, meanwhile, to persuade the directors that he could not and would not serve as superintendent if the other seven council members had an equal voice. It simply would not work. But he soon had a more immediate challenge to his tenuous executive role: Thomas Peters.

Without the latter's appeal to London, the people would still be in Nova Scotia and Freetown would be uncleared bush. The settlers respected Clarkson, but some had assumed that Peters would exercise formal leadership in Africa. When it dawned that this was not to be, Peters became a lightning rod for settlers' frustrations and their resentment of overbearing white behavior.

"Great dissatisfaction appears among the settlers," Clarkson wrote in his journal, "and many of them begin to be very troublesome. The bad example set them by the Europeans . . . the unfeeling manner in which they are often addressed, the promiscuous intercourse with so many dissatisfied sailors, and the old settlers . . . may in a great degree account for the irritability of temper."

Whites' transparent bias and verbal abuse was enough, Clarkson feared, to spark insurrection among people "who had just emerged from Slavery, and who were therefore jealous of every action, nay of every Look, which came from white Men, who were put in authority over them."[12]

Peters approached Clarkson on March 22 with several complaints on behalf of the settlers. "He was extremely violent and indiscreet in his conversation," Clarkson noted, "and seemed as if he were desirous of alarming and disheartening the people." Clarkson, on the verge of physical if not mental collapse, may have threatened to send Peters back to Nova Scotia. He then met with the settlers and felt confident that he had addressed their concerns. He had not.

Clarkson attended Easter service on April 8. Leaving the interdenominational gathering, which had been held under a large canvas, he was given several letters. He began reading them over dinner aboard ship. The first ruined his appetite. Two settlers warned Clarkson that some planned to make Peters governor.

Clarkson hastened back to shore. Summoned by the town bell, the people probably gathered beneath the majestic cotton silk tree that still stands at the upper end of central Freetown. With his sword buckled, there could be no doubt who was in charge as Clarkson stood before the assembly. Looking severely at Peters, he announced melodramatically that one of them "would be hanged upon that Tree before the Palaver was settled."

Palaver there was. Settlers vented the anger that Clarkson had detected earlier. He harangued them with the possible consequences of their ingratitude toward the company, which in any case had sole authority to appoint the governor. Clarkson later decided that Peters had not been trying to supplant him. Still he was someone to be watched, a "rascal who . . . would have driven all the Whites out of the Place and ruin'd himself and all his Brethren."[13]

"The struggle between the two men for the hearts and minds of the Nova Scotians now reached a new intensity," Ellen Gibson Wilson explains. Clarkson "realized that underlying these symptoms of discontent was a strong sense of betrayal." The settlers had received neither the land promised nor been treated as equals by the whites. Peters continued to spread what Clarkson called "strange notions . . . as to [the Nova Scotians'] civil rights" and alleged that the company had breached the agreement he personally had engineered.

Clarkson countered by meeting openly with the settlers and with their captains over the coming weeks. Some of the religious leaders were preaching forbearance. The people seemed to Clarkson to accept his message of patience and reassurance that all would be well. But he failed to understand that "yes" in African cultures often is a polite way of saying "no." As Wilson observes, Clarkson was the first in a long line of governors in Sierra Leone who underestimated "blacks' drive for liberty and self-government."[14]

The transparent weakness of the council encouraged the settlers to assert their own authority. They proposed to Clarkson in mid-June that they take charge of policing the settlement and presented a list of a dozen men, including Peters, to serve as constables. After another palaver Clarkson also agreed to an elected "jury." But he insisted on retaining veto power over those chosen. Some settlers saw this as tantamount to slavery and said as much in a petition delivered to Clarkson on June 25.

Clarkson had hinted more than once that he would leave the colony if the people were dissatisfied with his stewardship. The petitioners urged him to stay but reminded him "what your honor told ye people in America at Shelburn that is whoever came to Sierra Leone that they should be free . . . and all should be equal, so we take it that we have a right to chuse men that we think proper to act for us in a reasonable manner."

Another petition in the same vein came to Clarkson the following day. So did news that Thomas Peters had died.[15]

Peters was one of the colony's founding fathers. "Without his astonishing faith and courage in crossing the Atlantic to see the wrongs done to his people righted," Christopher Fyfe writes, "no Nova Scotian settler would ever have come to Sierra Leone."[16] Sierra Leone ultimately might have been founded by other means. However, it was Peters's initiative and the people's courageous decision to forsake America for Africa that drove their pilgrimage. They were not passive recipients of British philanthropy; they believed that the opportunity to create their own "country" was their due.

Clarkson also merits founding father status. Without his fortitude, organizational ability, humility, and common sense, the Nova Scotian exodus might have aborted altogether or ended in complete disarray. Planting settlements in Africa was proving more challenging than first thought. The original attempt in Sierra Leone had been a catastrophe. A similar venture involving blacks recruited in Britain was foundering at Bulama, about three hundred miles to the northwest. As the seasonal rains soaked the coast, that settlement's surveyor, Benjamin Marston, was dying of fever.[17]

Of the many British gentlemen and military officers who governed them, Nova Scotian elders decades later remembered Clarkson as the best. He came closest to regarding them as equals, people who deserved the same rights as their peers—their peers in English society being the working class. He was capable of empathizing with their treatment by white loyalists in Nova Scotia and by his white colleagues in Sierra Leone. Honest and, for the day, racially liberated, Clarkson had shared the Nova Scotians' trials and nearly died doing so. He was, in effect, one of them.[18]

The contentious relationship between Peters and Clarkson was inevitable. It reflected the settlers' and the company's very disparate expectations. The company's directors knew only Peters. They could not appreciate the depth of the Nova Scotians' desire to make a clean break from the life they had led in slavery and in loyalist exile. Nor could they conceive former slaves sharing in the management of the colony, which to them was their private enterprise.

Clarkson had the task of reconciling the settlers' republican instincts with the company's cost-centered conviction that development in Africa must pay for itself. Had the company retained his services, Clarkson might have shaped a colony in which blacks held positions of genuine leadership and accountability and played a commanding role in the colony's commercial life.

Clarkson knew that his sympathy for the settlers put him potentially at odds with the company's directors, but he had reason to believe they would support him. At the end of August he received word that the eight-man council would be replaced by a governor and just two councillors. The directors also wrote that they would give *"full justice to the free blacks from Nova Scotia* . . . [and fulfill] *every expectation we have raised in them.* Having crossed the seas on the faith of our promises to them by Mr. Clarkson . . . we consider them as the foundation of our Colony." He read the letter to the Nova Scotians in their church services, to their very evident satisfaction.[19]

Having finally initiated allocation of the first farm plots and resolved a dispute over land rights with the Temne king, Clarkson prepared to take leave. He intended to return. Forty-nine settlers, including John Kizell, petitioned the company that they wished to benefit from his continued leadership, "patience," and "love in general to us all."[20]

Clarkson responded in kind in a farewell address. "I really cannot at this moment see any employment of such magnitude and importance as that of my coming to this place again to be your friend and adviser."[21] He began calling upon the settlers in their homes to bid them a proper African farewell. The encounters were tearful, and Clarkson was soon too overcome to continue.

No individual had emerged to replace Peters as the settlers' nominal leader. Nor was the petition a unanimous expression of Nova Scotian sentiment. David George, Boston King, and Lazarus Jones signed. So did Richard Corankapone, a New Brunswick settler who became Kizell's business partner and a prominent member of the Freetown community. But the names of Isaac Anderson, Harry Washington, and many others are conspicuously absent.

Clarkson sailed for England on December 29. The Nova Scotians, waving and cheering from shore, could not know that they had just lost their other founding father.

Breaches in the Promised Land

Clarkson left behind a settlement of mixed blessings. Mortality had been decimating during the first year. Officially 138 Nova Scotians had perished since arriving in Africa. The Europeans had lost 57 souls, almost half their number. But the settlers had begun building wooden houses that offered greater protection against the rains. They were raising cabbages, pumpkins, beans, sweet potatoes, corn, rice, yams, and other foods in their gardens. Fruit was abundant, and hunters who had culled Nova Scotia's moose population were harvesting the peninsula's deer and wild boar.

A refugee from the failed colony at Bulama was impressed with the Nova Scotians' resilience and their joy of living. "It is impossible," he wrote, "to conceive the cheerfulness with which they go to their daily labour at five o'clock in the morning, and continue till the afternoon, when each attends his domestic concerns, and cultivates his garden. In the evening they adjourn to some meeting, of which they have many, and sing Psalms with the greatest devotion until late at night. It is a pleasing sight on a Sunday to see them go to church, attired in their gayest apparel with content and happiness imprinted on their countenance."[22]

Beneath the veneer of "content and happiness," the Nova Scotians grew uneasy. They regarded themselves as Clarkson's people and detected a mean spirit among the new men whom the company had placed over them. William Dawes, another naval officer, had arrived in the colony in mid-1792. He was on the rebound from four years of trying to manage a penal settlement in New South Wales. A man of rigid piety, Dawes was to act as governor until Clarkson returned.

The people were dubious. Dawes might be "a very good man," they told Clarkson before he left, "but he does not show it." He was joined in January 1793 by Zachary Macaulay as councillor, just twenty-four years old and Dawes's equal in religious zealotry. Having served as an overseer on a Jamaican plantation, Macaulay had become a committed foe of slavery and the slave trade. But what Fyfe describes as his "stern, intellectual passion for righteousness" was a liability in dealing with a proud and assertive community of free blacks.[23]

The settlers soon began to hear Clarkson spoken of disrespectfully—and in the past tense—by white officials, particularly Richard Pepys, the company surveyor. The Nova Scotians soon learned that the new men had no intention of abiding by Clarkson's promises. Dawes and Pepys were more interested in building a fort than in surveying the settlers' farms. Then on February 6 they announced in a public meeting that they were implementing an entirely new plan for the town, which excluded the settlers from the valuable waterfront. When the Nova Scotians recited Clarkson's pledge that they would have equal rights to wharf lots, Pepys ridiculed him as a man who "seldom knew or thought of what he said," and that at Birchtown he had been drunk when he made his unauthorized promises.[24]

Clarkson's return was beginning to look as uncertain as his assurances to the settlers. They refused, however, to abandon faith in Clarkson or in their prerogatives as free people. They would send two of their own, the outspoken Anderson and Methodist preacher Cato Perkins, to London to obtain direct answers from the company. By the time they arrived, however, Clarkson had been dismissed. On principle he had refused to resign.

Clarkson had heard from people in Sierra Leone that he was being abused but told the company he would try to mollify the settlers. To Corankapone he wrote in July 1793 that the people must "not be riotous." The company's intentions were "honourable . . . but you must give them time." As he had preached before, black people throughout the world "depend upon your honest industrious & peaceable conduct. I assure you I will always support your rights as Men and will recommend you for not suffering any people to take them from you, but you must be obedient to the laws or else the Colony will be at an end."[25]

In effect Clarkson was asking the Nova Scotians to bear the greatest responsibility for the success of the colony and to forgive supposedly well-intentioned European officials for their insensitivity and incompetence. Although in private he made no secret, in Fyfe's words, of his disdain for the directors' "cold-blooded parsimony and . . . meanness," he publicly supported the company. To do otherwise, Fyfe writes, would "provide a weapon for the Colony's enemies."[26]

The colony had enemies enough among the slave traders who operated with impunity in the immediate area and in the rivers penetrating the adjacent coast. They regarded the settlement as a trespass upon their long-held preserve and as a direct challenge to their livelihood. Their African allies and clients shared similar concerns. The slave trade dominated commerce up and down the coast and shaped trade relationships with the interior.

None of this came as a surprise to Kizell or to several other settlers who had been sold into slavery in or near Sierra Leone. As the Nova Scotians soon learned, the slave trade would be a dominant factor in the life of the colony. Hope that the slave trade was dying had proved premature. It had revived strongly after the American war, as the British called it, and it was the Americans who were descending upon the coast to meet the accrued demand for slaves.

European and Euro-African slave traders nested in the Rio Pongas and Rio Nunez to the north, and at the Isles de Los in the present-day Republic of Guinea. They were in the Sherbro and Gallinas areas to the south. And they were on Freetown's very threshold at Bance Island, twenty miles up the Sierra Leone River, and on the Banana Islands off the peninsula's southern tip. Slavers routinely called at Freetown, reminding the settlers how precariously they were perched on the edge of the slave traders' domain.

The company's white officials accepted the slave traders' presence as distasteful but unavoidable. The company's purpose was to generate revenue and trade. To do so it could hardly afford to provoke the slave traders and their African friends. Even Zachary Macaulay, a sworn enemy of the slave trade, was obliged to protect slave traders' interests. In August 1793, when five Africans escaped from a ship in the harbor, he demanded that the settlers hiding them give them up. They refused and whisked them to safety in the interior.[27]

Although slave trading was, in theory, taboo in Sierra Leone proper, the colony was too near to avoid contamination. Illicit sales of captive Africans, by white and black residents, were not uncommon. On the same day in January 1796 that Kizell, Corankapone, and a third partner launched a trading sloop, Corankapone—now the town marshal—alerted Dawes that a boy brought into the colony from the Isles de Los had been sold clandestinely to an American ship captain for a puncheon of rum. Dawes intervened and seized two other children from the seller.[28]

Other incidents involving American slavers mainly from New England had prompted Henry Thornton in March 1795 to appeal to Massachusetts governor Samuel Adams to stop these depredations. "We have been informed," he wrote, "by the Governor and Council of our Settlement in Africa . . . that several American vessels have . . . been trading in slaves on that coast contrary . . . to the laws of the states to which they respectively belong."[29]

The Americans were not deterred. Adam Afzelius recorded in May 1796 that the *Betsey*, from Providence, "had some time been in our harbour, collecting Slaves from all quarters. At last she moved nearer to the shore . . . with the intention . . . to carry off Slaves, if not from the very Freetown, at least from the neighbouring natives villages."

Three Kru sailors aboard the *Betsey*, claiming that they had been ill treated, came ashore to inform Macaulay that the captain had bought three slaves within the colony. Two company officials boarded the ship to confront the captain and found the

slaves—a man and two girls. The captain explained that they were pawns, received as
security for debts, but surrendered them for a receipt. Macaulay put the girls under
the care of Mary Perth, a Nova Scotian who was acquainted with the eldest.

But the captain was not done. "Some days after these slaves had been rescued,"
Afzelius resumed, "the Captain came . . . with a long retinue of black people, headed
by the Chiefs, who had delivered the Girls, and said this people would now prove that
they were only pawned, and desired the Governor therefore to let them come back to
the owners. But the Governor very properly answered, that every body knew, that they
were as safe in S. L. as anywhere else."[30]

Macaulay may also have sensed that the slave trade was weakening. The *Betsey's*
lingering near Sierra Leone to fill its quota of slaves suggested as much. War with
France and tensions with the United States were interrupting the availability of trade
goods to exchange for slaves. "The Foulahs have indeed brought down a great many
Slaves within these few weeks," Macaulay wrote in mid-1798, "but most of the traders
in the Rio Nunez & Rio Pongas are at present without goods, and unless Bance Island
can supply them . . . the Foulahs will have to carry them back."[31]

In London the company went on the offensive. Thornton introduced a bill in
Parliament in 1799 to prohibit British subjects from trading in slaves in the Sierra
Leone River and within five hundred miles in either direction along the coast. The
bill passed but lost in the House of Lords by four votes. The slave merchants in
London and Liverpool still retained veto powers.[32]

In reality the slave trade was the least of the infant colony's troubles. Even the war
with France, beginning in 1793, was more an annoyance than a direct threat. A
French fleet attacked Freetown in September 1794 and caused considerable damage
and mayhem. But the colony's most serious woes were self-inflicted, rooted principally
in the company's profit-based philosophy, in the moralistic management of Dawes
and Macaulay, and in the paternalism that suffused the entire undertaking.

Macaulay drove this home on March 4, 1794, when he swore in the Nova
Scotians' representatives. As acting governor in Dawes's absence, he defended the
company's discriminatory policies. "They [the directors] promise that none of you
thro' their means shall be reduced to Slavery," he lectured them. "You cannot say this
promise has been violated. They promise you that the rights of Blacks & Whites shall
be the same. And can you point out that they differ? . . . Whites live better than you
do. But why—because they can afford it—they have better salaries—but why should
not we have the same [you ask]. Because you don't deserve them. Write as well,
Figure as well, Act as well, think as well as they do & you shall have a preference."

Macaulay dispensed with the Nova Scotians' smoldering anger over the failure to
allot all the lands promised and the requirement of a quit rent on what few acres they
did receive. The company, he said, had redressed the lack of adequate land in the
colony by increasing the provision of food, health, and education. There was plenty
of land to be had, he said, as long as they were prepared to pay the quit rent. The settlers had complained that the plots offered were on the steep hillsides rising above the

town. Macaulay scoffed: "True the land is in the Mountains, but was it promised you that Mountains should sink into Plains?"

The council minutes note that "there appeared . . . a general acquiescence in the justice of Mr. Macaulay's observations."[33] This might read well at a directors' meeting in London but was a typical European misreading of polite African demurrals. Three months later the mask was dropped, and Macaulay discovered instead general and abiding disquiet.

Macaulay had dismissed two Nova Scotians, serving the company as porters, for threatening the captain of a slaver. The hundredors and tythingmen, no longer acquiescent, tendered their resignations if the two men were not rehired. Macaulay refused to accept their resignations and reasserted the company's right to hire and fire its employees. When a mob gathered by one of the dismissed men threatened the governor, the hundredors and tythingmen refused to protect him. Macaulay sent David George to summon the "well-affected" settlers to defend his house.[34]

Macaulay dared the disaffected by offering free passage to anyone wishing to return to Nova Scotia. He bought a ship and anchored it in plain view, but there were no takers. The hundredors and tythingmen finally returned to duty and arrested the rioters. Eight were sent to England for trial along with five witnesses. One was Kizell, apparently one of the "well-affected" who had rallied to Macaulay's defense.[35]

There is no evidence that any of the men charged with threatening the governor was tried or punished. Nor is there any official indication why Kizell was chosen—presumably by Macaulay—to travel to England as a witness. It is from this point, however, that Kizell begins to appear regularly in the colony's public record.

It helped that Kizell was a Baptist. Macaulay regarded them as the most loyal settlers. He had met at some length with Kizell and George several months earlier. He evidently trusted Kizell to represent events in Sierra Leone responsibly while in London. Macaulay later spoke of Kizell as one of the "more thinking settlers" and took his nine-year-old son, George, with him to England for schooling.[36]

If the Baptists were in Macaulay's good graces, the Methodists—especially those following the blind "Daddy Moses" Wilkinson—decidedly were not. All eight of the men sent to England for trial belonged to Wilkinson's church. "Their government is pure democracy," Macaulay fumed, "without subordination to anyone."[37] The Baptists seemed more amenable to the company's primacy. George himself had been reconciled to Clarkson's dismissal and made clear that his allegiance now lay with Dawes and Macaulay.[38]

Kizell and the witnesses, all for the prosecution, arrived in England in late September just days before the French burned and looted Freetown. Two months later Granville Sharp was reporting to his fellow company directors that the witnesses wished to return home. No legal charges appear to have been brought against the ringleaders. Rather than advertise that there had been an insurrection among their colonists, the directors may have considered it politic to banish the men quietly from the colony.[39]

Kizell and the other witnesses tarried in England for nearly three months at the company's expense.[40] Fear of further French activity along the West African coast may explain their delayed return. It was mid-February 1795 before they left aboard the company's brig, the *Amy*. Dawes, who had decided to continue as governor, sailed with them.

137

Kizell, as one historian suggests, made "useful friends" during his nearly five months in England. Apart from meeting with Thornton, Sharp, and other luminaries, he evidently spent productive time in Baptist circles. The Baptist Missionary Society was considering its first foray into Africa, and the presence of the Nova Scotian Baptists was serendipitous. Kizell especially seems to have made an excellent impression. Not only was he well-spoken, he may have struck English Baptists as a man with business sense, in addition to his native understanding of African conditions. He could be an asset to any missionaries sent to Sierra Leone.

When Kizell was reunited in Freetown with Phillis and the children, he discovered—to no surprise—that the family had lost much of their modest possessions in the French attack. But he had not returned empty-handed. Someone, possibly the Baptists, had given him trade goods to sell, presumably to help him recover and as an incentive to a budding entrepreneur. Kizell's stature in the colony and abroad was growing.

A Boston publication, excerpting a Baptist source in England, reported in 1798 that Kizell, "one of our negro Baptist brethren, who came to England in the [Sierra Leone] company's service . . . was enabled to take out a venture with him, which he sold extremely well. The profits were to have been solely for his use; but though . . . he lost what property he had in the colony, of his own accord, in the generosity of his heart, he divided the profits of his venture among his brethren"—probably fellow Baptists—"thus alleviating their distress as far as he was able."[41]

The Nova Scotians had shown generosity of heart as well in the wake of the French assault. Although their possessions had been looted by sailors and opportunistic villagers, they shared what they could with the company's European staff and gave them shelter. Macaulay rewarded them by alleging that some settlers had participated in the pillage and demanding that all pledge in writing to return any stolen goods. Otherwise they would be cut off from company jobs, education for their children, and medical assistance. The Methodists refused to sign; the Baptists complied. The absent Kizell was spared this indignity.[42]

As he sold his venture and distributed the boon to needy settlers, Kizell retained capital to launch his own enterprises. The first was retailing spirits. The council, with Dawes in the governor's chair, approved liquor licenses on May 5, 1795, for Kizell and several other settlers, including four women. One was the shopkeeper Mary Perth, a favorite of Macaulay's. The spirits were "not to be drunk in their houses," however.

Given his close friendship later with the teetotalist black ship captain Paul Cuffe, who bemoaned the amount of liquor consumed in Sierra Leone, Kizell may have abandoned this particular trade early on.[43] Liquor goes unmentioned in Kizell's subsequent business dealings. Moreover once he was established as a trader in the Sherbro, where rum was a staple of the slave trade, it is hard to imagine Kizell exploiting locals' taste for alcohol.[44]

Kizell was beginning to focus his entrepreneurial instincts on the interior. The settlement depended on rice and cattle brought from coastal areas and nearby rivers. Some settlers had already established themselves outside the colony. As early as 1793, three or four were cultivating rice plantations near the Rokel River—"so large," Macaulay wrote, "as to astonish the natives."[45]

The lack of reliable transport encouraged Kizell, Corankapone, and Abraham Smith (a fellow witness in London) to pool their resources and build a twelve-ton sloop to trade down the coast. It was an ambitious "first" in the colony.

Corankapone was the colony's most prominent settler at the time. The council had just raised his annual salary as marshal and inspector of farms to fifty pounds "in consequence of . . . good conduct."[46] Kizell, for his part, had demonstrated sound commercial skills in disposing of his venture. Having been born and raised in the coastal region, he was equipped to deal with the indigenous peoples.

When ambition exhausted their cash, the three asked the council for a loan to complete the ship's construction. Corankapone pledged his salary as security, and the council granted five pounds to finish the vessel "with a view to bring a quantity of cattle and other stock into the colony." The company may also have been hoping to encourage legitimate commerce with the Fulani and to deter the latter's heavy involvement in the slave trade.[47]

Kizell, Corankapone, and Smith launched the *Three Friends* on Saturday, January 16, 1796. It was an auspicious day, Afzelius remembered. The ship was "the largest that has yet been built here." A strong Harmattan wind was blowing, which the people considered healthy. The early morning sun blushed red through the ambient Saharan dust.[48]

The *Three Friends* soon began to return its investment, delivering five tons of rice from the Sherbro several weeks later.[49] Kizell's involvement in the Sherbro dates from this period, but he also was being drawn, possibly by his Baptist connections, toward the Temne country to the north.

Unsettled conditions had prevented George from going there on mission the previous year. He had planned to use Thomas London, another Birchtown Baptist born in Africa, as interpreter. London was a successful trader in the large town of Wongapung.[50] Now a fresh opportunity offered.

The Baptist Missionary Society had sent the reverends James Redway and Jacob Grigg to Freetown in December 1795. Grigg especially seemed miscast. As Wilson writes, he "brought to the colony a much more liberal, even radical outlook than any previous European. . . . He was steeped in English nonconformity and a sympathizer with the American and French revolutions. . . . He also represented the antiwar feeling among British Baptists during the American conflict. . . . In contrast, Evangelicals like Macaulay disliked 'French leveling and republicanism.'"[51]

What proved a tempestuous year for Grigg after Macaulay's return in March began well enough. Redway was soon sidelined by illness, but with the reopening of the Temne country, Grigg determined to plant a mission in Port Logo (today's Port Loko), a major town where Fulani caravans transferred slaves for the journey downstream to Bance Island. He left for Port Logo on January 5, 1796, accompanied by Kizell.

Grigg was aware of Kizell's standing with influential Baptists at home. They may have met in England. But bringing Kizell along was not Grigg's idea. The company had its own interest in extending its commercial reach outside the colony. Grigg's mission was an opportunity to locate a company trading post in Port Logo. Under the heading "Baptist Missionaries," Dawes reported in council on February 6 that Grigg had based himself in Port Logo and that "we have given encouragement to one of the Settlers [Kizell] with his family to go and keep a Factory at the same Town on his own acct."[52] Sending a Nova Scotian Baptist trader with Grigg seemed logical enough.

Returning to Freetown briefly at the end of January, Grigg said he had been well received by the people and was progressing in the Temne language. He was concerned, however, that the slave-trading Europeans on Bance Island were warning headmen in Port Logo against allowing the Sierra Leone Company to establish a presence in their midst. It would threaten their control of trade with the interior and potentially interfere with the flow of slaves.[53]

They need not have worried. Within weeks Grigg had abandoned his mission. Combining the company's interest in trade and the saving of Temne souls had been counterproductive. The Bance Island traders had deliberately undersold the company's goods, which Kizell was obliged to sell at higher prices. Grigg complained that the people assumed the company stock was his—the white man's, not Kizell's—and began turning away. So ended the first Baptist mission in Africa.

The council minutes are silent on Grigg's withdrawal and the fate of the company's initial business venture in the hinterland. But in Grigg's version, Kizell was at fault. "His excuse," one historian writes, "was that a fellow Baptist" had "made them so unpopular as to defeat his missionary intentions."[54]

If Kizell responded to Grigg, privately or otherwise, neither man left an account of their relationship in Port Logo. Kizell now busied himself with the *Three Friends* and commercial opportunities in the Sherbro. This led to long absences from Freetown during much of 1796 and distanced him from Grigg's controversial activities in the coming months.

David George was soon complaining to Macaulay, now confirmed as governor, that Grigg was "a man who made himself too busy with matters wh[ich] did not concern him." In May Grigg was preaching to the Methodists that it was unchristian to resist an enemy—a direct challenge to Macaulay, who had requested the settlers to build defenses against the rumored return of the French.

By September a contrite Grigg was confessing to Macaulay "his absolute unfitness for the situation in which he has been placed." At Grigg's request Macaulay secured passage to America for the unhappy young man aboard a ship carrying slaves from the Rio Pongas and Rio Nunez.[55]

140   Kizell's participation in the abortive Baptist mission was not his last attempt to help a foreign institution establish a foothold in Africa. The next, nearly a quarter century later, had more far-reaching consequences.

"Our children scatter"

Four days before Christmas 1796, Macaulay sat writing in his journal. He had before him the names of the tythingmen and hundredors who had been elected the previous day. Now he recorded his private estimation of their abilities. Of the thirty tything-men, only ten were "men who may be depended on at least at present to do their utmost to keep things quiet." John Kizell, chosen for the first time by his fellow set-tlers, was one of these.

Macaulay reserved less charitable judgment for the rest. Many of the tythingmen were "men of at best dubious character & some of them unquestionably bad." Abraham Elliott Griffith, recently suspected of counterfeiting paper currency, was "intelligent and outwardly decent" but otherwise "desperately bad as to principles." Among the hundredors Stephen Peters had substantial influence with the Methodists—"he being one of their great thundering orators." Ishmael York was "a noisy, fractious fellow . . . griping & selfish." Nathaniel Snowball "may truly be called a pestilent fellow." Isaac Anderson was "as disaffected as ever."[56]

Macaulay regarded the settlers' representatives, no matter how flawed or roguish, as an unavoidable concession to the African Americans' republicanism. "Had such an association as the above," he concluded his assessment, "been formed in our state of confusion after the departure of the French I should have entertained no small fear."[57]

Macaulay was critical of virtually every aspect of Nova Scotian society and culture. Given the company's avowed interest in promoting "civilization," he took a dim view of their supposed doctrinal deficiencies, their adulterous relationships, and their belief in spirits and witchcraft. Their very Americanness and lack of subservience com-pounded these sins.

To his credit Macaulay strongly promoted education. The adults might be a lost cause, he thought, but the children were not. They eventually became his principal concern and direct responsibility. With the assistance of Mary Perth as their caretaker, Macaulay by late 1796 had twenty-five children under his roof to receive schooling and religious instruction.

The children were his salvation. They appear frequently in his journal entries and in letters to Selina Mills, his fiancée in Bristol. Sunday school with the children "con-tinues to afford me great satisfaction," he wrote. They all lived "within one enclosure, so that I can have them entirely under my eye. I have them also removed from the evils of that indiscriminate intercourse with other Children."[58]

They were something tangible that Macaulay could control. They were evidence that the company's experiment in Africa was achieving genuine good. When he left in April 1799, he took the children with him to attend school at Clapham, a village near London. They included nine-year-old George Kizell and Chief Stephen Caulker's two sons. Macaulay would report to Selina in late May of that year that they were "in good health with no small admiration among our friends, who account them a highly favourable specimen of African youth."[59]

Sierra Leone was developing, however, in ways that defied the company's vision. Nowhere was this more apparent than in the agricultural sector. The company had sent out three specialists in tropical produce in 1791 to establish plantations. Various seeds and plants were provided by the royal gardens at Kew, but the experimental farms soon failed.

The Nova Scotians were expected to fill the void, which they did by raising much of their own food on their town lots. But the delay in allocating the promised farms, the hilly land where many would be situated and the disincentive of the quit rent discouraged settlers from engaging in commercial agriculture. In spite of premiums offered by the company, settlers relied more on trade and selling imported commodities—liquor, tobacco, and textiles. Many had never farmed before and pursued carpentry and other trades.

"The British sponsors," Ellen Gibson Wilson notes, "foresaw a community of yeoman farmers," but the Nova Scotians "did not share the evangelical mystique that manual labor, especially on the land, was a good in itself and the test of civilization. Having known little but hard labor, they were not likely to idealize it. For American blacks, above all, agricultural labor was inseparably linked with slavery."[60]

Macaulay tried to set a personal example in 1796 by establishing his own farm in the hills three miles from the town. He too failed to produce much, apart from a few cabbages and some sugar cane, in spite of having capital and labor. A few settlers, including Kizell on his nine acres, were working their farms on the hillsides, but to no great advantage. Macaulay ridiculed what he considered settlers' laziness and a desire for ready income.[61]

Looking back three decades later, Kizell saw things much differently. To the British commissioners examining conditions in the colony in 1826, he implied that the "unfortunate Nova Scotians" could have become successful farmers and created the agricultural foundation the company craved. He pointed out that in spite of all the obstacles placed in their way, including the quit rent, he and many other settlers had indeed become yeoman farmers. They had followed Macaulay's example on the mountainsides and begun producing sugar cane, cotton, pepper, ginger, and coffee.

Kizell did not mention in his testimony that the company in 1797 had started allowing its white officials to engage in private trade. They had been complaining about their salaries, so the company, counting its pence, simply let them supplement their income instead of raising their pay. But now, as Fyfe points out, the Nova Scotians "were given commercial rivals who were allowed credit at the Company's store, and had salaries which . . . provided capital." The company's servants "tended to neglect its interests for their own. Instead of trading through the Company's ill-supplied store they dealt with the better-stocked slave traders into whose orbit they were gradually drawn."[62]

142   The company's decision undermined settler agriculture. It not only licensed European officials to compete unfairly with the Nova Scotians, it allowed them to influence the direction of the colony's economic development toward trade and away from agriculture.

Kizell focused in his testimony on the role played by John Gray, the company's commercial agent. After Macaulay's departure in 1799, Gray as interim governor continued purchasing the settlers' produce. Then, Kizell recalled, he stopped "all at once and shut up the store against the produce of the land." Gray and other company staff had started their own farms. To discourage the Nova Scotians even further from competing, he restricted credit. Settlers could obtain trade goods on credit at the company store, but only if they were willing to "go abroad and traffeck" (in Kizell's words) outside the colony.

Kizell remembered the colony's flirtation with sugar cane. Settlers grew it in such quantity that James Wilson, one of the company's clerks, set up a mill. "We brought sugar cain to him, but when we came to ask him what price . . . he would . . . give only two or three pence per bundle." The settlers rejected Wilson's offer, but by then he was having second thoughts about the enterprise. "Wilson," Kizell claimed, "said if sugar was to be made in Sierra Leone it would spoil the West India trade. After this, John Gray and James Wilson left the Sierra Leone servis and went into the slave trade."

The next governor, Thomas Ludlam, "strove very much" to revive the settlers' interest in cultivation, Kizell said. "But the people was disappointed and taken in so very often that they paid no much heed to what he said."[63] In hindsight Kizell believed the company had failed the settlers—not vice versa—when it came to agriculture. "We know that coffee will grow on the mountains," he told the sympathetic commissioners. Kizell had grown and cured tobacco in the 1790s and assured them that "tobacco can grow in this place as well as in any part of America . . . but as we have no support and no encouragement, that cause us to withdraw our labour from the cultivation of such."[64]

The company had missed its chance. According to its own reports, half of the Nova Scotian households were engaged in farming in 1798. Considering the disincentives they had faced and continued to face, it is remarkable that so many were still farming. Although Kizell himself was inclining more and more toward trading, he still considered himself a farmer. But based on his 1826 submission, he understood early on that the Nova Scotians would have neither political nor economic leverage in the colony. This, more than mountain slopes or aversion to hard work, marginalized settler agriculture.

In perhaps his most trenchant comments to the commissioners, Kizell voiced Nova Scotians' enduring lament that "we cannot do any thing of ourselves. It was promised by the Hon. John Clarkson that the Noviscotian and the white should be as one, but instead of this they have set a parcel of white and mallater boys over us as magistrates. This is the very thing that makes our children scatter from one place to another."[65]

Kizell had begun to distance himself from whites. Although he continued to maintain good relations with many of the British governors, he did so at arm's length from his home and trading base in the Sherbro. His brief sojourn in Port Logo and the trading voyages to the Sherbro in the *Three Friends* were an opportunity to reconnect with the world he had known as a boy. He evidently found this environment more congenial than Freetown. By the end of 1796, he had effectively relocated to the Sherbro. Although elected in December as a tythingman, he was missing among those sworn in by Macaulay in January. The council gave no reason, but Kizell may have declined the position because he planned to reside outside the colony.[66]

Although Macaulay regarded him as one of the "more thinking" settlers, Kizell had to be concerned with Macaulay's unrelenting affronts to Nova Scotians' sense of personal liberty. Since returning to the colony, Macaulay had alienated the settlers time and again. He continued to insist on quit rents—albeit reduced—and threatened to withdraw allotments from those who refused to pay. He had ruffled settlers' feathers by demanding their labor on town defenses. And he launched an ill-advised campaign to draw the people into the stolid embrace of England's established religion, denigrating the Nova Scotians' "proud conceit of their own spiritual gifts."[67]

If Kizell thought he would be able to reside in the colony, free of white domination, Macaulay's dogmatic paternalism dispelled such illusions. Kizell retained his links to Freetown, settler society, and British officialdom. But by establishing himself in the Sherbro, not far from his origins, he had come full circle. He was an African again, living in a genuinely African milieu.

But could he be African to the core, living in complete harmony with his indigenous surroundings? He might understand the language and the culture. He might later have completed his initiation into Poro. But to people in the Sherbro, Kizell remained a stranger, disconnected from his extended family and ancestral terrain.

More than twenty years later, Kizell introduced Prince Kong Couber, King Sherbro's son, to two Americans. Samuel Mills and Ebenezer Burgess had come to scout a place of settlement for free blacks. Kong Couber told them that he wished to send his sons to the United States for education. "Whenever he looked at Kizell," Mills quoted the prince, "he wished that he too had been made a captive, if through slavery he could but learn the manners, customs and knowledge of other nations."[68]

In the privacy of his thoughts, Kizell might well have conceded that he was better off for having been dragged violently into slavery in America. Kizell placed a high premium on education. He had sent his own son with Macaulay to be schooled in England. He later explored sending his two grandsons.

Kizell himself was impressively self-schooled, functionally literate and numerate. But this underscored his anomalous status in the Sherbro, as someone neither native nor foreign. He bore the imprint of his formative experiences in Charleston, in

Revolutionary encampments, in New York's seething Canvas Town, and in Nova Scotia. He lived in two cultural skins, African and American. In the DuBoisian sense, he had internalized two opposing identities.[69]

144

While Kizell was integrating himself into the Sherbro, Isaac Anderson and many other Nova Scotians in Freetown were angrily confronting Macaulay over his renewed

Coastal Sierra Leone in the early 1800s. John Kizell established his village at Camplar (also spelled Campelar). Courtesy of Oxford University Press

demand in June 1797 that they pay a nominal quit rent. At David George's reluctant urging, the Baptists agreed to pay. Whether Kizell went along is unknown. He strongly criticized the imposition of the quit rent in his 1826 testimony, but the fact that Macaulay later took Kizell's son to England leaves open the possibility that Kizell had "paid his dues."

The Methodists furiously refused to pay and again charged the company with breach of faith. On August 5 the tythingmen and hundredors reminded Macaulay that "we have left Lands to come here in expectation to receive Lands in the same condition as we received them in Nova Scotia. But we find . . . that the Company says the Land is theirs. Sir if we had been told that, we never could come here." They then threatened to apply directly to the British government for redress or negotiate with the local Temne chiefs to obtain land to farm without encumbrance.[70]

Macaulay responded two weeks later with a long diatribe to a gathering of householders. He declared that they had known all along of the quit rent provision. "You still return like the sow to flounder in the same dirty puddle," he mocked. When Anderson asked to reply, Macaulay stalked out, leaving printed copies of his address to salt their wounded pride.[71]

Where Clarkson would have listened, reasoned, and sought common ground with the settlers, Macaulay was obtuse and unbending. He preferred dealing with his malleable children. He had no patience for adults such as Anderson and the recalcitrant Methodists, always jealous of their "rights" and freedom. A few of the Methodists had already determined to escape the company's hegemony and Macaulay's dictatorial management. Boston King, recently returned from religious training in England, persuaded some to remain in the colony. However, thirty families moved a few miles to the west, on Pirate's Bay, to establish their own settlement under the "pestilent" Nathaniel Snowball.[72]

Following an angry confrontation in August with Anderson and his people, Macaulay sniffed insurrection. He warned the company's white servants and George's loyal Baptists to be ready to defend the governor's house. Macaulay almost seemed to relish challenges to his authority, even to his life. Warned several months later of a plot to murder him, he shrugged off the threat. He wrote smugly in his journal that the informer was "chagrined at my indifference."[73]

No one attacked Macaulay's house or tried to kill him, but through his intransigence and his animus toward Anderson and others, Macaulay was seeding bloodshed to come after his departure. Far from plotting rebellion, Anderson's faction simply wanted to resolve once and for all the issue of their lands and the quit rent. This was their litmus test for freedom. Refusing to pay the quit rent, they surrendered their titles and began negotiating with the Temne for land to settle outside the colony.

They also appealed, as British subjects, for guidance from the king. When an English warship appeared in the harbor in January 1798, Anderson, Ishmael York, and Stephen Peters sent the captain, in his capacity as a royal official, a letter on behalf of the hundredors and tythingmen. The letter briefly rehearsed their grievances and asked whether they were indeed the king's subjects. For if they were, they wished to apply "to government to see ourselves righted in all the wrongs which are Due to us here." They closed by suggesting that the captain call "a hearing between us & the Governor."[74]

No threats of dire consequences here, no saber rattling, no hint of insurrection. Macaulay refused to acknowledge the appeal, although in an uncharacteristic act of common sense he rescinded the demand for quit rents. A short-lived calm ensued—until the company directors again instructed Macaulay to collect the quit rents. Still blind to the settlers' real grievance, the directors told him to assure them that all revenue would go to public improvements and not to the company.

The settlers were to apply for their new land grants—with the quit rent provision—by December 15, 1798. All but a few families refused to accept the new grants, whereupon Macaulay effectively reclaimed lands that Anderson, Harry Washington, and others had been farming productively.[75] By continuing to misapprehend the settlers' principled opposition to the quit rent, Macaulay and the directors were leading the colony toward its darkest moment.

The tension building within the colony found partial release in animated settler church services and in the withdrawal of Snowball's malcontent Methodists. Even rituals intended to "solve" crimes and punish wrongdoers outside the company's court helped alleviate some of the tension.

During a visit to Freetown, shortly after Anderson and York had petitioned the British naval commander, Kizell became embroiled with York over an alleged robbery of the latter's shop. York and Abraham Elliott Griffith had persuaded the two alleged culprits to submit to a *greegree* man's examination to prove their guilt or innocence.

The *greegree* man, a Mandingo from the interior, was staying in the home of an elderly Nova Scotian woman. She "had been taken from this country at an advanced time," according to Macaulay's account, "and . . . was therefore more imbued with African prejudices than most of the settlers."

The detainees were brought to the house where Saloo, the Mandingo, "procured a large stone which weighed about 15 pounds," Macaulay recounted, "& pronouncing some cabalistic words over it, placed it on the head of . . . Griffith who with great seeming artlessness consented to bear it. Saloo then called on the stone with great earnestness to speak truth & discover the guilty, & pronouncing several names." At last he called the names of Bob and Domingo, the accused. "Immediately Elliot['s] head began to shake as if paralyzed, and after various grimaces, down came the fatal stone and put the guilt of the two young men beyond doubt."

The two refused to confess, claiming that "country fashion" could not function properly within Freetown. But they were prepared to undergo the often-mortal "red water" ordeal outside the colony.

Word meanwhile had brought several settlers, including Kizell. He "interrupted . . . such disgraceful proceedings," Macaulay continued. An outraged Kizell exchanged harsh words with York. It was then that Kizell, apologizing to Macaulay the next morning, revealed how witchcraft had figured in his enslavement.[76]

Macaulay ordered York and Griffith to be prosecuted to "discourage the propensity the Settlers occasionally manifest to return to the superstitious & idolatrous practices of their fathers. The wellbeing of the Colony undeniably depends upon it."

When York charged Kizell with defamation, Kizell conceded that he had used strong language, but only because "what he saw practiced . . . roused his indignation" and because York had first "loaded him with abuse, to which he had imprudently replied." The jury dismissed York's suit.[77]

Macaulay and Kizell shared reformist instincts, but for very different reasons. Macaulay regarded witchcraft and superstition as inherently wrong and emblematic of an inferior culture. Kizell, however, understood these in the context of the people's worldview, in which spirits, ancestors, and occult forces interacted with the living. Kizell knew that witchcraft and magic were often manipulated for personal gain—to obtain slaves, for instance—but he also knew that these were more real than Macaulay and other whites could credit.

To Macaulay, in spite of his several years in Africa and the Caribbean, seemingly superstitious practices reflected a primitive and immature society, one that demanded the guiding hand of the white race, informed by Christianity. To the company's directors, none of whom would ever set foot in Africa, Sierra Leone was intended as the first step toward reclaiming an entire continent from heathen darkness.

Establishing a genuinely free society in Sierra Leone was incidental to this transcendent objective. Macaulay and the directors viewed the Nova Scotians through the same philanthropic prism as they did the uneducated working class in England. It was their moral duty to guide them, to raise them up from beggary and ignorance.

The Nova Scotians were free only because they were not slaves. It did not follow that they were free to shape their religious, economic, and political life. That was the responsibility of Macaulay and his elite cohort of reformers. They were the first in a long line of missionaries, colonial officers, and development workers who have since presumed to save Africa from itself.

Macaulay regarded Kizell as an ally in his crusade and had taken Kizell's son under his wing. He was now one of Macaulay's children, "uncontaminated" by African beliefs and practices. Kizell appears to have parted willingly with the boy. He believed in the intrinsic value of education. Whether he was confident that English schooling would prepare young George to reform Africa is problematic. Many an African youth, Kizell knew, had come back with an English education and turned to slave trading.[78]

"Thorough Jacobins"

The new century had turned, in this most revolutionary of times, and William Wilberforce was losing patience with the Nova Scotians. They had proved to be "the worst possible subjects," he wrote to a friend in April 1800. Wilberforce had dedicated his life and political capital to ending slavery and the slave trade. But reports from Sierra Leone, and no doubt from Zachary Macaulay directly, had jaundiced his respect for the former African American slaves. In his view they threatened the great cause he was championing.

They were nothing more than "thorough Jacobins as if they had been trained & educated in Paris," Wilberforce grieved. "They have lately become more unmanageable than ever & the sound part among them who . . . have hitherto kept the disaffected in awe, are become less equal to the Task." He feared that some settlers planned, with the neighboring Temne, to seize the colony "into their own hands."[79]

The settler "rebellion" that came six months later was an inevitable venting of frustration with the company's blinkered rule. Historians have exaggerated its racial character. James W. St. G. Walker has described the Nova Scotians as antiwhite. Ellen Gibson Wilson claims the dissidents' intent was "to overthrow the rule of white men." And P. E. H. Hair, writing at the dawn of African independence in the early 1960s, described the event as "a first step towards 'negritude' and black 'African nationalism.'"[80]

Walker's generalization that the Nova Scotians, as former slaves, would have "carried with them to Africa . . . a 'rooted hatred of whites'" is unsupported by the evidence. These are the same people who asked John Clarkson to return as their governor and continued to remember him warmly decades later. Many settlers indeed became impatient with arrogant, culture-bound whites who monopolized company offices and eventually dominated the colony's trade. Some certainly harbored racial animosity. And the distinct minority who "rebelled" in September 1800 certainly hoped to achieve a measure of autonomy.

But there was no intent to expel whites from the colony. In the end had the dissidents "won," they probably would have been satisfied with a government in which blacks—both elected and appointed—exercised substantial responsibility for the colony's affairs in conjunction with civil servants from England. It was to be a century and a half before anything resembling such a political accommodation was attempted.

To understudy and eventually replace Macaulay, the company sent a twenty-three-year-old neophyte. Clarkson had been tested as a naval officer; Macaulay had been a plantation overseer; but Thomas Ludlam was a printer's apprentice with no obvious qualifications to manage a distant colonial outpost.

Macaulay had his doubts. Ludlam was not physically robust and seemed too willing to indulge the settlers. His conciliatory and practical approach made him appear initially as a clone of Clarkson. He agreed with the Nova Scotian position on the quit rent and effectively shelved it. He later expanded school enrollments by removing Macaulay's restrictions favoring the more subservient colonists.

The mild-mannered Ludlam had inherited another issue, however, that he was neither able nor willing to redress. Even before leaving Nova Scotia, the settlers had believed they would be "magistrates in Africa"—able to dispense justice to themselves in a way that had been foreclosed in America. Macaulay and the directors adamantly opposed this. They told the settlers that no one among them possessed the necessary understanding of English law and jurisprudence. Ludlam also accepted the logic of what, to any Englishman, seemed self-evident.

This particular grievance had simmered throughout the 1790s. It still rankled in 1826 when Kizell reminded the British commissioners that Clarkson had promised that "every black and white should be equal and the blacks should be magistrates as well as the white."[81] As soon as Macaulay and his retinue of children had departed, the hundredors and tythingmen tested Ludlam's mettle by naming Mingo Jordan, a Methodist preacher, to be a judge. Anderson was to be one of two justices of the peace.

The elected representatives also began meeting as a de facto bicameral legislative body and tried to assert authority.[82] On September 7, 1799, they resolved that the Nova Scotians and the surviving Granville Town settlers "are the proprietors of the Colenney and no for enners shall com in as a right of making of Lawes with ought the concent of the Hundredors and tythingmen."[83]

Ludlam, awaiting confirmation as governor, hoped to avoid confrontation. He was privy to information not yet shared with the settlers: the company had been chartered to rule the colony on behalf of the king, and a detachment of British soldiers was to be stationed in Freetown.

Ludlam was aware, moreover, that settler opinion was divided on the issue of black-administered justice. Nowhere in the British Empire, he pointed out, were these positions elective. The majority of the settlers, given subsequent events, grudgingly accepted this. But when Ludlam announced in December that the company had rejected the settlers' elected magistrates, his "reasoning and concession only enflamed opposition," as Fyfe tells it.[84]

The power vacuum intensified in February 1800 when the captain of a Liverpool slaver refused to pay the customary anchorage fee to a local chief. Ludlam offered to mediate, but several Nova Scotians threatened to seize the unarmed captain and turn him over to the Temne king. Unable to honor his pledge of safe conduct, Ludlam was humiliated when the captain was compelled to pay.[85]

The rainy season, with its lowering clouds and thundering downpours, brought a confrontation that even Clarkson might have been unable to prevent. Nova Scotians' aspirations had been rubbed bare by the shackles of British paternalism. The turning point came on May 20. Ludlam reiterated that no settler was qualified to serve as a judge and none would be approved. He hinted that the company would soon represent royal authority. Opposition would be tantamount to treason.

The settler "Jacobins" realized that they needed to preempt the company's plans and establish their own government as soon as possible. After hearing Ludlam out, James Robinson Sr., one of Kizell's fellow witnesses in London, challenged the young governor's authority by suspending court sessions until the people had passed their own laws. The tythingmen purged themselves of those who opposed their revolutionary strategy. "There was even talk," Fyfe relates, "of putting the Europeans out to sea in an oarless boat. Most [settlers] disapproved strongly of violence, but few would join actively with a government they mistrusted against extremists."[86]

Those passing Abraham Smith's house on September 3 found a notice nailed to his door. It was a "Paper of Laws" signed on behalf of the hundredors and tythingmen by Robinson, Anderson, and Nathaniel Wansey, one of the more prosperous Nova Scotian farmers. At first glance it appeared to be nothing more than an attempt to control prices that the company and private traders were charging for salt pork and beef, palm oil, rum, and other goods. But that was not all.

There were sanctions against husbands and wives going to "another." There were restrictions on the killing of goats, hogs, and other livestock. Those who read further, or listened to someone reading it for them, were in no doubt of the document's real import: "The Governor and Council shall not have any thing to do with the Colony no farther than the Company's affairs." Anyone siding with the governor would be fined twenty pounds.[87]

The conciliatory Ludlam was losing command of events. His indulgence in other matters had emboldened the settlers. He also was aware that there were hotheads within the settler ranks prepared to seize control and, if necessary, to assault him and the European community.

As Kizell implied a quarter century later, Ludlam had informers among the Nova Scotians. He had sent "spies to see where the people mett" during the tense days of September. The Paper of Laws had been torn down but was restored on September 25, declaring settler rule to be in force. Ludlam responded by arming the company's officials and the few Nova Scotians who volunteered.

When Wansey and Robinson refused to explain their actions in person, Ludlam issued warrants for the arrest of the ringleaders. Knowing where they were meeting in town, Ludlam, in Kizell's account, "send down some men, under arms, on them; and these people had no arms whatsoever."[88]

The arresting party was headed by the town's long-serving marshal, Richard Corankapone. Christopher Fyfe agrees with Kizell's re-creation of the fray. It was evening as the marshal and his men descended upon the rebels' meeting. "Some got out of hand and rushed ahead, shouting and threatening," Fyfe writes. When the conspirators emerged with sticks and clubs, Corankapone's men started shooting without orders and used their bayonets. Several were wounded on both sides, and a number detained. Anderson and Wansey escaped and rallied their followers at the bridge leading east to Granville Town.[89]

Whether the forty-plus men with Anderson and Wansey genuinely acted in "open rebellion" is questionable. They had been meeting peaceably, without arms, when they were attacked in the dark by an undisciplined armed body. They had every right to defend themselves and understandably retreated into the night for safety. They were joined the next day by a few others who lived near the bridge, including Harry Washington.

Ludlam and the dissidents' leaders might have resolved the situation without further bloodshed. The governor, however, denounced Anderson and Wansey for "treasonable and rebellious practices" and posted a reward for their capture. Anderson responded on September 28 in a short, unsigned note, requesting the release of three colleagues. Ludlam chose to interpret this as an ultimatum threatening violence. Anderson unwittingly had written his own death warrant.[90]

A vulnerable Ludlam sensibly wanted to avoid bloodshed. He was backed only by about thirty Nova Scotians in addition to fourteen Europeans and some local Africans. More than two thirds of Nova Scotian household heads remained either neutral or awaited events.

The affair might have ended well but for two external factors. When the dissidents rejected Ludlam's offer to have the next visiting naval captain mediate, the neighboring Temne chieftain threatened to send his warriors to resolve the dispute. Ludlam believed that he now had no alternative but to act. As he organized an attack on September 30, a double-decked British warship appeared on the horizon. It carried five hundred former slaves who had thrown off English rule in Jamaica. These "militants" had been resettled briefly in Nova Scotia before agreeing to go to Sierra Leone. A contingent of British soldiers escorted them.[91]

The sudden arrival of troops and the so-called Maroons, many of them experienced fighters, doomed the rebellion as well as the chance to negotiate. At the Maroons' urging, Ludlam made a final offer, but Anderson and Wansey pleaded that the one man literate enough to "write an answer for them" was absent.[92] Ludlam considered this temporizing and ordered an attack. A heavy storm prevented serious fighting, but two dissidents died in a brief skirmish. Within days most had surrendered or been tracked down in the bush. Anderson, Wansey, and a few others escaped, but a nearby chief delivered Anderson to Ludlam's custody. The company's official version blamed the radicals for the violence. But Kizell and another Nova Scotian, Eli Ackim, agreed in their 1826 testimony that the dissidents had acted in self-defense.[93] The role of the Maroons also is ambiguous. Fyfe claims that they were happy to "stretch their legs in familiar warlike pursuits" and help crush the upstarts.[94] Kizell's account casts doubt on the Maroons' eagerness to intervene.

"The Maroons came," he said, "and not knowing that the Noviscotians had a dispute among themselves they was ordered, by the governor, to go and make an attack on the men that laid over the brook." Kizell's reference to his people's internal disagreement probably related to the anger many Nova Scotians expressed over the rebels' presumption to impose laws and threaten banishment.[95]

Kizell's farm lay along the mountain path that one of the Maroon columns took to surround the rebels. In all likelihood, however, he was in the Sherbro and missed the confrontation, as he had the French attack in 1794. He would have learned many of the details from Corankapone when the two met in early December in Freetown.[96]

Kizell's true sympathies are difficult to gauge. He implied later that violence could have been averted. He must have regretted that several settlers—men whose character had been vetted by Clarkson in Nova Scotia—were banished. In spite of his contentious history with Ishmael York, he would have been saddened by the man's pathetic downfall. York had lost an arm in the fighting and was exiled to the Rio Pongas.[97]

Nor would Kizell have celebrated the subsequent hanging of Isaac Anderson and Frank Patrick. They had merely claimed the rights that Clarkson had promised them. Patrick had been one of those who petitioned for Clarkson's return.

Because the royal charter had not arrived, treason per se was not a capital crime. They were hung nonetheless—Patrick for stealing a gun and some powder, probably to shoot game, and Anderson for his unsigned note. It was a low moment for Sierra Leone, the company, and the settlers as well as for Ludlam. Lower moments were just ahead.

For all his youth and inexperience, Ludlam had grasped that the colony's survival depended on economic development. That meant cultivating marketable crops and extending trade outside Freetown. Unlike Macaulay, Ludlam took settler views seriously. Given Kizell's active involvement in both agriculture and trade, it is likely that he was prominent among the Nova Scotians whom Ludlam consulted. The governor's trust in Kizell, who later represented him in resolving a long-standing war in the interior, probably dates to this period.

As one of the colony's more active farmers, Kizell would have explained to Ludlam why so many settlers opposed the quit rent. Dawes had returned in early 1801 to resume the governorship, but Ludlam remained on the council and began delving into the root causes of settler dissatisfaction. When Dawes made yet another attempt to collect quit rents, Ludlam addressed a lengthy letter to him and the council in which he essentially endorsed the settler view. He would dispense with the quit rent altogether, he said, if he thought such a recommendation would be accepted in London. He proposed at least reducing the charge for widows, orphans, and those who were cultivating a minimum amount of land.

"The time has been I know when such a proposal would not have been listened to for a moment," he explained, but he believed the issue had become irrelevant. "Most of these farmers who were determined not to pay the quit rent took an active part in the insurrection, & are no longer in the colony." The rest had "quitted their lands & suffered their lands to fall to ruin."[98]

Ludlam referred to the settlers' collective memory of Clarkson's pledge in Nova Scotia and called him "perhaps the most popular governor in the colony"—a judgment that Macaulay, now serving as the company's secretary in London, might have regarded as a gratuitous insult. Ludlam believed that imposing the quit rent was counterproductive to the company's interests. It undermined any incentive among the settlers to cultivate land in the colony.[99]

Ludlam was equally concerned that the company directors, alarmed by losses in the Sherbro, might withdraw from trading outside the colony. European traders had suffered from declining business activity. John Gray, the company's commercial agent, had been promising to support them in the Bagru and Boom rivers, but the company seemed indifferent.[100]

Ludlam later warned that "cessation of the Company's trade" would have serious consequences. "The natural inference among the natives will be, that the Colony is preserved merely for the purposes of ambition & conquest. . . . [Yet,] the advantages derived from trading with us are strongly felt by the natives, who find a ready market for all their produce." It was important to support traders such as Kizell in the Sherbro.

Settlers' involvement in trade enhanced "the permanent and real strength of the Colony," Ludlam maintained. This was "not the case with European traders"— including company employees who engaged in both commerce and the slave trade. Ludlam almost certainly had Kizell in mind when he asserted that "many of the most respectable [settlers] . . . now support themselves by an active and successful trade: which closely attaches them to the Colony."[101]

While Ludlam was sampling settler opinion and analyzing the colony's economic woes, King Tom and the Temne were plotting its destruction. The arrival of the Maroons and British troops suggested an expansionist policy, which threatened Temne hegemony and control of the local slave trade. The Maroons had been settled at Granville Town to separate them from the Nova Scotians, but the presence of more than five hundred strangers, many of them reputed warriors, alarmed King Tom.

With the outlaw Wansey counseling war, the Temne chieftain sent a substantial force early on the morning of November 18, 1801, to surprise the colony. Wansey led the attackers, storming into the town before dawn and killing more than thirty people, including women and children, before being driven back.

As Kizell sadly related, "a number of the principal men" among the Nova Scotians died. One was his friend and former business partner. Hearing the first shots, Richard Corankapone had rushed up to Fort Thornton and into the midst of the attackers. Wounded twice, he resisted until he was struck a third time and died.[102]

Recovering from his own wounds, Dawes launched a counteroffensive, burning several of King Tom's towns and driving his people from their farms between Freetown and Cape Sierra Leone to the west. By January King Tom was reported to be mobilizing allies for a fresh assault on the colony.[103] When he, Wansey, and four hundred warriors finally came—again at dawn, on April 11, 1802—the defenders were better prepared, and the attack quickly repulsed. Within months Wansey was delivered in irons. Although no record of his fate exists, presumably he was executed.[104]

There was little to celebrate. King Tom and another powerful war chief were an omnipresent threat. In the meantime an ongoing conflict between the Caulkers and Clevelands in the Sherbro was cutting off trade and rice supplies. Kizell and other farmers abandoned their lands near Freetown in fear when one of the original Granville Town settlers was found murdered nearby. Disease and death were decimating the garrison. Rumors abounded that the colony was to be abandoned.[105]

These were the colony's bleakest times. Fyfe pictures Dawes and Ludlam as "sickened with responsibilities [that] they felt unrewarded." Gray and other European employees were drifting off to trade in slaves. One company officer submitted his resignation, defending his involvement "in respect of selling my fellow creatures." The Africans, he argued to Dawes, "would have murdered yourself and all the rest of us in our beds . . . for what, I never did any of them any injury." The governor refused to release him from his contract.[106]

Kizell's mood had to be dismal, as well. Not only was the colony in jeopardy, but age and misfortune were thinning the Nova Scotian ranks. Of the three friends who had launched their boat a few years before, he alone remained. Corankapone had died a hero; Abraham Smith had been exiled for his role in the settler uprising. Boston King had died recently in the Sherbro. But the hardest loss to bear was that of his son, George, who had contracted measles. He lay now in a Clapham churchyard.[107]

6

ABOLITION AND ILLUSION

"The poor man saw nothing but death before him."
John Kizell, watching an accused witch die

The Sierra Leone Company and South Carolina both dropped pretenses in 1803. In London the company's directors concluded that the colony would never profit investors and began lobbying government to assume control. In Charleston legislators conceded that extensive smuggling of Africans into the state could not be arrested and repealed the unenforceable ban imposed sixteen years earlier.[1]

Settler unrest, the Temne attacks, and the failure to develop the colony's agriculture were disappointing enough to the directors. But it was the renewed demand for cheap labor in America and the West Indies that most damaged the settlement's economic viability. The slave trade dominated commerce and the colony's relationship with its African neighbors.

Palavers and Peacemaking

As a community of free people, Sierra Leone defined itself as the antithesis to slavery and the slave trade. But it was unable to avoid their enveloping influence. At least a dozen company employees had entered slave trading by 1803. So had several Nova Scotians, although they "of course tenaciously maintain their innocence," Macaulay remarked. He seemed affronted that there was "little or no indignation" among the other settlers.[2]

The colony had coexisted with slave traders since the establishment of Granville Town in 1787. Or rather the slave traders had, in their view, tolerated the intrusion into their domain by former slaves cosseted by meddling do-gooders. The fear promoted by whites in Nova Scotia that the settlers would be reenslaved proved groundless. No one foresaw that some of the Nova Scotians might do the enslaving.

The problem was serious enough to goad the governor and council in 1801 to ban settlers from holding and trading in slaves. After lengthy discussion on whether they had the authority, Dawes and the council resolved that anyone who retained another person "in his or her service by force or fear . . . shall be deemed a slaveholder."[3]

Domestic servitude was so institutionalized in the region that indigenous slaves were commonplace in the colony. They might come and go, often unidentified as slaves, but on occasion they sought freedom under the colony's aegis. In September 1801 an enslaved Sherbro man who had accompanied his owner's associate on business refused to leave Freetown with him. When Dawes summoned both men, the slave "declared explicitly & repeatedly that he would . . . remain here and subsist by his labour." Dawes then decreed that, "in conformity to the spirit and letter of the English constitution, the municipal laws of this Colony did not recognize or allow any such state or condition of slavery."[4]

The colony's fading promise reflected the resurgence of the slave trade. Liverpool alone by 1801 was home to 150 ships capable of transporting more than fifty-two thousand slaves—double the capacity in the first year of peace with America.[5] Slavers based in Charleston and in New England had filled the postwar vacuum, as well, in spite of official sanctions.

The Peace of Amiens, in 1802, allowed Napoleon to begin reviving French plantations in the Caribbean. His sale of the Louisiana Territory to the United States in 1803 further inflated demand for slaves. Aware that the twenty-year constitutional grace for the slave trade would expire in 1807, South Carolina reopened slave importation to take legal advantage of the market for labor in the Louisiana "purchase" and on the expanding cotton plantations of its own upcountry.[6]

In England a parliamentary committee in 1803 investigated whether to continue subsidizing the colony. It made more sense to take it wholly under the Crown, if only to avoid the huge cost of resettling the Nova Scotians and Maroons elsewhere. The Pitt government, however, preferred for the time being to leave the company to its own devices. It feared further alienating the West Indies and slave-trade interests if it became more directly involved in West Africa.[7]

Although there had been no further attacks by the Temne, the colony's position was precarious. A long-standing intramural dispute between the Caulkers and Clevelands had destabilized the entire coast between the Banana Islands and the Sherbro. European slave traders fomented the unrest by supplying weapons. Rice in the colony was chronically short as a result, and the once-thriving trade in camwood had been interrupted.[8] Control of the slave trade was the root cause of the feud, which ultimately embroiled the Sherbro chiefs and prompted Dawes to intervene without success in 1803.[9]

Following the departure of Dawes two years later, Ludlam tried his hand at defusing the internecine conflict. It was proving the "ruin of this country," Ludlam wrote, referring to the Sherbro. "The system on which the Native Chiefs seem uniformly to act has a natural tendency to poverty and depopulation. They live by the Slave Trade." This required "occasionally selling one of their own people, or an unprotected stranger, to help them out of their pecuniary difficulties." A chief was encouraged to sell, rather than retain, his domestic bondsmen. As a result, Ludlam explained, "his plantations . . . are small, and he is always poor. He must keep all his people as poor as himself; and therefore must bring a palaver against every aspiring subject."[10]

To negotiate Ludlam turned to a man he evidently trusted. John Kizell was known   **157** to the principal contestants and the Sherbro chiefs. He had been living and trading in the Sherbro for nearly a decade and probably found much in common with Stephen Caulker and William Cleveland Jr., the mixed-race brother of South Carolina plantation owner Elizabeth Clevland Hardcastle. Although both men were slave traders, each possessed "considerable intelligence and enterprise" in the estimation of an English visitor in 1805. Cleveland, like his sister, had been educated in England.[11]

Kizell had a vested interest in peace. The interruption of commerce between the colony and Sherbro affected him directly. So did the slave trade. The limits imposed on agricultural production prevented people from growing rice and other crops—his stock in trade—for sale to Sierra Leone. "The country," Ludlam understood, "is thus systematically kept poor, and the influence of the [slave] traders . . . is proportionably increased."[12]

Precisely how Kizell persuaded all parties to declare a truce is unrecorded. The colony itself was at its weakest. European slave traders were urging the chiefs to resist any attempt by the Sierra Leone Company to interfere with slaving. Because he had neither carrot nor stick, Kizell probably took advantage of general war fatigue. His first step would have been to engage King Sherbro and the chiefs, then summon Cleveland and Caulker, or their representatives, to a palaver. He may also have sought the intervention of Poro.

Kizell was uniquely qualified as a peacemaker. He could speak firsthand to the slave trade's horrors. Because he did not engage in slave trading—itself remarkable in that time and place for any businessman—he could appeal both in moral and practical terms. Trading in slaves was not only wrong, it was economic suicide. Kizell also was neutral. He had no known family ties or allegiances in the Sherbro. He was a stranger who nonetheless spoke the local language, understood the customs, and had settled there peaceably.

Kizell's task was complicated by the inherently weak authority of the king within the Sherbro political system. Ludlam later reported that he had been "strongly urged to interfere yet more actively in the concerns of this district & re-establishing the authority of their Supreme King, which now scarcely exists even in name, to secure the peace & order of the Country."[13]

As Ludlam's principal informant on Sherbro affairs, Kizell may have been doing the urging. Although a truce was finally achieved in late 1805 or early 1806, mediation continued well into 1808. By then the British government had banned the slave trade and assumed direct responsibility for the colony.[14]

Ludlam and Kizell were in regular contact throughout this period. There was concern, in England and in Freetown, regarding the impact abolition would have on the ground. Kizell was a well-positioned source of information and insight.

Ludlam believed that the slave traders had "a decided superiority over us" and would be difficult to dislodge. He respected Kizell's initiative both as a businessman and as someone willing to challenge the slave traders. Kizell had "opened" the Boom River to trade, in spite of the Sherbro war, but slave traders following in his wake were trying to evict him. "Kizell already complains, with good reason, of their conduct towards him," Ludlam wrote Macaulay in April 1807.

Ludlam was preoccupied with the "confused State of Sherbro . . . occasioned by the Slave Trade."[15] Kizell had written in April to describe just how "confused" affairs were. One of the Tuckers, whom Kizell identified only as a prominent mulatto, had used trickery to obtain slaves to clear his debt to two white slave traders. Kizell had met him earlier going to Kittam. His canoes were piled with goods to trade for slaves.

"He went," Kizell reported, "but did not get the slaves so soon as he had agreed." Two white slave dealers, who had advanced him goods for thirty slaves, became impatient when he failed to deliver them.

"Now think what [Tucker] did to get slaves to pay them," Kizell wrote. "He has ten wives; he sent for a greegree-man, who told him his wives were kept by other men. In order to prove the guilt of his wives, he got some oil and put it in a pot, and set it on the fire. He knew the poor women could not put their hands into it without being burnt. He nevertheless called them, and said they were the cause of his not being able to get slaves."

The women denied the allegation. Tucker ordered them to place their hands in the hot oil. If they were innocent, he assured them, they would not be harmed. Knowing they would be burned, they refused. Tucker then separated three of the women "who he pretended were not guilty." The others "must inform against some one. They knew he did not want old men, and they, to please him, mentioned the most likely young men they could think of. . . . They then sent people to catch the persons who had been accused. He afterwards sent to a town and caught eighteen."[16]

Kizell's outrage with Tucker and others fomenting the slave trade coincided with renewed abolitionist pressure in the United States and England. South Carolina's decision to legalize importation of slaves had "shocked the nation," W. E. B. DuBois wrote in his landmark analysis of the slave trade, published in 1896. It frightened the southern states "with visions of an influx of untrained barbarians and servile insurrections, . . . arousing and intensifying the anti-slavery feeling of the North, which had long since come to think of the trade, so far as legal enactment went, as a thing of the past."[17]

The fate of the eighteen men falsely accused of "damaging" Tucker's wives could well have been tied to South Carolina's action. From 1804 until the close of 1807, 202 ships—61 originating in Charleston—brought more than thirty-nine thousand Africans into the state. Most were sold into the territories added by Jefferson's unilateral acquisition.[18]

Many of these ships trolled the Windward Coast, some touching Sierra Leone and the Sherbro. The Venus sailed from Charleston in late March 1807, loaded with rum,

View of the Banana Islands from Cape Shilling, south of Freetown.
Author's photograph (1965)

textiles, and other goods, and traded for slaves between Senegal and Sierra Leone. Trade reportedly was slow and slaves for purchase difficult to find—as Tucker's dilemma in the Sherbro suggested. The *Venus* lingered on the coast much of the year before returning to Charleston in mid-December with eighty-eight slaves. It was one of the last slavers to arrive before the trade became illegal for Americans two weeks later.[19]

In England and America, political and humanitarian sentiment had been coalescing against the slave trade. While Ludlam and Kizell were trying to pacify the Sherbro, leaders on both sides of the Atlantic were concluding that slavery and the slave trade were dying institutions that could be interred someday without undue inconvenience to national interests. The easiest to bury, with the least consequences, was thought to be the slave trade itself.

British abolitionists achieved a critical breakthrough in 1806. "As a tactical maneuver," David Brion Davis writes, "they deliberately suppressed humanitarian arguments and concentrated their fire on the neutral (mainly American) slave trade to enemy colonies." Banastre Tarleton, now a member of Parliament, gave no quarter to the abolitionists but conceded that they had "by a side wind" obliterated much of Britain's slave trade. The shift in tactics, Davis concludes, "meant that a total abolition, even if demanded for true humanitarian motives, would not be regarded as a dangerous innovation."[20]

The government and Parliament knew that the time limit was about to expire in the United States and that the Americans were likely to ban participation in the slave

trade. The British navy had already substantially reduced slave trafficking by its enemies north of the equator. With the United States about to act, the slave trade's demise
seemed near.[21]

This reflected a naive understanding in England of the slave power in America.
Slavery might be declining in Britain's West Indian colonies; revolutionary blacks in
Saint Domingue (Haiti) might have signaled a cataclysmic beginning-of-the-end for
slavery in the Americas; but the opening of the trans-Mississippi had given new lease
to the expansion of American slavery.[22]

President Jefferson, aware that English abolitionists were about to succeed, asked
the American people to celebrate their own constitutional opportunity "to withdraw
the citizens of the United States from all further participation in those violations of
human rights which have been so long continued on the unoffending inhabitants of
Africa."

In a message to Congress on December 2, 1806, Jefferson invited legislation that
would honor "the morality, the reputation, and the best interests of our country."[23]
Three months later he signed the act that criminalized the slave trade for American
citizens from January 1, 1808. A week earlier Parliament had done likewise—almost
unanimously—for British subjects, effective May 1, 1807.[24]

The Atlantic world was to be transformed, or so it was thought. The *Venus* would
sail no longer between Charleston and Africa in search of chattel; Kizell would no
longer encounter Tucker's canoes laden with goods to exchange for slaves; European
traders would stop selling arms to warring parties in the Sherbro; and the people
would return joyously and productively to the land.

There would be no such transformation. The Americans saw to that. The fine
print in the British and American legislation foreshadowed the former's sincerity and
the latter's cynicism. One of the English act's essential provisions, Davis explains, was
that Africans recaptured from illegal slave traders "were to be forfeited to the government and eventually freed." The Americans' dispensation, however, was entangled in
the fate of slavery itself. After much bitter and sarcastic debate, one congressman predicted to his colleagues that the law placed beneath Jefferson's pen "will be broken
every day of your lives."

One section provided that "any negro, mulatto, or person of color" imported "in
violation of this law . . . shall remain subject to any regulations . . . which the
Legislatures of the several States or Territories . . . may make, for disposing of any such
negro, mulatto, or person of color."[25] The act of importing slaves would be illegal, but
slaves seized could be sold, indentured, or liberated according to local statutes. No
imagination was required to divine how this provision might be employed in the
South and in the vast Louisiana country.

American commitment to ending the slave trade was compromised further by
Napoleon's continuing war with England. Although the United States was neutral, its
shipping was routinely captured and condemned by both belligerents. The French
seized many American merchantmen in spite of having only a modest navy; losses to

the British were even greater during 1805 and 1806. As one historian writes of these troubled times, "there was little to distinguish the two foes of American commerce."[26]

Absent the prolonged international conflict with France, England and the United States might have worked in concert to hasten the end of the slave trade. "Had our relations with the United States been such as all must wish them to be," the recently formed African Institution reported in March 1810, "it might have been possible to come to such an arrangement . . . as would speedily have put an end to every vestige of the contraband American Slave Trade."[27]

Anglo-American cooperation in mutually enforcing their respective bans would have reduced slave trading substantially. In the immediate term, the war forced American slavers from the seas in any case. "Our dispute with America," Ludlam reported to the African Institution's directors in mid-1808, "has probably done more towards carrying [abolition] into full effect" than the act itself.[28] American sources also reported a decline in slave trading. Ivory and agricultural goods had begun to supplant slaves.[29]

Ludlam believed that abolition was having the desired effect, but mere parchment would not end the African trade. "Just as might be expected," he wrote Macaulay in May 1808, "the principal people of the Country are very much vexed." Yet there had been "none of those massacres which were predicted as an inevitable consequence of the Abolition." He took satisfaction in his (and Kizell's) having restored peace. "I do not say that [the wars] are suspended in consequence of the Abolition; but the Abolition is very likely to prevent their revival."[30]

Ludlam recommended direct action to interdict the more incorrigible slave traders. "I do not see that any thing except active Cruizers can prevent an illicit Slave Trade." Slave traders were resorting to new stratagems. "The first Scheme," Ludlam said, "seems to be, to keep the Slaves on shore at some independent place till everything is ready; then to proceed on the voyage and run off the Coast as quick as possible." He also predicted, correctly, that the Portuguese flag "will be made use of."[31]

Ludlam's guarded optimism was buoyed by the apparent reduction in "witch palavers," a further indication that the slave trade was atrophying. Ludlam knew the impact of witchcraft allegations on local life. Kizell, one of his informants, continued to intervene, as he had ten years earlier, when he saw superstition being misused. Another local man had told Ludlam that "two-thirds of those who were sent off . . . the coast were sold for witchcraft."

One chief had pleaded with Ludlam, during his effort to end the Sherbro war, that "should I succeed in establishing peace, to . . . abolish the red water" as well. "He had himself seen King S— —- kill six persons in one morning with it; and an equal number of the families of the victims were immediately sold."

Ludlam wrote Macaulay that he had heard of only one witch palaver for some time. At the last one, "the people were in sad distress because they could not sell the Witches for Rum. . . . I was really afraid from the first account that they would have killed them; however, they thought better of it."[32] Macaulay would have been pleased

to learn that the colony now had a law forbidding witchcraft, under which several settlers had recently been prosecuted.[33]

Even as Ludlam was sending encouraging news to London, he was receiving
unwelcome word from Kizell that European slave traders had stoked a new war in the
Gallinas. The dispute was over the prices that whites were willing to pay in a market
now "distorted" by abolition; and over which chiefs were entitled to receive certain
"duties" on the slaves sold.

The immediate cause was the demand of a young prince, Conay Billa, that the
white slave traders should pay duties to him, as they had to his late father, and not to
several minor chiefs. The prince complained that the latter had, figuratively, been his
father's slaves and that they were abusing his authority because of his youth. A palaver
would have to be called.

"The white people," Kizell wrote Ludlam, "learning that a war was threatened,
thought that if it was carried on, it would furnish them with the means of getting
slaves." One white slave trader decided to back the prince; two others supported the
main insurgents. When the prince discovered that the latter planned to kill him at the
palaver, he fled. "He . . . dug up the bones of his father and carried them with him,"
Kizell reported. When he refused to renew the palaver, the chiefs attacked his town.
War had come.

The prince was not without allies. "The Marno and [Tewo] people came to
palaver," Kizell explained, "and said to the chiefs: 'You . . . tell the whites not to give
us the same price with you. . . . You all know that Conay Billa is the king's son . . . and
you all know that you are his people. You want to be greater than your master. No: we
will join with him, and drive all the white people from us; for it is they who make you
all so proud. . . . We will have all the up country people to help us, for the king came
from them, and you will see that we will drive all the white people from you.'" These
words "put the chiefs in a rage," Kizell added.

In addition to the Marno and Tewo partisans, another young chief, Stephen
Rogers, joined the prince's cause. "Knowing him to be a dangerous man," Kizell
informed Ludlam, the chiefs failed twice to capture Rogers's town. Rogers then surprised one of his opponent's villages at night, seized nearly two hundred people, and
killed the chief. But as he and his men returned home, survivors of the attack
ambushed Rogers and recaptured many of the prisoners. In the darkness and confusion, Rogers was taken. "His enemies," Kizell said, "told him to sing a war song; he
would not: They then killed him, and cut him up, and sent a piece of him to all their
friends."

Having lost his ally, the prince "was at a loss what to do," Kizell wrote. He retreated
first to Kittam and then to the interior, where he requested help. The Gallinas people
took their chance to punish the Marno, burned three towns, and seized many people.
They came back, "dancing and rejoicing," paid their two white allies, and drove away
the third who had underwritten the prince. "I saw him afterwards," Kizell said, "and
he related to me how he had been used."

The prince was undaunted, Kizell related. He soon returned with several hundred men and collected many more. "He then fell on the chiefs in the Gallinas, and burnt many towns, and killed, and took many prisoners. . . . The white people were all driven away; and not one got off without great loss."[34] Kizell was all too pleased to write an epitaph for the white slave traders, premature though it proved to be.

Where Slaves Breathe

The outlawing of the slave trade was widely viewed, at least in England, as a watershed event. This was the conceit of William Wilberforce, Thomas Clarkson, Henry Thornton, and other elites who created the African Institution in 1807. "England," David Brion Davis writes, "had begun the nineteenth century with an act of sublime nobility." The new body was pledged "to institutionalize that transcendent impulse."[35]

The African Institution's backers knew that they needed first to erase public perception that the experiment in Sierra Leone had failed and that Africa was infertile ground for commercial and humanitarian endeavors. Conceding that "unforeseen and calamitous events" had subverted the Sierra Leone Company's objectives, its principals retained faith in the ultimate goal: the civilizing of Africa. The African Institution reported in July 1807 that it was "no part of our plan to purchase territory in Africa, to found a colony, or even to carry on commerce."[36]

Experience in Sierra Leone had been a hard teacher. The settlers had proved all too human in the view of many whites. They had refused to follow compliantly the course laid down by their European betters. They had resisted moral instruction and religious orthodoxy. The indigenous people had been a disappointment as well. Far from being children of nature, amenable to enlightenment and improvement, they had persisted in unreconstructed barbarism.

The slave trade had been struck a blow, opening Africa—it was thought—to genuine reformation. Beneath the surface of this celebration, however, was a subtle shift in perspective. Following the settler "rebellion" in 1800, the company had dispensed with the hundredors and tythingmen. There was to be no further pretense of democracy. The African Institution, for all its liberal notions, made clear in its first year that "free Negroes are capable of being governed by mild laws, and require neither whips nor chains to *enforce their submission to civil authority*" (emphasis added).[37]

In its final report, the Sierra Leone Company in 1808 congratulated itself for demonstrating "that the African does not labour under the intellectual inferiority, which had been so long imputed to him . . . and that he can feel with the same force as the Europeans, the considerations by which Christianity exalts the mind of man."[38]

"This was a fine ringing statement," Philip D. Curtin writes in his study of British thought and action regarding Africa, "but it has to be read in the light of [the directors'] other belief that Africans had a very long way to go" to realize their potential. There was a "new humanitarian assessment of Africans in general," Curtin explains. "There had always been an ambivalence between Christian acceptance of spiritual equality, and the obviously unchristian state of African culture. Humanitarians seldom defended African culture after 1800."[39]

164 Although Sierra Leone passed under royal responsibility on January 1, 1808, the government was content to leave it temporarily in the company's hands. It was not until early August that Ludlam welcomed the governor-designate—a twenty-five-year-old army subaltern on half pay.

Thomas Perronet Thompson was the son of a staunch supporter of Wilberforce who had helped to drive a parliamentary stake into the slave trade's heart on March 25, 1807. Having just returned from the Argentine campaign and now at loose ends, Thompson was introduced to Wilberforce. Impressed by the young man's interest in Africa, Wilberforce recommended him for Sierra Leone.

Thompson was to understudy Ludlam and assume the governorship in October. Ludlam soon realized the arrangement was untenable and proposed to Thompson that he take over immediately. Thompson eagerly obliged. A man of strong and quickly formed opinions, he had determined within his first day on land that there were two very contradictory versions of Sierra Leone.

One existed in the delusions of Wilberforce, Thornton, and even Macaulay; the other belonged to the Nova Scotians and, to a lesser degree, the Maroons. Thompson concluded that the company's leadership had been dangerously misinformed about conditions in the colony. He also sized up the whites and blacks in short order: "The state of European manners is bad beyond description," he wrote privately three days after arriving. "The black subjects are infinitely more orderly and decent."[40] He amended his good opinion of the settlers soon enough.

Thompson aimed his first salvo at the Sierra Leone Company. He had barely acquired his land legs when he wrote to Lord Castlereagh, his immediate superior in the colonial department, that the company's agents "have had just so much of the slave-trade in this Colony as suited their conscience & just so little as suited their character. . . . The Sierra Leone Company . . . have left to the British Government the shadow of what ought to be."[41]

"It is as I suspected," he wrote to his future wife in England. Thompson had been warned of "Macaulay's apprenticeships" before he left home. "These . . . have after sixteen years . . . at last introduced actual slavery into the colony. . . . I am writing to [Lord Castlereagh] and Mr. Wilberforce very plainly about the colony and shall assert roundly that if every step which has been taken in this affair of the apprentices is not retraced instantly the colony will soon be little better than a slave-factory."[42]

On August 18 Thompson and the council passed a bill to make slave trading illegal in the colony. Its real purpose was to end apprenticing, which Thompson regarded as de facto slavery.[43] Two days later he served public notice in an unsigned article in the *Sierra Leone Gazette*:

Apprenticing will always be a source of mischief in Africa. There are many good men within the Colony who have native children in their houses and use them like their own; but there are others who know they bought them for dollars and rum and tobacco from the native chiefs, and who think they may make use of them as they please. . . .

What African does not see that as long as a Slave is permitted to breathe in this Colony neither he nor his children are in safety? . . . A Slave cannot breathe in England, and a Slave cannot breathe in this Colony. . . . In defiance of the laws Slavery has existed in this Colony; it will exist no longer, though there are yet men who *always thought slavery necessary for this Colony and who think so still*. Africans, your King thinks otherwise, and the brave African people think otherwise. Surely we shall together be a match for a few men who wish to sell you.[44]

Ludlam waited several days before sending a strongly worded retort to Thompson and demanding evidence to support his charges. None was forthcoming. Thompson had already established to his own satisfaction that settlers were keeping "apprenticed" slaves. One of his first acts had been to liberate several who had run away from their masters, only to be returned by villagers and jailed. In front of a crowd gathered in the yard of Fort Thornton, Thompson ordered the gaoler to strike the irons from twenty men and one woman. Then he announced, through interpreters, that they were free.[45]

Thompson threatened to prosecute Ludlam under the British abolition law. He also advised Lord Castlereagh that he was thinking of charging the company and several of its employees with serious crimes. He had learned that "infant murders and the procuring of abortions among the women of colour, with whom the European servants of the Sierra Leone Company were connected, were systematically encouraged by the highest servants of the company." He supposed this was to preserve "uninjured the religious reputation of their Colony." Foremost among those supporting the "illegal practices" of the company "in opposition to the Government" were persons, he alleged, who had recently been appointed royal commissioners to investigate the state of British forts and settlements in Africa.[46] One of them was Ludlam.

The Nova Scotians soon joined Ludlam and the company in Thompson's litany of all that was rotten in the colony. He derided their "half-comprehended notions of American independence" and castigated their morals. "The Nova Scotian," he informed Castlereagh in November, "discourages his children from marriage, that the sons not be encumbered with families and that the daughters may have the chance of being supported by some European. I have no doubt that the natives of Africa are likely in every respect to make better subjects . . . and will prove themselves to be more deserving of the privileges of Englishmen."[47]

Thompson's priggish disdain for settlers' morals reflected outsiders' superficial understanding of local culture. His reaction was little different from that of Paul Cuffe, the African American shipowner and merchant who visited Freetown a few years later. Neither man spent enough time in the colony to perceive the underlying stability of family life.

Walker provides a more nuanced interpretation of the familial and sexual mores that prevailed. "Nova Scotian family life remained much as it had in Nova Scotia and during the 1790s," he writes, "with the difference that since the early nineteenth century adulterous relationships had been extended to include Europeans. They were neither prostituting themselves in order to gain favour nor copying the lax standards of the overseas white community. Disregard for the marital tie had prevailed among them for many years, and could be considered one of their characteristics."

The Nova Scotians had developed relationships and behavioral norms that, as Walker points out, "had long since been accommodated by their own moral system, and even the most prominent and religious Nova Scotians had common-law marriages or mistresses." The Nova Scotians openly recognized their children, legitimate and otherwise. They acknowledged relationships that were based on mutual respect and fidelity, regardless of their legal status. Europeans who chose to "marry" into the Nova Scotian community were accepted in the same spirit.[48]

Thompson's dismissive attitude toward the Nova Scotians moderated as he became better acquainted with them. Writing the following August, he praised the settlers' conduct "in the midst of . . . trying circumstances," under the "hostile" management of the company's white agents. Years later he sent seeds from his military posting in India, asking that they be distributed to the Maroon and Nova Scotian farmers.[49] But in 1808 the human resource best suited to Thompson's reformist instincts were the recaptured slaves. The navy was beginning to deliver them in Freetown in mounting numbers. As John Peterson notes in *Province of Freedom*, "the recaptives were untouched by those influences which had, in [Thompson's] mind, warped the Nova Scotians."

Thompson understood that apprenticing the recaptives would ultimately overwhelm the colony's capacity to absorb them. Why not settle them in their own communities in areas surrounding the town? "By putting them on the soil as free and independent agents," Peterson explains, "he hoped . . . that they would serve the original purpose of the colony and become the first wave of civilized Africans to penetrate the interior." They would also feed the colony and serve as a buffer against attack from inland.[50]

The headstrong governor proceeded to establish recaptive villages without direct approval or funding from London, which had yet to turn its attention to the full implications of abolition. Lacking means to return recaptives to their original countries, Thompson had no alternative but to resettle people who had been rescued hundreds, even thousands, of miles from their homes.

The growing recaptive presence was an opportunity to transform the tiny, flawed colony into a robust mercantile base and to expand British trade and influence deep into Africa. He blamed the Sierra Leone Company for failing to develop trade connections with the interior and for alienating "the only real power in the neighbourhood"—the Mohammedans.

Thompson believed the latter had been planning to attack the colony to revenge the Sierra Leone Company's role in abolishing the slave trade. To Thompson, however, the Mohammedans were a potential asset and ally. "Britain might supply the whole continent of Africa with manufactured goods," he predicted, if the government reached out boldly to the Muslims in the interior and beyond to Timbuktu, North Africa, and Suez.[51]

The feared attack never came. "There is strong reason to believe," Thompson reported to Castlereagh, "that [the rumors] proceeded . . . from the apprehensions of our own people."[52] Thompson continued, entirely on his own initiative, to promote expansion into the hinterland. The colony was too vulnerable to assault from both the sea and the interior. It made no sense, therefore, "to collect the vitality and existence of the Colony in a single point."[53]

Lord Castlereagh had heard enough. So had Wilberforce and his compatriots in the African Institution. The dispatches arriving from Sierra Leone deeply embarrassed Wilberforce, who had vetted the young man. They were worrisome to Castlereagh because they projected an undesired widening of British responsibility and expense in a region of peripheral importance.

The last straw was the minutes of the governor and council session of November 11, 1808. They recorded an unauthorized "treaty of alliance offensive and defensive," which Thompson, without Kizell's intervention, had just signed with several chiefs and headmen in the Sherbro and nearby coastal areas. The governor also had unilaterally renamed Freetown because it had been "perverted to Purposes of Insubordination & Rebellion." It was henceforth to be known (albeit briefly) as Georgetown, in honor of the king.[54]

Writing to Thompson for the first and only time, Castlereagh on April 3, 1809, recalled the governor to London to explain his actions, especially the treaty.[55] Wilberforce alerted Thompson in advance that he was being summoned home and that he would not be returning to Sierra Leone. "I wish," the pained Wilberforce wrote, "I had time to go into the particulars respecting the difficulties which forced us"—meaning his aggrieved associates in the Sierra Leone Company—"into acquiescing in the system of apprenticing."[56]

Thompson's high ideals, energy, and impatience collided with several hard realities: an established Nova Scotian community and culture; a government at home distracted by war and disinterested in colonial expansion; the quasi-defunct Sierra Leone Company, whose employees regarded the governor as their adversary; and the abolition of the slave trade itself, which disrupted the region's economic and political relations. Thompson's exhaustive work habits nearly killed him. He took so much calomel for frequent bouts of malaria that his front teeth fell out.[57]

His preconceived bias toward the company and apprenticing, his rush to judgment of the veteran Ludlam, and his lack of diplomacy prevented Thompson from developing a coherent understanding of the challenges and opportunities he faced.

He had little intercourse with the settlers. Kizell and Ludlam had developed a close working relationship, but there is no indication that Ludlam introduced Kizell to the governor or that Thompson sought out Kizell and other sources of African insight.

Thompson was drawn instead to fellow military officers who commanded troops stationed in the colony. As Fyfe remarks, these were men who "found service in Africa a refuge rather than a vocation." He befriended white slave traders, who welcomed his criticism of the company. He even entertained the supercargo of a Spanish-flagged slaver who was openly purchasing slaves on the opposite side of the estuary.

Thompson's attitude toward slavery was suspect, given his charge that the company was trying to deprive West India planters of a steady flow of fresh slaves.[58] His consorting with slave traders would have been widely remarked among the settlers. Nor was it conducive to establishing rapport with Kizell, who apart from his antislavery views was a known confidante of the despised Ludlam.[59]

Thompson, in the end, had little use for the Nova Scotians. They represented "everything . . . vile in the American." They had been spoiled by the company, as well, and by their relations with many Europeans in the colony who were now exciting "the lowest orders" against the government.[60] Thompson shared the prevailing view in England that the Islamic peoples of the interior were more civilized. In Fyfe's estimation "he contrasted the polished urbanity of visiting Muslims . . . with the degraded habits of the coastal peoples."[61]

Thompson continued to act as governor as though nothing had changed. He had been instructed by Castlereagh to surrender command of the colony to Edward H. Columbine, a naval captain affiliated with the African Institution. Along with Ludlam and Dawes, Columbine had already been appointed to a commission to review the state of Britain's settlements and forts in West Africa. But Columbine's ship foundered en route. He did not arrive in Sierra Leone until mid-February 1810.[62]

The changing of the guard was awkward. Columbine had taken exception to Thompson's characterization of Ludlam, his fellow commissioner. Thompson assured him that he did not regard Columbine in the same light. But to his fiancée he wrote that "Capt. Columbine is come out with all the rascals in his train you may imagine. . . . Their one single object since their arrival appears to have been to turn the Colony upside down."[63] The next day, as though in validation, fire destroyed thirty houses in the town.[64]

One of the "rascals" accompanying Columbine was Ludlam, who had returned briefly to England. He and Dawes were to conduct the commission's work along the coast while Columbine remained in Freetown to sort out the colony's disordered affairs. The commissioners were under instruction to "turn the attention of British Subjects resident on the coast as much as possible to the pursuit of agriculture & of a Trade in the natural Production of Africa." They were also to convey to African chieftains "a favourable impression of the Principles which have produced the abolition of the Slave Trade, & to point out to them the means they enjoy of improving the condition of their country."[65]

Ludlam no doubt had shared with Columbine his decade of experience in the colony, his assessment of the settlers, his knowledge of the slave trade, and his estimate of the colony's leading men. Given Kizell's role in negotiating a cease-fire in the Sherbro war and his reporting from the Gallinas two years earlier, Ludlam probably commended him to Columbine as an informed interlocutor among the coastal peoples. Within months, Columbine was sending Kizell—"my friend and ally"—to represent him to the Sherbro chiefs and to convince them to abandon slave trading.[66]

Columbine showed only passing interest in the actual state of the slave trade. He probably shared the widespread belief in England that the trade had been fatally wounded and was being supplanted by legitimate commerce. Bance Island, where Thompson had to quell rioting *grumettas* the previous October, had essentially wound up its century as a slave factory.[67]

In the meantime American merchants were taking advantage of an opening in Napoleon's restriction of neutral shipping to meet demand for an array of manufactures and commodities. American goods began flooding the colony via British traders at the Isles de Los in the second half of 1809. The United States had replaced a total embargo on trade with Britain and France with a more flexible nonintercourse policy. The latter allowed enterprising Americans to trade in ports—such as the Isles de Los—that were not formally governed by either belligerent.

"American commerce," writes George E. Brooks Jr. in his history of maritime trade in this period, "rebounded to new heights in West Africa. . . . The British garrisons welcomed the return of American vessels, and the decline . . . of slavers on the coast made trade . . . extremely profitable." They traded mainly for ivory, gold, and camwood. Some American captains sailed boldly into Freetown itself.[68]

Thompson wrote to Castlereagh, shortly before Columbine's arrival, that Sierra Leone was beginning to look more American than British. He was open to the Americans on purely economic grounds but appealed for official guidance in view of government sanctions against U.S. shipping. "Had the trade of Americans with Sierra Leone," he asked, "to stop in view of the quarrel with the United States?" They were extremely competitive, he said frankly, and could undersell the East India Company.[69]

Columbine preferred to play by the rules. National law governed trade in British ports and protected East Indian interests against American inroads. He ruled in October 1810 that foreign ships would require special permission to trade at Sierra Leone. India goods, however, were strictly limited to English bottoms. But in practice Columbine often permitted the Americans to land goods—except tobacco and India cloth—that the colony needed.[70]

Unusually heavy rains drenched the coast as Kizell carried Columbine's letter to the Sherbro.[71] Thompson had arrived in London, where he vainly sought official explanation for his recall. Dawes soon returned to Freetown on the *Crocodile* after investigating British posts as far east as the Bight of Benin. Ludlam did not; fever had claimed him at sea.

Ludlam went to his final rest with little faith in the continent's future. "Abolition," he had confessed to Macaulay, "will not prevent the Africans from remaining a savage and uncivilized people. To abolish the Slave Trade is not to abolish . . . violent passions. . . . Were it to cease, the misery of Africa would arise from other causes . . . : she might . . . be less miserable, and yet be savage and uncivilized."[72] To Ludlam Kizell had merely been an exception to the rule.

"We sell such as know not god"

The imam of the Futa Jallon, one of the polished Mohammedans Governor Thompson so admired, had appealed to the governor in early 1810 to "give us orders for the selling of slaves." Abolition was a great wrong to his people, he implied. "We sell such as know not god," he explained, "nor know any of the prophets, and they are the Kafirs, they are like the cattle." If the governor did not permit them to sell slaves, they would "perish through poverty."[73]

With Thompson gone, rumor abounded that neighboring chiefs were planning Sierra Leone's destruction as the only means to revive the slave trade. Dawes urged Columbine to strengthen Freetown's defenses and convinced him to keep the *Crocodile* anchored in the harbor throughout much of the rainy season as a deterrent.[74]

The slave trade, in fact, was reviving strongly. "The slave trade is now in the hands of the Americans," a Boston merchant wrote to a business associate in October 1810. "The prohibition of the slave trade by England has encreas'd very much our exports to Africa." British traders no longer had an incentive to send goods to Africa to exchange for slaves. Not only were the Americans taking advantage of legitimate commerce, they were filling the vacuum created by British withdrawal from the slave trade.[75]

President James Madison was abashed. "It appears," he advised Congress on December 5, "that American citizens are instrumental in carrying on a traffic in enslaved Africans, equally in violation of the laws of humanity, and in defiance of those of their own country." He urged Congress to devise "further means of suppressing the evil."[76] Meanwhile, the secretary of the navy was writing to officials in Charleston to express "great concern" over South Carolina's involvement in the illegal importation of slaves.[77]

At least three American-owned slavers, cleared from Charleston and flying Spanish colors, were captured by British warships and condemned in Freetown during 1810. A fourth, the brig *Amelia*, left Charleston in May 1810 for Cabenda (the present-day Angolan province of Cabinda) and was captured the following May off Cape Mount with Portuguese papers. Its eighty-five slaves were freed in Sierra Leone.[78]

In London Zachary Macaulay kept government officials and the abolitionist lobby informed of the slave trade's resilience. He estimated that at least seventy thousand slaves were being stolen annually from Africa between Cape Palmas and southern Angola. He listed fourteen slavers recently condemned, including those from Charleston.

Typical was the schooner *Doris*, which had been condemned in March 1810. It was owned, Macaulay reported, by a Charleston merchant "who conveyed her and her cargo, by a pretended sale, to a Spaniard residing at Amelia Island [in Spanish-controlled East Florida]; the Supercargo and the Crew, who were Americans, remaining the same as before the sale." Macaulay also mentioned that a British warship had chased into Havana a vessel belonging to William Broadfoot of Charleston carrying more than four hundred slaves.[79]

There was no pretending, in London or Washington, that the slave trade was not still in full vigor. While the United States was content to pass unenforceable laws, the British determined to go beyond pontifical gestures. In 1811 the reformer Henry Brougham, who looked to Macaulay for support, pushed through Parliament the Slave Felony Act, which applied to anyone trading in slaves on British-controlled territory.[80] But even the most knowledgeable British officials continued to underestimate the trade's staying power. In August Dawes, by then the sole surviving West Africa commissioner, recommended that the government mount a one-year naval blockade to suffocate the slave trade along the entire coast. "The Trade," Dawes predicted, "might receive a Blow . . . from which it would hardly recover."[81]

Columbine had approached the slave trade with similar simplicity: selling one's people was economically counterproductive. He asked Kizell to convey this obvious truth to the Sherbro chiefs and their people.

"You must be sensible that the Slave Trade cannot be carried on much longer," he wrote to the chiefs in August 1810. Only "cultivation of your land" would enable them to "rise above the poverty which renders you so dependent on Europe. . . . If the inhabitants of Europe had sold each other . . . do you suppose that we should have the ships and fleets, and armies, and riches, as we now have?"

Kizell's mission had two related objectives. He was to visit all parts of the Sherbro and urge the chiefs to block the selling of their people to slave traders. But he also was to propose an agricultural initiative, to be managed by Kizell, which would produce rice, coffee, palm oil, and other marketable goods. Columbine asked the chiefs to "allow my friend Mr. Kizell to have a sufficient portion of ground, or territory, for him to build a town, and to point out to you the proper mode of rearing those articles for trade, which will supply you with all European commodities. . . . I entreat you to forward his views as much as possible, and to join him in a noble endeavour to make yourselves and your children great, and your country happy."

Columbine's explicit reference to "his" views, meaning Kizell's, suggests that it was the latter who conceived the agricultural scheme, which they would have discussed in some detail. Columbine seemed satisfied that it might work and that Kizell was capable of implementing it. In his letter Columbine promised to furnish the necessary tools. He also pledged to send no Europeans. Whether at Kizell's insistence or to minimize costs, this was to be an African initiative.

Kizell was the linchpin. "You cannot have the least reason to be jealous of him," Columbine assured the chiefs. "He is one of yourselves; and he has the welfare of you and his country very earnestly at heart." Disclaiming any "personal advantage . . . from your taking my advice," Columbine left "the transaction entirely to yourselves." But given the whispered threats to the colony, he thought it prudent to observe in his final line that Kizell was "under my protection."[82]

Kizell had been living and trading somewhere on the Bagru River, in the northern reaches of the Sherbro. He had relearned the southern Bullom vernacular common in the Sherbro—similar to what he had spoken as a boy; he would have been acculturated, to the extent possible, for a stranger; and he probably had been initiated into Poro. Kizell was well-known throughout the Sherbro, Boom, and Kittam regions. He also was the bête noire of the eight or nine English slave traders based on the coast.

"I have got into the Sherbro," Kizell advised Columbine on September 30. He had gone first to William Cleveland Jr. on York Island, "dashed" him rum and tobacco, and showed him the governor's letter. Cleveland was impressed. "He said there never was a man that ever came to this country who spoke so well for the welfare of the people, and the happiness of the country, as you do; and that this was his wish for these many years past."

Kizell went next to Chief Sumano and read Columbine's letter to him and his people. "The young people were thankful for the word they heard," Kizell reported, "but there were some that did not like it. I then asked them, 'From the time your fathers began to sell slaves to this day, what have you got by it? Can any of you shew me how much money you have; how much gold; how many slaves, and vessels, and cattle; how many people you have?' They said, none. Then I turned to their king; I asked him in what was he better than his people? He said he was the poorest: he said he only talked palavers when any one brought them to him to talk. . . . I then told him, 'Our king wants to make you rich. . . .' He said that my king talked right; he wanted the country to be free."

As Cleveland had promised, Chief Sumano agreed to provide Kizell with land, but said "he cannot do any thing before he sees all the rest of the kings." Kizell of course understood the elaborate protocol required to obtain consensual support of all the region's traditional leaders. He now went to the sacred place of Yonie, on Sherbro Island.

"I sent for old King Sherbro's son, who is my friend," Kizell explained to Columbine in his long letter.

> I shewed him the things you had sent for the king: he was glad. I then shewed the letter to him: he said it was right. He told me to go with him into the town. We went. He called for him that stands as king, and all the people; and then he told me to read the letter to them. They said to me, "That book you bring is good."
>
> I then asked them if they never heard that there was an agreement between the King of England and King Sherbro? They said, "Yes, it was as I said: they had the cane that was given to King Sherbro, at that time, now in their hands.

The old people had told them that the King of England was to take care of them; and they were not to be made slaves; but he had forgot them."[83]

"To these words I could not give them an answer," a diplomatic Kizell told Columbine. "Not that I did not know how to answer it, but I thought . . . I might not answer it as you might wish." Notwithstanding the venerable "agreement," Kizell knew that the British government had disavowed Thompson's unauthorized treaty two years earlier and was not eager to extend sovereignty beyond the colony. "So I told them they had better send a man to you themselves."

By now some of the slave traders had learned of Kizell's presence and purpose. Because the river current would delay his progress up the Kittam to the east, he decided to head north to Bagru, traveling by night, "before my enemies should know where I was going. . . . When I got to Bagaroo, I sent to all the headmen to come to see me, as I had a letter from the Governor to them." Kizell waited eight days before the king appeared with some of his chiefs. He recited Columbine's message, which they acknowledged as the "truth and good," but demurred answering in the absence of some of the chiefs.

Kizell lectured them on the slave trade: "I told them that the blood of their people cried out against them, and that God had heard it. They had killed the poor of the land; the people that should work the land; and had sold them to fill their bellies. All their people were gone or going to other countries. They allowed the Slave Trade to stop their ears, and blind their eyes: for a little rum and tobacco they allowed their people to be carried off, and said nothing."

Kizell did not spare the chiefs and the big men. "I told them of their bad ways towards their wives. . . . when they get a little old, they . . . accuse [them] of being witches, so as to get rid of them to make room for young women: of these, some chiefs had thirty, some twenty, some ten. . . . Then they called themselves great men. And if any of the young men were caught with their wives, he must be sold; and if any of his family complained, all of them were likely to be sold too. They all knew this to be the truth. . . . As I spoke, they all hung down their heads. They said, 'All the letter says is truth: all you say is the truth; we can say nothing against it.'"

The Bagru people also remembered that the kings of England and Sherbro had been friends "in the old time. . . . But the King of England had thrown them away, and has sent his ships to buy them, although the agreement was, that they were not to be sold, as they were his people." Kizell advised them "to send a man to the Governor, and he would give them an answer."

Everywhere he went in the Sherbro, Kizell found a readiness to provide land on which to demonstrate the region's agricultural bounty. But in every case they would have to await the collective endorsement of King Sherbro and his senior chiefs. In the Banga River, however, the people implored Kizell to settle with them. The area had suffered badly during the Sherbro war. Now "God had sent me to them," Kizell wrote. "They would not let me go, but they would give me land to live upon." First, of course, they must send for "their father"—the chief—who had gone to the Plantains to attend the funeral of Stephen Caulker.

While he tarried in the Banga, awaiting the chief's return, Kizell went for a walk in the bush and was astounded by the number of wild coffee trees growing near the town. "Some places were entirely covered by them," he reported enthusiastically. "I pulled up three plants, and carried them to the town: I asked what it was. They said it was all over their country. I then told them it was coffee. . . . I told them if they would get a house full of it, I would buy it of them." Others came from the "upper country" and told Kizell they used the plant to fence their plantations. It grew everywhere, they said.

"I was glad to find there was another trade which might be put in the room of the Slave Trade," Kizell exulted, "and which might not lie in the hands of the white traders and the chiefs. The coffee trade is fit for women and boys, so that the poor women and the young people may get money as well as the chiefs; for at present they and the white slave traders keep the country under, because *they* can get goods, and the rest cannot. I have heard them [the traders] say that the natives are *their* money."

Kizell bemoaned the lack of genuine leadership. "There was no man to be found among them who had the welfare of this country and people at heart. . . . It will pro-duce . . . coffee, which is the natural plant of Africa. Her people are carried off to raise coffee to supply the markets of Europe, when they might as well get it from Africa, if the people were but directed what to do."

God, Kizell believed, was stepping forward with "his over-ruling power; he does all things in their season; and this is the time he has appointed in which to rouse the great men of England, and to put it in their hearts to consider the human race. . . . These men of sin"—the white and Euro-African slave traders—"wish to keep the black peo-ple in slavery, and their minds in darkness, so that they would enjoy neither the good of this world, nor the happiness of the world to come."[84]

Although the chiefs, in his view, were complicit in sustaining the slave trade, Kizell regarded them as virtual hostages to a system that had long dominated coastal societies. For the Euro-Africans, however, he reserved real hatred. These were men free to choose the path they trod. The governor needed to know this.

"There is a race of people in this district," Kizell wrote at length in a separate let-ter in December, "called the Mulattoes, that are a great plague to it. They think them-selves better than either the whites or blacks; and although they come from both, they do all they can to injure both. They will address [a] European with fair words, tell him they are the children of white men; they cannot treat their fathers ill; they will procure slaves for him; they know the price."

As a trader himself, Kizell understood how the Euro-Africans controlled the mid-dle ground between the people and the white slave dealers. If the European trader "refuses to give them his goods in advance to trade with," Kizell explained, "they will send round to all the people, requiring them not to trade with him; or if they do, to ask a particular price; and if he will not give that price, then to stop his fire and water, meaning to refuse him all supplies of every kind.

"If he consents to give them goods, they will demand 140 bars for a slave; and when they go to the blacks to make their purchases, they will give them only, perhaps, 40 bars for a slave: and even with this profit, if they receive goods for eight slaves, for instance, they will pay to their employer perhaps only four of them, and will amuse him with saying, that the remaining goods have been sent up the country for slaves which have not yet come down. . . . The truth is, that they have made their full purchase of slaves, but have sold them to some other European, from whom they have received goods in return."

The Euro-Africans returned Kizell's dislike in kind. "They are fond of a man who is newly-arrived in the country," Kizell continued, "because they can take him in; but a man like me, who knows their ways, they call a bad man; and if a stranger should arrive, who will not trust them, they say it is owing to me; I must have sent a letter to them."

Kizell related a story to illustrate what he regarded as the Euro-African's innate evil. "I cannot tell what these people are made of," he began. "I have seen them take their wives and sell them, even when they have had children in their arms, and these children are their own. They will take the child away and sell the wife, when they are in want of money . . . and they think nothing of it. . . . They will take no care of a sick person; not even of their own children; and should they die, they will say it was the family of one of their wives that killed them, and will sell all that family. In short, they are not bound by any ties of nature."[85]

Nor were the white slave traders. One of the worst was an Englishman named Crundell, who had helped incite the Gallinas war a few years earlier. If Kizell was despised and feared by any man, of any race, in the Sherbro, it was Crundell. In Kizell's eyes Crundell's only redeeming aspect may have been that he was not a mulatto. He sketched Crundell's character for Columbine in a story both poignant and cruel:

[Crundell] had a woman slave who had a child in her arms. The slave captains would not give so much for her as they would for a young [childless] woman. He ordered his boys to take the child and throw it into the sea. They took the child. . . . As they were going to fulfil their orders, they met with an old woman, who, learning that they were about to kill the child, stopped them, and went to Crundell, and begged him to give her the child. . . . He told her the child was too young; she could do it no good, and it would certainly die. She said she would give it to her people to suckle, and if it died she would bury it, and begged him not to kill it; it was not good for him to kill the child; it was bad.

Crundell finally relented and gave her the child. "She carried it home," Kizell said, "and gave it to her people; it is now as fine a child as any one would wish to see." But the mother's fate was sealed. As soon as her milk dried up, Crundell sold her.[86]

Kizell warned Columbine that mere persuasion and offers of development assistance would not suffice. Stopping the slave trade "must be done partly by force."

Evicting the European slave traders, most of them English, would be a start. In a short letter to Columbine in mid-November, Kizell urged the governor "to send the European Slave Traders out of this country, for they are a great hurt. They tell the people we are going to starve them; they speak very much against you to the people."

Kizell was in an awkward position. Although he carried the governor's letter, he was still an African. "I am the worst man you could get . . . to send to [the people]," he admitted candidly. "Even some of our own people, who come into this country, say, that I am a deceiver. . . . I have trouble enough; but I do not mind . . . if my country is freed from slavery. I will thank you to let Mr. Crundell be sent for . . . that I may have to do only with the natives, and not with both [whites and blacks]."[87]

English and other European slave traders had never had much to fear from British authorities in the colony. They had absolutely nothing to fear from Columbine, who was in failing health and anxious to be recalled. Although he clearly hoped that Kizell might wean some of the chiefs from the slave trade, Columbine was under orders to reduce costs. He had no mandate to exert British authority in the Sherbro—no matter what the old people fondly remembered from a long-ago generation.

Nor did he have jurisdiction over Crundell and other British subjects engaged in the slave trade. Had he lived and remained governor at Sierra Leone, Columbine by mid-1811 would have had legal authority to move against Crundell. But like governors who came before and after, he was content to decry slavery and the slave trade without using force, sanctioned or otherwise, to root out European slave traders from African soil.[88] Interdicting the slave trade was left by default to the navy.

Kizell cut short his November 15 note to Columbine. He had discovered a slave ship about to leave the coast. "The brig at Shebar is ready for sea," he reported. "She has all her slaves on board: if you do send to take her, let the boat go in the night; for if they see it coming, they will put all the slaves on shore before the boat can get up to her."[89]

His fear was borne out. The brig evidently was seized—emptied of its cargo—taken to Freetown, and then released. When Kizell returned to Shebar in January 1811, the brig had reappeared. "The slaves they were seizing in such a violent manner were for her," Kizell appealed to Columbine.[90] No boat came this time.

In the Slaver's Lair

The sea bar—or Shebar strait—was important to the peoples of the Sherbro and its tributaries. It afforded access to the sea while protecting them from its violent temper. For generations the people had honored Kasillah, a powerful spirit who inhabits the Shebar. Kasillah safeguarded them from the sea and from evil spirits that occasionally wandered down from the upper Boom and Kittam rivers.[91]

The strait also protected the slave trade. The slaver that Kizell had spied could load (or unload) its slaves inside the Shebar, beyond reach of the deeper-keeled British warships. The anchorage was normally tranquil, and slaves could be taken on board easily. European slave traders paid neither heed nor homage to Kasillah. The people, however, widely believed that Kasillah, like most spirits, was white and may have inferred that he was in league with the white men who traded in slaves.

Peter L. Tucker suggests in his family history that this would have been a logical assumption. Before he died in the 1770s, Henry Tucker "had become a legend. . . . In the Sherbro country, fabulous wealth in the hands of a native man was attributed to some mysterious association with a spirit of the sea who always brought him money. There was, therefore, widespread belief among the natives of Shebar that Henry was the son of Kasillah. People pointed to his frequent visits to ships at the sea bar . . . and his close friendship with the white men as proof." They later believed that Henry and his brother, when they died, had "joined Kasillah in his watery spirit world."[92]

As a boy, living fifty or sixty miles to the east, Kizell would probably have heard of the Tuckers. One day he would be known to the Tuckers—to Henry's son James, in particular. He and James became adversaries in the ongoing struggle over the slave trade.

By the time Kizell settled in the Sherbro, at the turn of the nineteenth century, the British-educated James had consolidated political hegemony over the region, which his late father and uncle had administered loosely for trading purposes. As the young chief of the Bullom, James respected the traditional autonomy of the headmen, elders who usually were senior officials of the local Poro. Eventually he began exerting more central authority, Peter L. Tucker writes, "as their overlord and political head of all the Poro societies in his territory. He maintained peace in the region and commercial traffic flowed smoothly down the rivers to the Shebar and other Sherbro ports."

By the time Kizell was broadcasting Columbine's appeal to the entire Sherbro, James had become "a powerful and highly respected warrior-king, generous and tolerant, but firmly in control," Tucker writes. To his people and the European traders alike, he was now known as James "the Great."[93] To Kizell, however, he and his extended family were "the greatest slave traders in Sherbro."[94]

The family's involvement in the slave trade dated to the 1750s, when Henry sold a few slaves to his friend John Newton. According to Peter L. Tucker, the slaves sold "consisted almost entirely of persons captured in war who had not been ransomed, or persons convicted of murder, witchcraft, theft or adultery." There were also "debtors and persons who could not pay the fines imposed on them by the [traditional] courts." Otherwise it was "a serious offence to sell a free man into this type of slavery."[95]

Tucker describes a "less obnoxious form of slavery"—domestic servitude—"which arose in the normal course of business or political settlements between . . . powerful Chiefs." As he explains, "a man would give his son or relative as security for a loan or guarantee of an agreement or pledge. It . . . had its own rules. Domestic slaves could not be sold into foreign slavery . . . except for a serious offence for which a free man might be . . . punished. This very rarely happened."

For their part, he maintains, the Tuckers were "known for treating their domestic slaves as . . . members of their family. . . . Some of them were from the families of their friends or business customers. Such slaves were given land of their own and encouraged to cultivate . . . them for themselves and their families. . . . Some were able to acquire enough wealth to buy their freedom or live as free men."[96]

In Kizell's telling, however, life in James Tucker's dominions was overshadowed by the slave trade. It pervaded people's existence, regardless of their status. In the following account of his visit to Shebar and vicinity in September 1810, Kizell provided Columbine with an African's-eye view of the slave trade's impact on the people and their communities.

Several Tucker family members—but apparently not James—had come to Shebar to meet Kizell and to receive the governor's message. Kizell distributed the obligatory rum and tobacco, then read the letter to the large gathering. They were not pleased.

"If you come to stop the Slave Trade, what shall we do for a living?" they asked. "You and your people, as the Governor says to you, must all work, as other people do," Kizell told them. "They must not look for any more slave ships here."

According to Kizell, the Tuckers replied "It was hard, but if it was so, they would settle a price on their camwood and rice, and on all that they had."

It was at the next gathering, where about one hundred people and their chief were waiting, that Kizell first encountered open hostility. When he arrived, "the first word was, 'Are *you* come? It is you that have got all the slave vessels taken out of our river. You are come to make war on us.' . . . There was a young man with the king, who said, 'Kizell says he is sent to you: why will you not wait till you hear what he has to say?' The king said this was right. I gave the Governor's letter to him: he had a white man that could read it to him." The king did not trust Kizell, as a black man, to convey the governor's words honestly and accurately.

When the European came, it was Crundell. He looked at the letter "and immediately cursed and swore, and raved: he told the king and his people that the Governor was a nuisance: 'He is like Buonaparte: he wants to take the country from you. As for Kizell, he is the worst man the Governor could pick out at Sierra Leone to send to you. Kizell is a troublesome, undermining man. The people of Sierra Leone want to take the country, as they have taken my goods from me.'" Kizell assumed Crundell was alluding to slave ships that had been confiscated.

Rising from his stool, Kizell asked a mulatto named Taylor "to bear witness to all that Crundell had said, as he would, sooner or later, be called to account for it. I told him I knew *he* [Crundell] did not want the Slave Trade to stop: he wished to kill the people's children and to drink their blood."

Crundell was unrepentant. God had ordered the people to sell slaves. "If God did not like it, why did he not put a stop to it?" Kizell responded that "God had ordered him not to swear: why did he not obey him in this too?" Taylor intervened and told Crundell "that what he had said against the Governor was not right: the Governor loved the people, and did not like they should continue in slavery: the letter he had sent was a friendly letter: if Kizell had not been a trusty man, the Governor would not have sent him; 'Yet you, Crundell, tell the people not to hear him.'"

Crundell began arguing vehemently that the Sherbro fell under the Europeans at Bance Island, not the government at Sierra Leone or even the English king. Crundell claimed that he "belonged to that place, and the people must hearken to Bance Island." Kizell was dismissive. "You say the people must hearken to Bance Island, and that you are one of them: I tell you Bance Island is now of no more consequence than the dirt under my feet."

The palaver was degenerating. Crundell "and the people about him got into a great rage," Kizell reported. "At one time they were so violent, I thought they would have beat me. They had got plenty of rum, and had all been drinking freely before I came to them. The same young man who had spoken . . . to the king now rose, and said to the king and the people, 'Some years ago, when we were in trouble, was it not John Kizell who was sent from Sierra Leone to make peace for us? We were then all glad to see him: then we all called him a good man. Is this not the same Kizell whom the Government sent to us before? Yet now you call him a bad man; and why? Where was Crundell at that time? Was he not at the Gallinas buying and selling slaves? He that troubles Kizell must first beat me.'"

"The speech turned things in my favour," Kizell continued in his account to Columbine, "and Crundell, finding he could do no more, went away. Then Taylor took the letter, and read it to the king and all his people; they were glad. [The king] said he did not think it had been such a letter. . . . The white people had told him that we were come to take his country from him." He promised to go see the governor and obtain his written assurance "that he might no longer be troubled with such reports."

Taylor and the young man had restored calm. "Why do you listen to foolish people?" the latter scolded the king. "If your people had done any harm to John Kizell . . . your name . . . would have gone for ever: then indeed you would have had need to be afraid."

The king called Kizell to sit next to him. "He said he would give me land: he said he was sorry he had talked to me as he had, but it was because they had told him so many things against me, and that I had come to make war." He then ordered two men to accompany Kizell as he continued his mission—up the Boom River to James Tucker's town—"so that when the people saw them, they might not be afraid; for they also had heard that I was come to make war on them."

Kizell and his two companions, including an old friend, spent two days warping upriver until they came within sight of a town. The women and children began running into the bush. "I sent my friend to them," Kizell recalled, "and told them not to run, for I brought good news to them." When they reached the town, Kizell presented the chief and village elders with rum and tobacco. Then he read them the governor's letter. "They said they were glad, and that you did right to send that letter; for the people did nothing but catch people's children and sell them."

Word of Kizell's approach had reached James Tucker at his home several miles farther upstream. He sent for Kizell to join him, aware that Kizell was bringing one of

Tucker's relations. He was an older man who had been liberated from a slave ship in Freetown. Crundell had not been idle, however, and had warned Tucker that Kizell "was come to bring war on them." But Tucker, Kizell reported, "said he did not believe it; because if the Governor meant to bring war on them, he would not release their people from slavery and send them home." Crundell "had done all he could to poison the people's minds against me" and had failed.[97]

In his communications to Columbine, Kizell left no doubt that it was the slave trade that had poisoned people's minds and the entire Sherbro country. Those engaged in the trade, Kizell said, "had made the country so bad, that a man was afraid of his own friends." What he saw in Shebar and Kittam in December 1810 bore witness.

Slave traders at Shebar were reloading the brig that had been released in Freetown, Kizell wrote Columbine on January 30, 1811. Several Kru were ferrying slaves to the ship. A coastal people who were prized as sailors and canoe men, they never sold fellow Kru into slavery, only others.

A young man at Shebar had failed to deliver slaves as promised to the traders. "When the traders saw the slaves were not procured," Kizell wrote, "they said they would seize his wives. . . . This was overheard, and the women and children escaped into the bush. In the evening, at dusk, the women ventured out. As they were going towards the town, they saw on the road two or three Kroomen. One of the young women, who was terrified at seeing them, ran back with such force that, meeting another woman with a bundle of wood on her head, she had not time to stop herself. . . . A splinter pierced one of her eyes about an inch."

Kizell heard the woman cry out. She was in agony when he went to investigate. "I went to the [slave] traders and . . . talked very sharp to them. I told them that they made the Kroomen their dogs, to seize people. They said I was a dog too, for the Governor sent me to tell him all I saw; but that I should never be able to stop the Slave Trade. I told them, if the Governor would but give me a few men, I would soon find men enough to help me."[98]

Wherever Kizell went the slave trade had become a way of life. The people had internalized it as something no less real and unavoidable as the spirits with whom they shared their world. Kizell knew this, but he may have believed that the trade's moment of truth was at hand. The British had abolished it and were about to make people such as Crundell outlaws. The navy was seizing slavers and liberating hundreds of captives. Columbine's sending him on this mission indicated that the government might be preparing even bolder action. Kizell approached his task with the courage born of knowing that the slave trade not only was evil, it was on its last legs.

No one had ever come among the people to say what Kizell was saying, to challenge and embarrass the chiefs, or to threaten the white slave traders in their petty fiefdoms. Although Kizell had been deputized by Columbine, he exuded a unique moral authority of his own. For a black man—especially one who had been a slave—to shame one traditional leader after another was unprecedented.

In retrospect Kizell was tilting at windmills. At the time, however, he probably saw this as a first step in a larger plan to disrupt the slave trade in the Sherbro. Columbine had promised to support agricultural schemes as an alternative to selling people. It is conceivable that Kizell believed the governor would "give [him] a few men" to choke the trade at its source. Whatever support Kizell may have anticipated, he displayed remarkable faith in his cause, as well as the physical and moral steel to stand alone before people whom he was calling out as sinners.

Reactions were mixed. Some of the people condemned him; others applauded. As an African, however, Kizell knew they would all remain essentially passive and fatalistic in the absence of concrete evidence that he and the forces he might represent would materially alter their circumstances. His vivid accounts of his palavers have to be read in that context. Much was said, often with great emotion; the wrongs of the slave trade were conceded, even by some directly responsible. In the end, however, Kizell was a lonely voice crying out against something the people had known for generations and expected to live with indefinitely.

The enduring nature of the slave trade stalked Kizell as he "quitted" Shebar and went into Kittam to confront Queen Messe. "I gave her the articles you sent for her," Kizell reported to Columbine. "All the old women and young people came to hear what I had to say. I then shewed your letter to her. She said the present sent was not enough. I interrupted her, and said the Governor did not send me to blind her eyes, but to open them; and to persuade her no longer to sell her people."

The crowd was delighted. "All the young people gave a shout," Kizell recalled, "and the women clapped their hands for joy." The queen was visibly displeased but said nothing. Kizell pressed on. "I told her it was she who had sold all her people, and that we meant to put a stop to it in the country if we could. All the young people shouted again, and said, 'the old people knew that *they* could not be sold, but that it was the young people who must be sold.'"

Queen Messe asked Kizell, "if you come to stop the Slave Trade," could they sell their rice, goats, wood, "and all other things" for a good price, "as in the old time?" Kizell replied that he had not been sent to negotiate prices. "Every man knew the price of his goods," Kizell told her. "But as for you, you have changed the old price of your goods for that of your sons and daughters. . . . The young people said that was the truth."

An old man rose to speak. "He said the letter was good, and they must give an answer. They then appointed a day for me to come. On that day I went to meet them, but not one was to be seen, except three old men who were sick! I was much displeased, and told them to tell Messe that, as she and her people thought the Governor not worthy of an answer to his letter, or of attention to his messenger, I would tell him of it: they had given us great affront."

This indeed breached local etiquette, as Kizell's anger made manifest. At his next stop, in Fad, he complained "how he had been used" by the queen and her people.

The people of Fad expressed sympathy. "They said that they would help me"—if, that is, "I should get men from the Governor"—to stop the slave trade. "All the poor and the young people said they would join me in this. I told the young men if the old people would join them, and do as they propose, I would place myself at their head." If the governor was willing to assist, "then we should fight for liberty and freedom against all who may stand up for the Slave Trade."

If Kizell was rallied by the young people in Fad, he was quickly reminded that he was effectively powerless to stop the slave trade singlehandedly. From Fad he had come on the second day of the new year to a place called Cotton. "There was a man there," Kizell wrote, "who brought two other men with him, strangers, who came from a short distance." The two strangers came to sell plantains, unaware that they were to be sold themselves by their traveling companion. Kizell described what ensued:

> In the evening the two men were quietly sitting down, when all the people rose upon them and tied them like pigs, hand and foot, very fast. I heard the cry, and went to see what was the matter. I asked what they tied the men for? They told me they were witches. One of the two men on the ground told me it was false; that the chief of this town had wished to sell his children; and because he would not consent to it, he had framed this charge against him. He said he had fourteen children. I then asked if it was so? They said, yes, he has fourteen children. I told them what the man said was truth, and why did they act so? I prevailed on them to loose the ropes, and ease their hands.

Kizell was unable to secure their release, however. Instead, that night "they were carried to James Tucker's. . . . I went there and found . . . seventeen in irons."

The European slave traders were beginning to have some success. At Tarbumpe Kizell discovered "the minds of the people . . . were poisoned against me" by Crundell and other slave traders in the area. The king was willing to receive Kizell, "but he was afraid: the old men would have nothing to do with me or the letter. I told them, 'I will let the Governor know what you are doing.' Some of them said, 'You come to stop us from selling people; what are we to do?'"[99] It was a familiar refrain, that slavery was in the natural order of things. He had heard it as a boy; he had heard it in America; he heard it to his last days.

King Sherbro framed the futility of Kizell's mission as politely as he could. All the chiefs deferred to the king on the matter of land, as Kizell had known they would. Nor would he have been surprised by the king's own prevarication; he was prepared to deal directly with the governor, or another white official, but not with a black commoner, even one of Kizell's stature.

"The situation of the country is so," the king wrote to Columbine in early 1811, "that it is not in my power to give you a full answer at the present." There were many reasons, "with respect to the late war, which our deceased friend Mr. Ludlam and Mr. Kizell interceded into." They had succeeded in making a truce, "which has been standing for this five or six years." The king had grown impatient, however, "waiting for Mr. Ludlam to come and assemble both parties"—the Caulkers and Clevelands— "to make a general and standing peace . . . to . . . abate all grievances, and . . . to nom- inate and crown the king of Sherbro."

There were many other matters to resolve, "too tedius to mention." The governor needed to come, "or send a white gentleman along with Mr. Kizell, that will be capa- ble of acting as yourself; far from saying Mr. Kizell is not capable of doing all himself, but it is my request. Then I would take infinite pleasure in giving you a full answer to yours by Mr. Kizell."[100] The king said nothing of the slave trade.

"THE LAND OF BLACK MEN"

"If we are as vile and degraded as they represent us, and they wish the Africans to be rendered virtuous, enlightened and happy people, they should not think of sending us among them, lest we should make them worse instead of better."

Reverend Peter Williams Jr.,
addressing blacks in New York City, July 4, 1830

On the morning of March 1, 1811, a single-decked, two-masted brig flying the American flag dropped anchor in Freetown's harbor.[1] The arrival of any ship was a notable event in the colony's languid day-to-day existence. The arrival of the *Traveller* was something more, for she was captained by a black man.

"As I am of the African race"

On the same day that John Kizell was trying to save a father of fourteen from enslavement, Paul Cuffe was sailing from Philadelphia to fulfill an abiding desire to visit Africa and to serve its people. "As I am of the African race," he had written two white acquaintances in 1809, "I feel myself interested for them, and, if I am favored with a talent, I think I am willing that they should be benefited thereby."[2]

Born on a tiny island off Martha's Vineyard in 1759, of a Gay Head Wampanoag mother and an emancipated Gold Coast father, Cuffe was possibly the wealthiest American of color.[3] He farmed along the Westport River, near New Bedford. His three ships had traded as far as the Baltic and the Caribbean. Prominent whites from Boston to Delaware considered him a friend and business associate. His Quaker neighbors had accepted him into their meeting.

Cuffe had come to believe that his purpose in life was to redeem Africa. He had shared his thoughts with leading Quakers. They in turn had alerted Friends in England of his interest in opening legitimate trade with Africa. As Cuffe gave increasingly serious attention to his plan, the founders of the African Institution began to receive intriguing reports from America of a remarkable black ship captain whose preoccupation dovetailed with theirs.

Cuffe's interest in Africa had coincided with sharpening Quaker concerns with slavery. So had his self-identity. For most of his life, he had "vacillated between his

Negro and his Indian origins," Sheldon Harris writes in a 1972 biography of Cuffe. His conversion to the Quaker faith in 1808 was a turning point. In the context of Quakers' commitment to service and their focus on abolition, Cuffe knew what he must do.

"I am what I am," he wrote that September to James Pemberton, explaining his newfound devotion "for my brethren the African race."[4] As a prime mover in Pennsylvania's abolitionist circles, Pemberton had written earlier to the African Institution of Cuffe's interest. Pemberton was dead by the time Zachary Macaulay responded the following August that Cuffe would find excellent prospects in Sierra Leone once trade sanctions were lifted.[5]

Macaulay was referring to the Non-Intercourse Act, passed by Congress in May 1809. The act banned American trade with British and French ports as long as both nations preyed on Yankee shipping. Some American captains nonetheless rushed to trade in West Africa but avoided touching Freetown or other British ports. Cuffe refused to take the risk, knowing that he would need to trade directly at Sierra Leone.

Cuffe and other American businessmen monitored political winds at home and abroad, hoping for a clear indication that they could again trade openly with one or both nations. In the fall of 1810, President Madison chose to trust Napoleon's apparent decision to allow American commerce with British ports. Madison announced on November 2 that the United States would reimpose nonintercourse with Britain in ninety days if it did not also drop its restrictions against neutral shipping.[6]

Cuffe by now had made up his mind to go. William Allen, a prominent London philanthropist, had been urging him, on behalf of the African Institution, to open trade with Sierra Leone. He thus had this influential body's blessing. In September he asked the Westport Friends, as he was obliged to do under Quaker discipline, to endorse his plan. They too gave their blessing. Dr. Benjamin Rush, a signer of the Declaration of Independence, promised support in the name of the Pennsylvania abolitionists.[7]

Madison's pronouncement complicated his decision, however. He risked having his ship and cargo seized upon return if Britain did not abandon its sanctions. New England merchants were wary. At first they doubted that the government would detain ships that had embarked during the grace period, but by the time Cuffe sailed for Philadelphia in early December, they were less certain. "No one thinks of adventuring," said Boston merchant Henry Lee, "except some small vessels for the Coast of Africa."[8]

The improbable appearance in Freetown of one of these small vessels came at a difficult time for Governor Columbine. He had been chronically ill, probably with malaria and dysentery, since arriving the previous year. He had been asking for several months without response to be relieved because of his health. While Kizell had been carrying the governor's letter throughout the Sherbro, Columbine had spent several weeks at sea "as the only means of saving my life."[9] He had returned to the colony to deal with unpleasant administrative tasks. Theft had been increasing, he reported in late January, and he had been forced to execute a notorious criminal.[10] He also had to cope with the influx of recaptives.

Domestic slavery had resurfaced as an issue. Days before Cuffe's arrival, Columbine disclaimed any attempt by the government "to interfere with the ancient customs of Africa." He announced that domestic slaves "taking refuge in Sierra Leone will be given up when properly claimed." He was at Bance Island to explain to the British proprietors that the same policy applied there when he learned of Cuffe's presence.[11]

Columbine came down from Bance early the next morning and began negotiating the purchase of Cuffe's cargo of beef, flour, and bread. He was impressed with the American's business instincts. He was no "mere babe in the ways of the trading world."[12] As a paid subscriber to the African Institution, Columbine must have been impressed as well by its endorsement of Cuffe's plans. The governor invited the captain to dine on March 4. Cuffe wrote in his journal that "an extensive observation took place on the slave trade and the *unsuccessfulness* of the colony" (emphasis added).[13]

Cuffe was aware of the colony's checkered history and that his initiative threatened the commercial dominance of the European traders. They would try to sabotage him, but Columbine was supportive. The two mariners met frequently to consider the future of the colony and of Africa. When Cuffe raised the possibility of other African Americans settling in Sierra Leone, the governor applauded the idea.[14]

In their discussions of the slave trade, Columbine would have shared the essentials of Kizell's reports from the Sherbro. Although Cuffe's journal entries during his first weeks dwell largely on the off-loading and sale of his cargo, he was taking careful note of the slave trade. It was hard to ignore. Two captured slave ships were anchored in the harbor when he arrived. News arrived a few days later of Portuguese slave traders operating with impunity along the coast. On March 9 he took time from business to attend the trial and condemnation of a slaver.[15]

Kizell also had heard of Cuffe's arrival and came up from the Sherbro in early April. He brought Columbine a list of five English slave dealers in the Sherbro, including Crundell. There were two or three others in the Gallinas whose names he did not know.[16]

How Kizell and Cuffe actually met is unknown, but two days later Cuffe attended Sunday services at the Baptist meetinghouse—Kizell's church. That afternoon Cuffe and Kizell, along with a few other settlers, rowed out to the *Traveller*. After much discussion they drafted—in Cuffe's words—"a petition to Lay before the pepple for their apperbation."[17]

Cuffe already was preparing to sail for home. Columbine had been cordial and cooperative, but he had no instructions regarding official policy toward Cuffe's proposed commercial links with Sierra Leone. Cuffe saw no alternative but to depart for America. There had been no word about reimposition of nonintercourse. He could only hope that the British government would eventually endorse his plan.

The ailing Columbine also was planning to return to England. Kizell had briefed the governor on recent developments in the Sherbro. As one of the West African commissioners, Columbine would be recommending actions to the government. Kizell had provided ample evidence that more direct engagement was needed to suppress the slave trade, as well as the British subjects who were promoting it. Kizell may also have urged Columbine to negotiate with the Sherbro leadership for British sovereignty.

Cuffe's appearance and Columbine's imminent departure also were an opportunity to address the economic frustrations of the Nova Scotian and Maroon settlers. Cuffe's vision of African-driven commerce was tantalizing to Kizell and others who chafed under white domination of Sierra Leone's trade and business. Cuffe was looking for settlers such as Kizell to take responsibility for marketing his goods.[18]

The petition sketched aboard the *Traveller* probably was Kizell's initiative. He is the only settler Cuffe mentions by name in his journal entry—which asserts no claim of his own copyright—and Kizell appears first among the dozen signatories. A sympathetic Columbine was to carry their appeal to England.

Kizell and his fellow petitioners asked that "Encouragement . . . be given unto all our Breatheren who may Come from the British Colonies or from America and Become farmers in order to help us Cultivate the Land." This spoke to Kizell's focus on agricultural development during his recent travels throughout the Sherbro. Also envisioned was an alliance with "our foreign Breatheren who may have Vessels"— an obvious reference to Cuffe—"that Encouragement may be given to Establish Commerce in Sierra Leone." Finally the petition proposed introducing whaling to take advantage of Cuffe's experience in that critical industry.[19]

European traders responded to this direct challenge to their primacy only when they learned that Cuffe would be sailing for Britain, not America. The Privy Council had granted Cuffe a temporary license to trade between England and Sierra Leone. He also had been invited to meet members of the African Institution. One Freetown merchant immediately wrote Zachary Macaulay to beware Cuffe and anything he might say about conditions in the colony. Alexander Smith claimed that "he had never known a more mercenary or unprincipled man, except perhaps a slave trader."[20]

Cuffe, Kizell, and the colony's other black entrepreneurs now had reason to believe that Sierra Leone could achieve its long-delayed economic promise. The advent of a wealthy black American shipowner was galvanizing. He was proof that a person of color could possess the skills and integrity to succeed mightily in business, even in the treacherous waters of international commerce. He had the cachet and access to represent the settler business community in England in a way that no one else could. And he owned a vessel that could break white merchants' stranglehold on limited shipping capacity to and from the colony.

The European traders, including Smith, had treated Cuffe condescendingly at first. He was nothing more than a curiosity who would soon be gone back to America.

When it dawned that the Privy Council and the principals of the African Institution were giving Cuffe leeway to trade between the colony and England, they persisted in underestimating the black Yankee.

Smith hoped that his defamation of Cuffe's character would precede the captain in England, as it did. Macaulay showed the scurrilous letter to Allen, stressing that Smith was "a *most respectable* person." Allen, however, was suspicious. Smith had "showed every kindness . . . to Cuffe," he noted, "*till he* found him determined to come to *England*."[21]

Several weeks passed before Cuffe could depart. Curiously the pages of Cuffe's diary for this period have been excised. They would have recorded mundane matters, such as the off-loading from the *Traveller* of goods intended for America and their replacement with commodities for the English market. If Cuffe offered Kizell and other settlers space for their produce, there was little time to organize cargo. Cuffe mentions no settler shipments in the surviving portion of his diary, which covers his sojourn in England.

The missing pages might have revealed how Cuffe disposed of six valuable bales of India cloth, which Columbine had not allowed him to land due to British trade restrictions. The white merchants had been circumventing these by arranging to rendezvous with American ships outside the colony, buying forbidden goods, and smuggling them into Freetown at night. Columbine was aware of their subterfuge, and when one European asked permission to buy Cuffe's precious bales, the governor saw an opportunity to have the last laugh.

Henry Warren, writing two years later as president of the petitioners' newly formed Friendly Society, reported the episode to Allen with some relish: the governor had denied the British merchant's request and instead sent for Kizell. "Those fellows have done enough to put me out of temper with them," Warren quoted Columbine. "I would proceed against them but there is no one to swear to the goods." The governor then offered Kizell the chance to buy Cuffe's India cloth, as long as he sold the goods outside the colony.[22] The incident underscored Columbine's trust in Kizell.

Columbine had packed the settlers' petition with his papers as he prepared for the homeward voyage. He had promised Cuffe, Kizell, and the others that he would present it in Parliament. Columbine dutifully waited for authorization to leave, but it never came. Thundering storms heralded the approach of the rainy season when he finally sailed on May 11. The *Traveller* and Cuffe departed in his wake. Physically exhausted, and perhaps embittered by unresponsive superiors, Columbine died soon thereafter at sea.

During their final weeks in Freetown, Cuffe and Columbine continued to discuss the colony's prospects. The governor seemed hopeful that the slave trade was ebbing. More than one thousand men, women, and children had been rescued from slave ships in the past year and settled near Freetown. He was proud that he had improved the handling and welfare of the recaptives. He also believed that Africans now saw that "all white men are not their enemies." He was convinced that England was determined to end the slave trade. This, he believed, would encourage the people "to liberate themselves from this horrible thralldom."[23]

Cuffe may have spoken tentatively of moving his family, business, and shipping interests to Sierra Leone and of encouraging other African Americans to contribute their talents to the colony's development. Both men understood that expanding trade with the United States was conditional on resolving the continental war, which had compromised Anglo-American relations. But Columbine was impressed that Cuffe had secured official approval for his venture. This boded well, in spite of the political tensions. So did Cuffe's standing with the African Institution.

As a fellow seagoing man, Cuffe probably told Columbine that he planned to take Aaron Richards, one of the Nova Scotians, to England and to teach him navigational skills. Richards's seventy-eight-year-old father, Thomas, was a cooper who had signed the petition aboard the *Traveller*. Ten years earlier he had been among the loyal settlers wounded in the confrontation with Isaac Anderson and his ill-fated comrades.

Aaron was a shipwright and may have impressed Cuffe as a likely candidate to become the colony's first black ship captain.[24] To the European merchants, this too was a threat. If the younger Richards complemented his shipbuilding ability with navigational expertise, his next step might be to establish an independent shipping link with England. When Cuffe arrived in Liverpool on July 12, a press-gang plucked Richards—and only Richards—from his crew. No proof was ever found that Richards had been targeted at the instigation of white commercial interests. William Allen interceded at the admiralty and gained Richards's release, but he considered the incident as suspicious as Smith's poison-pen letter.[25]

Cuffe became the toast of Liverpool and London during the remainder of the summer. Two reformed slave dealers entertained him at dinner and "treated [him] politely."[26] Allen took him under his wing in London and introduced him to Thomas Clarkson, Macaulay, and other friends of the African cause. Allen was encouraged by Cuffe's opinion of Sierra Leone's fertility. "Clarkson and I are both of the mind," Allen wrote, "that the present opportunity for promoting the civilization of Africa, through the means of Paul Cuffee, should not be lost; he seems like a man made on purpose for the business."[27]

Macaulay also seemed reconciled to the disarming Cuffe, who dined at his London home in late August. Macaulay gave him letters for the new governor, Col. Charles Maxwell, and for Smith. Allen hoped this "will soften the latter." Allen meanwhile had met a New Bedford ship captain who had known Cuffe "from a boy" and considered him of unparalleled "integrity and honour in business."[28] He and his African Institution colleagues later probed the dealings of the colony's European business community. "The principle [*sic*] thing attended to by the white people of Sierra Leone," Allen concluded, ". . . has been getting money, and that in the shortest way. The mystery of poor Paul Cuffee's ill usage is now unraveled."[29]

Cuffe returned to Freetown on November 12 after eight weeks at sea to find tensions brewing. The governor was concerned that the colony's defenses were inadequate to withstand another rumored attack by neighboring African chiefs. Colonel Maxwell had demanded that male settlers between ages thirteen and sixty enlist in a militia. They would be subject to military discipline, including flogging, and in theory could be deployed outside the colony.

The Maroons and Nova Scotians united in protest. They were prepared to defend Sierra Leone but not to submit to army regulations—and certainly not to be whipped. Maxwell responded by mobilizing recaptives to suppress any settler "turbulence." He still insisted on enforcing his militia act.[30]

Matters came to a head on December 23, the same day that a schooner arrived from the Sherbro. It carried twenty-eight tons of camwood, which Kizell planned to send with Cuffe to America—possibly in payment for the India goods. "There was a meeting of the inhabitants called together today," Cuffe wrote in his journal, "to take the oath of allegiance to [the] Crown. . . . but . . . [they] refused signing. It was then told to them that they forfeited their houses and lots of land, but all this did not prevail on the men."[31]

In the meantime Cuffe had met with signers of the April petition to frame a constitution for what they would call the Friendly Society. According to Cuffe's notes on December 18, the group would "take every matter unto their care that appeared to be for the beneficial good of the universe." A more defined purpose awaited Kizell's arrival from the Sherbro on January 6.

Cuffe had brought a letter from William Allen, written in late August and addressed to Kizell. The society met that evening to hear Kizell read Allen's encouragement to promote the colony's economic development and civilization in Africa. The letter, which has been lost to history, was received, Cuffe recorded, with "love and unity."[32]

If Cuffe hoped that the Friendly Society could be a vehicle to foster legitimate commerce between Sierra Leone, England, and America, he soon had cause for concern. "There appears to be more debating than business done," he wrote following one meeting. "Many . . . are willing to lade[n] other men's shoulders with burdens, and they themselves to be excused. . . . But if we in Sierra Leone would rouse ourselves to more industry and sobriety we would . . . make better progress. They seem to be much agitated because the Governor will not permit foreigners to land tobacco and rum."[33]

Cuffe—alone, it appears—called on the governor the next day to discuss "the matter of improvement among the inhabitants . . . and on the propriety of [his obtaining] grants of land, and building a saw mill." He asked Maxwell what African Americans could expect in exchange for aiding Sierra Leone. Maxwell subsequently promised that "every protection and encouragement will be given to persons of industrious habits who will remove to the colony."[34]

After more than a year away, the Yankee merchant was anxious to return home. His plans to establish trade between African Americans and Africa had been well received in England and in the colony. In his journal he betrayed no concern about the political impasse bedeviling Anglo-American relations. He was preoccupied instead with collecting payments, particularly from Alexander Smith, for goods he had brought from England and with laying the groundwork for his next visit.

The Friendly Society was critical to his success, but the infant body was having teething problems. As Cuffe prepared the *Traveller* to sail, the society met again and agreed "unanimously" to a response to Allen's letter. Whereupon two members abruptly resigned.[35]

Allen ultimately received *two* letters on the society's behalf. One was written on February 4, 1812, by Warren, the society's president, and James Wise. They accepted Allen's paternal chiding of the settlers' shortcomings but assured him that they would gladly return to farming if Allen could direct "the master of some vessel" to carry their produce to England. But they avoided directly criticizing their English business rivals.[36]

The second letter, written five days later, came from Kizell, who claimed responsibility for taking the lead in the society's formation. The new organization would "excite industry" among the settlers, Kizell agreed. But he reminded Allen that support for African agriculture was paramount. This would discourage people from selling one another.

"If we had factories on the coast to purchase the African produce," Kizell explained, the people would have an incentive to harvest and sell coffee, rice, and other valuable crops—not people.[37] It was the mantra he had been delivering to the chiefs and people of the Sherbro.

Kizell expressed unease over what was looking more and more like a lonely crusade against the slave trade. The two British governors who had enlisted his help in that cause, Columbine and Ludlam, were dead. He feared that the extensive commentary he had prepared for Columbine on the slave trade had gone astray. Columbine had assured Kizell that he planned to share this with Africa's friends in England, but he had heard nothing. Kizell offered to send Allen a copy.

Although Kizell wanted to continue pressing the Sherbro chiefs to cease trading in slaves, he complained that he lacked the material means to secure their attention. The chiefs expected the usual presents before they would sit with Kizell or anyone else to discuss serious matters. "I am not weary in welldoing," Kizell assured Allen, but hinted that assistance would be appreciated. "I am unable to defray such expenses."

The real constraint remained British policy. Since Ludlam's demise, Kizell lamented, "I do not hear much about the civilization of Africa." His Majesty's ships were diligently seizing slavers and liberating their cargoes, but the "country people" in the Sherbro were forever asking Kizell, "What do England intend to substitute for the Slave Trade?"[38] He could not say.

Stopping the slave trade had become an end in itself. Britain had no coherent and dedicated strategy to begin repairing the damage done or to provide Africans with an opportunity to meet the outside world on any but subservient and paternalistic terms. Civilizing Africa, it seemed, was to be left to a few brave souls—such as Cuffe and Kizell.

The Uncle and an African Ring

Kizell's palavers with the Sherbro chiefs, the Tuckers, and Crundell had been unprecedented in scope and portent. They spawned rumor and fear that the British government had ulterior designs not only on the coast but along the trade routes to the interior. Why else had British "explorers" suddenly shown such interest in traveling far inland to seek the source of Africa's fabled rivers and meet the great chiefs beyond the Futa Jallon?

The story had rippled widely, as far as the Gallinas, as far as Cusso country, maybe farther. Seated on their wooden stools and carved chairs, elders in countless villages had heard variations of the same story: how an African—he was a trader in the Sherbro . . . he had been a slave in America . . . he had gray hair . . . no, it was white—had brought important words from the governor at Sierra Leone, had confronted the Tuckers, had been insulted by Queen Messe, had threatened the white men!

This remarkable tale had traveled along paths through forests and high grass, watched by omnipresent spirits. Forty years had passed since a thirteen-year-old boy had walked one of these same paths, perhaps to visit his uncle. In a village somewhere in the Gallinas watershed, there were people who remembered the boy. He was one of the living dead. Only he had not died.

How this revelation arrived and how it was received in the uncle's village may have survived for a few generations in local tradition. Now it is known only to the ancestors. What prompted the uncle to believe that Columbine's emissary might be his nephew, reborn from another world? As he circulated the governor's message, Kizell must have revealed a kernel of his origins. It had been enough, however, to persuade the uncle that the man who had confronted the slave traders might be the boy who had been stolen one horrible night from his village.

Kizell's own reaction is opaque. Writing to William Allen in March 1813, Kizell promised to "pay all attention to what you shall say to me about going to the Interior"—an apparent reference to Allen's encouragement to promote agricultural development as an antidote to the slave trade. Then he added, almost apologetically: "I did not open my mind to you but now I will. My Uncle, that is my Father's Brother, came to me after hearing of me and wants me to go with him to my Country to see my Mother's brothers and friends. That is my reason for informing you of it. I do not wish that it may trouble you, or any of the friends. If you think it will answer I think it will be good."[39]

These few lines, interred in a long letter devoted to business concerns and the Friendly Society, are the sole evidence that Kizell was reunited with his extended family. Kizell appears anxious to assure Allen that he would not be diverted from strengthening the society. If he did return with his uncle to "my country," there is no mention, direct or otherwise, of his people in subsequent correspondence with Allen, nor in the reports and recollections of others who knew him in these years.

Kizell must have been overwhelmed to meet his uncle, a figure of great importance in the raising of an African boy, and to rediscover his ancestral ties to the land and extended family. "I think it will be good" is all that he confided to Allen.

The reunion, coming as it did so many years after Kizell had established himself in the Sherbro, raises intriguing questions: Why did he not seek out his people? Did he hold some responsible for his enslavement? Was he uncertain of how he might be perceived? Was he reluctant as a man of some means to assume responsibility for impoverished relatives?

Kizell's apparent reluctance to reconnect with his roots, at least until his uncle appeared, is not easily explained within the context of African cultures. It may in fact reflect the degree to which he truly had become—and felt—a stranger. Kizell was African, but he was many other things as well: an American, a Nova Scotian, a Baptist preacher, a businessman, a diplomat entrusted by white men to represent English might and English ideas.

In the same letter to Allen, Kizell enclosed a gold ring for Thomas Clarkson "as token of [his] love and respect" for the man who had long crusaded against the slave trade. "It is an African made ring," Kizell added with pride, to grace Clarkson's writing hand.

He also revealed that he had retained legal counsel—the colony's new chief justice, Robert Thorpe—to represent him in a debt dispute with the Sierra Leone Company. "I have made him my attorney. . . . he has got all my papers and documents." He asked for Allen's assistance.[40]

For Kizell to place his affairs in Thorpe's hands was as curious as it was courageous. Although his immediate objective was to resolve financial matters, Kizell in effect was challenging the British government and the humanitarian elite who had once directed the Sierra Leone Company and were now reconstituted as the African Institution. Thorpe was about to call them and Governor Maxwell to account for their dereliction in promoting civilized ideals in the colony.

By giving Thorpe authority to represent him in England, Kizell was associating himself with the former's allegations of slave trading and abuse of power. It was a bold step for any settler and reflects mounting Nova Scotian and Maroon resentment of Europeans' control of economic opportunity.

Thorpe had arrived with Maxwell in mid-1811. The young Irish barrister was being transferred from a controversial judicial posting in Upper Canada. In Freetown he took over from Alexander Smith, who had been acting on the bench in addition to

A shrine to a bush spirit,
typical of those guarding paths
throughout Sierra Leone.
Author's photograph (1963)

trading. He soon determined that the white business community was colluding against black competitors.

Thorpe focused on the same issue that had led to Governor Thompson's recall: the virtual enslavement of recaptives by white officials. He blamed Thompson's downfall on "the little select party"—the men behind the Sierra Leone Company and the African Institution—"because he would not become an instrument of delusion. . . . Thompson was English oak, unbending, and sound to the heart."[41]

Thorpe left for extended leave in England in March 1813. He probably carried Kizell's letter to Allen and the ring for Clarkson. In England he made no secret of his sympathy for Thompson's critique of the Sierra Leone Company and its successor. In *A Letter to William Wilberforce*, which he later published, Thorpe summarized his well-advertised dismissal of the philanthropists' claims for Sierra Leone. The African Institution had "completely failed." No schools had been built. Agriculture was a lost cause. And the "liberated Africans" were being abused by white officials.[42]

The directors tried to refute Thorpe, but Allen believed that hard truths hid among the less tenable accusations. He already suspected that the settlers were being exploited, based on reports from Kizell and the Friendly Society. Thorpe's attack on the African Institution effectively undermined any influence it might eventually have exercised in the colony.[43]

Thorpe's sharpest allegations were aimed at Maxwell, who returned to London in mid-1814 for medical treatment. They were based in large part on a lengthy bill of particulars that some of the settlers, probably including Kizell, sent to Thorpe after Maxwell's departure. As Thorpe later explained, the settlers, whose names are lost, "dared not have forwarded the Charges while Governor Maxwell was in the Colony" because they feared his *"violent and arbitrary conduct."*

Thorpe submitted the settler petition, which he endorsed, to the government. Among the more serious claims was Maxwell's alleged use of recaptives as virtual slave labor on large farms he had established for his own profit. He was also suspected of sexually abusing young female recaptives. Other white officials, including Zachary Macaulay's nephew Kenneth, were implicated.[44]

Kizell may have been a source for one of the most incriminating allegations. Thorpe cited him as one of four men who could prove that Maxwell had forced several chiefs to collude in an elaborate scheme to defraud the government. The settlers charged that Maxwell had seized a slaver under Spanish colors, which had "arrived at the Plantains . . . to obtain 200 slaves." The governor brought the empty vessel to Freetown and had the acting vice admiralty judge condemn the two hundred nonexistent slaves. Maxwell allegedly pocketed the proceeds for the ship and its cargo of ghosts. To cover his tracks, he threatened to destroy the chiefs' "factories and habitations" if they failed to provide two hundred slaves, whom he could then "liberate." The chiefs apparently complied.[45]

In addition to Kizell in Sierra Leone, Thorpe claimed to have witnesses in London who would verify this extraordinary tale. Maxwell had ingratiated himself with the abolitionists, Thorpe said, by hypocritically professing "his abhorrence of the slave trade." Maxwell denied the charges in very general terms and ignored the Plantains scheme altogether in a written response. He managed to avoid an official investigation, but his reassignment to the small Caribbean island of Dominica suggested that the charges had not been entirely unfounded.[46]

Thorpe's confrontational strategy was not helpful to Kizell. Although he was the colony's chief justice and Kizell's attorney, he alienated many in the African Institution who might otherwise have made greater efforts to redress Kizell's two grievances.

The first involved services he claimed to have performed for the Sierra Leone Company. Instead of being compensated, he had been told that he owed the company a substantial amount accrued over several years. In June 1810, as the company was winding up its affairs, Kizell had signed over a Freetown lot and house as security. Macaulay and the other directors interpreted this as acknowledgment of his debts. In fact it had been a good-faith gesture recommended by Ludlam to facilitate an amicable settlement.

"Kizell was an illiterate man in matters of account," Thorpe later wrote. "I assured him the best mode would be to propose settling it by arbitration, and he sent his papers to Mr. Allen for that purpose."[47] Kizell argued that he was being victimized by Alexander Smith, Cuffe's nemesis, in his capacity as acting chief justice. "He had the books of the Company in his hands," Kizell claimed, "and with the authority that was vested in him, might bring a man to say any thing." Governor Ludlam, Kizell said, had scolded Smith for trying to bring Kizell "in debt to the Company, for they were greatly in debt to me."[48]

Thorpe finally got a hearing in January 1814 before a committee of the African Institution. The Sierra Leone Company, he alleged, had failed to compensate many of the settlers, including Kizell, who had labored for it. "Poor Kizil," he lamented, "the old black settler . . . requested of the worthy Mr. William Allen to purchase a mill from the money he had so justly earned, and send it out; but neither the Chairman of the [company] nor the Committee . . . would attend to the poor old man's demand."[49]

The African Institution absolved itself and the company of any debt to Kizell—what he described to Allen as a "considerable balance."[50] In its report the committee documented Kizell's apparent acknowledgment of his debt to the company incurred between 1802 and 1809. It dismissed his substantial claim for services rendered, which conceivably included the peace negotiations he undertook on behalf of Ludlam. Those "services" may have included quantities of rum and tobacco to bring the chiefs to palaver.

"In short," the committee concluded, "never was any charge more completely falsified than this." The committee was alluding, it appears, to Thorpe rather than to "poor" Kizell. "It may be proper to add," the committee noted, "that Kizell's assignment of his house had not been put into force by the Company or their agents." This suggests that some on the committee—Allen, for certain—believed that Kizell's claims had merit. There the matter ended. Kizell paid nothing and kept his Freetown property, but he no longer sought reimbursement.[51]

Kizell entertained greater hope that a separate grievance—"my late received act of injury," as he wrote Allen in June 1813—would secure "some final redress. It is Sir to England we can only turn . . . for a deliverance from . . . heavy handed oppression."[52] He was now corresponding not only with Allen, but also with the revered Thomas Clarkson. Kizell was humbled to be "noticed by a person of your consideration and interest. I can now say that the hand of God is in this."

He outlined his dilemma to Clarkson in a lengthy letter on May 30, 1813. As the affairs of the Bance Island proprietors were being wound up, its longtime surgeon had made Kizell his agent. Kizell also had agreed to be guardian of his infant child by an African mother. In lieu of wages, the company had given the doctor a small schooner that lay derelict on the island's shore. Kizell bought the vessel for thirty pounds, but only after obtaining Thorpe's legal opinion that the schooner was the doctor's to sell.

Two shipwrights went to Bance to refurbish the ship. "When I got her Seaworthy," Kizell explained to Clarkson, "I brought her down to Sierra Leone and securely placed her, when she was seized by the Sheriff . . . together with whatever I had on board." Altogether Kizell had invested 215 pounds to buy and rehabilitate the vessel.

The sheriff had acted at the request of a British merchant, George Nicol, who was responsible for liquidating the proprietors' assets. Nicol claimed that the abandoned schooner still belonged to the company and quickly auctioned it for 150 pounds. When Kizell complained to the sheriff and Smith, they dismissed him. The latter told him that Thorpe, now gone to England, "had led me into an error and had spoke whimsically." Kizell was told he would not be compensated from the auction proceeds.

Kizell regarded the incident as part of a larger problem. "I considered their proceedings as actual oppression," Kizell told the sheriff, "and added that our grievances had been repeated and continued so long that I would . . . inform certain persons in England respecting it. The Sheriff returned for answer he would . . . report me and ordered me away from his door!"

Kizell obviously believed that Thorpe's testimony and the good offices of Allen and Clarkson boded well. "Sir," he wrote to Clarkson expectantly, "we suffer many grievances sore and oppressive in this Colony and because we have no one to tell our complaints, we did not know or imagine any one would deign to take up our cause until I received that kind letter from my respected good friend Mr. Allen which . . . has emboldened me to write to you thus."

There were other "oppressive things that have come under my notice," which Kizell offered to share. He was aware that official reports from the colony were circulating in England. "As I am informed we are represented as a riotous set of people . . . could you be so kind as to procure one or two of the reports of this Colony. . . . I shall be able to . . . refute [what] . . . is reported against us."[53]

When he had finished writing to Clarkson, Kizell drafted a letter to Allen. It reveals just how "considerable" an amount he believed was owed to him by the Sierra Leone Company, and how optimistic he had been that his allies in England would secure these funds. He no longer wanted Thorpe to buy him a rice mill; two already were being built in the colony. Instead he wanted to purchase "a vessel of about 100 Tons Burden, or more, not however under"—in other words the same size as Paul Cuffe's *Traveller*. The balance of his anticipated compensation was to be "laid out" for trade goods. "The surrounding Natives are in great want of Neptunes," he advised Allen, referring to large iron cooking pots.[54]

Allen, whom Clarkson once described as "the greatest man in Europe," was beginning to perceive a systematic effort by officials and merchants in the colony to retard settlers' economic advancement. However, he and Clarkson proved powerless. Whatever documentation Thorpe carried to England failed, in the eyes of African Institution colleagues schooled in business and the law, to validate Kizell's claims. Indeed the evidence appears to have been completely disregarded.

Allen reminded Kizell that he had had the opportunity to submit his accounts when the Sierra Leone Company was closing its affairs. As for the beached schooner, which Kizell had rescued from Bance Island, Allen chastised him for not resorting to the local court. He thus ignored or simply forgot what Kizell had written earlier concerning the local authorities' refusal to act. The case had "occupied our serious attention," but proof was needed that the retiring surgeon had legally sold the vessel to Kizell. "I understand [he now] denies the transaction," Allen added parenthetically.[55]

Allen's letter crossed at sea with one Kizell had written to his "Esteemed Friend" on February 14. Composed in apparent haste, to catch a ship departing for England, Kizell returned to his theme "that we have many enemies, men who say we are indolent and had we ever so much money it would do us no good." These were the English merchants who controlled commerce in the colony.

"We take the goods at the highest price and go into the Country and trade them off and pay them," Kizell continued. "There is not a black man in the Colony that keeps a shop on his own account. . . . The men that comes to this Colony as Traders are a set of Speculators whose sole aim is to make money—they care not a copper for the Colony nor for no black man—they endeavour to keep us down below the rank of freemen."[56]

The colony's demographic complexion, meanwhile, was changing dramatically. The mounting influx of liberated slaves introduced new opportunity for economic development, but it also began to alter the labor market and the social dynamic. Freetown "exhibited some features of a caste-like society," writes Arthur T. Porter in *Creoledom*, a study of the young colony's sociology. "There was little association between . . . different groups, and the few relations permitted were severely limited and formally prescribed."[57]

Although he spent most of his time in the Sherbro, Kizell would have realized that the Nova Scotians and Maroons were gradually being overwhelmed by the recaptives. As many as half of the male settlers may have been manual laborers, placing them in direct competition with the newcomers.[58]

Settler fears surfaced in December 1814 when they asked for arms to defend themselves against a rumored alliance of Sherbro warriors and black troops who had been recruited among the liberated slaves. (Kizell had told Governor Maxwell that he considered enlisting recaptives as soldiers "nearly as bad as slavery.") The acting governor ignored the settlers' "rather imperious demand."[59] No attack came, but Sierra Leone clearly was entering a new phase in its development.

With the condemnation of more and more slaves recaptured by the navy, Maxwell wanted to know the colony's effective boundary and whether he had authority to settle new arrivals in the nearby mountains.[60] Many of the earlier recaptives had been apprenticed to the settlers. But their increasing numbers and cost demanded a longer-term solution.

In June 1811, shortly before Maxwell arrived to replace the departed Columbine, the acting governor and council formally approved settling about one hundred Cabindans on Signal Hill. These were the people who had been captured on the Charleston slaver *Amelia*. The council recognized the "good conduct and promising appearance" of recaptives who had been settled earlier on Leicester Mountain. The Cabindan and Leicester settlements anticipated a policy of establishing recaptive villages largely according to people's origins.[61]

Kizell took more than passing interest in the liberated Africans, as they were coming to be called. The *Maria Primeiro* had been brought into Freetown in 1812 with 383 slaves. Fifty-nine died on board—not an unusual number—while Thorpe, sitting as vice admiralty judge, considered the evidence. When the survivors were at last freed, 225 were taken into Maxwell's new military force or engaged on public works. Many were listed in His Majesty's "Land Services"—meaning they were assigned to work on the governor's private holdings.

Only eighteen were apprenticed, including Ajo, a fourteen-year-old boy who was placed in Kizell's care.[62] Ajo's eventual fate is unknown, but Kizell must have felt special kinship to a youth who could have been himself forty years earlier.

There was no shortage of Ajos and other Africans lucky enough to be liberated. Maxwell reported in June 1813 an "extensive traffick in slaves, carried on by American citizens in the Rio Pongas, and by one or two Englishmen & some Mulatto traders in the Sherbro."[63] Thorpe was a busy man, judging by the cases of the *Maria Primeiro* and many other slavers.

One was the *Dolphin*, a fifty-two-ton schooner that Robert Short Long, its captain, had bought in Charleston in 1811. He, his ship, and small crew, including three free black men, had been taken on June 12, 1812, by a British cruiser off present-day Guinea-Bissau. Described in court documents as a "notorious, confirmed, successful and incorrigible slave trader," Long had taken at least two shiploads of slaves in the *Dolphin* from the Rio Pongas and Rio Nunez to Havana, sailing under American colors in violation of United States law.[64]

In spite of disappointment regarding his appeals for compensation, Kizell was opening eyes—if not of Queen Messe in Kittam, then of Allen, Clarkson, and others in England. They were beginning to comprehend the extent to which whites in Sierra Leone were willing to go to prevent settlers such as Kizell from becoming economic freemen. Allen refused "to contradict the whole" of Thorpe's allegations and said so, to the discomfort of old friends such as Henry Thornton and Zachary Macaulay.[65]

Allen and Clarkson decided to act. Because the African Institution was proscribed from engaging directly in commercial activity, they took the lead in forming a "Society for the purpose of Encouraging the Black Settlers at Sierra Leone and the Natives of Africa generally, in the Cultivation of their Soil, by the Sale of their Produce."[66] This would enable them to capitalize the Friendly Society by advancing trade goods. They could also serve as the settlers' agents in England. Allen had been considering this course since personally sending Kizell and the society seventy pounds worth of commodities in October 1812, to be repaid in rice and Indian corn. He too had offered to represent them in London.[67]

War with America, declared by President Madison a few days after the seizure of the *Dolphin*, cleared the West African coast of Yankee shipping. This benefited the new venture in the immediate term. "Our little plan for the settlers promises very fair," Allen wrote a friend in October 1814. But the war blocked Cuffe from returning to Sierra Leone and providing the independent transportation link crucial to developing commerce between the Friendly Society and its English benefactors. In the meantime Allen was looking to the future. He lobbied Maxwell's replacement "to have a favourable eye on the Friendly Society"[68] and presumably on Kizell, who had become its president earlier in the year.

Kizell also was looking to the future. He wished to send a thirteen-year-old son to Allen "for the improvement of his education and a good trade." It was his "earnest wish and desire that he should be useful to Society, if not in one thing, it may be in another." He would send "African produce to pay for his learning." Kizell was now a grandfather, as well. "I have also two grandsons of my daughters," he added proudly, "that I intend to send after I know your mind about my son; the grandsons are young yet."[69]

Kizell disclosed nothing further in surviving letters about his uncle, his mother's relatives, and others among his rediscovered extended family. "I was in the Country," he wrote to Allen in February 1814, apologizing for a prolonged silence.[70] He might have meant the Sherbro, but he may have been down paths he had not trod in a very long time.

He also had been preparing documents—none of which has been found—requested separately by Allen and Clarkson. In his February letter, he asked Allen to inform "my friend Mr. Clarkson . . . that the work he desired me to do is finished, all to copying which I shall get done, to send him by the next ship that sails for England." Clarkson was deeply involved at this time in international consultations on the slave trade. He may have sought Kizell's insights and updated information on the status of slaving along the coast.[71]

Allen had requested a "journal," which Kizell copied and sent later. "If you wish for any further information in these matters, whatever falls under my immediate observation, I will most willingly furnish you with."[72] Given Allen's preoccupation with African agriculture, trade and education, the journal may have provided material for his new publication, the *Philanthropist*. Its nature and purpose remain to be discovered.

Finally Kizell asked Allen to pass an enclosure to "the gentleman that brought us from Nova Scotia." Perhaps it was another African ring. John Clarkson had not been forgotten.[73]

"When will you become a nation?"

With peace restored with Great Britain, Cuffe assembled nine black families who sailed with him for Sierra Leone in early December 1815. They survived what Cuffe described as "the most tremendous weather that I ever remember" and arrived in Freetown on February 3.[74] The storms were a harbinger of a year of extreme events. Heavy snow fell in New England in June. Racial apocalypse threatened in America.

Freetown was a safe haven for people such as Samuel Wilson, a thirty-six-year-old Methodist from Philadelphia, who planned to farm tobacco; for Perry Lockes, thirty, another Methodist who had left Boston with his wife and four children; for Peter

Wilcox, a tanner; and for two African-born men who hoped to return to their homes in Senegal and the Congo country.

More would have come if Cuffe had possessed a larger ship and if they could have defrayed his costs. Cuffe had written Allen as soon as he learned of the peace treaty, asking assistance in obtaining a vessel to accommodate more of the blacks wishing to immigrate to Africa. Allen suggested that he take the *Traveller* to Sierra Leone, carry Friendly Society goods to England, and then sell his ship for a larger one that would be under English registry.[75]

The new governor, Col. Charles MacCarthy, detested American republicanism and believed another war with the United States was inevitable. American ships were not welcome,[76] but MacCarthy received Cuffe and his settlers "kindly" and ensured that they were granted land. He even invited others to come. Cuffe was impressed and believed the governor "has the good wishes of all the colony."[77] MacCarthy's decade-long tenure indeed became known for its relative racial harmony. The confirmed bachelor fathered two children with his settler mistress and took pride in advancing African education.[78]

Cuffe had taken a dim view of the people's delight in rum when he first visited the colony. He found the situation unchanged. The African Institution had claimed publicly in 1812 that Cuffe applauded the moral climate in Freetown. Thorpe knew better. He remembered Cuffe "as a man of truth and observation; and I know he constantly lamented, while in the Colony, the dreadful state of depravity into which it was sunk."[79]

Thorpe, Cuffe—and perhaps Kizell—shared a dismay with the colony's alcoholic consumption. But as Walker reminds, drinking was an "honoured tradition among the Nova Scotians. . . . It had never been considered immoral." Kizell himself had once sold spirits, as had David George. In the judgmental view of Cuffe and Thorpe, tippling may have reflected deeper flaws in the settlers' culture.

Walker provides a more open-minded context. The "institution of all-night dancing, drinking and song" had come with them from America, he notes. "In addition to their mixed gatherings . . ."—similar to colonial Charleston's interracial cotillions—"the Nova Scotians continued to hold dance-nights limited to their own community. . . . The entire night would be spent singing songs in chorus and dancing in a circle. Many of the songs were brought from Africa, and others originated in Freetown, often satirizing their supposed white models."

Nova Scotian entertainments "would usually be accompanied by drinking and humour," Walker writes, "but sometimes they were devoted to religious themes, with hymns and testimonies and the visitation of the Holy Spirit. . . . Those nocturnal sessions[,] . . . which were banned by insomniac whites in Shelburne, had characterized the settlers' social life through slavery [and] Loyalist Nova Scotia."[80] Now they were assimilated into a gregarious, vivacious, and tolerant lifestyle, which the Quaker Cuffe was bound to find objectionable.

Another evil had worsened during Cuffe's four-year absence. The slave trade was being pursued with "rigor," he informed Allen. "There has been numbers brought in since I have been here, & it's sufficient that far greater number [of slaves] leaves than what is taken [by the British navy]." British naval officers were rumored to be taking bribes from European slave traders in the Gallinas and Cape Mount.[81]

Cuffe and MacCarthy may have discussed the scourge, which British merchants were complaining would be their ruin. Not long after Cuffe returned home to a chill summer, he wrote to thank the governor for "thy Very friendly care and attention," then asked for information on the slave trade. "The Abolishing Society in New York Informed me That There was 297 Vessels cleared from the Savannah for The Coast of Africa [in] 1815." If MacCarthy could provide the names of American citizens and ships engaged in the slave trade, it would facilitate their prosecution under United States law.[82]

The slave trade—rebounding in spite of the American peace, the defeat of Napoleon at Waterloo, and European negotiations to abolish the slave trade—was no better news for the Friendly Society. Its success was dependent on the production and export to England of agricultural commodities. As long as the selling of people satisfied the chiefs' appetite for rum, tobacco, guns, and other goods, they were unlikely to rely on the farming schemes that Kizell and Columbine had envisioned.

There is no evidence that Kizell received anything other than vague promises of land from the several chiefs in the Sherbro. Columbine appears to have abandoned the idea in his final months. He apparently did not respond to King Sherbro's request to come himself or send a white man to negotiate for land on which to develop commercial agriculture.

In his correspondence with Allen, Kizell had focused on the subversive attitude of the European merchants. Another Friendly Society member, however, looked to potential allies in an unconventional quarter. William Henry Savage, born in England of an African father and a white mother, had come to Sierra Leone in 1808 as a schoolmaster and dabbled in the slave trade. "From my long intercourse with the Natives," he wrote Allen in March 1815, "I am sure they are willing to enter into all your views respecting the Slave Trade, cherishing it only . . . because they find much difficulty to procure by any other means the different articles which . . . Europeans have taught them to consider necessary."[83]

Savage was now a junior clerk in the colony's government but evidently trusted by the Temne chiefs. He informed Allen in May that the new Temne king wished to establish direct contact with the African Institution. "I must say," he wrote of this novel— almost revolutionary—idea, "that the observation of the Chiefs . . . that their improvement is not wished by the Colonists is but too true." He added that the Friendly Society "does not think fit to interfere in any manner with the Natives around us."[84]

By now president of the society, Kizell makes no reference in his correspondence with Allen to the possibility of drawing people outside the colony into direct association with its activities or its benefactors in England. Nor is there any record of Allen's response to Savage. The concept probably died a quiet and natural death. Intriguing as it may have seemed to Savage and perhaps even to Kizell, the divide between the colony and its indigenous neighbors was entrenched. It would endure through the twentieth century and continues to bedevil what Savage described in 1815 as "this suffering country."

The Friendly Society itself was doomed from the start. It had to contend not only with the united opposition of the white merchants, the slave trade, and wars; it suffered congenital weaknesses and the inability of Allen and his cohorts to mobilize the financial resources needed to make a real difference.

Of the society's twenty-eight members in early 1814, only the former South Carolina landowner Lazarus Jones was described—in a list prepared at Allen's behest—as a farmer, and "very poor" at that. If the society was to rely on agricultural production, then the shoemakers, coopers, baker, joiner—even the colony's gaoler—composing the membership were ill equipped to launch a concerted agricultural campaign. That opportunity had passed. The society's adherents were advancing in years and lacked capital to invest in any major enterprise. Most, as did Kizell, listed their "circumstances" as poor or worse.

Kizell had replaced Henry Warren, an African American settler, as president. According to the shopkeeper Duncan Campbell, one of two European members, "Friend Warren's ignorance and misconduct disqualified him. . . . But as [Kizell] lives for the most part in Sherbro, I think he cannot hold the office long."[85]

Kizell had offered the use of one of his two Freetown houses, presumably to store goods, but his long absences deprived the society of consistent leadership. Members were largely traders or tradesmen who were obliged to attend to their own business affairs. Kizell was no exception, as Friend Campbell intimated to Allen in July 1814.

"None of our Trading members bring anything from the country for our consideration," he complained. He gave the society president as a case in point. "Friend Kizell had a very excellent bullock brought from Sherbro, which he had killed and sold at a rate double the market price." This had offended so many people that the society called a special meeting. "After a sharp . . . and long defence," Kizell "submitted to a resolution . . . that the money thus extorted should be reinstated for the benefit of the Poor."[86]

In London, meanwhile, Allen and the organization that he and Thomas Clarkson had created to foster trade and agriculture through the Friendly Society began keeping meticulous accounts of the goods sent out and the settlers' in-kind remittances. They believed on faith that their philanthropy would be repaid in produce sent by the society. The two accounts never balanced. A disillusioned Clarkson wrote to the society in February 1819, just as an economic panic in America was beginning to affect England, that they were ending support. He complained that the society had "never attended to the object *for which alone we had associated with it.*"[87]

Had Paul Cuffe lived to return to Sierra Leone and to establish an independent shipping link to England, and had Clarkson and Allen persuaded their wealthier colleagues to buy a trading vessel for the Friendly Society, the settlers might have succeeded in loosening the grip of the white merchants. But even under the best of circumstances, the Friendly Society was little more than a noble and early attempt to improve the terms of trade for Africa in an international economy controlled by external forces.

Relations between the society and its English backers ended awkwardly. Clarkson proposed a schedule by which the society should repay the 779 pounds sterling that it supposedly owed. These funds, he said, had been promised for "other benevolent purposes." Clarkson made clear that he and his friends expected to be repaid. "Do *not* disappoint us," he wrote to James Wise. "Do not allow us to forfeit our *word*. Nor your own *Characters to suffer in our Estimation*."[88]

Clarkson claimed that unnamed members had benefited at the expense of the society. They had received trade goods from London charged to the society's account, which were sold for personal benefit. Judging from their correspondence in 1812–15, Kizell received some goods directly from Allen and probably from others. Whether he reconciled his accounts is unknown.

What is apparent, given the lack of any evidence of contact after 1815, is that Allen ceased communicating regularly with Kizell. By mid-1817, when he addressed a letter to seven other settlers, he feared the Friendly Society was "not doing well." As he confessed a few months later, "It seems impossible to induce them to turn their attention to the raising of produce."[89]

Although Allen retained an abiding interest in promoting agricultural development in the colony, he gradually lost faith in the original settlers. He looked more hopefully to the liberated African community.[90]

Cuffe's death at home in September 1817 removed an essential link between the Friendly Society and its English allies. His high repute in England, business instincts, moral compass, and vision for Africa might have helped the society to steer a steadier course and to sustain English support.

Cuffe had returned in April 1812 from his first voyage to Sierra Leone to discover the United States on the verge of war with Great Britain. His ship and cargo had been seized, obliging him to appeal in person to President Madison for their release. He was the first person of color officially received by an American president. Madison arranged immediately for the restoration of the *Traveller* and probably asked Cuffe for his opinion of England's settlement of free blacks at Sierra Leone.

Madison was deeply concerned with the rapidly increasing number of manumitted slaves in America and believed that "freed blacks ought to be permanently removed beyond the region occupied by . . . a White population." As early as 1788, he had considered colonization of free blacks as an incentive to manumission in the slave states.[91]

"The objections to a thorough incorporation of the two people are . . . insupera-ble," he had written. "If the blacks, strongly marked as they are by Physical and last-ing peculiarities, be retained amid the Whites, under the degrading privation of equal rights, political and social, they must always be dissatisfied . . . [and] secretly confed-erated against the ruling and privileged class."[92]

When Cuffe arrived back from his second African pilgrimage in early spring of 1816, Madison's worst fears were being realized. Newspapers were rife with reports of slave insurrection and racial bloodshed. *Niles' Weekly Register* in Baltimore passed along the rumor that Africans had destroyed Sierra Leone and "murdered nearly all the white inhabitants." Slaves in Barbados were said to have burned dozens of planta-tions and killed all the whites they could find.

Closer to home, editors in the South were demanding that three hundred armed fugitive slaves be driven from a former British fort in Spanish Florida. In February a black woman had betrayed a planned slave uprising in Virginia. Another plot intended to erupt on July 4 in South Carolina was uncovered in Camden. "I think it is time for us to leave a country where we cannot go to bed in safety," a white resident wrote to a northern newspaper.[93]

Blacks had been thinking much longer of leaving a country where they could not be full citizens. For the many African-born, especially, returning to Africa—in life or in death—was the stuff of dreams, of silent reflection and subliminal longing. The African Union Society in Newport, Rhode Island, had seventy members ready to emigrate in 1787. A dozen volunteered to visit Sierra Leone and report on conditions. Another sev-enty-three "African blacks" had appealed in the same year to the Massachusetts legisla-ture for help in returning to "our native country."[94] They had seen the newspaper reports of British philanthropists' sending hundreds of blacks to Sierra Leone.

In the immediate post-Revolutionary decades, no issue more preoccupied the evolving American national consciousness than the mounting presence of free blacks. Although slavery and the slave trade visibly contradicted the ideals of American inde-pendence, it was widely assumed by many whites and even some blacks that these blights would be effaced in their own time. But what was to be done about the eman-cipated slaves? Northern whites were alarmed over the increasing numbers of people whom they regarded as degraded and unassimilable. Southern slaveholders were equally anxious to be rid of this anomalous class, which they regarded as a bad influ-ence on their chattel and a source of slave unrest.

Whites were compelled to consider the implications of blacks' existence among them. Were free blacks citizens? Or were they a permanent underclass that mocked the pretensions of American democracy?

Blacks were no less interested in resolving these questions. Most believed that their place, for better or worse, was in America. Africa might beckon in darker moments, but as the percentage of African-born declined among both slaves and free blacks, Africa receded as a remote and fearsome refuge of last resort.

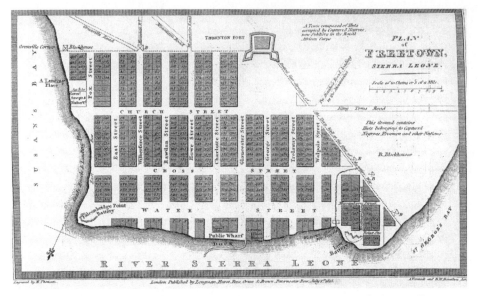

Freetown city plan published in the Philanthropist *in 1815. Two of John Kizell's
plots were located at the upper end of Wilberforce and Rawdon streets.
A third was on the corner of Water and Rawdon streets.*

For Cuffe, during the frigid summer of 1816, these *were* dark moments. He was
shocked by inflammatory news from the slave states and what it portended. To Samuel
Mills, a seminarian who had queried him about settling blacks in Sierra Leone, Cuffe
wrote from Westport on August 6 about slave owners' being "much alarmed on
account of the Africans rising. I have thought it would be prudent for them to have
early seen to this in order to prevent this evil, but it appears that they have made use
of the very means to bring this destruction among them." To his friend James Forten
in Philadelphia, he hinted at the possibility of a racial Armageddon.[95]

Free blacks peppered Cuffe with inquiries about Africa. "I have many applications
for settlers to remove from America to Africa," he wrote to Kizell on August 14. He
wondered, if Sierra Leone were problematic, "could not there be a settlement made
at some other place or port with prudence and equal safety? I only mention this for
thee to consider upon as it appears that there are motions of insurrection in the
Southern states. I imagine that many will be glad to find some place where they could
send them for the peace and tranquility of the world."[96]

Cuffe probably had read a pamphlet that had recently appeared from the pen of
Robert Finley, a Presbyterian minister in New Jersey. *Thoughts on the Colonization of
Free Blacks* had been prompted by Finley's horror of the poverty he observed among
free blacks and his conviction that they could never be happy if shackled to inferior

status in America. "If the people of color remain among us," he wrote, ". . . their presence will be unfavorable to our industry and morals."

Finley, who as a young man had seen slavery at close hand while teaching in Charleston, was the first to distill the essence of colonization for popular consumption. His eloquence was seductive:

> Most nations have had their colonies. Greece and Rome planted many which grew and flourished, and which, as they grew, added strength and luster to the mother country. . . . The people of color, observing the constant emigration of whites [from Europe], would soon feel the common impulse, if they could see a place where they might remove, and which they could fondly call their own. . . . Who can tell the blessings which might in this way be conferred on Africa herself, when her strangers should be restored, and she should receive her children redeemed from bondage by the humanity of America.[97]

Finley's articulation led directly to the formation in Washington of the American Colonization Society in December 1816. Defenders of slavery such as Henry Clay found common cause, albeit uncomfortably, with such opponents as the lawyer Francis Scott Key.

Each side had misgivings about the others' motives. Some doubt was expressed that the free blacks wanted to emigrate. The expense, all conceded, would be enormous. But as Elias B. Caldwell, the clerk of the Supreme Court, argued, colonization was "a great national object and ought to be supported by a national purse. . . . There ought to be a national atonement for the wrongs and injuries which Africa has suffered. . . . We cannot rid ourselves entirely from the guilt and disgrace attending that iniquitous traffic until we, as a nation, have made every reparation in our power."[98]

This was a moment of truth—one among many—in Americans' self-identification as a people of "color." Colonization was a lightning rod. Over the next two years, it became the flash point for an emotional public debate: Were blacks—free and slave—Americans? And if they were, what did that ultimately mean?

Free blacks were the first to react. Three thousand met in Philadelphia in January 1817 and warned against any program "which will stay the cause of the entire abolition of slavery." In New York blacks assembled to protest "the unmerited stigma" that had been applied to them and resolved that "we will never separate ourselves voluntarily from the slave population of this country."

Finley rushed to Philadelphia to assure black leaders that the colonization society's motives were the purest. But one of its founders—all of whom were white men—was less diplomatic: "Be [blacks'] industry ever so great, and their conduct ever so correct," he wrote in a letter published in the society's first annual report, "we never would consent . . . to see the two races placed on a footing of perfect equality." Even Paul Cuffe, "respectable, intelligent and wealthy as he is, has no expectation of ever being invited to dine with any gentleman . . . [or] of marrying his daughter."[99]

Free blacks were wary of manipulation by either wing of the colonization move-ment. They neither rejected voluntary emigration out of hand nor openly endorsed it. Black leaders' fear that large-scale emigration would undermine efforts to abolish slavery remained an overriding concern.

Recognizing that government support would be critical, the colonization society proposed to Congress that free blacks be settled "in some salubrious and fertile region . . . [under] the authority and protection of the United States." A congressional com-mittee in February 1817 applauded the idea in principle and recommended collabo-ration with the British initiative in Sierra Leone. It was silent, however, regarding whether the government had the constitutional authority, not to mention the where-withal, to establish an American colony in Africa.[100]

Finley and Mills had written to Cuffe, even before the formal creation of the col-onization society, to elicit his advice. "Their [sic] is a River about 50 leagues south of Cape Sierra Leone called Sherbro," he informed Mills on January 6, 1817. He had been told by Kizell that there were good soils. "The man [Kizell] has ever been extream earnest that a settlement Should be established at that Place, With those — people that may come from America. He is a man of good Character, not so . . . much given to liquir as the general run of that People."

Sherbro would do for "small beginnings," Cuffe believed, but if there were "a will-ingness" for a more general "removal" of free blacks, he recommended "the South Part of Africa." He shared the same information with Finley and recommended Kizell by name.[101]

Mills possessed strong missionary instincts and had served in the Mississippi region before being ordained in 1815. He had worked in New York City's impover-ished black neighborhoods in the summer and fall of 1816 and hoped to start a school to train black ministers and teachers. Now he had turned his attention to leading free blacks — whom he privately described as mostly "ignorant and vicious" — to Africa. He had been corresponding with Thomas Clarkson, who also recommended the Sherbro, probably based on information provided by Kizell.

Mills was raising funds to support an exploratory trip to Sierra Leone and had recruited Ebenezer Burgess, a mathematics professor from Vermont, to accompany him. "Paul Cuffe has been requested by some of the citizens of Sierra Leone to com-mence a colony at Sherbro," he wrote enthusiastically to Burgess that summer. Cuffe had told him that "more than half of the people of color in Boston . . . would embrace the first opportunity to go out to Africa. My brother, can we engage in a nobler effort? We go to make freemen of slaves."[102]

Mills was convinced that colonization would end slavery in America and civilize Africa. In late August he appeared at Cuffe's threshold, hoping to obtain more details about Sierra Leone and to receive his personal blessing for the mission. Instead he found Cuffe confined to bed, near death and barely able to speak. He was permitted to read Cuffe's notes from his visit to Sierra Leone the year before but left the next morning without discussing colonization or anything else of substance. Cuffe was dead within a week.[103]

Kizell was aware that colonization was being actively canvassed in America. Under the heading "Slave Trade," the *Royal Gazette and Sierra Leone Advertiser* reported on August 23, 1817, that Congress had authorized the new president, James Monroe, "to entertain a convention with . . . Great Britain, for receiving into the colony of Sierra Leone, Such of the free people of colour of the United States, as, with their own consent, shall be carried thither."[104] Kizell would not have been entirely surprised, therefore, when Mills and Burgess, having stopped in England to meet with the leading lights of the African Institution, arrived in Freetown the following March. They immediately sought his assistance in surveying prospects for an American colony in the Sherbro.

Kizell quickly convened the Friendly Society, over which he still presided. The two Americans were advised not to alarm the kings and local headmen by requesting large tracts of land, at least not at first. Otherwise they might conclude, Mills wrote in his diary, that "we should take their country from them."

There was another concern: "Some of the kings have a suspicion lest those whom they have sold to slave traders should return and revenge on them their wrongs. . . . One man, who was sold from the Sherbro nearly thirty years ago, has lately returned. He openly asserted that if any person should take any of his family and sell them, he would kill that man without the least hesitation."[105] A third fear, frequently expressed as they toured the Sherbro in the coming weeks, was that white men would govern any American colony and seize control of the region.

Mills had been looking forward to meeting Kizell, whose published reports on the slave trade he likely had read. He was not disappointed. "Mr. K. is a second Paul Cuffee," he concluded. "He has a good mind and considerable knowledge. His writings discover him to be a man of sense and worth."

Kizell was a living icon of colonization's potential. "Africa is the land of black men," Mills quoted Kizell, "and to Africa they must and will come. . . . They have not forfeited a right to the inheritance of their forefathers, by being carried by force from their country. . . . Mr. K. thinks the greater part of the people of colour, who are now in America, will yet return to Africa."[106]

Kizell might have been a second Paul Cuffe, but Mills avoided hinting in his journal that he would be a suitable choice to lead the settlement. He left open the possibility that "a judicious man of colour" might be found but mentioned neither Kizell nor any other candidate.[107]

It may have seemed a curious omission, but Mills had the political instincts to sense that the colonization society would insist on a white governor. Nonetheless he described Kizell's standing effusively. "No man's heart can be more ardent for the success of our object," he wrote on April 3 at Yonie, where he had just met with King Sherbro. "And no man in Africa could probably be so useful to us under present circumstances." Kizell "has great influence in Sherbro," he added three days later. He "owns considerable tracts of land here, and is acknowledged by the natives to be the head man of the country."[108]

Although he had brought together most of the chiefs and the king, in spite of differences that had lingered since the great Sherbro war, Kizell was unable to get them to agree formally to a specific area for the Americans to settle. It was clear, however, as they traveled up the Bagru and Mano rivers that there was abundant land, but few people to populate it. Prince Kong Couber assured them, "You are our strangers." Let the free people of color come, he said. "We cannot hate them, we will receive them." But where they would settle was left to another day, to palavers yet to come.[109]

Mills had found one of Cuffe's settlers living on the Bagru. Samuel Wilson seemed to be prospering. He had made a fortune from nothing, he told Mills, and was strongly critical of black leaders in America, especially the Methodist bishop Richard Allen, who rejected colonization.[110] Kizell had seen either a letter or an American publication reporting Bishop Allen's opposition. He had shared this information with Wilson, who asked Mills to carry a response back to the "brethren" in America.

"I am surprised to hear from brother John Kizell," Wilson wrote, "that . . . you oppose coming to a land which your fathers went from. You may be rich, but do you think you will be respected as real Americans? . . . Do you not know that you are strangers in that land? Your fathers were carried into that land to increase strangers' treasures, but God has turned it all to good, that you may bring the gospel into your country. When will you become a nation, if you refuse to come? . . . If you refuse to come and deliver Africa out of darkness, God will send deliverance from another quarter."[111]

In Freetown another of Cuffe's followers requested that Mills take his message to blacks at home. "Which of you is lord over America," Perry Lockes asked, "that you do not want to come to your birth right? It is the will of God for you to come into the possession of your ancestors."[112]

These letters were soon circulating in the United States as part of the colonization society's proselytizing among free blacks. Mills's diary was disseminated widely, conveying Kizell's views.

Kong Couber had asked Mills, hopefully, when he planned to return to Africa. Perhaps through a premonition, Mills told the prince not to expect to see him again. He did not: Mills died before his ship reached England. It remained for Burgess to report to a meeting of the colonization society soon after returning to Washington in October 1818.

Burgess supported colonization, but unlike Finley and many other adherents, he blamed blacks' "debasement and subordination" on whites' prejudice, not on blacks' alleged inferiority. He endorsed Cuffe's proposal to send blacks, who had the necessary skills and experience to redeem Africa's "children of nature," as he termed them. But it was not the clarion call to exodus that Mills might have delivered. Burgess did

Mr. Kizell introduced by Couber to his father King Sherbro.

John Kizell is supposedly pictured in this 1851 engraving published in Africa Redeemed. The caption on the image is incorrect. Kong Couber (center) is introducing to his father, King Sherbo (seated), Samuel Mills and Ebenezer Burgess (the two white men wearing hats) during their 1818 mission to scout for land to settle free American black people in the Sherbro. Kizell, who was short and gray haired, may be the man between the king and his son. Manuscripts, Archives and Rare Books Division, Schomburg Center for Research in Black Culture, New York Public Library, Astor, Lenox and Tilden Foundations

not quote Wilson and Lockes. He said nothing of Kizell's conviction that all blacks in America should return to Africa.[113] It too was a curious omission.

The Race Card Face Up

"The slave trade—that scourge of Africa; the disgrace of humanity." President Monroe held forth his glass, waiting for the toast to be completed. "May it cease forever, and may the voice of peace, of Christianity, and of civilization, be heard on the savage shores."

Monroe and his hosts in Athens, Georgia, drank to the end of the slave trade, but not of course to the end of slavery. The president was making a grand tour of the southern states. The date was May 21, 1819.[114]

Reverend William Meade was no tourist. He had hastened earlier that month from Virginia to the Georgia capital at Milledgeville. The American Colonization Society had sent him to prevent the sale into slavery of more than thirty smuggled Africans. They had been brought up to Milledgeville to await their fate. Others from their ship already had been sold, enriching the state by fifty thousand dollars. Fortuitously the second auction had been delayed when Meade arrived on a Saturday evening. The next morning he walked to their encampment outside town.

"As I approached," he reported to the society, "I found them gathered round a good old man, into whose care they had been given, and who was telling them that some good people had sent me to prevent their sale, and carry them back to Africa.

"I wish you could have been with me to have witnessed their joy; they crowded around me and by turns took hold of my hands, and in broken English expressed their gratitude. They at first . . . would scarcely believe it; they had never heard of any such thing before. . . . One of them said . . . 'white people never send negroes back to Africa; I never see my children again.'"

They included Angolans and others taken along the West African coast. They had been shipped from the Rio Pongas, but several were familiar with Sierra Leone and the Sherbro. Some knew John Kizell and told Meade that "he was a good man." When he mentioned Paul Cuffe, several cried out, "Yes! Yes!"[115]

Reverend Meade persuaded the governor to postpone the Africans' sale, allowing the colonization society time to raise funds to purchase their freedom. Without the means to send anyone to Africa, however, the society apparently resettled these involuntary refugees on Smith Island, at the mouth of the Chesapeake Bay. George Washington Parke Custis, the island's owner, had "cheerfully offered" it, according to the society's managers. Monroe had personally approved the site "till they can be sent to Africa."[116]

The president still opposed granting government funds to the colonization society. Slavery was becoming an even more divisive issue. Missouri was about to apply for admission to the Union as a slave state. This would ignite a bitter struggle over preserving a precarious balance in Congress between slave and "free" state representation.

American complicity in the slave trade also continued apace. Efforts in Washington to restrain it were contradictory. Senator James de Wolf of Rhode Island, whose brother George was an active slave trader, amended an Anglo-American treaty in early 1819 to delete mutual rights of inspection of one another's ships. But he could not prevent Congress from instructing Monroe—twelve years after making the slave trade illegal—to send navy ships to cruise the African coast for American slavers.

The president also was authorized to appoint an agent to establish liberated slaves "on the island of Sherbro, or elsewhere on the coast of Africa" and to construct barracks to hold people freed from slave ships. The agent, however, was to have nothing to do with colonization.[117]

Monroe chose Samuel Bacon, a Harvard-educated teacher, literary editor, lawyer, and recently ordained cleric. He had been a captain of marines in 1814 at the battle of Bladensburg and prominent in the Sunday school movement. There was nothing for Bacon to do, however, until Francis Scott Key and another leading adherent of colonization convinced the attorney general and then Monroe that it would be legal to send a few free black carpenters and mechanics to establish an American station—just not a colony.

Bacon rushed to New York—it was now late fall—to charter a ship and "hire" blacks to go on the mission. Everyone from the president down knew its true character. If there were any doubts, they were dispelled by the women and children who made up two thirds of the passenger manifest.[118]

At Campelar, his village on Sherbro Island, Kizell waited. He had built more than a dozen traditional structures to house settlers but had heard nothing from America since Mills's departure nearly two years earlier. Burgess apparently had not written. If the colonization society had communicated with him, the correspondence is absent from its annual reports and papers. Kizell had no idea when, if at all, the first settlers would come—Mills had vaguely suggested in a year—nor how many. He had no idea precisely what would be expected of him.

Kizell was aware that the prospect of an American settlement was causing consternation among British officials and merchants in Freetown. Although MacCarthy had been cordial to the American visitors, he had earlier warned London that an American colony would be "highly prejudicial" to British commerce. He could not have been pleased to learn, after Mills and Burgess had left, that the Privy Council discerned no reason to prevent the Americans "from forming an Establishment on the Coast of Africa, if they shall think fit to do so."[119]

Even as Mills and Burgess toured the Sherbro in 1818, Freetown's white merchants had launched their own campaign to block a competing American colony. A long letter, signed "Two Africans," in the *Royal Gazette and Sierra Leone Advertiser* of April 25 quoted private American sources that more than twenty thousand settlers— ten times Sierra Leone's population—were anticipated. This was no exaggeration. During their stopover in England, Mills and Burgess had spoken to William Allen of "many thousands." For the "Two Africans," this would be "most injurious to our increasing prosperity to share what we now possess with others."[120]

Kenneth Macaulay, the leading trader in Sierra Leone, tried to steer Mills and Burgess in other directions. Sherbro "would take away a great deal of our trade," he told them, "and so become the foundation of envy and ultimate hatred between the two settlements. . . . Sherbro would become a complete smuggling depot . . . the evils which must result from each place becoming a refuge to the criminals and debtors of the other."[121]

Kizell was part of the problem, Macaulay believed. The American agents "have given themselves up to such persons as Mr. Kizell," he wrote his uncle Zachary, "and ... look upon every person else as quite ignorant of the Country. . . . What their reception may have been in the Sherbro I do not exactly know.—I have been told it was very cold and forbidding."[122]

Macaulay proposed that American blacks be settled close to Sierra Leone "under our jurisdiction." Mills and Burgess were amenable but doubted their black settlers would agree. According to Macaulay, the governor planned to recommend that Britain invite the Americans to settle between Cape Sierra Leone and the Camaranca River to the south, or on the banks of the Sierra Leone River itself. "The number of good industrious people that we should receive would give an incalculable increase to the importance and improvement of the colony," Macaulay suggested.[123]

If this was MacCarthy's thinking, it belied his anti-American instincts. Kizell had written Cuffe in early 1817 that the governor "seems dissatisfied with those [settlers] that you brought out afore." An open-door policy would have reflected a complete reversal of Britain's decision, nearly twenty years earlier, to reject more free blacks from America. In the wake of a major slave plot in Virginia, President Jefferson had inquired in 1802 whether the United States could send its free blacks to Sierra Leone. The American ambassador conveyed Britain's profound disinterest: "It was exactly that portion of settlers"—meaning the Nova Scotians—"which . . . by their idleness and turbulence, had kept [Sierra Leone] in constant danger of dissolution."[124]

Bacon had been tireless in making preparations and in defending the mission against its many critics. During the summer he had written a series of articles in a Pennsylvania newspaper arguing that colonization would benefit free blacks and undermine slavery. In New York, as he readied a three-hundred-ton merchantman, the *Elizabeth*, he found many people eager to see the venture abort. "Satan literally 'has his seat' in Africa," Bacon wrote. "But we have too much reason to believe he is not confined entirely to foreign shores."[125]

The *Elizabeth*, with its eighty-six pilgrims and four white agents, was to sail on January 31, 1820. They were to be blessed at the African church. Friends and well-wishers would then escort them to the Liberty Street wharf on the North River.

It was to be a joyous farewell, but little connected with this enterprise went according to plan. So many people congregated at the church that Bacon, fearing the crush of what seemed the city's entire black populace, barred their entry. While he addressed the crowd, the emigrants were led secretly through the frigid streets to board the ship. It was six days, however, before the *Elizabeth* could be cut from the ice. Thousands lined the shore on a Sunday afternoon as she finally headed toward Sandy Hook lighthouse and wintry seas.[126]

Hundreds had expressed interest in leaving America for Africa. They had been winnowed by the colonization society to sixteen families—all but one from New York and Philadelphia—and some others, mostly single men.[127]

The most notable pioneer was thirty-five-year-old Daniel Coker. The alabaster son of a slave and an indentured Englishwoman, he had fled slavery on Maryland's eastern shore. Years later he reappeared in Baltimore under an alias, secured his freedom, and began teaching at the African school. More recently he had helped Richard Allen to found the breakaway African Methodist Episcopal Church and risen to leadership among Baltimore's black Methodists.

Coker had met Cuffe when he passed through Baltimore, soon after his first return from Africa in 1812. They had discussed how Coker and a fellow teacher could assist settlers' education in Sierra Leone. They agreed to correspond with their African counterparts in Freetown. Coker began turning his students' minds—and his own, evidently—to Africa.[128]

Coker's identification with Africa evolved in part from his desire, in spite of his Caucasian features and color, to be considered a black man. Historian Mary Corey suggests that it was his class identity, however, that divorced him from Baltimore's black society. Coker "acted like a white man," she writes. It was this, not his complexion, that progressively distanced Coker from his community.[129]

Coker's "excommunication," in 1818, from the black denomination he had helped found remains a mystery. Although his color may have been a contributing factor, Corey's class-oriented thesis may best explain Coker's alienation from the mass of Baltimore's blacks and his ultimate decision to expatriate himself to Africa.

Coker initially was suspicious of colonization. Influential whites, however, persuaded him to join the first emigrants. His talents would be wasted in America, they told him patronizingly, implying that he might one day preside over the African settlement. In Baltimore his leadership aspirations seemed foreclosed. In effect, Corey writes, Coker "defected" from a "burgeoning free black culture" in which he felt increasingly marginalized and out of place. He bid his wife and children farewell and joined the historic pilgrimage to Africa.[130]

"We believe that there are dangers and trials ahead," Coker wrote in his journal aboard the *Elizabeth* on February 24, halfway across the Atlantic. They had already come through the first. A gale had forced Capt. William Sebor to lash the helm and had inspired the passengers to pray. When the storm subsided, they encountered the lifeless hulk of another ship named the *Elizabeth*, out of Boston.

On the same day that Coker predicted more trials to come, the pet dog of African-born Peter Small got into a fight with the captain's mongrel. Words were exchanged between Small and Sebor, who called for his pistols. "The captain soon got over his passion," Coker recorded, and the people went below. To Bacon, however, the incident was "an awful judgment upon us."

Coker met alone with the people—"it was a weeping time"—and Small apologized to the captain. Increasingly cast in the role of the emigrants' de facto representative, Coker believed the white agents had been well chosen. Bacon was "only wanting a sable skin to make him an African."[131] Within a few weeks, Coker may have wished that *he* had a sable countenance.

The dogfight had reflected the unavoidable racial tensions and misunderstandings aboard a crowded ship sailing into the unknown. According to Coker, the agents had begun hearing "improper expressions" from some of the emigrants. When Bacon revealed that he and his white colleagues were to negotiate for land—according to the colonization society's instructions—the emigrants' suspicion was confirmed: they would have no real authority.

Their anger prompted Coker to summon the men on deck and demand their confidence in the agents' judgment and goodwill. Coker, who shared a cabin with the agents, had to defend his close relationship with Bacon and the other whites. It allowed him to "see and hear for you what was going on," he pleaded. Only two of the men openly refused to accept the whites' leadership, but the race card was now face up.[132]

Race aggravated a more fundamental problem: the mission's barely disguised duality. The colonization society was interested in demonstrating the viability of settling free blacks in Africa; the United States government, opposed to incurring expenses and political entanglement in a colonial venture, saw mainly an opportunity to become more directly engaged in driving Americans from the slave trade; the emigrant blacks were almost incidental.

As had been the case with the Nova Scotians, the settlers' ultimate political role and identity in Africa had been ignored in the conceptualization and planning. Yet it was they who were taking the greatest risk. Their very lives were at stake, and their talents and dedication would be critical to achieving both the society's and the government's purposes.

The agents and colonists aboard the *Elizabeth* had no formal or consensus understanding of how the colony was to be organized and managed. "Many [of the blacks] simply assumed they would be sovereign in all territorial and political matters," Floyd J. Miller writes in *The Search for a Black Nationality*. "No one really knew where the government's responsibility ended and where the Society's started, or where the agents' authority stopped and where the blacks' right to make decisions for themselves began."[133]

Governor MacCarthy quickly perceived the mission's divided nature. He welcomed the white agents a few days after the *Elizabeth* anchored on March 9 amid several recently captured slavers. He urged Bacon to land his passengers and provisions, free of duty, and to consider settling them in or near the colony. He could tell that the agents "had different objects in view, and were in fact sent by different Departments."

Bacon was "inclined to accept my offer," MacCarthy thought. But the Americans remained fixed on the Sherbro. "I had to steer clear of British claims," Bacon wrote to Navy Secretary Smith Thompson on March 21, "as they look with jealousy upon even this modest and humane effort to do good."[134]

Bacon had already sent his deputy, John Bankson, to alert Kizell at Campelar of their presence. While Bankson's return was expected daily, Freetown was gripped with rumor and gossip. The people also were mourning King George III. His death on January 29 was announced in the black-bordered March 11 edition of the *Royal Gazette and Sierra Leone Advertiser.*[135]

There was much speculation whether the governor would assert British authority in the Sherbro, thus preempting an American settlement that might draw away many of Sierra Leone's own people.[136] Residents also were intrigued by the sudden appearance in Freetown of George Caulker, the chief of the Plantains, who had not visited the colony in seven years. Coker and Bacon met with the urbane Caulker and found him, in Bacon's estimation, "far from approving our errand to the coast."[137]

Had the British officials and merchants in Freetown fully comprehended the dysfunctional nature of the American initiative, they would have expressed little concern that it threatened Sierra Leone's own viability. By the time MacCarthy reported to London on May 27, it was obvious that the danger had been exaggerated. Bacon and the American agents were dead. So were a quarter of the settlers. The effort to establish a competing American colony had self-destructed.

Confrontation at Campelar

Because so many—Mills, Burgess, Thomas Clarkson, William Allen, Paul Cuffe, and others—had placed high expectations on John Kizell, blame for the venture's demise quickly fell upon his now very grey head. The British took no satisfaction in the Americans' failure in Sherbro and certainly not in the many deaths. There is no circumstantial or other evidence that the governor or any of the merchants in Freetown tried to bias the Sherbro leaders against the Americans.[138]

Journals kept by Bacon, Coker, Samuel Crozer—the colonization society's agent—and at least one settler provide considerable information regarding the difficult first weeks in Africa. The diary of Christian Wiltberger, an agent who followed in 1821 with the second group of settlers, is an important complementary source. Two American naval officers added their own postmortems.

These sources support the conclusion that the pioneering free blacks who came on the *Elizabeth* were betrayed neither by the British, the local chiefs, or the slave traders. They were victims largely of poor planning, haste, false assumptions, and impatience with deliberative African protocol. Their inherent cultural myopia—as Americans and as strangers—blinded the agents and most of the settlers to the workings of their new world.

All had started promisingly. Bacon's journal for March 20, the day that he, Coker, and the settlers arrived at Campelar, captures a transcendent moment: "I went on shore and was received with joy by Mr. Kizzel and his people. He wept as we walked together to his house." They dined on fish, rice, and palm oil while the settlers arranged themselves in the thatched huts prepared for them. At seven they adjourned to Kizell's chapel. Two oil lamps provided a warm glow as Kizell and Bacon stood together at the pulpit.

"We . . . had a joyful season of evening prayer," Bacon remembered. "About twenty native Africans, nearly naked, were present. . . . Mr. Kizzel is a pious man; and has kept up worship amongst them a long time. I exhorted in English, and he in Sherbro. This was an affecting season of devotion! It was worth living an age to partici-

pate in it, with our feelings!"[139]

Bacon presented Kizell with a written vote of thanks from the colonization society's board of managers "for his kindness and attention" to Burgess and Mills.[140] Kizell was so touched by this gesture and by the settlers' long-wished presence that he wrote immediately to Bushrod Washington, the society's slave-owning president, to acknowledge "the confidence you . . . repose in me." He also thanked Washington for the "very useful and very beautiful" gift—possibly a church bell—that the society had sent.

Kizell was transported by the fulfillment of his vision for an "African return." Africa is "wide and long," he wrote to Washington, who served on the Supreme Court. "Africa is fertile and healthy—Africa is afflicted—'Rachel mourneth for her children,' and 'will not be comforted till they come home.' . . . You must . . . send my brethren home."

Kizell sought to counter black leaders in America who opposed colonization. "You must not mind the talk of those coloured people. . . . They are ignorant of our climate, and soil, and fruit, and cattle. It may be, they are wicked too . . . and do not wish their 'Zion well.'"

Colonization was God's will, Kizell concluded. "God has sent me here and set me down to make a place for my brethren. . . . You cannot send too many. Let them come down and sit in our valleys, and on our hills, and near our rivers, and all the country will soon break forth into a song. The Sherbro country is full of meat, and fish, and bread, and oil, and honey. Send us people to eat them."[141]

Campelar was anything but a place of milk and honey. It was located on the swampy northern shore of Sherbro Island. Crozer, a medical man, described it ominously as "a low marshy situation." The houses Kizell had built perched on a long, narrow beach. Behind the beach were mud flats, which Kizell's wife (possibly a local successor to Phillis) diked to produce salt. Mangroves fringed the village.

The available water had a sulfuric taste, according to Crozer, but was "by no means unwholesome."[142] Kizell claimed that his "meridian," as he called the well, provided water with unusually healthy properties. But he was accustomed to supplementing this with drinking water from the mainland.[143] Unaware until a few days before that he was about to receive nearly one hundred guests, Kizell could not have stored adequate fresh water to sustain them safely through their gastrointestinal adjustment to Africa. There were fatal consequences.

The settlers had arrived at the end of the long dry season. Crozer noticed that nothing was growing on the few cleared acres where Kizell cultivated rice and cassava. According to Mills, Kizell had secured more than five hundred acres in 1814 but had angered neighboring villagers when he burned the surrounding bush. "It was said," Mills wrote, "that some serpents were involved in the conflagration. The natives, who have a particular veneration for serpents (believing them to be the abode of evil spirits . . .), asserted that the devils were so disturbed . . . that they came into their towns, raising the most bitter complaints against John Kizell."[144]

This is an intriguing anecdote. None of the agents, including the ordained Bacon and Coker, refer to Kizell's pouring a libation to the ancestors and ritually seeking the spirits' hospitality and protection on behalf of the settlers. It would not have been unusual, even for a Christianized African such as Kizell, to acknowledge the spirits and to acculturate the newcomers to an African cosmos. Perhaps he had embraced his own Christian beliefs so firmly that he no longer gave serious credence to the spirit world or to the "surprising things" emanating from it. But he may also have been intimidated by the fervor of the white agents and Coker.

The latter remarked in his diary that Kizell, after their meeting, had professed to being converted. His command of scripture impressed Coker, as apparently it did Bacon.[145] Kizell indeed was "a pious man." As such he seems to have set himself apart from local traditions and from a deeper connection with the people and their beliefs.

As headman of Campelar, a village with as many as one hundred people, Kizell was required to notify King Sherbro and the chiefs of his visitors. Word was sent immediately to request a palaver, but as Kizell counseled, "these men must have their own time; they cannot be hurried."[146] The agents, however, were under enormous pressure to negotiate for land and—as the people rapidly sickened—to locate a permanent site where they also could receive slaves liberated by American cruisers. Their navy escort, the *Cyane*, already was preparing to patrol to leeward.

King Sherbro lived at Yonie, about ten miles away at the island's southeastern extremity. Why Kizell and the agents initially invited the king to Campelar instead of paying him the customary courtesy call is unclear. A frustrated Bacon had just left to obtain provisions in Freetown when the king sent word to Kizell on March 24 that he would not come to Campelar. The country, he complained, was ablaze with reports that the Americans had driven Kizell away and stolen some of his people. Crozer dismissed this as "a trifling alarm that we are enemies of Mr. Kizell," who was "staunch as a rock in our favour."[147]

In the absence of the white agents, Coker and Kizell agreed that as soon as Bacon returned they should lead about thirty of the women and children to greet the king and present the obligatory gifts.[148] This seemingly peculiar strategy—to exclude the men from their delegation—implies that the king and other chiefs feared that they were dealing with an armed advance guard of Americans who intended taking control of the country and not with innocent and defenseless families.

Kizell understood that negotiating for a place to settle would be anything but straightforward. What he could not have anticipated was the racial animosity beginning to reveal itself in the Americans' camp.

Before arriving in Freetown, the settlers had elected a seven-man council. Coker, as "first justice," was titular head. The day after they had received King Sherbro's message, Coker had to sit in judgment of a settler accused of stealing. In front of the people, assembled probably in Kizell's chapel, the man declared that he would not be interrogated by a mulatto.

In spite of Kizell's dislike of mulattoes, he and Coker had quickly developed a rapport. Each strongly believed that blacks in America must come to Africa. Kizell rose angrily in Coker's defense.

"Mr. Coker was a descendant of Africa," Coker quotes Kizell in his journal, "and [said]. . . that he would suffer no such reflection [of color] to be cast; and that if *we* had not men enough to support Mr. Coker, *he* had, and it should be done. . . ; that some would not be governed by white men, and some would not be governed by black men, and some would not be governed by mulattoes; but the truth was, they did not want to be governed by anybody."

Kizell told Coker to proceed with his examination. The man was found guilty and received twelve lashes.[149]

Bacon still had not returned when Kizell, Coker, and thirty of the settlers decided the time had come to visit King Sherbro. In a long canoe hollowed from a tree trunk, they paddled to Yonie on March 29. There they briefly greeted the recently installed king before continuing to Prince Kong Couber's nearby village to spend the night. It was the prince, Kizell told them, who wielded the real authority. The prince assured them a place to settle would be found, but Coker could extract few specifics.

The settlers feasted the next morning on a goat provided by the prince, then used his small cannon to salute their host. But they had been sobered to learn that, just a few miles across the Shebar strait, one hundred slaves in irons were about to be loaded onto a schooner. "Our coloured men," Coker wrote, "talk of going up in the small boat and releasing them, or trying for it. Had we ten thousand of our coloured people from America . . . what we might not do!"[150] In this instance the settlers apparently thought better of challenging armed slave dealers on their own ground.

A fretful Bacon awaited them at Campelar. His mission was teetering dangerously. Although he met with several chiefs in the early days of April, nothing was decided. He was beginning to doubt not only Kizell's sincerity but also his influence. He had learned that the chiefs on the mainland, where Burgess and Mills had recommended the Americans settle, indeed regarded Kizell as a stranger. They also resented his special relationship to the Americans and his perceived access to the wealth and influence they represented.[151]

When the settlers complained to Bacon about the poor water, Kizell told them there was excellent water on the mainland, up the Mano River. Bacon instructed Elijah Johnson to ask the people there for assistance. When Johnson reached Mano, he told the headman he had come for water in Kizell's name. The headman was contemptuous and called Kizell a "bad man." "He take you all to his town," Johnson paraphrased later, "now let him give you water, we will not. . . . You came for Kizzell; if you had come for yourselves, we would give you water."[152]

The settlers vented their frustration on Bacon. In an April 6 petition, they announced that "we have now arrived to the trying point; we are sick, almost naked and really do suffer of such things as was said to be in store for us." Bacon was not sympathetic: "They complain of every thing they have; and are clamorous for every thing they have not." They even blamed him for not seizing land by force.[153]

The people had begun to sicken and die; so had the agents. In the midst of the death and dying, a racially tinged power struggle continued to play out. At an assembly, which Bacon had called to respond to settlers' grievances, he accused Kizell of turning them against him. This startling charge was prompted by one of the men's assertion that the chiefs "will not let a *white* man have the land," but that Kizell as a British subject was prepared to negotiate on the settlers' behalf if he was given "full power." Kizell protested that he had been misunderstood, but Bacon's trust in him was ended.[154]

The first agent to die was Crozer, the colonization society's sole representative, on April 15. As the settlers' nominal leader, Coker evidently made clear to the other agents and to the people that Crozer's authority now devolved upon him. Kizell supported him. Judging from an undated entry in Johnson's journal, Bacon did not.

"This M[orning] I saw Mr. Coker walking up and down slinging his hands," Johnson observed. "I came near to him and heard him say I will not submit to it, and bring my brethren into bondage, that after I am dead and gone they will say I have been the cause of this. I will not go without I have full power as our agent."

According to Johnson, Kizell insisted that Coker deserved the same power as Crozer. Bacon, Bankson, Coker, and Kizell went inside a house to confer. When they emerged Bacon reached his hands toward the sky and cried, "My God, I am ruined."[155]

Kizell no doubt had supported Coker's assumption of Crozer's mantle. Bacon and Bankson, too ill to object strongly, evidently conceded. Both were soon to be dead. Bacon, indeed, expected to die a missionary's death. But now it was largely Coker's responsibility to satisfy the settlers' demands, dispense scarce provisions, police the pilfering, and find a healthier haven as malaria and dysentery decimated their ranks.

Kizell had stood by Coker up to now, but their relationship had begun to deteriorate. Coker was under great duress. Much of the provisions that had been brought out were reserved for the slaves who were to be liberated by the American navy. His refusal to share these with the colonists stoked their resentment of a man they saw as neither "white" enough nor "black" enough.[156]

Coker's ego and self-esteem also were interfering with his ability to accept advice, particularly from Kizell, and to exert genuine leadership of the settlers. Mary Corey suggests that Coker's "contentious" personality made it difficult to work with those he deemed beneath him. "He identified with the rulers," Corey writes, "not the ruled and tended to form his alliance with other powerful men"—such as Paul Cuffe and Richard Allen—"or white clergymen who were friendly to his cause."[157]

Coker's preeminence also complicated negotiations for land. Impatient and frustrated with attenuated African palavers, Coker—against Kizell's advice—tried to accelerate the process. This further alienated the chiefs and headmen, who rebuffed the approaches of the mixed-race Coker. As one of the settlers later intimated, Kizell had tried to warn Coker of his racial liability: "White blood is good, and black blood is good, but they [the natives] know that mulattoes are bastards, and will have no dealings with them."[158] Coker also had rejected Kizell's counsel and steadfastly refused to indulge the chiefs' expectation of the accustomed rum.[159] According to Kizell, Coker also made no secret of his disdain for the chiefs as "nothing but imposters and blood suckers."[160]

Coker blamed Kizell for the breakdown in negotiations, for setting the colonists against him, and for trying to block their move to supposedly healthier higher ground at Yonie. With Bankson, the remaining white agent, having just died, Coker's status was now paramount. Johnson could see that Coker and Kizell were "divided in mind and doing all they can against each other." Kizell had told Johnson that "they cannot get the headmen together to the palaver . . . [and] that he and Mr. Coker are not good friends, that Coker thinks himself above him."[161]

In spite of Kizell's reluctance to have them abandon Campelar, Coker finally removed most of the surviving colonists to Yonie. There they remained until the colonization society sent new agents and a second group of settlers early the next year. A despondent Coker, rejected by the settlers, retreated to Freetown and began writing to the society's directors of Kizell's alleged treachery.[162]

Coker already had the ear of two American naval officers aboard the *Cyane*, which was cruising the coast for slavers. Without having participated directly in the settlement's affairs or having known any of the settlers well, both made serious allegations against Kizell. Coker was their primary source.

Lt. William Mervine informed the commander of the *Cyane*, Edward Trenchard, that the settlers were unlikely to obtain land in the Sherbro because of "the villainous frauds and deceptions practiced on the [deceased white] Agents by Mr. John Kizzell." Mervine wrote on November 1, 1820, that "all his transactions . . . have been influenced from motives of self-interest and speculation." He claimed that Kizell had assisted "a few disaffected men" among the settlers in their attempt to take control of the colony. Kizell had "expressed in strong language his disapprobation of White Agents having been sent out to govern." He also charged that Kizell had misappropriated presents that the colonization society had intended for the chiefs.[163]

John Dix, the *Cyane's* surgeon, wrote Trenchard three weeks later that Kizell was the "true and main cause" of all that had befallen the settlers at Campelar. Dix had spoken with Kizell and read his narrative of the past several months' events. He also claimed to have listened to both Kizell's supporters and detractors.

"It is apparent," Dix wrote of Kizell, "that he has acted the part of a speculator, deceiver and tyrant. . . . Yet, with the most sanctified spirit and looks, he professes to wish to live to see the good work begin, though he has put an end to this attempt, in which many lives have been lost . . . merely to further his own self-interested views."[164]

Dix believed Kizell was "ambitious to be at [the] head" of the colony. "The colonists," he advised Trenchard, ". . . say 'they have seen enough of slavery, that they are now in a free country where they mean to enjoy liberty, ease and comfort and will not be under a government of the whites, and'—he conceded—'particularly under that of Mr. Coker, a mulatto.'"

The surviving colonists had another conceit worth noting, Dix remarked. They "consider themselves also as citizens of the United States, and entitled to support . . . and protection as such, and threaten the natives with our vengeance for every wrong done them."[165] Even if land were available, this did not bode well for an African American presence in the Sherbro.

According to Dix, Kizell "imputes the failure of the settlement to the agents not [following] his advice, in getting more rum, etc., to their arrival while people were planting, to the bad quality of the presents, and a selection of bad settlers."[166]

Kizell evidently rehearsed these and other factors in the commentary that he prepared for Justice Washington and shared with Dix. The surgeon promised to forward it, but there is no mention of it in the records of the colonization society or in Washington's papers. Dix believed, however, that Kizell's own words "confirm the conclusions [Dix had] drawn respecting his conduct."[167]

Several historians of the colonization movement—starting with Archibald Alexander in 1846—have recycled the largely unsourced and undocumented innuendo that Kizell was responsible for the failure to establish an American colony in the Sherbro. According to Alexander, Kizell "fell under strong suspicion of being a selfish and deceitful man."[168] Yet the colonization society itself absolved Kizell of any blame for the chiefs' refusal to grant land and acknowledged that he "was no traitor."[169] In late October 1820, Caldwell, the society's respected secretary, made no reference to Kizell when he informed members and the public of "the distressing intelligence received from the coast of Africa."[170]

If Caldwell had received distressing and credible intelligence about Kizell, he would have divulged it to deflect criticism of colonization. The society's annual reports during the early 1820s make only passing mention of Kizell and reiterate that poor timing and "the want of preparation" were to blame for the failure in the Sherbro.[171]

The most reliable testimony regarding Kizell's conduct appears in the diary of Christian Wiltberger, a young Philadelphian who accompanied the second wave of settlers. They arrived in Freetown on March 8, 1821, along with Coker's family. In the coming months, Wiltberger had considerable contact with Kizell, with the *Elizabeth's* survivors—now down to sixty—and with Coker. Wiltberger took his time to form his judgments, then rendered them frankly.

"The Board of Managers," he wrote on August 4 from Freetown, "have been deceived . . . principally by Mr. Coker. It is my firm opinion that that man has done more injury to the cause than any other man living." Three months earlier he had listened to Elijah Johnson's version of events at Sherbro. "They were very different from what Coker gave us," Wiltberger noted, concluding that Coker "has given very incorrect information to us."[172]

Kizell was in Freetown in June to discuss an invoice that he had submitted to Coker the year before for goods and services provided to the settlers at Campelar. Coker apparently had ignored it, but Wiltberger found most of the charges "plausible."

When he went to hear Kizell preach at the Baptist meeting, as Kizell often did when in Freetown, Wiltberger was moved. Kizell "appeared to be very well-acquainted with Scripture and . . . to speak the language of Zion. I don't know how a man that has [been] represented to be as bad a character as he has . . . can preach as he did."[173]

By the middle of July, Wiltberger had gone to Yonie and shepherded the colonists to Freetown. Kizell asked to meet with them to explain his claims on the society and to solicit their endorsement. "His object in having the palaver," Wiltberger wrote, "was to . . . let them say wether he spoke true or false. I am informed the people attested to the truth of almost all he said." That satisfied the agents, and they settled Kizell's account.

In his August report to the society's principals, Wiltberger felt duty-bound to rehabilitate Kizell's reputation. "It is my humble opinion," he wrote, "that poor man's character has been greatly abused, that he has acted rightly in all the business that he has been engaged . . . in affairs relative to the Society + Government. . . . His character has been greatly maligned, I have no hesitation in saying, and by the *very man* [meaning Coker] that should hold his Peace, because he was much more at fault. I have seen him and conversed with him . . . [and] he has told his tale before all the Sherbro people, of all transactions, and they have been substantiated by the People's saying in almost every instance, yes *these things are so.*"[174]

Kizell hoped to have the last word. His written account, which Dix presumably sent to Bushrod Washington in late 1820, either was lost or pigeonholed. However, as Wiltberger was drawing his own conclusions several months later, Kizell was drafting a lengthy defense against Coker's allegations, which had been circulating locally and in the United States. In a covering note dated August 17, 1821, Kizell authorized Ebenezer Burgess—if he thought proper—to publish his facetiously titled "John Kizell's Apology in Two Letters to Daniel Coker."

Burgess chose not to burden the public with Kizell's rambling discourse. In the florid and verbose style of the time, Kizell countercharged that Coker had betrayed the settlers, their agents, and his own generosity. "Sir," he wrote, "the old saying is true: Never take a frozen snake in the house, for as soon as he gets warm he will bite you."

Distilled to their essentials, Kizell's claims were that Coker had deliberately undermined the white agents; that he had tried to convince the Sherbro chiefs that Kizell was a British subject bent upon taking their country for England; and that Coker's stubborn refusal to provide two hogsheads of rum for the palavers had killed an imminent agreement for land in the Bagru.

Two hogsheads of rum would have been a small price to pay. According to Kizell, Coker at first said he would have to write the colonization society managers for authority to purchase the rum. The settlers themselves, according to Kizell, were ready to pass the hat. Finally Kizell offered to lend them the rum and absorb the loss if the chiefs reneged on their promise of land. Again, in Kizell's telling, Coker adamantly refused.

Whether it was to flaunt his power or out of sheer mean-spiritedness, Coker later stripped Kizell's village of every item, small or large, that had been provided by the colonization society or the American government. "As soon as you came into power," Kizell reminded Coker, "and was going away from my place, orders were given to your people to nock down all the sheds that the former agents put up, without regard to my property. The little chapple that I bilt for me and my people . . . was ransacked and the seats that was given me by your agents ripped up." Even the bell presented by Bacon was confiscated.[175]

What actually transpired during these turbulent months will never be entirely clear. There is no evidence, however, that the Sherbro chiefs wished to forestall an African American settlement in their midst. The chiefs and Kizell had a mutual interest in the economic activity that would have been generated. A bit more patience—and rum—might well have changed West African history. The future nation of Liberia might have risen in the Sherbro instead of farther down the coast on the banks of the Mesurado River.

Coker did not accompany the settlers to Mesurado. Governor MacCarthy—whom Coker described as "one of the kindest of friends"—appointed him to manage the liberated African village at Hastings. He lived the remainder of his days in Sierra Leone but felt obliged to justify why he had not gone to Liberia. "I could be more useful" in Sierra Leone, he wrote to a white Methodist bishop in early 1824. "Here let me live, here let me die."[176] He and Kizell were agreed on this, if nothing else.

8

"WHAT A CREATURE MAN IS!"

"Some compensation was due to Africa, for the countless miseries which our criminal conduct had for ages inflicted upon her."

Thomas Clarkson, writing of the struggle against the slave trade, 1839

The African American colonists, banded together in Freetown, had been taking part in raucous Christmas festivities and enjoying the advent of the Harmattan. Wiltberger and a fresh cadre of colonization society agents had been preparing them for the final journey to Mesurado, where they were to establish their haven. As their brig finally headed out to sea in the first days of 1822, they may have passed a small, inbound schooner.[1]

"The works of our Forefathers"

The *Calypso* was captained by James Creighton of Charleston. It probably had been a difficult crossing, but no less daunting than Creighton's first, half a century earlier, when he had been carried from the Congo country. Arriving in Charleston at about the same time, he and Kizell had been youthful age-mates in the city's black community. They had known the same Revolutionary scenes. They had shared the slave experience.

Creighton had brought his family and a few other free people of color—a dozen in all—to escape the tightening regulatory vise controlling free blacks in South Carolina. He was not the first to contemplate leaving for Africa. In 1818, as national interest in colonization intensified, at least forty Charleston free blacks had expressed interest in leaving for Sierra Leone with a mixed-race South Carolina rice planter.[2]

As a popular barber on East Bay Street, which paralleled the Cooper River wharves, Creighton had acquired his freedom and "some little Property." He explained to Governor MacCarthy and his council that he had found the laws in South Carolina "very oppressive on persons of my color, and [desired] to end my days in the country of my nativity." The governor immediately granted his petition to settle.[3] Sierra Leone was the richer, Charleston the poorer.

Creighton did not mention in his petition that he had owned several slaves. He had offered to bring them to Africa as free people. Otherwise he would be obliged under South Carolina law to sell them. Only one chose freedom in Africa versus continued servitude in America.[4]

The free black population in Charleston had increased 50 percent between 1800 and 1820. The state legislature, alarmed by this trend, in 1820 effectively banned manumission and the emigration of free blacks. Other restrictions were contemplated.[5] In Charleston, where blacks had withdrawn in droves from white churches, members of the free black Methodist congregation at Hampstead asked permission in 1818 to worship independently. Although this was denied, the Hampstead church managed to continue services until 1822, when, in historian John Lofton's account, "its use as a seedbed for revolt brought a still more severe subjugation."[6]

Concluding that he and his descendants could never be truly free, Creighton reluctantly sold his bondsmen and sailed away. Denmark Vesey, one of the Hampstead parishioners, considered leaving with Creighton but decided to remain. According to a witness at his subsequent trial, Vesey wanted to "see what he could do for his fellow creatures."[7]

In the early months of 1822, as Creighton replanted his African roots and black American colonists planted their flag at Mesurado, Vesey, a free black carpenter, began planning a massive slave insurrection in Charleston and beyond. He was betrayed and executed that summer, but several other free blacks—though acquitted—were exiled.[8]

One of the accused, a free black named Prince Graham, asked to go to Africa. He joined a small group of free blacks who were leaving Charleston on August 19, with the intention of joining the black colonists at Mesurado. Their ship traveled instead to the Rio Pongas, where several of the blacks died. A few found their way to Sierra Leone late in 1822, joining the Creightons, Kizell, and others in the growing African-Charlestonian diaspora.[9]

Kizell must have been astounded when he learned that all but one of Creighton's slaves had preferred remaining in America and in slavery. Their decision, likely based on family and other ties, contradicted his oft-stated faith that blacks in America had little to hold them. Uprisings such as Vesey's, he believed, were bound some day to bathe the slave states in blood. The logical alternative was to open the way to African American resettlement in the motherland.[10]

Kizell's critics in Freetown meanwhile blamed him for driving away the first American colonists. Had they been integrated into Sierra Leone, they would have strengthened the local economy. If Sherbro had been a nonstarter, Mesurado looked even less inviting. The Americans had been forced to beat back a ferocious assault by several hundred warriors; seven of their children had been taken captive; and they were facing the same difficulties with the chiefs that had confronted them in the Sherbro.

The *Royal Gazette and Sierra Leone Advertiser*, reflecting the sentiments of the white merchants, reminded readers that the colonization society had "rejected the advice of intelligent and disinterested persons who were friendly to their benevolent

objects; and though warned of his character [meaning Kizell's], listened to the suggestions of one greatly interested in the course he recommended; and whom their various agents since have heaped with every vituperative epithet."[11]

The colonists at Mesurado had provoked local African hostility by interfering with
the slave trade. Not long after arriving in early 1822, they had defended—with the loss
of one settler's life—an English prize crew and the slaves they had rescued from a
Spanish schooner. An American naval officer, appealing to MacCarthy for assistance,
said the colonists were "in great danger."[12]

The Liberian settlers' first years coincided with a substantial increase in slaving
along the coast. British officials in Freetown credited the American settlement in
1823—"by its mere presence and object"—with diminishing slaving between
Mesurado and the Gallinas.[13] Through the coming decade, the colonists, with occasional support from American warships, restricted slave trading in their quarter.

The escalation of the slave trade in the Gallinas and in neighboring portions of the
Sherbro during the 1820s ironically was an indirect result of Liberia's establishment.
The active collaboration of the Mesurado colonists and the American navy, which
began to patrol the area more regularly, deflected slaving activity toward Sierra Leone.

Other factors also were at play. As the Gallinas historian Adam Jones suggests, the
"very *un*productivity" of the area may have drawn slave traders. "There was little that
slaves could be used to produce," he writes, "either for home consumption (with the
exception of salt) or for export." If wars produced surplus workers, selling them was a
logical business decision. "Once this process began," Jones explains, ". . . slave dealers were encouraged to settle; they offered credit; and the . . . country found itself con-
tinuously inhabited by a larger population than it could support, except through the
slave trade."[14]

Many of the slaves being sold in the Gallinas were generated by a fresh wave of
warfare in Mende country and in the Mano River region on the Sherbro periphery.[15]
It was along the Mano that Mills and Burgess had envisioned settling thousands of free
blacks from America. In that event their "mere presence" might have muted local conflict and dampened slave trading in the vicinity. The same Freetown merchants who
had opposed an American establishment in the Sherbro now complained that the war
raging in the interior was penetrating the region "to the great detriment of the colonial trader."[16]

The benign MacCarthy's governorship ended abruptly in early 1824 when he lost
his head—literally—in an ill-advised campaign against the Ashanti in the Gold Coast.[17]
His replacement, Gen. Charles Turner, a one-armed veteran of the Peninsular War,
arrived in Freetown in February 1825. He soon embarked on his own ill-considered
and unauthorized campaign to exert British sovereignty in the Sherbro to protect trade
and reduce slaving.

Reports in the *Gazette* in May and June spoke of desolation and mayhem in the
Sherbro. The Cussoes (or Mende) and the Sherbro chiefs were fighting a proxy war
allegedly on behalf, respectively, of the Clevelands and George Caulker, the chief of

the Plantains. Neither faction, it seemed, had felt completely reconciled by the peace brokered two decades before by Ludlam and Kizell.

"So destructive has [the war] now become, that the plantations are entirely deserted," the *Gazette* reported. The people preferred "the abandonment of their homes to . . . being . . . seized as slaves." A month later the *Gazette* claimed that a massive assault by the Sherbro chiefs on a fortified Cusso town at Peypurra had been repulsed "with great slaughter. . . . Some hundreds of lives have been lost, and a large supply of victims for the slave mart have thus been obtained."[18]

Turner urgently sent a messenger offering his mediation to both sides. Caulker and the Sherbro chiefs, on the defensive against Cusso encroachment from the interior, readily agreed. But in exchange for British protection, Turner demanded that they collectively cede sovereignty between the Camaranca River and the southern extremity of King Sherbro's supposed realm. The treaty was ratified at Yonie on October 1, 1825, but neither the Cussoes nor the powerful Tuckers in the Boom-Kittam participated in the negotiations. Although the Tuckers came to Yonie to observe, they refused to sign and soon departed to plot resistance.[19]

Turner knew that British policy opposed extension of colonial responsibility and expense, but the spreading violence provided an excuse to act without explicit instructions from London. He gave no hint in his dispatches that he contemplated such a bold initiative. When Turner finally informed his superiors, on October 15, of "the complete success of the *little* expedition to the Sherbro" (emphasis added), he justified it as "a great blow against the slave trade in one of its strongest holds in this country."[20] Earlier he had complained that the "inefficiency of our Squadron" was encouraging the slave trade. "Dealers in Slaves are now so daring," he had reported in July, ". . . that Residents in our Territories are engaged in it."[21]

Turner's concern with ending the slave trade appears to have been genuine. The merchants may also have had his attention, but Turner's designs in the Sherbro, especially his crusade against the Tuckers, were prompted by other factors as well. The first was the Cussoes' increasingly aggressive incursion into what any British governor at Sierra Leone would have regarded as the colony's sphere of interest.

Cusso messengers in Freetown had informed Turner that their people "were resolved to conquer the whole territory and sell it to the Governor," according to the *Gazette* in early September. Although the Cussoes said they wanted to stop the slave trade and to establish "direct communication with the Colony," Turner—again in the *Gazette*'s words—"was dreadfully alarmed."[22] He would not have trusted Cusso pledges at face value and may have seen his intended treaty with the Sherbro leaders as a means to preempt Cusso control of the interior. Ransoming the Sherbro from the Cussoes would be costly and distasteful.

Having achieved his immediate aims in the Sherbro through treaty, Turner decided to use force against the recalcitrant Tuckers. His ostensible purpose was to stop them from trading in slaves and—according to the *Gazette*—providing weapons to all sides in the Sherbro conflict. However, Turner had also been greatly impressed by the Sherbro region's agricultural potential. The Boom River, the Tuckers' domain, was "the most fertile and promising country he had ever seen, not excepting the banks of the Nile."[23] The Boom and Kittam country was too attractive to resist. Turner meant to have it under British dominion.[24]

While the Tuckers repaired from Yonie to their main town of Bohal, Turner and an armed retinue went to Shebar and discovered five French slavers, some of which had already taken slaves on board. "But on seeing me," he recounted, "they landed them at night and hid them in the woods, in chains." Turner allowed the French to leave empty-handed, warning them not to return. He sent the largest ship, fitted to carry five hundred slaves, to Freetown to be condemned.[25]

Before leaving Shebar, the governor sent Kizell to Bohal with a blunt warning to James Tucker. Kizell's brief was not to reason with Tucker or discuss an accommodation; he was to threaten Tucker with execution if he did not cease slave trading.

Pleading innocence several months later to Turner's successor, Tucker described Kizell's visit. "I was afraid," he confessed, ". . . by hearing Sir Charles Turner was swearing . . . to hang me if he should get hold on me at the mouth of the Seabar. . . . Mr. Kizell came and call me, whether I go or not [to meet Turner at Shebar]. He swear that he would surely hang me, which caused me to flee further back with dread into my own native country." Tucker claimed that he would have gladly met with Turner if he had not been intimidated.[26]

Turner evidently made no effort to communicate directly again with the Tuckers or to resolve their differences. Kizell had long regarded the Tuckers as among the most active traders in slaves in the region. He would have applauded Turner's aggressiveness and likely was one of his principal informants. Kizell would not have been disappointed when the governor reappeared in the Sherbro in early February 1826 to attack the Tuckers.

Turner's official objective was to consolidate "arrangements for the Abolition of Slavery" under what he now termed the Sherbro "convention." But his real aim was to eliminate the Tuckers' influence in the Boom and Kittam Rivers and to capture—and presumably to execute—James Tucker.

"I discovered," Turner wrote London, after returning to Freetown on March 2, "that the Great Slave Dealers who had retired from the Sherbro and Sea Bar . . . had joined with those of the Gallinas." With help from French slave traders there, they had reestablished the trade in the Sherbro and "assembled in force, up the Boom River. . . . These Slave Dealers are all Mulattoes, Descendants of Europeans, Strangers to the Soil, and I grieve to say, Men, generally educated in England."[27]

With the help of a naval contingent that had been surveying the coast, Turner burned the stockaded town of Bolome on February 16 and found a large cache of weapons and gunpowder. Three days later, after a tortuous fifteen-mile approach up the snaking Boom, he assaulted Moccabba. According to family lore, several Tuckers helped to repel Turner and his men. Neither of the governor's main quarry, James and his nephew Harry, was found.

Unaware that London had disavowed his treaty with the Sherbro chiefs, Turner proclaimed a naval blockade of the Gallinas on March 4. The proclamation, which Turner was too sick to sign personally, charged James Tucker with slave dealing, insurrection, and restoring the slave trade "within the . . . ceded Territories."[28] Turner died two days later,[29] believing, as he had written during his last sentient hours, that he was making "rapid progress . . . towards the total extinction of the Trade in these seas."[30]

General Turner's obsession with James Tucker overlooked the real power in the family: English-educated Harry. Family tradition credits Harry, in Peter L. Tucker's account, as "the moving spirit behind the resistance to Governor Turner and the reprisals that followed. . . . But for him, James Tucker might have discontinued the resistance to annexation."[31] Kenneth Macaulay, the Freetown merchant who acted as interim governor following Turner's death, also believed that James was prepared to accept British dispensation in the Sherbro, "but he is an Old Weak man" subject to "the influence of his 'Gris-Gris Men' and young relations."[32]

Macaulay regarded Harry as "a most determined Slave Trader, and an enemy of Sierra Leone," but saw an opportunity to appeal to James's more accommodating instincts. When Macaulay sent a small force in April to retrieve an English trader's sloop and goods seized by the younger Tuckers, he cautioned against arousing the uncle's fears. James reportedly chastised his nephew for yanking the British lion's tail.

Harry was unrepentant. Although he returned the ship and its contents, he spurned peace overtures.[33] Fearing that a "confederacy" of mulatto slave traders was regaining a foothold in the Gallinas with the Tuckers' support, Macaulay in April dispatched a detachment of black soldiers to attack Harry at Commenda. He had already fled, however.

Kizell anticipated the wrath of the Tuckers—probably Harry's most of all. On May 7 he wrote from Campelar to the colonial secretary in Freetown to request protection. Given Macaulay's frequent criticism of Kizell, the acting governor would have had little concern for the latter's security. Nevertheless he soon stationed an armed brig and soldiers inside Shebar to deter slaving and protect King Sherbro's domain.[34]

Heavy rains doused war spirits on all sides. By early September the newly arrived governor, Gen. Neil Campbell—like Turner, an elderly Scot—saw an opening to reconcile with the Tuckers. He instructed a Royal Africa Corps lieutenant to meet with James and Harry at Bolome. "You will tell them that I confide in their promise not to permit any vessel or boat or canoe, engaged in the slave trade, to enter the Sherbro', or Shebar, that they will neither directly nor indirectly be engaged in this odious traffic."[35]

The lieutenant waited vainly at Shebar for the Tuckers to present themselves. After receiving nothing but "saucy messages" from them for nearly a week, he left with the ceremonial swords and medals he was to have given them as tokens of their fealty. The Tuckers said they wished to meet Campbell in person and to ask his permission to continue trading in slaves.[36]

James seemed particularly anxious to profess his peaceful intentions, both toward the colony and British trading interests in the Sherbro. In an extraordinary letter, apparently addressed to the English lieutenant, James tried as well to explain why he and his people traded in slaves. Writing on September 28, 1826, from his seat at Mamu, Tucker portrayed the slave trade as "the works of our Forefathers, that they have been carrying on from their youth up until their old age. When we were brought forth by our parents, they brought us up in that line, and we knowing no better so we carry on the same business. Unless we are told the consequences of these things in a better manner, it is most impossible for us to leave of the Slave trade."[37]

The Tuckers may have had intelligence from sources in Freetown that Campbell was in no position to compel them to abandon the "family business." Campbell was under orders not to attack the Tuckers. The strategy was to choke access to the Sherbro and Gallinas slaving grounds, but Campbell complained that English cruisers provided only cursory attention while focusing on the Bights of Benin and Biafra to the east.

"The Tuckers," he reported in November, "assert that the Ashantees drove us into the sea and that the French are to have the Coast from the Gallinas to the Camaranca." This was widely believed by the chiefs and the slave traders, he said, because "no Governor has been there since the death of General Turner, nor any British man of war."[38]

Campbell lifted the Gallinas blockade in January 1827, "confident that . . . [the Tuckers] will shortly . . . partake of the benefits of British Subjects." In March he visited the Sherbro and reported that the Tuckers and other chiefs "consider this infamous traffick . . . drawn to a close."

Campbell was whistling in the dark. He may also have believed that the slave trade could be weakened by chopping its mangrovelike roots, which fed on domestic slavery. Slaves in the Gallinas had recently "risen upon their masters," the *Gazette* claimed, "and declare that they will be as free as the people at Sierra Leone."[39]

The so-called Zawo war, in Vai country, reverberated widely. "I find," Campbell wrote in March 1827, "that among all the Powers, who surround this Colony . . . there is a very strong fear that our Policy is not only to prevent them from exporting their slaves (who are the great mass of the people . . .) but also to destroy the whole system of their Domestic Servitude, the consequences of which would be a general Rebellion."[40] In short any attack on the foreign slave trade threatened the "social contract" of domestic slavery and the political hierarchy it sustained.

On July 28, 1830, Kizell wrote to the Liberated African Department in Freetown that he had custody of a slave trader at Campelar.[41] It was Kizell's final recorded moment in the twilight of a long life.

Since October 1825—the same month he conveyed General Turner's death threat to James Tucker—Kizell had been serving as superintendent of liberated Africans in Campelar and Shebar. It was in this capacity that he had recently helped rescue five liberated African boys who were being taken by canoe to the Gallinas to be shipped to Cuba.[42] The boys had been sold to a nephew of James Tucker and then to a French slave dealer who lived in one of the Tuckers' towns on the Boom River.[43]

In this letter to a British
military officer, James Tucker
explained that slave trading is
"the works of our Forefathers."
National Archives of the
United Kingdom

Nearly twenty thousand Africans had been liberated by the British navy and resettled in the colony. As their numbers swelled, however, they had become easy prey for slave traders—including other liberated Africans.[44] Children were the most vulnerable. Many were apprenticed. "Any person in the colony of respectable appearance may have several liberated African children," wrote a British naval surgeon who visited Sierra Leone in 1830. They needed only to pay a pittance. The children often vanished. Even a schoolmaster had been tried for selling some of his students.[45]

The governor, notwithstanding his many years in West Africa, was appalled. "I am astonished," Lt. Col. Alexander Findlay reported that July, "that the kidnapping system had not been detected before this time. . . . I do believe instead of Sierra Leone being a free colony, slavery has been carried on in it to a very great extent."[46] Another governor, T. Perronet Thompson, had lost his job for expressing similar outrage more than twenty years earlier.

By the late 1820s, the slave trade had been substantially internalized in the colony's culture. "Slave and legitimate trade were inextricably mixed," Fyfe observes. Sailors from condemned slavers wandered the streets, boarded with settlers, and lived on government rations. "Inevitably there was less public feeling against the slave trade than might have been expected among a population of former slaves."[47]

People had reconciled themselves to the slave trade's resiliency and what by then may have seemed inevitable. British and American naval squadrons intercepted a few of the slavers—enough to salve the humanitarian conscience. But they were powerless to stifle a trade that rose to meet sustained demand. The new Baltimore clippers, fast and armed, were making it easier to evade capture. As one British official warned in May 1828, "if fresh measures with augmented means" were not employed to counter this American innovation, the slave trade "must flourish in greater force instead of diminishing as we have been led to hope."[48]

The man whom John Kizell was holding at Campelar was a fellow Nova Scotian named Peter Jorden. He had been implicated in the kidnapping of the five boys. His alleged accomplice, an African American, was also caught, convicted, and sentenced to hang. Perhaps conceding the crime's "inevitability," the governor commuted the sentence to ten years' hard labor.

In the colony's prison, described by the surgeon as an "unvarnished pile of stone, several stories high," twenty-eight men were being held in late 1830 for decoying and selling liberated Africans. One presumably was Kizell's detainee. Another, in all likelihood, was his accomplice, Samuel Wilson, who had accompanied Paul Cuffe in 1816 and urged blacks in America to return to Africa, where they could become a nation.[49]

The Dark and the Light

> The white man is not strong—he's scared. His whiteness is made of terror, or otherwise he would not be white. He is consumed by his terror and wrestles with it to stay alive. Until he is at peace with himself, no one around him ever will be. (A Dagara villager in French West Africa, circa 1960)[50]

> Black . . . is a hiding place . . . black or Darkness. . . . This black can hide you from your enemies. (A Poro diviner in Makeni, Sierra Leone, 1978)[51]

Slavery and the slave trade defined John Kizell's life, as they did for millions of black and white people. In ways that will never be truly understood, on either side of the Atlantic, the legacy of the "African trade" remains embedded in the souls of black folk and white folk as well. All carry history's "slavery" gene—recessive but never entirely expunged.

The pathologies of race and poverty in North America are well documented and often laid at slavery's door. The pathologies left by slavery and the slave trade in Africa have received less attention. They are often considered, largely by non-Africans, as innate to African cultures.

The slave trade already had begun to distort Kizell's world when it swallowed him in 1773 and excreted him in a Charleston slave market. By the time, nearly six decades later, that Samuel Wilson prepared to answer kidnapping charges, the slave trade had become institutionalized in much of West Africa, just as slavery and racial bigotry had in America.

In her unsettling exploration of the slave trade's residual impact on Temne communities to the immediate north of the Sherbro, Rosalind Shaw argues that Sierra Leoneans continue to live with its consequences. "The slave trade is not forgotten in Sierra Leone," she wrote in 1999, near the end of a decade-long civil war symbolized by drugged child soldiers, gratuitous amputations, and blood diamonds. "Memories of the slave trade . . . keep open a vision of the predatory nature of modernity that resonates all too strongly with the violence of Sierra Leone's rebel war. These memories often take ritual, 'magical,' and phantasmagoric forms."[52]

In 1885 Samuel Lewis, a prominent Sierra Leonean barrister, lamented that the people "bordering on this coast are unable to forget the lesson of rapine and bloodshed . . . fostered in them under the now obsolete European slave-trade system."[53] By more than a century, he anticipated Shaw's observation that Sierra Leone's inheritance from the slave trade is "a landscape of terror and capture; the exchange of commodified people for imported money and goods; and the growth of new kinds of leaders whose power and wealth were derived from the exchange."

Although Great Britain abolished the internal slave trade in Sierra Leone in 1898 and domestic servitude in 1928, "these assumed new forms under colonial rule and postcolonial domination," Shaw writes. "'Big men' . . . are rumored to have (secretly, ritually) exchanged human beings for wealth and power, while money and Western commodities are often linked to the image of an invisible city of witches whose influence is built upon the theft of human lives."[54] Among the Temne, who were both its victims and its agents, the Atlantic slave trade is remembered, Shaw explains, "in the dangerous invisible presences that pervade the landscape itself, and in the protective ritual techniques that people use in order to live in this landscape."[55]

Kizell reviled Africans' superstition. His own life had been traumatically altered by people's belief in witchcraft, and by its manipulation in the hands of the powerful — the chiefs and slave traders among his people. He had seen men, women, and even children murdered as witches and whole families sold abroad in consequence.

In spite of his horror of witchcraft, Kizell may have understood, at some deeper level, that it fulfilled a "legitimate" function — as among the Yoruba, where it counterbalanced male domination and prevented dangerously excessive accumulation of personal wealth, or among the Bakongo, James Creighton's people, where it enhanced the importance of elders who possessed the knowledge to pacify offended ancestors.[56]

Kizell could not entirely discount the existence of occult forces, of the "darkness." In 1810 he described in detail the autopsies he had seen conducted on a boy, a man, and a woman to determine if they were witches. When the abdomens of the boy and the man were cut open, nothing was found. "But in the body of the woman," Governor Columbine recorded in his notes, "something appeared which staggered Kizell so much, that being unable to refute the assertion that this strange appearance was a witchbag, and unwilling to concede so incredible a point, he felt obliged to retire out of the house."[57]

Witchcraft, John Mbiti suggests, has to be viewed in the context of rural African societies. These "are deeply affected and permeated by the psychological atmosphere which creates both real and imaginary powers or forces of evil that give rise to more tensions, jealousies, suspicions, slanders, and scapegoats."

Unless one grows up in village life, Mbiti explains, it is impossible "to get an idea of the depth of evil and its consequences upon individuals and society. A visitor . . . will immediately be struck by African readiness to externalize feelings of joy, love, friendship and generosity. But this must be balanced by the fact that Africans are men, and there are many occasions when their feelings of hatred, strain, fear, jealousy and suspicion also become readily externalized."[58]

All that Africans knew, believed, and valued came with them to America. Many considered darkness as sacred and protective. "It is forbidden to illuminate it," writes Malidoma Patrice Somé, "for light scares the Spirit away. Our night is the day of the Spirit and of the ancestors, who come . . . to tell us what lies on our life paths." Villagers, he adds, "are expected to learn how to function in the dark."[59]

For enslaved Africans in America, darkness became a real and metaphysical refuge, a technique of survival in the country of white people, a people who preferred light to darkness. As Shaw implies, certain slaves who were carried from Sierra Leone (and elsewhere in Africa) brought with them knowledge of "darkness medicine" that could prevent their being seen by others, including their masters and other whites.

The Poro in Temneland, Shaw writes, is "renowned for its control of states of Darkness through its medicines and its practices of verbal and ritual secrecy." The medicines enabled "Poro adepts to enter 'crossed' . . . states in which the distinction between this world . . . and the spirits' world . . . is collapsed, giving them miraculous capacities."[60] These were among the "surprising things" that Kizell left unexplained.

Americans have tried, with considerable success, to obliterate the memory and guilt of slavery and the slave trade. For most African Americans, this has meant obliterating their connection to Africa. African complicity in the slave trade is an unwelcome reminder of that link. It is not something that people are eager to remember, let alone to acknowledge.

For Africans, however, their complicity and victimization are not easily ignored or ultimately forgotten. They become not part of the "past" but part of a closed existential loop. The slave trade and colonialism "happened" in a time framed by the white people's calendar. To the African cultures affected, however, these are experiences that now and forever belong to the ancestors, the living dead, the living, and those yet to be born.

Because their cultures recognize the importance of reconciling good and evil and of maintaining harmony with the spirits who cohabit their world, Africans have internalized the slave trade within their corporate memory. Sierra Leoneans thus live with what Shaw calls a "perilous potential" for evil in a society that, in effect, has lost some of its faith in the spirits' goodness.

The "ritual landscape" among the Temne was transformed radically during the slave trade, Shaw argues. Benign spirits, who once resided in people's homes, had failed to protect them from being sold into slavery. Most spirits are now regarded as "amoral and destructive beings." They have been "banished . . . to the bush, where they had changed into 'rogue' spirits with bad intentions."[61] The violence visited upon Sierra Leone in the 1990s—unimaginable to outsiders who had long taken the country's peaceful veneer at face value—could be understood, at least partially, in the context of the slave trade.

The violence may also be traceable to the *internal* slave trade and the endemic domestic servitude that filled the vacuum left when the foreign slave trade ended in the midnineteenth century. In *War and the Crisis of Youth in Sierra Leone*, Krijn Peters documents the motivations of rural youth who served in the rebel Revolutionary United Front. "Many [RUF] conscripts," Peters writes, "were from a labouring class that was a product of incomplete emancipation from domestic slavery during the colonial period. . . ." They were youth still largely at the economic and social mercy of chiefs, village elders, and "big men," who virtually controlled their destiny through allocation of land and marriage partners. "Many of the practices," Peters explains, "'codified' in customary law are still recognisably related to the exploitation of the labour of youths under domestic slavery."[62]

Looking back in 1839 on his half-century struggle to abolish the slave trade, Thomas Clarkson considered the lessons he had learned. One was foremost: "The slave trade has proved what a creature man is! How devoted he is to his own interest! To what a length of atrocity he can go."[63]

Kizell would not have contested Clarkson's assessment of human nature. Yet he gave no hint of his own experiences as a slave in South Carolina—not in his surviving correspondence with William Allen, not in his reports to Governor Columbine, nor in the recollections of Paul Cuffe, Daniel Coker, Samuel Mills, and others who had known him. Perhaps he considered his experience too commonplace to shock or instruct. But it was not something he would have forgotten.

There were reminders enough. Kizell would have read the *Royal Gazette and Sierra Leone Advertiser* of September 18, 1824, which excerpted the travelogue of an Englishman who visited Charleston about the time that Creighton was weighing anchor for Africa and Denmark Vesey was planning his apocalypse.

In *Letters from North America*, Adam Hodgson described a slave auction in a street around the corner from "a fashionable promenade, enlivened by gay parties and glittering equipages. Several merchants and planters were walking about examining the unhappy creatures. . . . A poor woman . . . with a child at her breast, [and] her two little boys . . . composed the *first lot*. They were mounted on a platform . . . taking hold of each other's hands, and the little boys looking up at their mother's face with an air of curiosity, as if they wondered what could make her look so sad."[64] Kizell knew.

The future of Sierra Leone did not look promising in the latter part of the 1820s. Observers in England questioned the colony's salubrity, its intrinsic worth and cost. There was talk of transferring the mixed courts and the business of condemning captured slave ships to Fernando Po, an island off the Nigerian coast. As real estate values plunged in consequence, John Kizell and others sold their properties in Freetown. Yellow fever revisited in 1829, taking poor and prosperous alike, including Kizell's former critic Kenneth Macaulay. His death—after more than two decades on the coast—seemed to mark the end of an era.[65]

A select committee of Parliament reprieved Sierra Leone in 1830, recommending that it not be abandoned. The deciding rationale was that the European merchants and surviving Nova Scotian–Maroon settlers would otherwise be overwhelmed by the growing recaptive presence.[66] In the meantime the slave trade expanded in the Gallinas. Settlers in the Sherbro abetted the trade by selling their rice, at favorable prices, to feed slaves being held for shipment in the Gallinas—as Kizell had been nearly sixty years earlier.[67]

Precisely when Kizell joined the living dead may never be known. He remained alive at Campelar as late as mid-1830. It is there, in his thatched chapel, that villagers must eventually have gathered to commend him vocally to the Christian god and probably silently to the ancestors.

Kizell outlived most of his Nova Scotian contemporaries. It would be nice to think that he also outlived slavery in the British Empire, which was made illegal in 1833. As it did for William Wilberforce, William Allen, and Thomas Clarkson, who all lived to see that day, abolition would have brought closure to Kizell and a life lived in the conviction that slavery, in any form, was wrong.

NOTES

Chapter 1. Chained Together

1. Henry Laurens to John Knight, March 17, 1773, *Papers of Henry Laurens*, 8:628.

2. *South Carolina Gazette and Country Journal*, May 31, 1773.

3. The number of slaves imported directly into Charleston in 1771–74, before the trade was suspended by the American colonies, was at least 16,000, based on customhouse records held by the South Carolina Department of Archives and History. W. Robert Higgins gives a figure of 19,215 in "Geographical Origins of Negro Slaves." Elizabeth Donnan estimated that 21,198 slaves were imported into South Carolina in this period, including 11,641 in 1773 alone. She warned that her numbers were not precise, and it is likely that Donnan included imports from the West Indies as well as Africa. (See Donnan, "Slave Trade into South Carolina," 807.) Based on the Charleston customs records, which recorded 7,238 slaves in calendar year 1773, Laurens retained a good sense of the market.

4. Details regarding the Blossom in 1773 are available on the Trans-Atlantic Slave Trade Database, voyage 91849, available on-line at www.slavevoyages.org/tast/index.faces (accessed August 18, 2010). Kizell's known biography suggests that he arrived in Charleston in 1773, but he may have come as late as September 1774. Because ship and customs records do not mention the Gallinas as the "place of slave purchase," Kizell most likely was carried on a ship that also stopped for slaves at Cape Mount, near the Gallinas. The *Blossom* is one of three slave ships that arrived in Charleston in 1773 from Cape Mount. At least two others arrived the following year.

5. In 1810 Kizell recounted to a British governor of Sierra Leone that a woman slave aboard his ship was flogged to death on the captain's orders. See the African Institution's *Sixth Report*, 145.

6. Sellers, *Charleston Business*, 166.

7. Wilberforce, *Sherbro and the Sherbros*, 18.

8. Donnan, "Slave Trade into South Carolina," 807. Data on the number of slaves imported into South Carolina and Georgia in the late colonial period varies substantially. Precise numbers for Charleston are unavailable because the imports for the two provinces tended to be aggregated. However, David Eltis estimates that as many as 9,700 slaves were imported altogether in 1773 (March 28, 2009, e-mail to the author), suggesting that those brought into the Charleston slave market numbered about 9,000.

9. Smith, *New Age Now Begins*, 2:275.

10. Ibid., 2:296.

11. Sellers, *Charleston Business*, 220.

12. Walsh, *Charleston's Sons of Liberty*, 57.

13. *South Carolina Gazette and Country Journal*, June 7, 1773.

14. Donnan, *Documents Illustrative of the History of the Slave Trade to America*, 4:466.

15. Donnan, "Slave Trade into South Carolina," 828; Davis, *Problem of Slavery*, 120. Davis believes South Carolina "complied more willingly with the non-importation agreements, in part to reduce debts and allow merchants, as one manifesto put it, 'to settle their accounts, and be ready with the return of liberty to renew trade.'"

16. Laurens to Knight, March 17, 1773, *Papers of Henry Laurens*, 8:628.

17. Rogers, *Charleston in the Age of the Pinckneys*, 27; *South Carolina Gazette*, May 25, 1773.

18. Rogers, *Charleston in the Age of the Pinckneys*, 26.

19. Coclanis, *Shadow of a Dream*, 7.

20. Will Book 55, 1771–1774, 285, South Carolina Department of Archives and History (hereafter SCDAH).

21. Holcomb, *South Carolina Deed Abstracts*, 39; Donnan states that in spite of "the unprecedented numbers [of slaves] offered for sale [in Charleston] in May and June of 1773, prime men sold for 350 pounds and women for 290 pounds." Donnan, "Slave Trade into South Carolina," 823.

22. Laurens to George Appleby, February 28, 1774, *Papers of Henry Laurens*, 9:317.

23. *South Carolina Gazette*, May 31, 1773. Senegambia ports were notoriously dangerous for slavers. Slaves—such as those aboard the *New Britannia*—were many times more likely to revolt than elsewhere along the African coast. See Richardson, "Shipboard Revolts," 77.

24. Kup, *History of Sierra Leone*, 112. "For the eighteenth century," Kup notes, "it is practically a rule that if a ship's documents mention a swivel-gun, but contain no Letters of Marque (which would have created her a legal privateer) then she is a slave ship."

25. Afzelius, *Sierra Leone Journal*, 158. Smeathman later played a controversial role in sending black settlers to Sierra Leone in 1787. He is quoted from correspondence held by the Uppsala University Library.

26. Charleston customhouse records show that the *Africa* arrived on or about May 31, 1773, with 185 slaves. Given the normal four- to six-week voyage back to Africa, the ship could have refitted quickly in Charleston and reached the Isles de Los by the time Smeathman visited the ship about July 10; *Papers of Henry Laurens*, 9:75.

27. Morgan, *Slave Counterpoint*, 444–45.

28. Olwell, *Masters, Slaves and Subjects*, 222–23.

29. Donnan, *Documents Illustrative of the History of the Slave Trade to America*, vol. 4. The *South Carolina Gazette* of May 16, 1773, quoted a correspondent who was "sorry to see Guineymen permitted, at a season when no bad Weather is apprehended, to come up from Rebellion Road, before they have performed the Quarantine required by Law; by which he apprehends the Inhabitants of the Town may be exposed to some terrible Calamity worse than the Rage to buy Negroes."

30. According to J. Russell Cross, planters realized in the late 1750s that "the mixture of silt and peat that had washed down to form the marshy sections of the tidal streams could be used for the cultivation of rice by construction of dams and dikes" (Cross, *Historic Ramblin's through Berkeley*, 83); Sellers, *Charleston Business*, 154, 157.

31. *Papers of Henry Laurens*, 8:635; Berkeley and Berkeley, *Dr. Alexander Garden*, 58–59. Garden believed that "the loss of many . . . [slaves'] lives testified the Fatigue they Underwent in Satisfying the Inexpressible Avarice of the Masters." Their owners "pay dear for their Barbarity, by the loss of many so . . . Valuable Negroes" (Garden to William Shipley, April 2, 1755).

32. Littlefield, *Rice and Slaves*, 103.

33. Carney, *Black Rice*, 81.

34. Littlefield, *Rice and Slaves*, 27.

35. "Journal of Josiah Quincy," 441.

36. Higgins, "Charleston," 118.

37. Sellers, *Charleston Business*, 109.

38. Ibid., 59, 147.

39. Ibid., 51–52; Charleston Customs House Records, 1771–1774, SCDAH.

40. Sellers, *Charleston Business*, 109.

41. Ibid., 97–98.

42. Ibid., 133.

43. Donnan, "Slave Trade Into South Carolina," 816; Littlefield, "Charleston and Internal Slave Redistribution," 97.

44. Sellers, *Charleston Business*, 141.

45. *Papers of Henry Laurens*, 8:529.

46. The consensus of two experts on Charleston history, Michael Coker and Dr. George Williams, is that in 1773 the bells of St. Michael's and St. Philip's churches "would have rung at night to mark the time. . . . They also doubled as city bells, so would have rung for any type of warning." E-mail to the author, October 9, 2008, from Jane Aldrich, South Carolina Historical Society.

47. Coclanis, *Shadow of a Dream*, 121.

48. Gibson, "Costume and Fashion," 232–33.

49. Walsh, *Charleston's Sons of Liberty*, 3.

50. Stephenson, *Scotch-Irish Migration*, 8.

51. Henry Laurens to William Fisher, November 9, 1768, quoted in Sellers, *Charleston Business*, 118.

52. Sellers, *Charleston Business*, 203; Walsh, *Charleston's Sons of Liberty*, 24.

53. See Bridenbaugh, *Cities in Revolt*, 358.

54. Walsh, *Charleston's Sons of Liberty*, 17.

55. Woodson, *Palatines of Londonborough*, 5; Holcomb, *Petitions for Land*, 5:42–45; Bell, *Anomaly of Charleston*, 23.

56. Holcomb, *South Carolina Marriages, 1688–1799*, 144; Migliazzo, *To Make This Land Our Own*, 80. Conrad Kysell did not receive a town lot in Purrysburg, which suggests that he did not take up permanent residence.

57. Roeber, *Palatines, Liberty, and Property*, 220.

58. Riley, "Michael Kalteisen," 35.

59. Gongaware, *History of the German Friendly Society*, xx. German-speaking Charlestonians are conspicuously absent among the names of those who swore allegiance to the Crown following the fall of the city to General Clinton in May 1780. Although some English-speaking citizens questioned German sympathies, Roeber believes Kalteisen and members of St. John's Parish "were ardent patriots." See Roeber, *Palatines, Liberty, and Property*, 318.

60. Loans were made "to the Publick Treasury" in August 1777, May 1778, and February 1780. The last loan came as British forces laid siege to Charleston. See the German Friendly Society Fair Minute Book, SCDAH, 1971.

61. Conrad "Keysell" pleaded not guilty when indicted for perjury in October 1770 and was found innocent on January 22, 1771. See the *Journal of the South Carolina Court of General*

Sessions, 1769–1776, SCDAH, 81; German Friendly Society Fair Minute Book, minutes for April 3, 1771, and December 30, 1772.

62. Roeber, *Palatines, Liberty, and Property*, 229.

63. Ibid., 224.

64. Will Book 55 1771–1774, 285, SCDAH.

65. *South Carolina Gazette*, February 8, 15, and 22, 1773.

66. Roeber, *Palatines, Liberty, and Property*, 226.

67. Migliazzo, *To Make This Land Our Own*, 288.

68. Equiano, who was close to leading English abolitionists, published *The Interesting Narrative of the Life of Olaudah Equiano, or Gustavus Vassa, the African*, in 1788. He claimed to have been born and enslaved in Africa, but it is now believed that he was born in South Carolina about 1747 and that he based parts of his autobiography on secondhand accounts of the slave trade. See Vincent Carretta, *Equiano the African*, xiv–xv.

69. "Memoirs of the Life of Boston King" was published in the *Methodist Magazine* in 1798 while he was living temporarily in England.

70. The Charleston Negro School was established in 1743 under the Society for the Propagation of the Gospel. It closed in 1764 when its black instructor died and no competent replacement could be found. See Klingberg, *Appraisal of the Negro*, 121.

71. I am indebted to the linguist Tucker Childs, who in 2007–10 conducted field research on the nearly extinct language of the Kim in southeastern Sierra Leone, for confirming birth names traditionally given to boys. The names are virtually the same as those used among the neighboring Sherbro. The Kim language has no "r" sound. Thus the term "Krim," which historians have long used to describe Kim speakers, is incorrect. E-mail to author, March 16, 2010. See also Wilberforce, *Sherbro and the Sherbros*, 16–17.

72. Heuman and Walvin, *Slavery Reader*, 358.

73. Morgan, *Slave Counterpoint*, 559.

74. Ibid., 442; Morgan, "Black Life in Eighteenth-Century Charleston," 189.

75. Berkeley and Berkeley, *Dr. Alexander Garden*, 32.

76. Frey and Wood, "Survival of African Religions," 402.

77. Morgan, "Black Society in the Lowcountry," 134.

78. Zornow, "Troublesome Community," 39.

79. Seeber, *On the Threshold of Liberty*, 14–15.

80. Morgan, "Black Life in Eighteenth-Century Charleston," 187.

81. Berlin, "Time, Space, and the Evolution," 135.

82. *South Carolina Gazette and Country Journal*, January 25, 1772, and October 31, 1774.

83. Ibid., March 23, 1773, and April 20, 1773.

84. Wood, "Taking Care of Business," 273.

85. Olwell, *Masters, Slaves and Subjects*, 168–72.

86. *South Carolina Gazette and Country Journal*, September 24, 1772.

87. Morgan, "Black Life in Eighteenth-Century Charleston," 194; *South Carolina Gazette and Country Journal*, November 15, 1770.

88. Morgan, "Work and Culture," 203; Berlin, "Time Space, and the Evolution," 135.

89. Sellers, *Charleston Business*, 93–94.

90. *South Carolina Gazette and Country Journal*, September 24, 1772; *Journal of the South Carolina Court of General Sessions*, May 16, 1775.

91. *South Carolina Gazette*, October 10, 1772.

92. Zornow, "Troublesome Community," 42.

93. Morgan, "Black Society in the Lowcountry," 134.

94. Sellers, *Charleston Business*, 96. Slaves were required by law to wear "Negro cloth, Duffils . . . Osnabrugs, blue linen, check linen, coarse garlix, coarse calicoes, check cottons, scotch plaids."

95. Zornow, "Troublesome Community," 39, 48.

96. Wood, "Taking Care of Business," 273.

97. Morgan, "Black Life in Eighteenth-Century Charleston," 191.

98. Sellers, *Charleston Business*, 105; *South Carolina Gazette and Country Journal*, November 3, 1772.

99. Morgan, "Black Life in Eighteenth-Century Charleston," 224. In South Carolina, Morgan writes, "Africans of similar ethnicity established or renewed ties with one another even when they lived on separate plantations." Morgan, *Slave Counterpoint*, 447.

100. Bolster, *Black Jacks*, 62.

101. Sellers, *Charleston Business*, 106; Morgan, "Black Life in Eighteenth-Century Charleston," 197.

102. "Journal of Josiah Quincy," 463.

103. Merrens, "View of Coastal South Carolina," 190.

104. *South Carolina Gazette*, August 27, 1772.

105. Olwell, "Becoming Free," 10–11. Only 61 manumissions were recorded in Charleston in the 1770s (Morgan, *Slavery and Freedom*, 115). The number nearly doubled in the 1780s to 118.

106. Moss and Scoggins, *African-American Loyalists*, 123, 169, 300.

Chapter 2. The Uprooting

1. For a detailed description of the physical characteristics of the Gallinas region, in particular see Jones, *From Slaves to Palm Kernels*.

2. Kup, *History of Sierra Leone*, 30.

3. Ibid.

4. Fyfe, *History of Sierra Leone*, 2; Afzelius, *Sierra Leone Journal*, 4.

5. Kup, *History of Sierra Leone*, 144.

6. Ibid., 153; Afzelius, *Sierra Leone Journal*, 5.

7. Elizabeth Clevland married William Hardcastle, a British military surgeon, in 1771, the same year she inherited her brother's large plantations near Moncks Corner. Educated, wealthy, and apparently light-skinned, she was considered white by the conventions of the day. Her darker-hued niece Catherine never married but bore several children, probably by local white planters. Several of her children are described in census records as mulatto or free persons of color. See Louise, *Elizabeth Clevland Hardcastle*, 71–72, 431; Fyfe, *History of Sierra Leone*, 10.

8. Tucker, *Tuckers of Sierra Leone*, 1.

9. Ibid., 2.

10. Owen, *Journal of a Slave-Dealer*, 76.

11. Day, "Afro-British Integration," 82–84.

12. Ibid., 84.

13. Tucker, *Tuckers of Sierra Leone*, 8. Tucker writes that the "first Tuckers, in spite of their western education and life-style, were members of the Poro. They could not otherwise have been Chiefs and achieved the success they did in business."

14. Wadstrom, *Essay on Colonization*, 84–85.

15. William Smith, *A New Voyage to Guinea* (London, 1744), 65, quoted in Kup, *History of Sierra Leone*, 104.

16. Owen, *Journal of a Slave-Dealer*, 62.

17. Ibid., 45.

18. Jones, *From Slaves to Palm Kernels*, 27.

19. African Institution, *Sixth Report*, 125.

20. Somé, *Of Water and the Spirit*, 3.

21. Owen, *Journal of a Slave-Dealer*, 51; African Institution, *Sixth Report*, 137.

22. African Institution, *Sixth Report*, 125, 127.

23. Ibid., 126.

24. Ibid.

25. Mbiti, *African Religions and Philosophy*, 19; Somé, *Of Water and the Spirit*, 8.

26. Mbiti, *African Religions and Philosophy*, 97.

27. Morgan, *Slave Counterpoint*, 631.

28. Mbiti, *African Religions and Philosophy*, 29–30.

29. Wilberforce, *Sherbro and the Sherbros*, 18.

30. Owen, *Journal of a Slave-Dealer*, 49. Owen found "little or no religion" among the Sherbros in the mid-1700s, and "therefore conscience is but a small burden. . . . They belive [sic] that there is a god who has made the world and all things, but they never worship him in any set place . . . giving more honour to thier [sic] idols or devils then [sic] they do a divine being."

31. Mbiti, *African Religions and Philosophy*, 257.

32. Ibid., 34–35.

33. African Institution, *Sixth Report*, 136.

34. Ibid., 139.

35. Ibid., 136.

36. Ibid.

37. Ibid., 138.

38. Ibid., 139.

39. Ibid., 140–41.

40. I am grateful to the late Christopher Fyfe and to Adam Jones for their insights regarding Kizell's origins. In a personal discussion on May 14, 2008, in London, Fyfe accepted the possibility that Kizell came from an area closer to the Gallinas than to the Sherbro. Jones likewise regards the Gallinas hypothesis as "plausible" (e-mail to the author, December 28, 2007). Jones cautions against trying to guess Kizell's ethnic identity. "Generally," he wrote in a December 20, 2007, e-mail to the author, "research on Africa has shown in the past 20 years that it seldom makes sense to project ethnicity back into the eighteenth century. The kind of ethnicity documented in the 20th century was a very modern phenomenon. It would have been meaningless . . . to say . . . in the 1750s 'I am a Sherbro,' since [one] had no reason to identify himself in such a way."

41. African Institution, *Sixth Report*, 144–45.

42. Somé, *Of Water and the Spirit*, 60–61.

43. Newton, *Thoughts upon the African Slave Trade*, 25–26.

44. John Matthews, *A Voyage to the River Sierra Leone* (London, 1788), quoted in Afzelius, *Sierra Leone Journal*, 82.

45. Jones, *From Slaves to Palm Kernels*, 19. According to Sierra Leonean historian Arthur Abraham, "exposing Poro secrets carries death" (July 7, 2009, e-mail to author).

46. Grace, "Slavery and Emancipation," 428.

47. Afzelius, *Sierra Leone Journal*, 128.

48. Grace, "Slavery and Emancipation," 416–17.

49. MacCormack, "Slaves, Slave Owners, and Slave Dealers," 421.

50. Miers and Kopytoff, *Slavery in Africa*, 53; MacCormack, "Slaves, Slave Owners, and Slave Dealers," 428.

51. Arthur Abraham, e-mail to author, July 7, 2009.

52. Heywood and Thornton, *Central Africans*, 9.

53. Shaw, *Memories of the Slave Trade*, 26–27.

54. Kup, *History of Sierra Leone*, 121.

55. Shaw, *Memories of the Slave Trade*, 232.

56. Kup, *History of Sierra Leone*, 40.

57. Ibid., 38, 89.

58. Jones, *From Slaves to Palm Kernels*, 21.

59. Kup, *History of Sierra Leone*, 67.

60. Eltis, "Labour and Coercion," 66.

61. Ibid., 65.

62. Ibid., 66.

63. Ibid., 67.

64. Ibid., 68.

65. Curtin, "Epidemiology and the Slave Trade," 13. In reality blacks and whites suffered alike in tropical conditions. Black mortality was high on Caribbean plantations and in the Carolina lowcountry.

66. Eltis, "Labour and Coercion," 69.

67. Ibid., 70.

68. Manning, *Slavery and African Life*, 25.

69. Ibid., 32, 35.

70. Eltis and Richardson, "West Africa and the Trans-Atlantic Slave Trade," 44–45.

71. Kup, *History of Sierra Leone*, 89.

72. Jones, *From Slaves to Palm Kernels*, 25–26.

73. Holsoe, "Slavery and Economic Response," 293.

74. Owen and Newton, as quoted in Kup, *History of Sierra Leone*, 57–59.

75. Knight, *New Republic*, 34–35.

76. Zachary Macaulay Journal, February 16–20, 1798, Manuscript Division (call number MY 418), Huntington Library (hereafter MDHL).

77. Macaulay, who must have read Governor Columbine's biographical note on Kizell when it was published in London in 1812, never commented publicly on what he would have regarded as a glaring discrepancy in Kizell's recollection of his enslavement. He might have wondered why Kizell had not told Columbine of the witchcraft accusation. But as an active

opponent of the slave trade, he would not have wished to undermine the credibility of Kizell's damning reports by questioning the consistency or veracity of what he had told Columbine about his enslavement. Christopher Fyfe, who first drew the author's attention to the witchcraft version, believed this was a credible story (personal conversation, August 27, 2007); Kizell implied to Macaulay that he actually drank the red water. This scenario is consistent with the slave trader Matthews's 1788 account of life in the Sherbro. As an accused witch, Kizell could have been permitted to "escape" to a nearby village, where he would have asked the headman to administer the red water ordeal. An influential person could have intervened at this stage and enabled him to vomit the liquid, which was concocted from sasswood. This would have proved his innocence. On the other hand, if he "spoiled the red water" by defecating within a day of regurgitating, he would have been sold. See Matthews, *Voyage to the River Sierra Leone*, 125–26.

78. Holsoe, "Slavery and Economic Response," 289–90.

79. Ibid, 290.

80. Tucker Childs, a linguist who spent 2007–10 among the last Kim speakers and neighboring peoples in southeastern Sierra Leone, e-mail to the author, March 16, 2010.

81. Afzelius, *Sierra Leone Journal*, 164.

82. Shaw, *Memories of the Slave Trade*, 24. Shaw reports present-day "images of an invisible witch city [where] the slave trade has been 'remembered' through images of modernity and globalization as fundamentally predatory, witch-like processes."

Chapter 3. The Overturning

1. Henry Laurens to John Knight, March 17, 1774, quoted in Donnan, *Documents Illustrative of the History of the Slave Trade to America*, 4:469.

2. Laurens to John Lewis Gervais, February 5, 1774, *Papers of Henry Laurens*, 9:264.

3. Laurens to Gervais, April 9, 1774, *Papers of Henry Laurens*, 9:395.

4. Charleston Customs House Records, 1771–1774, SCDAH.

5. *South Carolina Gazette*, October 20, 1774. The Continental Congress, in Philadelphia, adopted the nonimportation resolution on September 5, 1774.

6. *South Carolina Gazette*, November 21, 1774, and March 6, 1775.

7. The *South Carolina Gazette* reported on December 19, 1774, that several vessels had arrived with foreign goods, "but no person refused to conform to the Resolutions."

8. Force, *American Archives*, 1:511, 526.

9. Boyd, *Papers of Thomas Jefferson*, 1:426.

10. Ibid, 1:314. Jefferson, July 2, 1776, in his "Notes of the Proceedings in the Continental Congress"; DuBois, *Suppression of the African Slave Trade*, 49.

11. Frey, *Water from the Rock*, 54.

12. *South Carolina Gazette*, September 17, 1772.

13. Drayton, *Memoirs of the American Revolution*, 1:231.

14. Frey, *Water from the Rock*, 54.

15. Morgan, "Black Life in Eighteenth-Century Charleston," 208–9.

16. Olwell, *Masters, Slaves and Subjects*, 232.

17. Frey, *Water from the Rock*, 57.

18. Sellers, *Charleston Business*, 229.

19. Frey, *Water from the Rock*, 4.

20. Morgan, "Black Society in the Lowcountry," 108.

21. Frey, *Water from the Rock*, 56. See Ryan, *The World of Thomas Jeremiah*, 45–46, regarding Charleston slaves' open discussion of the freedom they believed Lord Campbell's arrival portended.

22. Force, *American Archives*, 2:1129. Force quotes a Charleston letter dated June 29, 1775.

23. June 23, 1775, *Papers of Henry Laurens*, 10:191.

24. Having extensively researched the events leading to Jeremiah's execution in August 1775, William R. Ryan concludes that it is impossible to know "with absolute certainty" whether the prosperous black slave owner truly intended "to turn his world upside down and fan the flames of a British instigated [slave] insurrection in South Carolina." Ryan, *The World of Thomas Jeremiah*, 160; see also Wood, *Black Majority*, 284.

25. Walsh, *Charleston's Sons of Liberty*, 71–73.

26. Olwell, *Masters, Slaves and Subjects*, 237.

27. Henry Laurens to John Laurens, August 14, 1776, *Papers of Henry Laurens*, 11:225.

28. In the council of safety minutes for December 10, 1775, a British commander was reported to have claimed that "he could have had near five hundred [blacks], who had offered," requesting protection. See *Collections of the South-Carolina Historical Society*, 3:75.

29. Ibid., 3:95.

30. *Papers of Henry Laurens*, 10:576.

31. Pybus, *Epic Journeys of Freedom*, 21; Olwell, *Masters, Slaves and Subjects*, 239.

32. Pybus, *Epic Journeys of Freedom*, 23.

33. Parramore, *Norfolk*, 90–91; Smith, *New Age Now Begins*, 1:621–22.

34. Parramore, *Norfolk*, 93.

35. Smith, *New Age Now Begins*, 1:622.

36. Ibid.

37. *Collections of the South-Carolina Historical Society*, 3:208.

38. Spring, *Memoirs of the Rev. Samuel J. Mills*, 157.

39. Pybus, *Epic Journeys of Freedom*, 22. Anderson claimed in Nova Scotia to have been born free in Charleston. Pybus says that he later admitted to being from Angola. He may in fact have been owned by a free Charleston black, Robert Lindsay. For a discussion of west Central Africans' impact on the formation of African American culture, see Heywood and Thornton, *Central Africans*.

40. *Papers of Henry Laurens*, 9:333. Three "New Negroes" absconded in late 1772 from Laurens's plantation at Wright's Savannah. His brother James had published notices and distributed handbills widely, but during the ensuing year and a half there had been no trace. "I fear they are lost," James wrote.

41. Massey, *John Laurens*, 93.

42. Edelson, *Plantation Enterprise*, 239.

43. Henry Laurens to John Laurens, August 14, 1776, *Papers of Henry Laurens*, 11:225.

44. Ibid., September 16, 1776, 11:269.

45. John Laurens to Henry Laurens, October 26, 1776, *Papers of Henry Laurens*, 11:276–77.

46. Wilson, *Black Phalanx*, 43.

47. Borick, *Gallant Defense*, 61; Olwell, *Masters, Slaves and Subjects*, 244.

48. Coldham, *American Loyalist Claims*, 365.

49. Henry Laurens to John Laurens, September 16, 1776, *Papers of Henry Laurens*, 11:269.

50. John Lewis Gervais to Henry Laurens, August 2, 1777, "Letters from John Lewis Gervais to Henry Laurens," 19.

51. Edelson, *Plantation Enterprise*, 202.

52. Morgan, "Black Society in the Lowcountry," 108, 121.

53. *South Carolina Gazette*, June 30, 1777; *Papers of Henry Laurens*, 11:546.

54. Gervais to Laurens, August 2, 1777.

55. Frey, *Water from the Rock*, 67.

56. Gen. Augustine Prevost, desperate for men, armed several hundred black volunteers to defend Savannah against a Franco-American force in September–October 1779. They saw little combat and may have been forcibly disarmed and disbanded before the British withdrew. More than three thousand other tidewater slaves tried to attach themselves to General Prevost's army during his 1779 attempt to take Charleston and his retreat to Savannah. As three years before, the British considered them a burden. See Wilson, *Black Phalanx*, 149.

57. Frey, *Water from the Rock*, 117.

58. Ibid., 93.

59. Ibid. James Simpson to Lord George Germain, August 28, 1779.

60. Piecuch, *Three Peoples*, 7.

61. Public Record Office (hereafter PRO) 30/11/3/80–1, National Archives of the United Kingdom (hereafter NAUK).

62. Rogers, *Charleston in the Age of the Pinckneys*, 45.

63. Ibid.

64. Gervais to Laurens, June 26, 1778; "Letters from John Lewis Gervais to Henry Laurens," 31.

65. Ibid., 34, Gervais to Laurens, September 9, 1778.

66. Walsh, *Charleston's Sons of Liberty*, 78.

67. Watson, *Men and Times*, 54.

68. Ibid., 66–68.

69. Ibid., 69.

70. Nash, "Thomas Peters," 179.

71. Foote, *Africa and the American Flag*, 111.

72. Muster Book of Free Black Settlement in Birchtown.

73. Frey, *Water from the Rock*, 86.

74. Massey, *John Laurens*, 120.

75. The black Rhode Island regiment served for five years and fought in several battles, including Yorktown. The unit was demobilized, without pay, at Saratoga, New York, in June 1783. Some of the troops had to resist being reclaimed by their masters. See Greene, "Some Observations on the Black Regiment."

76. Davis, *Problem of Slavery*, 78.

77. Massey, *John Laurens*, 63; John Laurens to Francis Kinloch, April 12, 1776, quoted in Miscellaneous Papers (John Laurens), New York Public Library; in Massey, *John Laurens*, 63.

78. Kaplan, *Black Presence*, 32. Five thousand blacks are estimated to have served in patriot ranks. One quarter of the Continental troops paraded at White Plains, New York, in the summer of 1781, were black.

79. John Laurens to Henry Laurens, January 14, 1778, *Papers of Henry Laurens*, 12:315.

80. Henry Laurens to John Laurens, January 28, 1778, *Papers of Henry Laurens*, 12:368.

81. John Laurens to Henry Laurens, February 2, 1778, *Papers of Henry Laurens*, 12:390–92.

82. Henry Laurens to John Laurens, February 6, 1778, *Papers of Henry Laurens*, 12:412–13.

83. John Lewis Gervais to Henry Laurens, March 16, 1778, *Papers of Henry Laurens*, 13:5.

84. Frey, *Water from the Rock*, 86; Davis, *Problem of Slavery*, 79.

85. Moultrie, *Memoirs of the American Revolution*, 1:258–61.

86. Frey, *Water from the Rock*, 87.

87. "Philipsburg Proclamation," Carleton Papers, PRO 30/55, NAUK.

88. Frey, *Water from the Rock*, 114.

89. Wilson, *Black Phalanx*, 41–42; Massey, *John Laurens*, 140.

90. Massey, *John Laurens*, 135.

91. Borick, *Gallant Defense*, 13–15. Governor John Rutledge and the Privy Council had offered terms that would have surrendered Charleston to the British in exchange for South Carolina's "neutrality." Moultrie and John Laurens strongly opposed what was tantamount to capitulation. The British in any event rejected what they regarded as a "legislative" proposal. This was war.

92. Massey, *John Laurens*, 141–43.

93. Henry Laurens to John Laurens, September 27, 1779, *Papers of Henry Laurens*, 15:177.

94. Gen. Benjamin Lincoln to Gov. John Rutledge, January 30, 1780, quoted in Borick, *Gallant Defense*, 40.

95. South Carolina General Assembly committee report, presented by Henry Laurens on February 1, 1780. *Papers of Henry Laurens*, 15:232–33.

96. Gervais to Henry Laurens, April 28, 1780: "Col [Andrew] Pickens . . . had been down with a party within 5 miles of Savannah, had killed about 60 Negroes in Arms & some white Men with them." *Papers of Henry Laurens*, 15:287.

97. Massey, *John Laurens*, 96.

98. Ibid., 228.

99. Borick, *Gallant Defense*, 81.

100. Piecuch, *Three Peoples*, 214. Piecuch cites a single anecdotal reference to there being fewer blacks in Charleston during the siege. Several sources provide credible evidence that blacks continued to be a majority in Charleston throughout the Revolutionary era.

101. Uhlendorf, *Siege of Charleston*, 207.

102. Quarles, *Negro in the American Revolution*, 128.

103. Borick, *Gallant Defense*, 101–2.

104. Frey, *Water from the Rock*, 141.

105. Records of Loyalist Claims Commissions, Audit Office, AO13/4/321, NAUK.

106. Borick, *Gallant Defense*, 148–49; Scoggins, *Day It Rained Militia*, 39.

107. Scoggins, *Day It Rained Militia*, 39.

108. Scoggins cites the recent judgment of military historians who believe the "slaughter" (113 killed and 150 badly wounded against 5 British dead) was as much the result of "the chaotic and confused nature of the engagement, and the tactical mistakes of the American commanders" as it was "any bloodthirsty desire on the part of the British soldiers to kill Americans who had already surrendered." Scoggins, *Day It Rained Militia*, 46.

109. Dameron, *King's Mountain*, 14.

110. Smith, *New Age Now Begins*, 2:1426–27.

111. Borick, *Gallant Defense*, 98.

112. Quotation from PRO30/11/2/44, NAUK; Clark, *Loyalists in the Southern Campaign*, 1:xiii–xiv.

113. Borick, *Gallant Defense*, 25–26.

114. Lambert, *South Carolina Loyalists*, 185–86.

115. Pybus, *Epic Journeys of Freedom*, 40.

116. Schama, *Rough Crossings*, 105–6.

117. Ibid., 106.

118. Uhlendorf, *Siege of Charleston*, 297.

119. Lambert, *South Carolina Loyalists*, 192–93.

120. Fenn, *Pox Americana*, 118.

121. Moore, *Diary of the American Revolution*, 802.

122. McCowen, *British Occupation of Charleston*, 93–94; Samuel Massey to Henry Laurens, June 12, 1780, *Papers of Henry Laurens*, 15:305. Laurens purchased Massey in 1764 and relied upon his ability to mediate relations between his overseers and slaves. Given that he wrote regular reports to Laurens on all aspects of the plantation's management, including overseers' performance, Laurens must have regarded him as the most dependable and literate person at Mepkin, which he rarely visited.

123. McCowen, *British Occupation of Charleston*, 94. See also Olwell, *Masters, Slaves and Subjects*, 262.

124. German Friendly Society Minute Book, South Carolina Historical Society.

125. Frey, *Water from the Rock*, 119.

126. Ibid., 120. At Mepkin plantation Massey reported to Laurens in his June 12, 1780, letter that all the slaves were staying put because his fields and *theirs* "are in a flurishing way."

127. James Simpson to John André, June 6, 1780, quoted in McCowen, *British Occupation of Charleston*, 101.

128. Board of Police Proceedings, June 13, 1780, Colonial Office (hereafter CO), CO5/520, NAUK.

129. Walker, "Blacks as American Loyalists," 59–60.

130. McCowen, *British Occupation of Charleston*, 101. McCowen notes that slaves of "'unfriendly persons' were now considered public property under the supervision of John Cruden, commissioner of sequestered estates. . . . At war's end, these slaves would be granted their freedom provided that they had performed their assigned tasks faithfully."

131. Kizell related in later years that he joined the British when they took Charleston. This implies that he was *in* the city and still a slave. His writing ability indicates that he also learned early in his enslavement to speak "proper" English as opposed to slave patois or pidgin. Of the several people who wrote of their acquaintance with Kizell as an adult, none demeaned his speaking ability.

132. George Fulker owned land in Orangeburg and was executed in May 1781 after surrendering at Fort Motte. See "A List of Loyalists and Tories Hanged in South Carolina to April 19, 1782," CO5/82/597–600, NAUK.

133. Borick, *Gallant Defense*, 5.

134. Lambert, *South Carolina Loyalists*, 103.

135. "Instructions to Major Ferguson of Militia," May 22, 1780, PRO30/11/2/44-5, NAUK.

136. Stedman, *History of Origin*, 192.

137. Patrick Ferguson to Lord Cornwallis, May 30, 1780, PRO30/11/2/58/xv, NAUK.

138. Gilchrist, *Patrick Ferguson*, 62; Piecuch, *Three Peoples*, 186–88.

139. Smith, *New Age Now Begins*, 2:1426.

140. Gilchrist, *Patrick Ferguson*, 61.

141. Ferguson to Cornwallis, June 4, 1780, PRO30/11/2/86, NAUK.

142. Cornwallis to Francis Rawdon, July 13, 1780, PRO30/11/78/12-3, NAUK; Scoggins, *Day It Rained Militia*, 128.

143. Lambert, *South Carolina Loyalists*, 133.

144. Ibid., 47.

145. McCowen, *British Occupation of Charleston*, 45.

146. Ibid., 55.

147. Ibid., 242. See also Moss and Scoggins, *African-American Loyalists*, for in-depth information on black combatants who fought against the Whigs. Benjamin Quarles agrees that loyalist companies seldom included blacks, except early in the war; see Quarles, *Negro in the American Revolution*, 147.

148. Greene, *Black Courage*, 47. Isom Carter described himself in a June 5, 1818, pension application as a "free man of color descended from an Indian woman and a Negro man."

149. Gilchrist, *Patrick Ferguson*, 63.

150. Smith, *New Age Now Begins*, 2:1427.

151. Scoggins, *Day It Rained Militia*, 23.

152. Ibid., 146–47.

153. Ibid., 143. Some of Ferguson's men fought on the losing side at Musgrove's Mill on August 18, but the major himself was absent.

154. Ferguson to Cornwallis, July 11, 1780, PRO30/11/2/267, NAUK; Lambert, *South Carolina Loyalists*, 139.

155. Smith, *New Age Now Begins*, 2:1437.

156. Scoggins, *Day It Rained Militia*, 15.

157. Cornwallis to Henry Clinton, August 6, 1780, quoted in Willcox, *American Rebellion*, 448.

158. Nisbet Balfour to Cornwallis, June 24, 1780, PRO30/11/2/191-6, NAUK.

159. Frey, *Water from the Rock*, 130–32; Salley, *Documents Relating to the History*, 51.

160. Greene, *Black Courage*, 55; Dunkerly, *Battle of King's Mountain*, 46 (Federal Pension Application S32243); Massey, *John Laurens*, 267.

161. Allaire, *Diary of Lieut. Anthony Allaire*, 27.

162. Rawdon to Alexander Leslie, October 24, 1780, PRO30/11/3/267-70, NAUK.

163. Draper, *King's Mountain*, 202; Dunkerly, *Battle of King's Mountain*, 136.

164. Virginia approved raising a militia body on September 21, 1780. Clark, *Loyalists in the Southern Campaign*, 1:xviii, says its "objective was to help check the British invasion of North Carolina and to gain intelligence of the proposed invasion of Virginia."

165. Lambert, *South Carolina Loyalists*, 140.

166. Moss, e-mail to author, June 18, 2008; Dunkerly, e-mail to author, June 13, 2008.

167. Draper, *King's Mountain*, 204–6; Powell survived the battle, according to Gilchrist, *Patrick Ferguson*, 69. The "breakfast incident" is based on Anthony Twitty's recollections,

written in 1832. Twitty was born in Pennsylvania in 1745 and served as a Whig scout during the Revolution.

168. Smith, *New Age Now Begins*, 2:1427.

169. Ibid., 2:1425, 1428.

170. Moss and Scoggins, *African-American Patriots*, 34; Draper, *King's Mountain*, 267–68.

171. Dunkerly, *Battle of King's Mountain*, 79.

172. Smith, *New Age Now Begins*, 2:1429.

173. Dunkerly, *Battle of King's Mountain*, 88.

174. Smith, *New Age Now Begins*, 2:1429.

175. Dunkerly, *Battle of King's Mountain*, 18.

176. Moss and Scoggins, *African-American Patriots*, 84.

177. Abraham DePeyster to Cornwallis, October 11, 1780. PRO30/11/3/210-1, NAUK.

178. Graves, *James Williams*, 53; Dameron, *King's Mountain*, 70.

179. PRO30/11/3/210-1, NAUK.

180. Dunkerly, *Battle of King's Mountain*, 19.

181. Smith, *New Age Now Begins*, 2:1430–31.

182. Ibid., 2:1434.

183. Dameron, *King's Mountain*, 79; Gilchrist, *Patrick Ferguson*, 69. A second woman traveling with Ferguson, Virginia Paul, deserted to the Whigs before the battle and may have informed them how to identify the British commander. Dunkerly states that recent archaeological analysis confirms that the body buried with Ferguson was a woman's. *Battle of King's Mountain*, 10.

184. Dunkerly, *Battle of King's Mountain*, 82.

185. Moss, *Journal of Capt. Alexander Chesney*, 32–33.

186. Dunkerly, *Battle of King's Mountain*, 73.

187. Lambert, *South Carolina Loyalists*, 143.

188. Moss and Scoggins, *African-American Patriots*, 84, 233–34. The younger Ferguson also fought at Cowpens. He died in Indiana in 1856 at age 91. Titus moved to New York after the Revolution and later settled in Vermont, where he died in 1855 at the age of 112. Dameron lists seventy-four sets of brothers at Kings Mountain in addition to twenty-nine fathers and sons.

189. Dunkerly, *Battle at King's Mountain*, 73–74.

190. Moss, *Journal of Capt. Alexander Chesney*, 32–33, 159.

191. Lambert, *South Carolina Loyalists*, 143.

192. Cornwallis to Henry Gates, December 1, 1780, PRO30/11/91/13-4, NAUK.

193. Nathanael Greene to Cornwallis, December 17, 1780, PRO30/11/91/19, NAUK.

194. Dunkerly, e-mail to author, December 3, 2008.

195. Showman, *Papers of Nathanael Greene*, 544, 546.

196. Moss, *Journal of Capt. Alexander Chesney*, 35–36. When Chesney escaped near the Yadkin River, he slept in the woods and subsisted mainly on haws and wild grapes.

197. Dunkerly, *Battle at King's Mountain*, 15; Allaire, *Diary of Lieut. Anthony Allaire*, 36.

198. Showman, *Papers of Nathanael Greene*, 448; Smith, *New Age Now Begins*, 2:1433.

Chapter 4. Exodus

1. Smith, *New Age Now Begins*, 2:1454–58.

2. McCowen, *British Occupation of Charleston*, 69.

3. Piecuch, *Three Peoples*, 275; Lambert, *South Carolina Loyalists*, 201.

4. Ibid., 14, 35, 41.

5. Lord Cornwallis to Nathanael Greene, February 4, 1781, PRO30/11/91/19, NAUK. Cornwallis wrote that the "close manner in which we were obliged to confine the prisoners . . . to prevent their escape, must prove fatal to many of them when the warm weather commences."

6. Walsh, *Charleston's Sons of Liberty*, 98–99.

7. Ibid., 102.

8. *Royal Gazette*, November 7, 1781.

9. Statement dated December 22, 1781 and issued December 26, quoted in *Aging Database for Nova Scotian Black Cultural History*.

10. Walker, *Black Loyalists*, 62.

11. Ibid. "Charleston posed . . . a serious problem," Walker writes. "Here were concentrated the largest numbers of blacks within British lines, and already difficulties had been met in trying to feed and organize them."

12. Moss, *Journal of Capt. Alexander Chesney*, 42.

13. Alexander Leslie to Henry Clinton, March 30, 1782, quoted in McCowen, *British Occupation of Charleston*, 102.

14. Frey, *Water from the Rock*, 138–39.

15. Lord Dunmore to Clinton, February 2, 1782, CO5/175/264, NAUK; John Cruden to Dunmore, January 5, 1782, CO5/175/267, NAUK; Showman, *Papers of Nathanael Greene*, 2:490.

16. Schama, *Rough Crossings*, 123.

17. McCowen, *British Occupation of Charleston*, 102.

18. Walker, *Black Loyalists*, 62.

19. Ibid.

20. Pybus, *Epic Journeys of Freedom*, 58.

21. Wilson, *Loyal Blacks*, 12.

22. "Return of the Number of Persons and Quantity of Effects to Be Removed from Charleston," August 29, 1782, PRO30/55/97, NAUK.

23. Henry Laurens to Joseph Vesey, December 3, 1775, *Papers of Henry Laurens*, 10:532–33. The slave trader Joseph Vesey bought a fourteen-year-old boy in St. Thomas in 1781 and named him Denmark. Thirty-one years later, as a free man in Charleston, Denmark Vesey was executed for plotting insurrection.

24. Frey, *Water from the Rock*, 176; "The Memorial and Humble Representation of Divers Loyal Inhabitants of South Carolina, September 8, 1782," CO5/397/428–31, NAUK.

25. John Mathews to Leslie, August 17, 1782, CO5/1093/44–5, NAUK.

26. Carleton Papers, PRO30/55/51, NAUK.

27. Frey, *Water from the Rock*, 178.

28. Moultrie, *Memoirs of the American Revolution*, 2:351–52.

29. Olwell, *Masters, Slaves and Subjects*, 269.

30. Frey, *Water from the Rock*, 178.

31. "Return of Loyalists at Charleston Wishing to Leave, August 13, 1782," PRO30/55/97, NAUK.

32. Walker, *Black Loyalists*, 62; McCowen, *British Occupation of Charleston*, 106.

33. John Lewis Gervais to Henry Laurens, September 27, 1782, *Papers of Henry Laurens*, 16:30.

34. Moultrie, *Memoirs of the American Revolution*, 2:355–56.

35. "Return of People Embarked from South Carolina, 13th and 14th Dec., 1782," *Charleston Yearbook 1883*, 446. Of 5,333 blacks evacuated, 56 went to England and 2,613 to Jamaica. The balance went to East Florida. Wilson, *Loyal Blacks*, 68, 83.

36. Pybus, *Epic Journeys of Freedom*, 59.

37. David Ramsay, *History of the American Revolution*, 2:32–33.

38. Wilson, *Loyal Blacks*, 62.

39. "Memoirs of the Life of Boston King" (April 1798), 157; see also Wilson, *Loyal Blacks*, 13.

40. Pybus, *Epic Journeys of Freedom*, 60–61.

41. Wilson, *Loyal Blacks*, 50.

42. Schama, *Rough Crossings*, 150.

43. Ibid., 146; Wiencek, *Imperfect God*, 258. Wiencek says that Washington, as president, "continued to press for the return of the slaves until 1790."

44. Wiencek, *Imperfect God*, 258, 356.

45. Hodges, *Black Loyalist Directory*, xvi.

46. Carleton, October 13, 1783, CO5/111, NAUK.

47. Heywood and Thornton, *Central Africans*, 262–64.

48. Ottley and Weatherby, *Negro in New York*, 63; Jordan, *White over Black*, 116.

49. Sabine, *Biographical Sketches of Loyalists*, 564; Muster Book of Free Black Settlement of Birchtown, 35. There is no definitive evidence that Phillis actually worked for George Patten in New York, but the muster book implies a relationship to the Patten household prior to their sailing for Nova Scotia.

50. Hodges, *Black Loyalist Directory*, xx, notes that more than 40 percent of single blacks evacuated from New York were female, suggesting the degree to which the war ravaged family and social ties.

51. Muster Book of Free Black Settlement in Birchtown.

52. "The Memorial of John Lownds," April 8, 1786, Shelburne, Nova Scotia. Audit Office, AO13/24/329–33, NAUK. Lowndes variously spelled his name with and without an *e*.

53. Port Roseway Associates Minutebook, 1782–83, 13; Coldham, *American Loyalist Claims*, 1:550. Lowndes owned three houses in Norfolk and one in Portsmouth, where he kept three slaves.

54. Audit Office, AO13/24/329–33, NAUK.

55. The Norfolk area was ravaged for years thereafter by predatory groups and civilian violence. The enmity between Tory and Whig was intense and probably explains in part Lowndes's reference to abjuring "politics" after he returned to Norfolk in the early1790s.

56. Guy Carleton to Sir Andrew Swope Hammond, August 25, 1782, quoted by Robertson, *King's Bounty*, 32.

57. Joseph Durfee to Hammond, August 20, 1782, quoted by Robertson, *King's Bounty*, 32.

58. Port Roseway Associates Minutebook, 1782–83, 27, quoted in Robertson, *King's Bounty*, 33.

59. Muster Book of Free Black Settlement in Birchtown.

60. Audit Office, AO13/58 (Virginia New Claims, M, 256–8), NAUK; Port Roseway Associates Minutebook, 1782–83, 14.

61. Robertson, *King's Bounty*, 34–35.

62. Joseph Pynchon to Port Roseway Associates in New York, January 23, 1783, quoted by Robertson, *King's Bounty*, 38.

63. Ibid., 41–43.

64. Schama, *Rough Crossings*, 151; CO5/8/112–4, NAUK.

65. Schama, *Rough Crossings*, 151.

66. Ibid., 150.

67. Ibid.

68. Ibid., 146.

69. Robertson, *King's Bounty*, 86.

70. Ibid. Robertson claims that "a few" black loyalists came later by themselves.

71. Benjamin Marston's Diary, May 22 and 24, 1783, Public Archives of Nova Scotia, Halifax (hereafter PANS), Manuscript File, Shelburne County; Marston, May 24, June 8 and 9, 1783, PANS, White Collection, Document 308.

72. Schama, *Rough Crossings*, 231.

73. Ibid., 228–29.

74. Raymond, "Founding of Shelburne."

75. Robertson, *King's Bounty*, 1.

76. Ibid., 4; Berkeley, *Dr. Alexander Garden*, 123.

77. Robertson, *King's Bounty*, 77.

78. Ibid., 87. Robertson believes that the black quarter in Shelburne may have been the block on Harriot Street marked *L* in the North Division. Joseph Restine, the only black known to have received a town lot, was granted land in that block.

79. Ibid., 52.

80. Ibid., 55–56.

81. Guy Carleton to Brigadier General Fox, September 5, 1783, CO5/111, NAUK. Carleton had received intelligence "from many persons who have returned from Nova Scotia . . . that the same persecuting spirit which has driven them into the woods of Nova-Scotia, will not suffer them to remain there in peace and tranquility."

82. Carleton to Lord North, October 5, 1783, CO5/111, NAUK.

83. Gov. John Parr to Evan Nepean, January 22, 1783, quoted in Robertson, *King's Bounty*, 60–61.

84. Ibid., 63.

85. Gov. John Parr to Lord Shelburne, July 25, 1783, quoted in ibid., 65.

86. Ibid., 69.

87. Ibid., 70.

88. Muster Book of Free Black Settlement in Birchtown, 35.

89. Robertson, *King's Bounty*, 86.

90. Hodges, *Black Loyalist Directory*, xxi.

91. Robertson, *King's Bounty*, 87; Richard Bulkeley to Joseph Pynchon, August 9, 1783, PANS, RG1, 136:321.

92. Wilson, *Loyal Blacks*, 85.

93. Capt. William Booth's Journal, PANS; Hodges, *Black Loyalist Directory*, 88.

94. Robertson, *King's Bounty*, 87–88.

95. Acker and Jackson, *Historic Shelburne*, vi–vii.

96. Robertson, *King's Bounty*, 88.

97. Wilson, *Loyal Blacks*, 86.

98. Ibid., 88; Gilroy, *Loyalists and Land Settlements*, 77.

99. Hodges, *Black Loyalist Directory*, xxi.

100. Dennis, *Down in Nova Scotia*, 359.

101. Raymond, "Benjamin Marston of Marblehead," 90; See also Wilson, *Loyal Blacks*, 98.

102. Wilson, *Loyal Blacks*, 93–94.

103. Ibid; Robertson, *King's Bounty*, 128.

104. Robertson, *King's Bounty*, 128.

105. See George, "Account of the Life of Mr. David George."

106. Robertson, *King's Bounty*, 89.

107. Capt. William Booth's Journal, March 14, 1789, PANS.

108. "Government—Shelburne 20th Nov. 1787," PANS, NG100, vol. 256 no. 30, microfilm 21819; "Names of Settlers Located on the 1st Nova Scotian Allotment," original document in the South Carolina Historical Society. See also Schama, *Rough Crossings*, 250.

109. Robertson, *King's Bounty*, 194; Gilroy, *Loyalists and Land Settlement*, 84.

110. Robertson, *King's Bounty*, 86.

111. Schama, *Rough Crossings*, 235; Robert Wilkins offered a five-dollar reward for his "Negro Wench" Dinah, who ran away in July 1786. "Masters of vessels and others are hereby forbid to carry off or Harbour said Wench, at their Peril." *Royal American Gazette* (Shelburne), July 24, 1786.

112. The *Royal American Gazette* advertised on June 19, 1786, the sale of a fourteen-year-old "NEGRO BOY" who "has been brought up in a Gentleman's Family, is very handy at Farming, Housework, or attending Table, is strictly Honest, and has an exceeding good Temper." Schama, *Rough Crossings*, 250.

113. Spray, *Blacks in New Brunswick*, 21.

114. Ships frequenting West Indian ports often touched Shelburne. A few weeks after visiting Birchtown, Capt. William Booth of the Royal Engineers in Shelburne was negotiating passage for "my black servants" to Grenada. See "The Diary and Letters of Capt Booth of the Royal Engineers Stationed in Shelburne, 1789," PANS, MG1, Box 1911, Folder 16, C. B. Fergusson Papers.

115. Schama, *Rough Crossings*, 244–45.

116. Jeffery, *Dyott's Diary*, 1:57.

117. "Memoirs of the Life of Boston King" (May 1798), 208–12.

118. "Memorial, Overseers of the Poor, Shelburne, February 3, 1789," Public Archives of Canada, MG9, B6 (1).

119. Walker, *Black Loyalists*, 78.

120. Frey, *Water from the Rock*, 25.

121. Fergusson, *Clarkson's Mission to America*, 104.

122. Wilson, *Loyal Blacks*, 122.

123. Robertson, *King's Bounty*, 98.

124. Wilson, *Loyal Blacks*, 121.

125. Brooks, *John Marrant's Journal*, 11.

126. Ibid., 7–8.

127. Wilson, *Loyal Blacks*, 128.

128. Brooks, *John Marrant's Journal*, 11.

129. Ibid., 12, 18.

130. "Memoirs of the Life of Boston King" (May 1798), 209.

131. John Lowndes to Frederick Weiser, May 2, 1795, original letter in the Shelburne County Museum. Only three hundred white loyalists remained in Shelburne by 1800. Finn Bower, curator of the museum, attributes the decline mainly to the area's not being conducive to agriculture (conversation with the author, August 29, 2008).

132. Spray, *Blacks in New Brunswick*, 31.

133. Capt. William Booth's Journal, March 14, 1789, PANS.

134. Walker, *Black Loyalists*, 78.

135. Wilson, *Loyal Blacks*, 218.

136. Gerzina, *Black London*, 5. Gerzina cites estimates ranging from ten thousand to thirty thousand blacks in the city in the mid-1780s but believes the figure was closer to fifteen thousand.

137. Ibid., 136.

138. Ibid., 140–41.

139. Hoare, *Memoirs of Granville Sharp*, 2:95–96.

140. Fyfe, *History of Sierra Leone*, 23–25.

141. Fergusson, *Clarkson's Mission to America*, 21.

142. Wilson, *Loyal Blacks*, 149.

143. Fergusson, *Clarkson's Mission to America*, 23.

144. Ibid., 47.

145. Ibid., 40.

146. Hodges, *Black Loyalist Directory*, xxiv.

147. Fergusson, *Clarkson's Mission to America*, 53.

148. Ibid.

149. Ibid., 53–56.

150. Ibid.

151. Wilson, *Loyal Blacks*, 219.

152. Fergusson, *Clarkson's Mission to America*, 56–57.

153. Ibid., 56.

154. Stephen Blucke to John Parr, November 1, 1791, CO217/63, NAUK.

155. John Wentworth to King George III, September 12, 1792, Public Archives of Canada, CONS, 21:286; Robertson, *King's Bounty*, 106.

156. Carretta, *Unchained Voices*, 340. "Almost all the Baptists went," George wrote, "except a few of the sisters whose husbands were inclined to go back to New York." James W. St. G. Walker describes the emigrants as "the more advantaged group among the black loyalists. Indentured servants and debtors . . . were not allowed to leave." Walker, "Establishment of a Free Black Community," 221.

157. Capt. William Booth's Journal, March 14, 1789, PANS.

158. Fergusson, *Clarkson's Mission to America*, 60.

159. Ibid., 85. John Clarkson to William Wilberforce, Halifax, November 27, 1791.

160. Stephen Skinner to Henry Dundas, Secretary of State for the Colonies, March 10, 1792, PANS Micro Reel 13863; CO217/63, NAUK.

161. "Skinner Land Grants, 1791," appendix 2 in Niven, *Birchtown Archaeological Survey*. Receipts are in the T. H. White Collection in the Shelburne County Museum.

162. Fergusson, *Clarkson's Mission to America*, 81.

163. Wilson, *Loyal Blacks*, 230.

Chapter 5. Ransomed Sinners

1. Carretta, *Unchained Voices*, 340.

2. Fergusson, *Clarkson's Mission to America*, 169.

3. Wilson, *Loyal Blacks*, 229.

4. Fergusson, *Clarkson's Mission to America*, 170.

5. Ibid., 167.

6. Ibid., 171; Fyfe, *Sierra Leone Inheritance*, 120.

7. Fergusson, *Clarkson's Mission to America*, 169; Wilson, *Loyal Blacks*, 191.

8. Wilson, *Loyal Blacks*, 189.

9. Henry Thornton to John Clarkson, December 30, 1791, quoted in Wilson, *Loyal Blacks*, 189–90.

10. Ibid.

11. Fergusson, *Clarkson's Mission to America*, 172–73.

12. Wilson, *Loyal Blacks*, 244, 248; *Clarkson Journal*, March 27, 1792, and May 19, 1792, New-York Historical Society.

13. Wilson, *Loyal Blacks*, 249–50.

14. Ibid., 252–53.

15. Ibid., 253–55.

16. Ibid., 256; Fyfe, "Thomas Peters."

17. Raymond, "Founding of Shelburne," 276.

18. John Clarkson retained an abiding interest in Sierra Leone and eagerly sought news of the Nova Scotian settlers. See Wilson, *John Clarkson*, 176–77.

19. Wilson, *Loyal Blacks*, 269.

20. Ibid., 277. The original petition is held in the special collections of the University of Illinois at Chicago Library.

21. Ibid.

22. Wilson, *Loyal Blacks*, 275; Montefiore, *Authentic Account of the Late Expedition*, 47–48.

23. Pybus, *Epic Journeys of Freedom*, 172; Fyfe, *History of Sierra Leone*, 49.

24. Wilson, *Loyal Blacks*, 285.

25. Ibid., 288–89.

26. Fyfe, *History of Sierra Leone*, 49–50.

27. Zachary Macaulay Journal, August 31, 1793, MY418 MDHL. Fyfe writes that it was unclear "whether the Company could legally free slaves. The directors laid down a general rule that runaways ought not to be given up to their masters, but agreed that prudence and local circumstances [should] determine how strictly it be enforced. . . . Macaulay warned the Nova Scotians against sheltering fugitives until there was some legal power to free them." Fyfe, *History of Sierra Leone*, 53.

28. Afzelius, *Sierra Leone Journal*, 50.

29. Donnan, *Documents Illustrative of the History of the Slave Trade to America*, 3:99.

30. Afzelius, *Sierra Leone Journal*, 153–54.

31. Zachary Macaulay to Sierra Leone Company directors, June 5, 1798, CO268/5/234, NAUK.

32. African Institution, *Special Report*, 39.

33. Council minutes, March 4, 1794, CO270/3/56–7, NAUK.

34. Wilson, *Loyal Blacks*, 314.

35. Fyfe, *History of Sierra Leone*, 56.

36. Zachary Macaulay Journal, November 21, 1793, and February 16, 1798, MY418 MDHL.

37. Ibid., November 26, 1794, MY418 MDHL.

38. Wilson, *Loyal Blacks*, 340.

39. Ibid., 315–16.

40. Upon their return to Freetown, Kizell and four witnesses received compensation for 204 "working days" of lost wages, in addition to per diem in England and allowances for their families. CO270/3/90–1, NAUK.

41. American Colonization Society, *Annual Report* 2 (1819): 68.

42. Pybus, *Epic Journeys of Freedom*, 181; Eli Ackim's 1826 testimony to the British Commissioners for West Africa, CO267/92, NAUK. Three Methodists appeared before the council on April 16, 1795, conceding that they were "a people of a ranglesome nature" and expressing the Methodists' desire to live in harmony under the Sierra Leone Company. CO270/3/130–1, NAUK.

43. Wilson, *Loyal Blacks*, 348. Wilson notes that David George gave up his alehouse in 1796 after Macaulay, having returned from England, rebuked him for selling liquor. Macaulay might have exerted moral pressure on Kizell, as well.

44. Council minutes, May 5, 1795, CO270/3/143, NAUK. The council gave notice on March 7, 1796, that persons selling liquor without a license would be prosecuted.

45. Zachary Macaulay Journal, September 21, 1793, MY418 MDHL.

46. Council minutes, May 19, 1795, CO270/3/161, NAUK.

47. Council minutes, November 5, 1795, CO270/3/255, NAUK; Afzelius, *Sierra Leone Journal*, 14, 62, 93.

48. Afzelius, *Sierra Leone Journal*, 50–51. The Harmattan is an annual meteorological phenomenon tied to the north-south transit of the intertropical convergence zone. Prevailing winds carry fine Saharan soil out to sea and as far as North America during West Africa's driest months, from December to March.

49. Wilson, *Loyal Blacks*, 370.

50. Ibid., 340–41; Afzelius, *Sierra Leone Journal*, 54. "Wangapung," Afzelius wrote in his journal for January 21, 1796, "is a great trading place and larger than Freetown."

51. Wilson, *Loyal Blacks*, 348–49.

52. Council minutes, February 6, 1796, CO268/5/103, NAUK.

53. Afzelius, *Sierra Leone Journal*, 62.

54. Ibid., 94; no mention is made of Muslim influence, which was expanding in Port Logo; see Shaw, *Memories of the Slave Trade*, 75.

55. Zachary Macaulay Journal, May 2, 1796, July 29, 1796, and November 30, 1796, MY418 MDHL; Macaulay to Sierra Leone Company directors, April 5, 1797, CO268/5/371, NAUK. In America Grigg joined the Emancipating Baptists, who advocated full and immediate freeing of the slaves. See Wilson, *Loyal Blacks*, 353.

56. Zachary Macaulay Journal, December 21, 1796, MY418 MDHL. Griffith's house was searched, "but nothing was found to confirm the suspicion." See governor and council minutes, August 15, 1796, CO270/4/55, NAUK.

57. Zachary Macaulay Journal, December 21, 1796, MY418 MDHL.

58. Zachary Macaulay Journal, October 29, 1796, December 11, 1796, MY418 MDHL.

59. Zachary Macaulay to Selina Mills, undated [late May 1798], Zachary Macaulay Journal, MY418 MDHL; Louise, *Elizabeth Clevland Hardcastle*, 34.

60. Wilson, *Loyal Blacks*, 363–64.

61. Ibid., 364; Afzelius, *Sierra Leone Journal*, 84.

62. Fyfe, *History of Sierra Leone*, 72.

63. Commissioners of Inquiry of the Western Coast of Africa, 1826, CO267/92/22–3, NAUK. Kizell may have been referring to premiums, which the governor and council approved on December 1, 1799, to encourage expanded cultivation, coffee planting, and raising of livestock. See also CO270/4/317–9, NAUK.

64. Commissioners of Inquiry, 1826, CO267/92/26, NAUK; Wilson, *Loyal Blacks*, 368.

65. Commissioners of Inquiry, 1826, CO267/92/26, NAUK.

66. Council minutes, January 3, 1796, CO270/4/96, NAUK.

67. Macaulay to Mills, May 20, 1796, Zachary Macaulay Journal, MY418 MDHL.

68. *Africa Redeemed*, 40.

69. In *The Souls of Black Folk*, originally published in 1903, W. E. B. DuBois wrote that a black in America "ever feels his twoness—an American, a Negro; two souls, two thoughts, two unreconciled strivings; two warring ideals in one dark body, whose dogged strength alone keeps it from being torn asunder" (5).

70. Fyfe, *Our Children*, 56–57.

71. Council minutes, August 17, 1797, CO270/4, NAUK; Wilson, *Loyal Blacks*, 329.

72. Zachary Macaulay Journal, December 21, 1796, MY418 MDHL; Pybus, *Epic Journeys of Freedom*, 185, 193.

73. Zachary Macaulay Journal, June 21, 1798, MY418 MDHL; Pybus, *Epic Journeys of Freedom*, 193.

74. Fyfe, *Our Children*, 57–58. The letter was entered into the minutes of the governor and council for January 16, 1798; Pybus, *Epic Journeys of Freedom*, 193.

75. Pybus, *Epic Journeys of Freedom*, 194.

76. Zachary Macaulay Journal, February 16, 1798, MY418 MDHL. Witchcraft, according to Macaulay, was not recognized at the time as a crime in the colony. He believed that local Africans were reluctant to be "permanently attached" to a place where witchcraft was "sure to escape both detection and punishment." See Macaulay, *Letter to His Royal Highness*.

77. Zachary Macaulay Journal, February 20, 1798, MY418 MDHL.

78. The French cleric and revolutionary Henri Gregoire visited Macaulay's children at Clapham village in 1802. "I found that between them and European children," he later wrote, "there existed no difference but colour." Gregoire, *Enquiry Concerning the Intellectual and Moral Faculties*, 155.

79. William Wilberforce to Henry Dundas, April 1, 1800, quoted in Wilson, *Loyal Blacks*, 388.

80. Walker, *Black Loyalists*, 205; Hair, quoted by Wilson, *Loyal Blacks*, 383, 397.

81. John Kizell to Commissioners of Inquiry, 1826, CO267/92/24, NAUK.

82. Fyfe, *History of Sierra Leone*, 82; Pybus, *Epic Journeys of Freedom*, 195.

83. Fyfe, *Our Children*, 60.

84. Fyfe, *History of Sierra Leone*, 82.

85. Ibid., 83.

86. Ibid.

87. Fyfe, *Our Children*, 63–64.

88. Kizell to Commissioners of Inquiry, 1826, CO267/92/24, NAUK.

89. Fyfe, *History of Sierra Leone*, 84.

90. Pybus, *Epic Journeys of Freedom*, 198–99.

91. Fyfe, *History of Sierra Leone*, 84–85.

92. "A Narrative of the Rebellion Which Broke out in This Colony on the 25th of Sept. 1800," CO270/5/106 (appendix 3), NAUK.

93. Wilson, *Loyal Blacks*, 392.

94. Fyfe, *History of Sierra Leone*, 85.

95. "Narrative of the Rebellion." This "official" report states that "many of the Settlers," when they "flocked together to hear [the Paper of Laws] read" after it was posted again on September 25, "expressed in general great indignation at the power assumed . . . in pretending to bind them by new laws; objected particularly to the Clauses imposing fine and banishment on the Nova Scotians who—should side with the Governor and Council." CO270/5/100 (appendix 3), NAUK.

96. Campbell, *Back to Africa*, 18, 47; CO270/5, NAUK.

97. "Narrative of the Rebellion"; CO270/5/144–5 (appendix 3), NAUK.

98. Thomas Ludlam, council minutes, November 11, 1801, CO270/6/286–7, NAUK.

99. Ibid., 295.

100. John Gray to governor and council, April 6, 1802, CO270/8/72–3, NAUK.

101. Thomas Ludlam, council minutes, undated, CO270/8/133–4, NAUK.

102. Fyfe, *History of Sierra Leone*, 89.

103. J. Wilson, James Carr, and Michael Macmillan to governor and council, council minutes, January 24, 1802, CO270/8/13, NAUK.

104. Fyfe, *History of Sierra Leone*, 90; Pybus, *Epic Journeys of Freedom*, 217.

105. Fyfe, *History of Sierra Leone*, 91. In his 1826 testimony to the British commissioners of inquiry, Kizell said that following the second Temne attack in April 1802, "every man of us left the farms, and came into towns and we was in a very great distress, fearing our own people [probably a reference to Wansey] and the natives. After this we took in notion to go on our farms again. . . . The first that went . . . was shot and cut up. This again put a stop to us going on the farms." CO267/92/25, NAUK.

106. John Pease to William Dawes, council minutes, September 17, 1802, CO270/8/128, NAUK.

107. George Kizell's death and burial are officially recorded in Clapham, according to the Oxfordshire Black History Web site (Search: "Clapham Sect Kizell"). Many of the students brought from Sierra Leone in 1799–1802 by the Sierra Leone Company experienced health problems.

Chapter 6. Abolition and Illusion

1. Fyfe, *History of Sierra Leone*, 93; DuBois, *Suppression of the African Slave Trade*, 86.

2. Fyfe, *History of Sierra Leone*, 92; Zachary Macaulay Journal, August 27, 1797, and December 1, 1797, MY418 MDHL.

3. CO270/19/16, NAUK. The governor and council also considered inserting a condition in the settlers' renewed land grants to prohibit slaveholding and slave trading but decided this "could not be generally obtained" from the Nova Scotians, "however desirable it might be."

4. Council minutes, September 11, 1801, CO270/6/256, NAUK.

5. Sellers, *Charleston Business*, 126.

6. Davis, *Problem of Slavery*, 150; Michael E. Stevens, "To Get as Many Slaves," 187.

7. Fyfe, *History of Sierra Leone*, 93.

8. Ibid., 90, 96. The *Charleston Courier* of December 10, 1807, quoted an American slave ship captain that every slaver in the Rio Pongas was "much in want of rice for their slaves."

9. Fyfe, *History of Sierra Leone*, 81; Afzelius, *Sierra Leone Journal*, 89; Zachary Macaulay to the Sierra Leone Company directors, February 9, 1798, CO268/5/436, NAUK; Scotland, "Notes on the Banana Islands," 153.

10. African Institution, *Second Report*, appendix D: "Extract from a Letter of Governor Ludlam 29th October 1806," 44.

11. Corry, *Observations upon the Windward Coast*, 9; Louise, *Elizabeth Clevland Hardcastle*, 34.

12. African Institution, *Second Report*, 44.

13. Thomas Ludlam, "Observations Respecting the Relations of the Colony with the Neighbouring Countries," May 1, 1808, CO267/24, NAUK.

14. In May 1808 Ludlam wrote that "a truce was concluded, about three years ago, through our mediation, which continues . . . unbroken." His undated letter was published as annex M (page 35) in the African Institution's *Third Report*, published in London in 1814.

15. Thomas Ludlam to Zachary Macaulay, May 8, 1808, CO267/24, NAUK. Ludlam implied that relative peace had been restored in the Sherbro. The "Cussos" (or Mende) who had been prevented from coming down to the coast to sell their fine woven country cloth—for fear of being "caught in the Paths" and sold into slavery—were now trading them freely, mainly for salt; Ludlam to Macaulay, April 14, 1807, in Macaulay's *Letter to His Royal Highness*, appendix 9, 55.

16. African Institution, *Sixth Report*, 148–49.

17. DuBois, *Suppression of the African Slave Trade*, 86.

18. Ibid, 90; Stevens, "To Get as Many Slaves," 187.

19. Stevens, "To Get as Many Slaves," 189–90.

20. Davis, *Problem of Slavery*, 348. Davis credits Roger Anstey with effectively rebutting Adam Smith and others who argued that "British self-interest led to the abolition of the slave trade and to West Indian emancipation." See Anstey, "Re-interpretation of the Abolition."

21. Davis, *Problem of Slavery*, 117.

22. Ibid., 55, 416.

23. DuBois, *Suppression of the African Slave Trade*, 95.

24. Davis, *Problem of Slavery*, 118. Davis notes: "In the crucial vote of February 23, 1807, the West Indians were overwhelmed 283 to 16. After hearing their forecasts of ruin and disaster, Lord Howick, who . . . had introduced the bill in the Commons, agreed to change the preamble; instead of referring to the injustice and inhumanity of the African trade, it would simply read that 'it is expedient that the slave trade be abolished.'"

25. DuBois, *Suppression of the African Slave Trade*, 101.

26. Perkins, *Prologue to War*, 71.

27. African Institution, *Fourth Report*, 11.

28. African Institution, *Third Report*, 35.

29. The *New Bedford (Mass.) Mercury* reported on May 19, 1809, that chiefs in Sierra Leone had halted trading slaves in preference to selling agricultural commodities; an American ship captain wrote in the same period that "since the destruction of the slave trade the [coast] . . . is full of ivory." See Brooks, *Yankee Traders*, 26.

30. Thomas Ludlam to Zachary Macaulay, May 18, 1808, CO267/24, NAUK; African Institution, *Third Report*, 15–16.

31. Thomas Ludlam to Macaulay, May 18, 1808, CO267/24, NAUK; Holsoe, "Slavery and Economic Response," 293. Holsoe notes that from 1807, "with the increased danger involved in shipping slaves, the price per slave rose sharply, and it became imperative that waiting slave vessels be loaded with great speed."

32. Ludlam to Macaulay, May 18, 1808, CO267/24, NAUK; African Institution, *Second Report*, 46. Ludlam's letter, dated October 29, 1806, is quoted: "K [probably John Kizell] found even so intelligent a man as T_____ himself one day about to give red-water to his father's sister. With much difficulty he and another trader prevailed on him to desist."

33. Fyfe, *History of Sierra Leone*, 104.

34. Kizell based his account largely on what he had been told by two young men from the Gallinas who visited him in the Sherbro on April 21, 1808. His undated letter to Ludlam is extracted in the African Institution's *Sixth Report*, 149–53. Adam Jones believes Kizell may have "overstated the role of slave dealers in inciting people to fight." Jones, *From Slaves to Palm Kernels*, 60.

35. Davis, *Problem of Slavery*, 452.

36. African Institution, *First Report*, "Read to the General Meeting on the 15th of July, 1807," 35.

37. Ibid., 51.

38. *Sierra Leone Company Report* (1808), 13.

39. Curtin, *Image of Africa*, 138–39.

40. Johnson, *General T. Perronet Thompson*, 25, 39–40.

41. T. Perronet Thompson to Lord Castlereagh, August 8, 1808, CO267/24, NAUK.

42. Thompson to Nancy Barker, August 1808, quoted in Johnson, *General T. Perronet Thompson*, 40–41.

43. Council minutes, August 18, 1808, CO270/10/50, NAUK.

44. *Sierra Leone Gazette*, August 20, 1808, CO267/25, NAUK.

45. Thomas Ludlam to Thompson, August 26, 1808, CO267/25, NAUK; Johnson, *General T. Perronet Thompson*, 42.

46. Ludlam to Castlereagh, undated, CO270/11/146–7, NAUK.

47. Johnson, *General T. Perronet Thompson*, 49; Thomas Thompson to Lord Castlereagh, November 2, 1808, CO267/24, NAUK.

48. Walker, *Black Loyalists*, 310.

49. Thompson to Edward Cooke, August 15, 1809, CO267/25, NAUK; Thompson to William Allen, July 18, 1815, Allen's African correspondence (hereafter AC).

50. Peterson, *Province of Freedom*, 53.

51. Thompson to Cecil Jenkinson, June 6, 1810, CO267/28, NAUK.

52. Thompson to Castlereagh, February 17, 1809, CO267/25, NAUK.

53. Council minutes, April 8, 1809, CO270/11, NAUK.

54. Council minutes, November 11, 1808, CO270/11/27–9, NAUK.

55. Castlereagh to Thompson, April 3, 1809, CO268/6/61, NAUK.

56. Johnson, *General T. Perronet Thompson*, 51–53.

57. Ibid., 54.

58. Fyfe, *History of Sierra Leone*, 108–9. Thompson and his council on November 11, 1808, amended the act forbidding association with slave trading by anyone within the colony to apply only to acts committed within the colony. In effect residents of the colony could engage in the slave trade as long as they did so outside the colony. See CO270/10/83, NAUK.

59. Thompson certainly knew local people, such as George S. Caulker, who was one of the signatories of the treaty "offensive and defensive," executed in November 1808. Many of the signers, including Caulker, were implicated in the slave trade.

60. Pybus, *Epic Journeys of Freedom*, 205; Thompson's address to the Freetown mayor and aldermen, July 24, 1809, CO270/11/84, NAUK.

61. Fyfe, *History of Sierra Leone*, 109.

62. Castlereagh to Thompson, April 3, 1809, CO268/6/61, NAUK. Thompson told Capt. Frederick Forbes on July 29, 1809, that he was "to return to England . . . for the purpose of communicating with His Majesty's Ministers on subjects connected with the administration and general situation of the Colony." He did not reveal that his recall was permanent. Possibly he believed he could argue successfully for a reprieve. CO270/11/87–8, NAUK.

63. Thompson to Edward H. Columbine, March 1, 1810, CO270/11/208–9, NAUK; Thompson to Nancy Barker, March 1, 1810, quoted in Johnson, *General T. Perronet Thompson*, 63.

64. The log of Columbine's ship, the *Crocodile*, notes tersely on March 2, 1810, "at 3 observed the town to be on fire[.] man'd the Boats and sent the people on shore to assist." Admiralty Office, ADM51/2198, NAUK.

65. Lord Liverpool to Columbine, December 27, 1809, CO268/6/161–3, 183, NAUK.

66. See African Institution, *Sixth Report*, 114, for Columbine's letter of introduction to the Sherbro chiefs in August 1810. Neither Columbine's papers (at the University of Illinois at Chicago) nor Colonial Department records and other sources from the period shed light on why Columbine chose Kizell for the mission to the Sherbro. Ludlam is the logical connection between the two men.

67. Council minutes, June 24, 1810, CO270/11/196; CO267/28; CO270/11/93, NAUK. The local African workers briefly seized control of Bance Island on October 13, 1809. Thompson and Columbine both blamed the agitation on disgruntled British employees of the Sierra Leone Company and on colonial officers.

68. Brooks, *Yankee Traders*, 59–61.

69. Johnson, *General T. Perronet Thompson*, 61.

70. Brooks, *Yankee Traders*, 58–62. Brooks quotes Capt. Samuel Swan, a thirty-one-year-old Medford, Massachusetts, man who traded in Sierra Leone, that "Columbine throws every thing in [the] way [of American trade] & wished to prevent their coming to the coast but get their supplies from Halifax." However, Swan also reported that "the trade & consumption of American articles are very great" and that Columbine allowed most items to be landed, although at a relatively high duty.

71. Columbine in October 1810 ordered replenishment of depleted medical supplies following "a most severe rainy season." CO267/28, NAUK.

72. Ludlam to Macaulay, April 14, 1807, in Macaulay's *Letter to His Royal Highness*, 49. Kizell and Ludlam disagreed strongly on the horrors of the slave trade. Abolition in Ludlam's view undermined slavery as a benign tool of African justice. "When <u>so effectual</u> a punishment as Slavery is done away," he wrote Macaulay, ". . . the power of every hereditary chief must now be sustained by blood. . . ."

73. Imam of Futa Jallon to T. P. Thompson, undated, 1810, CO268/8, NAUK.

74. William Dawes, "Observations on the Situation of Sierra Leone with Respect to the Surrounding Natives," November 1, 1811, CO267/29/60,66, NAUK.

75. Henry Lee to Edward A. Newton, October 19, 1810, quoted in Porter, *Jacksons and the Lees*, 900.

76. *House Reports*, 17th Cong., 1st sess., 4, no. 92, 32.

77. *House Documents*, 15th Cong., 2nd sess., 4, no. 84, 5.

78. African Institution, *Sixth Report*, 39.

79. Zachary Macaulay to C. Yorke, September 21, 1811, CO267/43, NAUK.

80. Fyfe, *History of Sierra Leone*, 120; Davis, *Problem of Slavery*, 360; CO267/43, NAUK.

81. William Dawes, August 27, 1811, CO267/29/80, NAUK.

82. African Institution, *Sixth Report*, 113–14.

83. No treaty was signed (or implied) with the Sherbro chiefs in the 1700s. The Royal African Company had started paying "cole" to the king of Sherbro in the early 1700s, which included "rent, tribute and the right to trade" on York Island, according to Fyfe (*History of Sierra Leone*, 4). However, in his "Additional Memoranda with Respect to the Recent Cessions of Territory at Sierra Leone," dated June 9, 1826, Zachary Macaulay quotes his letter of May 7, 1807, to Lord Castlereagh, that "it is admitted by the Chiefs . . . that in consequence of some services conferred on them by the King of Great Britain about the beginning of the last century, he was then formally acknowledged as their Superior Lord." CO267/79, NAUK. Walter Rodney puts this in context when he writes that the "exchange of presents was a standardized procedure known as 'service.'" This was more truly a business than a political relationship. Rodney, *History of the Upper Guinea Coast*, 85.

84. African Institution, *Sixth Report*, 120–22.

85. Ibid., 134–35.

86. Ibid., 135.

87. Ibid., 123.

88. Council minutes during Columbine's governorship from February 1810 to May 1811 are conspicuously silent on the state of the slave trade in the Sherbro and Gallinas.

89. African Institution, *Sixth Report*, 123.

90. Ibid., 141.

91. Tucker, *Tuckers of Sierra Leone*, 10–11.

92. Ibid., 13.

93. Ibid., 14–15. Much of Peter Tucker's family history is based on oral tradition as well as colonial documents.

94. African Institution, *Sixth Report*, 116.

95. Tucker, *Tuckers of Sierra Leone*, 12.

96. Ibid., 12–13.

97. African Institution, *Sixth Report*, 116–20.

98. Ibid., 140–41.

99. Ibid., 141–43.

100. Ibid., 144.

Chapter 7. "The land of black men"

1. *Lloyd's Registry* for 1812 describes the *Traveller* as a 109-ton brig, built in Massachusetts in 1807 and captained and owned by Paul Cuffe.

2. Cuffe to John James and Alexander Wilson, Westport, Mass., June 10, 1809, Cuffe Papers.

3. James Forten, a Philadelphia sailmaker and close friend of Cuffe's, also possessed considerable wealth for any American, black or white, in that period.

4. Harris, *Paul Cuffe*, 38. Harris notes that Cuffe's correspondence after 1808 "scarcely mentions his Indian legacy. . . . Cuffe began to identify totally with Africa and his African heritage."

5. Miller, *Search for a Black Nationality*, 26.

6. Perkins, *Prologue to War*, 255; Brooks, *Yankee Traders*, 59–60; Porter, *Jacksons and the Lees*, 902.

7. Harris, *Paul Cuffe*, 49.

8. Porter, *Jacksons and the Lees*, 902, 944–46. On December 8, 1810, Treasury Secretary Albert Gallatin announced that if nonintercourse were revived after ninety days, ships would be seized "no matter when they sail'd."

9. Edward H. Columbine (at sea aboard the *Crocodile*) to Lord Liverpool, October 21, 1810, CO267/28.

10. Edward H. Columbine to Lord Liverpool, January 24, 1811, CO267/30, NAUK.

11. Columbine's proclamation of February 26, 1811, referred to "a mistaken notion" that the government "will harbour and retain" domestic slaves owned by "the neighboring Kings, Chiefs or other principal men." CO270/12/2, NAUK.

12. Cuffe's Journal, March 2, 1811, New Bedford (Mass.) Public Library (hereafter NBFPL); Miller, *Search for a Black Nationality*, 28.

13. Cuffe's Journal, March 4, 1811,

14. Ibid., March 26, 1811.

15. Ibid., March 9, 1811.

16. African Institution, *Sixth Report*, 153.

17. Cuffe's Journal, April 7, 1811. Harris, in his 1972 biography of Cuffe, mistakenly transcribed John Kizell as "John Hazwell" in Cuffe's entry for that day. Lamont D. Thomas and Rosalind Cobb Wiggins agree that Kizell was with Cuffe on April 7.

18. Cuffe's Journal, March 12, 1811.

19. Thomas, *Paul Cuffe*, 54.

20. Fyfe, *History of Sierra Leone*, 116; Allen, *Life of William Allen*, 136–37. Macaulay showed Alexander Smith's letter to Allen. The quotation is Allen's paraphrasing.

21. Allen, *Life of William Allen*, 136–37.

22. Henry Warren to Allen, June 20, 1813, AC.

23. Peterson, *Province of Freedom*, 56; African Institution, *Special Report*, 73.

24. Wilson, *Loyal Blacks*, 392; Friendly Society to Allen, February 14, 1814 (AC), lists the age, occupation, and status of all Friendly Society members. Thomas Richards is listed as eighty-one and "poor."

25. Allen, *Life of William Allen*, 136–37.

26. Cuffe's Journal, August 9, 1811.

27. Allen, *Life of William Allen*, 139 (journal entry for July 30, 1811).

28. Ibid., 140 (August 27, 1811).

29. Ibid., 185.

30. Walker, *Black Loyalists*, 278.

31. Cuffe's Journal, December 23, 1811.

32. Ibid., January 6, 1812.

33. Ibid., January 23, 1812.

34. Ibid., January 24, 1812; Charles Maxwell to Paul Cuffe, February 8, 1812, Cuffe manuscripts, NBFPL.

35. Cuffe's Journal, January 26 and 27, 1812.

36. Thomas, *Paul Cuffe*, 70.

37. Ibid.

38. Kizell to Allen, February 9, 1812, AC.

39. Kizell to Allen, March 14, 1813, AC.

40. Ibid.

41. Fyfe, *History of Sierra Leone*, 115; Thorpe, *Reply "Point by Point,"* 33.

42. Ackerson, *African Institution*, 118.

43. Fyfe, *History of Sierra Leone*, 122.

44. The National Archives of the United Kingdom includes a large file (CO267/88) devoted entirely to Thorpe's charges, including his petition to the House of Commons on May 25, 1821, in which he summarizes the settlers' specific allegations. In a private letter written in early 1827, Thorpe blames his dismissal "from [his] judicial appointments," by Lord Bathurst in 1814, on his submission of the settler grievances.

45. Ibid., 20.

46. Privy Council decision, August 3, 1816, CO267/44, NAUK.

47. Thorpe, *Reply "Point by Point,"* 19.

48. Ibid., 21. Kizell to Thorpe, March 18, 1815.

49. "Special Report of the Directors of the African Institution respecting THE ALLEGATIONS contained in A Pamphlet Entitled 'A Letter to William Wilberforce, Esq. Etc BY R. THORPE, ESQ Etc.," Annual General Meeting, London, April 12, 1815, 33.

50. Kizell to Allen, June 3, 1813, AC.

51. Ibid., 34. Kizell assigned title for Freetown lot 278 "with all buildings, outhouses, Etc." to the Sierra Leone Company on June 19, 1810; Thorpe appears not to have communicated directly with Kizell regarding the status of his claims against the Sierra Leone Company once he had testified to the committee of the African Institution. In August 1815 Kizell asked Allen, through James Wise, whether Thorpe had said anything about the case. Wise to Allen, August 16, 1815, AC.

52. Ibid., 35.

53. Kizell to Thomas Clarkson, May 30, 1813, AC.

54. Kizell to Allen, June 3, 1813, AC.

55. Ibid.; Allen to Kizell, March 27, 1814. Kizell responded at length on July 17, 1814, explaining to Allen that the late Thomas Ludlam had suggested he pledge his Freetown property as security while the Sierra Leone Company accounts were reconciled. Ludlam, he wrote,

"told me *privately* that [Alexander] Smith's acts [as keeper of the company's books] will not stand law." Meanwhile Kizell had approached George Nicol "to settle the matter [of the schooner] amicably, as you recommended, but he does nothing"; Wilson, *Thomas Clarkson*, 73; Davis believes that Allen, who refused to use sugar until slavery was abolished on the West Indies plantations, "weakened his effectiveness by engaging in such an incredible number of benevolent activities." Davis, *Problem of Slavery*, 242–45.

268

56. Kizell to Allen, February 14, 1814, AC.

57. Porter, *Creoledom*, 43.

58. African Institution, *Ninth Report*, 52.

59. "Petition of the Freeholders and Principal Inhabitants of the Colony of Sierra Leone," December 19, 1814, CO267/40, NAUK; Kizell to Allen, June 3, 1813, AC.

60. Governor's secretary, September 3, 1811, CO267/31, NAUK.

61. Walker, *Black Loyalists*, 277; African Institution, *Sixth Report*, 36; Council minutes, June 11, 1811, CO270/12/11, NAUK.

62. "Disposal of Captured Negroes Arrived in the Colony of Sierra Leone during the Year 1812," dated August 2, 1813, CO267/35, NAUK. Of 4,224 recaptives landed in Sierra Leone in 1812, 2,233 had died by the end of the year. Only 13 "returned to their own country." Mortality among slaves on board and after being landed was typically high, according to similar reports over the next several years.

63. Maxwell to Lord Bathurst, June 12, 1813, CO267/36, NAUK.

64. CO267/29, NAUK. Thorpe condemned the *Dolphin* on July 13, 1812. The *Amelia* sailed from Charleston to Bahia, Brazil, to obtain Portuguese papers. It then crossed the Atlantic to Cabinda and took on board 275 slaves. According to Ned Brown, an African American crew member, the slaves took control of the ship soon after it set sail. About 30 were killed, including Jack White, the captain's slave, who had been flogged frequently in Charleston. He showed the slaves his scars and told them this was what awaited them in "the white man's country." It was White, apparently, who opened the hatches to enable the slaves to rise up. They put the captain and crew in a boat, with a sail and provisions. Brown asked to go with the captain, but he was told, "you are black, the slaves won't kill you." The slaves and a skeleton crew tried to sail back to Cabinda but ended up four months later off Cape Mount, south of Sierra Leone, and were brought to Freetown. The majority had died of hunger. See African Institution, *Sixth Report*, 36–39.

65. Allen, *Life of William Allen*, 186–87.

66. Ibid.

67. Ibid., 155.

68. Ibid., 214. Allen to Richard Reynolds, October 26, 1814.

69. Kizell to Allen, April 1814, AC.

70. Kizell to Allen, February 14, 1814, AC.

71. In her biography of Thomas Clarkson, Ellen Gibson Wilson provides a succinct image of this remarkable advocate of human rights: "Clarkson was a private citizen of very moderate means. He held no public office, had limited access to government departments, commanded no political or religious faction and dispensed no patronage. He did not even make his home in the capital. His position as a director of the African Institution gave him a quasi-official status, perhaps, but he had become a kind of institution himself, distinguished by far-flung contacts and a voracious appetite for information and hard work." Wilson, *Thomas Clarkson*, 143.

72. Kizell to Allen, February 14, 1814, and July 17, 1814, AC.

73. Kizell to Allen, July 21, 1814, AC.

74. Paul Cuffe to William Rotch Jr., February 1816, Cuffe Papers.

75. Cuffe to William Allen, March 13, 1815, AC; Allen to Cuffe, May 6, 1815, Cuffe Papers; Cuffe to Allen, April 1, 1816, Cuffe Papers.

76. Brooks, *Yankee Traders*, 167–69. With a few exceptions, American trading ships were barred from Freetown for fourteen years, starting on September 1, 1817. Governor MacCarthy was mainly concerned with protecting British commerce in the rivers near Sierra Leone.

77. Cuffe to Allen, April 1, 1816, Cuffe Papers.

78. Fyfe, *History of Sierra Leone*, 146.

79. Cuffe to Allen, April 1, 1816, Cuffe Papers; Thorpe, *Reply "Point by Point,"* 14.

80. Walker, *Black Loyalists*, 309–10.

81. Cuffe to Allen, April 1, 1816, Cuffe Papers; Brooks, *Yankee Traders*, 91, quotes a letter in 1816 from George Howland, a young seaman, alleging that British officers socialized on shore with slave traders in the Gallinas and protected their operations from unannounced inspection of suspected slave ships.

82. Cuffe (in New Bedford) to MacCarthy, August 14, 1816, Cuffe Papers; MacCarthy to Bathurst, September 15, 1815, CO267/40, NAUK. MacCarthy wrote again to Bathurst on June 11, 1817, to report a resurgence of the slave trade, mainly in American, Portuguese, and French ships. The increased slave trading had turned "the minds of the Natives from peaceful habits of industry to rapine and plunder. . . . The British Merchants . . . cannot bear the competition with Slave dealers." CO267/45, NAUK.

83. Fyfe, *History of Sierra Leone*, 142; W. Henry Savage to Allen, March 24, 1815, AC.

84. Savage to Allen, May 29, 1815, AC.

85. Duncan Campbell (Freetown) to Allen, March 1814, AC.

86. Campbell to Allen, July 22, 1814; James Wise to Allen, July 3, 1814, AC.

87. Thomas Clarkson to James Wise, February 25, 1819, AC.

88. Ibid.

89. Allen, *Life of William Allen*, 312–13 (June 5, 1817), 338 (January 27, 1818).

90. Allen remained sanguine about Sierra Leone's future. Writing on December 16, 1828, to R. W. Hay, the undersecretary of state in the Colonial Department, Allen said he was convinced, "notwithstanding the disasters it has experienced," that Sierra Leone could be "made a blessing to the continent of Africa and highly useful to the mother country." Much of his faith was based on the liberated Africans. He believed they would pursue agricultural development where the Nova Scotians and Maroons had not. See CO267/97, NAUK.

91. Hunt, *Life in America*, 51–52. Madison shared his thoughts in 1788 with William Thornton, one of the earliest proponents of colonization and later the architect of the U.S. Capitol.

92. Madison to Robert J. Evans, June 15, 1819, quoted in Ruchames, *Racial Thought in America*.

93. *Niles' Weekly Register*, April 6, 1816, and May 18, 1816; Dangerfield, *Era of Good Feeling*, 125; *New York Evening Post*, July 18, 1816.

94. Wilson, *Loyal Blacks*, 136–37.

95. Cuffe to Mills, August 6, 1816; Cuffe to Forten, August 14, 1816, Cuffe Papers.

96. Cuffe to Kizell, August 14, 1816, Cuffe Papers.

97. Finley, *Thoughts on the Colonization*, 92.

98. *National Intelligencer* account of the American Colonization Society meeting on December 21, 1816, quoted in Adler and Van Doren, *Negro in American History*, 374.

99. Aptheker, "One Continual Cry," 31; American Colonization Society, *First Annual Report*, 1818; Ottley, *Negro in New York*, 69–70.

100. "Report on Colonizing the Free People of Color of the United States," House of Representatives, February 11, 1817, quoted in *Niles' Weekly Register*, April 12, 1817.

101. Cuffe to Mills, January 6, 1817; Cuffe to Finley, January 8, 1817, Cuffe Papers.

102. Douty, *Forten the Sailmaker*, 123; Spring, *Memoirs of the Rev. Samuel J. Mills*, 107–10.

103. Mills's visit to Cuffe on August 29, 1817, is described in the *African Repository* of January 1872. Stephen Gould, a close Quaker acquaintance from Newport, Rhode Island, visited Cuffe in his final days. His coughing "was almost continuous" and they spoke only of "temporal affairs." Gould later wrote that Cuffe received his fellow townspeople to bid farewell in his final hours. The last to see him were "his neighbors of his own colour . . . to [whom] he imparted many deep + instructive remarks." The original of Gould's May 20, 1822, letter to Thomas Thompson, a Liverpool Quaker, is in the Friends Library in London, portfolio 29/38.

104. *Royal Gazette and Sierra Leone Advertiser*, August 23, 1817, CO271/1, NAUK.

105. Spring, *Memoirs of the Rev. Samuel J. Mills*, 141–42.

106. Ibid., 157.

107. Ibid., 173.

108. Ibid., 151, 160.

109. Ibid., 164–66.

110. Wesley, *Richard Allen*, 219. In 1827 Bishop Allen wrote, "Why would they send us into a far country to die? See the thousands of foreigners immigrating to America every year; and if there be ground sufficient for them to cultivate . . . why would they insist to send the tillers of the soil away?"

111. American Colonization Society, *Second Annual Report*, 1819, 151.

112. Ibid; Miller, *Search for a Black Nationality*, 56.

113. Burgess, *Address to the American Society*.

114. *Niles' Weekly Register*, June 19, 1819.

115. Ibid., May 29, 1819.

116. *African Repository* 29 (May 1853): 147. The recaptives' ultimate fate is unknown.

117. Brooks, *Yankee Traders*, 107–8; DuBois, *Suppression of the African Slave Trade*, 121, 157.

118. Ashmun, *Memoir of Rev. Samuel Bacon*, 228–30.

119. Brooks, *Yankee Traders*, 171; Thomas Lack, Office of the Privy Council Committee for Trade, to Henry Goulburn, Colonial Department, April 25, 1818, CO267/48, NAUK.

120. Allen, *Life of William Allen*, 335 (January 5, 1818); *Royal Gazette and Sierra Leone Advertiser*, April 25, 1818, CO271/1, NAUK.

121. Kenneth Macaulay to Zachary Macaulay, May 19, 1818, CO267/48 (appendix M), NAUK.

122. Ibid.

123. Ibid.

124. Kizell to Cuffe, February 17, 1817, Cuffe Papers, NBFPL; Wilson, *Loyal Blacks*, 406.

125. Ashmun, *Memoir of Rev. Samuel Bacon*, 235.

126. Alexander, *History of Colonization*, 114; Coker, *Journal of Daniel Coker*, February 6, 1820.

127. The name, age, and state of residence for the passengers on the *Elizabeth* are listed on the "Roll of Emigrants That Have Been Sent to the Colony of Liberia, Western Africa, by the American Colonization Society and Its Auxiliaries, to Sept, 1843," 28th Cong., 2nd sess., Senate Document 150, Serial Volume 458. The predominance of New York and Philadelphia blacks among the first settlers is notable. The *African Repository* for December 1834 recorded few additional New York and Pennsylvania free blacks among the nearly three thousand who had gone to Africa since 1820. Most came from Virginia, North Carolina, and Maryland. The data suggest that organized black leadership in New York and Philadelphia remained strongly opposed to colonization. In New York Reverend Peter Williams Jr., who at first was open to African emigration, had turned against it by the early 1830s. See Woodson, *Negro Orators*, 77–81.

128. Cuffe Journal, May 6, 1812, NBFPL.

129. Corey, "Daniel Coker," 28.

130. Ibid., 36; Smith, *Biography of Rev. David Smith*, 36–37.

131. Coker, *Journal of Daniel Coker*, February 12, 24, and 25, 1820.

132. Ibid., March 1, 1820; Miller, *Search for a Black Nationality*, 60–61.

133. Miller, *Search for a Black Nationality*, 59.

134. MacCarthy to Bathurst, May 27, 1820, CO267/51, NAUK; Huberich, *Political and Legislative History of Liberia*, 114.

135. *Royal Gazette and Sierra Leone Advertiser*, March 11, 1820, CO271/1, NAUK. The same issue reported the arrival of the *Elizabeth* "with four Agents and 88 settlers for the purpose of establishing an Asylum on the coast for liberated Africans."

136. MacCarthy had made no secret of his desire to establish direct British authority in the Sherbro. Writing to his uncle Zachary in May 1818, Freetown merchant Kenneth Macaulay said MacCarthy "has declared openly his determination to take possession of York Island . . . and claim all British pretensions in the River; and no person there will or dare say him *no*." CO267/48 (appendix M), NAUK. MacCarthy instead requested official permission to annex the Sherbro, which was not forthcoming. An American naval officer who interviewed the governor, before Bacon's death in May 1820, believed the "English . . . look with a jealous eye upon the American settlers. They are fearful . . . the Sierra Leone settlers will pretty generally remove to the new country; and it is my opinion their fears are well founded." Quoted in the *Royal Gazette and Sierra Leone Advertiser*, January 13, 1821, CO271/2, NAUK.

137. Ashmun, *Memoir of Rev. Samuel Bacon*, 259.

138. In "The Debt to Africa—The Hope of Liberia," Reverend A. N. Bell asserted in the July 1881 issue of *American Church Review* that "influential agents from Sierra Leone . . . succeeded . . . in breaking up the negotiations which Kizell had instituted with the natives for Sherbro" (97). Bell provides no evidence or source to support this statement.

139. Ashmun, *Memoir of Rev. Samuel Bacon*, 257–58; *African Intelligencer* 1 (July 1820): 19.

140. Huberich, *Political and Legislative History of Liberia*, 95.

141. *African Intelligencer* 1 (July 1820): 17–18. Unapologetic about owning slaves, Bushrod Washington told his slaves that, unlike his Uncle George's chattel, they would not be manumitted after his death. In March 1820, as John Kizell was urging Washington to "send my brethren home," the latter was summoning his slaves at Mount Vernon to hear a stern warning: "I assured them most solemnly that I had no intention to give freedom to any of them. . . ." He later sold more than fifty to slaveholders in Louisiana. See Bushrod Washington letter, dated September 18, 1821, quoted in *Niles' Weekly Register* for September 29, 1821.

142. Ibid., 13–17.

143. Notes in Crozer's handwriting, for March 28, 1820, are appended to Christian Wiltberger's diary in the Library of Congress Manuscript Division; Miller, *Search for a Black Nationality*, 63.

144. Samuel Mills, April 20, 1818, quoted in the American Colonization Society's *Second Annual Report* (1819).

145. Coker, *Journal of Daniel Coker*, March 21, 1820. Settler Elijah Johnson, in a transcribed extract of his brief journal attached to Christian Wiltberger's diary, says that Kizell remarked, "I had almost given you up. I have been waiting for you these two years," since the departure of Mills and Burgess. Library of Congress Manuscript Division.

146. Ibid.

147. *African Intelligencer* 1 (July 1820): 13–17.

148. Coker, *Journal of Daniel Coker*, March 24, 1820.

149. Ibid., March 25, 1820; Miller, *Search for a Black Nationality*, 61.

150. Coker, *Journal of Daniel Coker*, March 30, 1820.

151. Bacon, *Abstract of a Journal*, 35.

152. Elijah Johnson's journal.

153. Miller, *Search for a Black Nationality*, 63; Ashmun, *Memoir of Rev. Samuel Bacon*, 265–66.

154. Elijah Johnson's journal.

155. Ibid.

156. Ibid. Johnson wrote, "Mr. Coker said the Society has sent out no thing for you, for all that is here is for the Captured Africans and I have no right to give them to you, and if you want them you must buy them."

157. Corey, "Daniel Coker," 28.

158. Edward T. Wigfall's journal, quoted in Miller, *Search for a Black Nationality*, 65.

159. *African Intelligencer* 1 (July 1820): 17. Crozer quotes Kizell's assertion that "the natives will do nothing without" rum, and that like a child being weaned from its mother's breast, "the poor natives of Africa cannot be torn at once from the use of ardent spirits, but must be gradually weaned."

160. Miller, *Search for a Black Nationality*, 67. James Doughen, a young Episcopalian from Pennsylvania who accompanied the *Elizabeth* but had no official position, was the only white member of the party to survive. Doughen is the sole source for the claim that Coker had succeeded in negotiating a grant of land in Mano, an area Burgess and Mills had visited in the Bagru River. Elijah Johnson, however, claims the Mano headman refused a palaver. Given Kizell's unpublished account in 1821, Doughen may have been correct that a land deal was near. Doughen's letter to Elias B. Caldwell is quoted in an American Colonization Society circular dated October 28, 1820, and published in the *Christian Spectator* 2 (1820).

161. Elijah Johnson's journal.

162. Miller, *Search for a Black Nationality*, 67; Alexander, *History of Colonization*, 130–31. One of the colonists, Thomas Camaraw, may have remained at Campelar with his family. Camaraw reportedly was a contentious individual. The colonization society's agent wrote to the board of managers on December 11, 1821, that "Camaraw says that Kizell was going to murder him and his family. I do not pretend to know how much of it is true. . . . I did not like his conversation and behavior." Judging by his surname, Camaraw may have been born in the Sierra Leone hinterland. American Colonization Society, *Fifth Annual Report*, 56.

163. Huberich, *Political and Legislative History of Liberia*, 121–23.

164. Ibid., 128.

165. Ibid., 131. Free blacks were not recognized as American citizens under federal law. In 1857 the Supreme Court ruled in *Dred Scott v. Sandford* that African Americans were not citizens. Citizenship for American-born and naturalized blacks did not become legal until ratification of the Fourteenth Amendment in 1866.

166. Ibid.

167. Ibid.

168. Alexander, *History of Colonization*, 98. One of Alexander's principal sources would have been Ephraim Bacon's account of his visit to the scenes of his late brother's demise. Bacon, accompanied by his wife and several other white colonization-society agents, escorted the second group of African American settlers to Sierra Leone in early 1821. After meeting with Daniel Coker in Freetown, Bacon and his colleagues abandoned all thought of settling in the Sherbro. Bacon then ventured down the coast to present-day Liberia, where he negotiated with local chiefs for land on which to settle the free black colonists. While sailing back to Freetown, Bacon appeared unannounced at Campelar late on Sunday afternoon, April 22. He found Kizell there. "I probably did not go on shore," he confessed in his journal, "without possessing some prejudices against Kizzell. But, indeed, I was very much surprised at his malignant conduct. . . . [H]e appeared somewhat disconcerted at seeing the successors of our deceased friends. He, doubtless, felt some compunctions on account of his baseness." Bacon regarded Kizell as a "huckster" who had demanded rent from the colonization society for the accommodation he provided the settlers at Campelar and for various supplies. When Bacon stopped next at the Plantain Islands, the English-educated chief George Caulker further stoked the American's animus toward Kizell. Bacon wrote in his journal that Caulker, "like all others, who have had any intercourse with Kizzell, consider him an unprincipled man, and 'a stranger' in the country, and that our people could not have stopped at a more unsuitable spot than Campelar." Perhaps he had hoped they would come to the Plantains, but this was the same Chief Caulker who had expressed to Bacon's brother reservations about any African American settlement along the coast, and who understandably may have resented Kizell's benefiting financially. For a full account of Ephraim Bacon's visit to Sherbro and his encounter with Kizell, see *Abstract of a Journal of E. Bacon*, 33–44.

169. *African Repository* 46 (November 1869): 11.

170. *Christian Spectator* 2 (November 1820): 603–5.

171. American Colonization Society, *Fourth Annual Report*.

172. Wiltberger diary, August 4 and May 6, 1821. Divisions within the American colonization movement were public knowledge in Freetown. In a long article appearing in the April 21, 1821, edition of the *Royal Gazette and Sierra Leone Advertiser*, it is implied that Coker, not Kizell, had been responsible for the failure to obtain land. "The colored agent," the newspaper reported, ". . . was proved not to be trustworthy, and the native chiefs were known to be unfavourably disposed by the treacherous influence of this very agent, and to be disinclined to fulfil their engagements respecting the lands purchased from them." CO271/2, NAUK. The "colored agent" was almost certainly Coker. He was acting as the sole surviving "agent" of the American Colonization Society and, in the racial lexicon of the day, would have been considered "colored." Kizell was not an agent, either in an official or de facto sense; and he was notably dark in complexion. The *Gazette* article resurfaced as an appendix to the *Abstract of a Journal of E. Bacon*, published the following year by the same man who published Coker's journal.

"The colored agent," in the reprinted version, is identified at the bottom of page 57 as "Kizzell." Bacon clearly sided with Coker and may have held Kizell culpable for his brother's fatal illness. Whether inspired by Bacon, the publisher or even Coker, using the *Gazette* article to blame Kizell for what transpired at Campelar was disingenuous at best.

173. Wiltberger diary, June 12, 13, and 17, 1821.

174. Ibid., August 4, 1821.

175. Kizell to Ebenezer Burgess, August 17, 1821, and attached "John Kizell's Apology in Two Letters to Daniel Coker," Ebenezer Burgess Papers, Massachusetts Historical Society.

176. Coker (from Hastings, near Freetown) to Bishop James Kemp, undated in early 1824, Maryland Diocesan Archives, Baltimore.

Chapter 8. "What a creature man is!"

1. The surviving colonists from the *Elizabeth* and those brought by the *Nautilus* arrived at Mesurado on January 7, 1822. Allowing for the three-day journey, it is conceivable that they witnessed James Creighton's *Calypso* coming into the Freetown harbor on January 4. See American Colonization Society, *Sixth Annual Report.*

2. Rev. William Meade, on a mission to Georgia on behalf of the American Colonization Society, met either John Holman Jr. or his brother Samuel in Charleston. Both were sons of a slave-trading Englishman and his African mistress, who had moved in 1791 from the Rio Pongas to take up the safer pursuit of rice farming in the South Carolina lowcountry. The sons later returned to Africa. In the colonization society's second annual report, published in 1819, Meade claimed that at least forty free blacks had asked to accompany Holman to Sierra Leone. Holman apparently was corresponding with Governor Charles MacCarthy in Freetown regarding land to settle African Americans. He said he was familiar with Paul Cuffe's settlers in Freetown and with conditions in the Sherbro. Both Holmans, who had owned as many as fifty slaves each in South Carolina, almost certainly knew John Kizell. There is no record that any Charleston blacks went to Sierra Leone with Holman. See Koger, *Black Slaveowners*, for a detailed account of the Holman family in Africa and South Carolina.

3. Governor and council minutes, January 5 and 7, 1822, CO270/16/6–8, NAUK.

4. Pearson, *Designs against Charleston*, 319. Pearson quotes the *Pendleton (S.C.) Messenger* of October 31, 1821, that Creighton had just sailed for Sierra Leone. Pearson incorrectly gives the year as 1820.

5. Lofton, *Insurrection in South Carolina*, 81–82.

6. Ibid., 94; Pearson, *Designs against Charleston*, 317. Free blacks in the African Methodist Episcopal Church had erected a "house of worship" at the corner of Hanover and Reid streets on Charleston Neck. They petitioned "to open said building for the purpose of Divine worship from the rising sun until the going down of the sun."

7. Hamilton, *Negro Plot*, 38; Pearson, *Designs against Charleston*, 110. Pearson quotes the testimony of Frank Ferguson, a slave, that Creighton had invited Vesey to come with him to Mesurado, apparently his original intended destination.

8. Rucker, "River Floweth On," 119.

9. The Official Report (page 163), written by magistrates Lionel H. Kennedy and Thomas Parker, published in 1822, states that Prince Graham—found guilty and banished from the state—requested that he be "transported to Africa on board a vessel which sailed from Charleston." Graham left aboard the *Dolphin*, owned and commanded by Benjamin Pearson of

Charleston, which arrived in the Rio Pongas in October. According to a report prepared in April 1823 by two British officials in Sierra Leone, the passengers aboard the *Dolphin* "were chiefly persons of colour . . . required to remove themselves in consequence of having taken part in some disturbances in Charleston. Some of the individuals were accompanied by their families." The British officials inferred, incorrectly, that all the blacks had been banished. Some may have been crew members. Graham was the only one exiled. Many perished from fever, the report continued, but "most of the survivors found their way to Sierra Leone" before the end of 1822. Commissioners Gregory and Fitzgerald to George Canning, Principal Secretary of State for Foreign Affairs, April 29, 1823, Foreign Office, FO84/21/79, NAUK. A subsequent British report suggested that the *Dolphin* later carried slaves from the Rio Pongas to Havana. See Acting Gov. D. M. Hamilton to Canning, May 15, 1824, CO84/28, NAUK.

10. Sierra Leone's expatriate black Charlestonians were joined in 1831 by Edward Jones, the son of Jehu Jones Sr. The father, a member of the mixed-race Brown Fellowship Society, owned what many regarded as Charleston's finest hotel, on Broad Street next to St. Michael's Church, in the 1820s. Edward graduated from Amherst College and was the second American black to receive a university degree. He was ordained as an Episcopal priest in Connecticut and went to Sierra Leone to teach. He also managed a settlement of liberated Africans and served two decades as principal of Fourah Bay College. When he retired in 1860, Jones wanted to reside in Charleston but was blocked by a state law that prohibited African Americans who had left from returning. He died in England in 1864. See Nicol, "Jones Family."

11. *Royal Gazette and Sierra Leone Advertiser*, December 28, 1822, and February 8, 1823, CO271/2, NAUK. Kizell may also have faced mounting debt in the early 1820s. He and other prominent blacks were forced to sell Freetown properties to meet financial obligations. Kizell was briefly imprisoned in mid-1824 by the British authorities at St. Mary's, in the Gambia River. He was returned to Sierra Leone in late August, in "custody," but allowed to go free. The charges against him, if any, have not survived. See the Colonial Secretary's Letter Book, Sierra Leone National Archives, for letters to Capt. Alexander Findlay, August 7 and September 1, 1824, in the Sierra Leone National Archives.

12. Harry D. Hunter, Sailing Master aboard U.S. Navy Schooner *Augusta*, to Governor MacCarthy, April 20, 1822, CO270/16/101–7, NAUK.

13. Report from West African Commissioners, April 29, 1823, FO84/21/88, NAUK.

14. Jones, *From Slaves to Palm Kernels*, 41.

15. Ibid., 47.

16. *Royal Gazette and Sierra Leone Advertiser*, May 28, 1825, CO271/2, NAUK. The war had broken out in late 1823, precipitated by the Mende. They were retaliating against the coastal peoples, principally the Sherbro and Vai, who kidnapped Mende traders coming to barter for salt and other commodities. The Sherbro and Vai were said to be under the sway of slave-trading chiefs and Europeans in the Gallinas and Cape Mount areas. See George Caulker's letter to George Rendall, February 28, 1824, requesting British assistance to resist Mende encroachment, CO270/17/15–20, NAUK.

17. Fyfe, *History of Sierra Leone*, 152.

18. *Royal Gazette and Sierra Leone Advertiser*, May 28 and June 25, 1825, CO271/2, NAUK.

19. Treaty agreement with local chiefs, CO879/35/piece 1, NAUK. The treaty was negotiated and signed on September 24, 1825, at George Caulker's headquarters on the Plantain

Islands. It was ratified at Yonie on October 1 by King Sherbro and other chiefs. See also Tucker, *Tuckers of Sierra Leone*, 18.

20. Charles Turner to Lord Bathurst, October 18, 1825, CO267/66, NAUK.

21. Turner to Bathurst, July 19, 1825, CO267/66; Turner to Canning, July 25, 1825, Foreign Office, FO84/38/187, NAUK.

22. *Royal Gazette and Sierra Leone Advertiser*, September 10, 1825, CO271/2, NAUK. The Cussoes (more properly, the Kpaa-Mende) seized control of the Banta territory on the Sherbro mainland by neutralizing the Mano chief's protective spirit (a mermaid) and beheading him. See Arthur Abraham's account in *Introduction to the Pre-Colonial History*, 144.

23. In "Additional Memoranda with Respect to the Recent Cessions of Territory at Sierra Leone," dated June 9, 1826, Zachary Macaulay records Turner's opinion of the Boom country as reported to him by someone—almost certainly his nephew Kenneth—traveling with the governor. CO267/79, NAUK.

24. In his family history, Peter L. Tucker writes that "the Colonial Government was really after . . . the revenue from the flourishing Boom/Kittam trade." *Tuckers of Sierra Leone*, 18. The Tuckers' alleged slave trading, he writes, was a pretext for Turner's attempt to control the area.

25. Turner to Bathurst, October 18, 1825, CO267/66, NAUK.

26. James Tucker (from Mamu), September 20, 1826, to Lt. Gov. Neil Campbell, in Freetown. The letter was included with Campbell's letter of January 22, 1827, to the Secretary of State for the Colonial Department, CO267/71, NAUK.

27. Turner to Bathurst, March 2, 1826, CO267/71, NAUK.

28. Proclamation, CO267/71, NAUK. The proclamation was signed by Walter W. Lewis, acting colonial secretary.

29. *Royal Gazette and Sierra Leone Advertiser*, March 7, 1826, CO267/71, NAUK. The *Gazette* blamed Turner's death on his "arduous and unremitting exertions . . . during the late expedition to the Sherbro."

30. Turner to Bathurst, March 2, 1826, CO267/71, NAUK.

31. Tucker, *Tuckers of Sierra Leone*, 30.

32. Kenneth Macaulay to Bathurst, July 2, 1826, CO267/72, NAUK.

33. George Rendall to Macaulay, May 5, 1826, CO267/72, NAUK; Kenneth Macaulay to Bathurst, July 2, 1826, CO267/72, NAUK.

34. Kizell to J. Reffell, May 7, 1826, Colonial Secretary's Letter Book, Sierra Leone National Archives; Macaulay to Bathurst, March 9, 1826; Rendall to Macaulay, May 5, 1826; and Macaulay to Bathurst, July 2, 1826, CO267/72, NAUK.

35. Neil Campbell (Freetown) to Lieutenant Hawkins, September 9, 1826, CO267/73, NAUK.

36. Hawkins to Lt. Col. Hugh Lumley, September 21, 1826, CO267/74, NAUK.

37. James Tucker (Mamu) to Hawkins, September 28, 1826, CO267/81, NAUK.

38. Campbell to Bathurst, October 27, 1826, and November 1826, CO267/74, NAUK. The British government's disavowal of Turner's "convention" in the Sherbro was never publicly revealed in Sierra Leone. It was probably no secret, however, to the Tuckers and other chiefs, who had sources of information in Freetown and among country traders. They may also have been aware that the British commissioners, who were inquiring into the state of the colony during 1826, believed Turner's military adventure had been counterproductive. In their final report,

submitted in April 1827, they questioned the wisdom of "offensive military operations in this part of Africa." CO267/91/5.

39. Campbell to Bathurst, January 22, 1827, CO267/81, NAUK; *Royal Gazette and Sierra Leone Advertiser*, October 15, 1825, CO271/2, NAUK. See Jones, *From Slaves to Palm Kernels*, 89–92, for an analysis of the Gallinas uprising. According to Jones, "It would be incorrect to regard the Zawo War as an attempt to secure the abolition of slavery or the slave trade. The Zawo themselves used slaves for farming and probably sold slaves to Spanish slave dealers on the Mano River. . . ."

40. Campbell to Bathurst, March 9, 1827, CO267/81, NAUK.

41. Liberated African Department Letter Book, July 28, 1830, Sierra Leone National Archives. Kizell's employment with the Liberated African Department is curious, given his belief, stated to the British commissioners in 1826, that the recaptives had been "set before our children and us ourselves." Walker quotes one liberated African that the "spirit of exclusiveness ran rampant among [the Nova Scotians]." *Black Loyalists*, 319.

42. Alexander Findlay to R. W. Hay, Undersecretary of State for the Colonies, July 1830, CO267/105, NAUK.

43. Constable Frederick Campbell (Freetown) to Thomas Cole, Assistant Superintendent of the Liberated African Department, July 15, 1830, CO267/105, NAUK.

44. Leonard, *Records of a Voyage*, 80–82.

45. Ibid., 79.

46. Findlay to Hay, July 1830, CO267/105, NAUK.

47. Fyfe, *History of Sierra Leone*, 196.

48. Col. Dixon Denham to Hay, May 24, 1828, CO268/10, NAUK.

49. Constable Frederick Campbell, CO267/105, NAUK; Findlay to Hay, November 29, 1830, CO267/105, NAUK.

50. Quoted in Somé, *Of Water and the Spirit*, 177.

51. Quoted in Shaw, *Memories of the Slave Trade*, 60.

52. Ibid., 17. For a discussion of occult practices during Sierra Leone's civil war, see Bergner, *In the Land of Magic Soldiers*. In Sierra Leonean communities closer to the coast, the slave trade and its consequences are not forgotten. Imodale Caulker Burnett, a historian of the Caulker family in Sierra Leone and the diaspora, acknowledges that some Caulker descendants "fear that our ancestors were cursed by those who were sold . . ." (e-mail to author, July 19, 2010).

53. Kup, *History of Sierra Leone*, 193.

54. Shaw, *Memories of the Slave Trade*, 11–12.

55. Ibid., 50.

56. Thompson, *Flash of the Spirit*, 74, 107.

57. "Notes on the Correspondence of Kizell, by Governor Columbine," in African Institution, *Sixth Report*, 146. Among the Temne, a witch—unlike other people—is thought to have a separate stomach capable of digesting human flesh. See Shaw, *Memories of the Slave Trade*, 207.

58. Mbiti, *African Religions and Philosophy*, 273–74.

59. Somé, *Of Water and the Spirit*, 175.

60. Shaw, *Memories of the Slave Trade*, 60.

61. Ibid., 50–56.

62. Peters, *War and the Crisis of Youth in Sierra Leone* (London: Cambridge University Press, 2011), 95, 240.

63. Clarkson, *History of the Rise*, 613.

64. *Royal Gazette and Sierra Leone Advertiser*, September 18, 1824, CO271/2, NAUK.

65. Fyfe, *History of Sierra Leone*, 175.

66. Ibid., 178–80.

67. Ibid., 184.

BIBLIOGRAPHY

Primary Sources

Manuscripts and Unpublished Sources

Allen, William. African correspondence. Box number AH064, GlaxoSmithKline, Brentford, Middlesex, U.K.

American Colonization Society Records, Manuscript Division, Library of Congress.

Booth, Capt. William. Diary and Letters. Fergusson Papers. Public Archives of Nova Scotia, Halifax.

———. Journal. Public Archives of Nova Scotia.

Burgess, Ebenezer. Papers. Massachusetts Historical Society, Boston.

Carleton, Guy. Papers. PRO30/55. National Archives of the United Kingdom (formerly Public Record Office), Kew, London.

Charleston Customs House Records, South Carolina Department of Archives and History.

Clarkson, John. Papers. New-York Historical Society.

Coker, Daniel. Letters. Maryland Diocesan Archives, Baltimore.

Cuffe, Paul. Papers. New Bedford (Mass.) Free Public Library.

German Friendly Society Fair Minute Book, vol. 1 (January 15, 1766–January 17, 1787), South Carolina Historical Society.

Johnson, Elijah. Journal. Manuscript Division, Library of Congress.

Laurens, John. Miscellaneous Papers. New York Public Library.

Macaulay, Zachary. Journal. Manuscript Division (call number MY 418). Huntington Library, San Marino, Cal.

Marston, Benjamin. Diary. Public Archives of Nova Scotia.

Millidge, Thomas. Papers. Public Archives of Nova Scotia.

Muster Book of Free Black Settlement in Birchtown, August 1, 1784, Shelburne County Museum, Shelburne, Nova Scotia.

Port Roseway Associates Minutebook, 1782–83, Public Archives of Canada, Document MG9 B9.14, vol. 1.

Sierra Leone Governor and Council Records. National Archives of the United Kingdom.

The Trans-Atlantic Slave Trade Database, www.slavevoyages.org/tast/index.faces (accessed August 18, 2010).

Will Book 55, 1771–1774. South Carolina Department of Archives and History.

Wiltberger, Christian. Diary. Manuscript Division, Library of Congress.

Books, Journals, Articles, and Published Reports

Africa Redeemed; or, the Means of Her Relief Illustrated by the Growth and Prospects of Liberia. London: Nisbet, 1851.

African Institution, *First Report*. London, 1811.

——. *Second Report*. London, 1808.

——. *Third Report*. London, 1809.

——. *Fourth Report*. London, 1810.

——. *Fifth Report*. London, 1811.

——. *Sixth Report*. London, 1812.

——. *Eighth Report*. London, 1814.

——. *Ninth Report*. London, 1815.

——. *Fifteenth Report*. London, 1821.

——. *Special Report*. London, 1815.

African Intelligencer (Washington, D.C.).

African Repository and Colonial Journal (Washington, D.C.).

Afzelius, Adam. *Sierra Leone Journal 1795–1796*. Edited by A. P. Kup. Uppsala, Sweden: Almqvist & Wiksells, 1967.

Alexander, Archibald. *A History of Colonization of the Western Coast of Africa*. Philadelphia: Martien, 1846.

Allaire, Anthony. *Diary of Lieut. Anthony Allaire*. New York: New York Times, 1968.

Allen, William. *Life of William Allen, with Selections from His Correspondence*. Vol. 1. London: Gilpin, 1846.

American Colonization Society. *Annual Report*. Vol. 1. Washington, D.C., 1818. Vol. 2. Washington, D.C., 1819. Vol. 5. Washington, D.C., 1822.

Bacon, E. *Abstract of a Journal of E. Bacon, Assistant Agent of the United States, to Africa*. Philadelphia, 1821.

Boyd, Julian P., ed. *The Papers of Thomas Jefferson*. Vol. 1, 1760–1776. Princeton, N.J.: Princeton University Press, 1950.

Burgess, Ebenezer. *Address to the American Society for Colonizing the Free People of Colour of the United States*. Washington, D.C.: Davis & Force, 1818.

Caldwell, Elias B. "American Colonization Society," *Christian Spectator* 2 (1820).

Charleston Yearbook 1883. Charleston, S.C., 1883.

Chesnutt, David R., et al., eds. *The Papers of Henry Laurens*. 16 vols. Columbia: University of South Carolina Press, 1968–2003.

Coker, Daniel. *Journal of Daniel Coker: A Descendant of Africa*. Baltimore: Coale, 1820.

Coldham, Peter Wilson. *American Loyalist Claims*. Vol. 1. Washington, D.C.: National Genealogical Society, 1980.

——. *American Migrations, 1765–1799*. Baltimore: Genealogical Publishing, 2000.

Corry, Joseph. *Observations upon the Windward Coast of Africa*. London, 1807.

Donnan, Elizabeth. *Documents Illustrative of the History of the Slave Trade to America*. Vols. 3 and 4. Washington, D.C.: Carnegie Institute, 1935.

Drayton, John. *Memoirs of the American Revolution, from Its Commencement to the Year of 1776, Inclusive: As Relating to the State of South-Carolina*. Vols. 1 and 2. Charleston, 1821.

Finley, Robert. *Thoughts on the Colonization of Free Blacks*. Washington, D.C., 1816.

Force, Peter. *American Archives: Consisting of a Collection of Authentick Records, State Papers, Debates and Letters and Other Notices of Publick Affairs*. Fourth series. 9 vols. New York: Johnson Reprint, 1972.

Bibliography

Fyfe, Christopher, ed. *Our Children Free and Happy: Letters from Black Settlers in Africa in the 1790s.* Edinburgh: Edinburgh University Press, 1991.

George, David. "An Account of the Life of Mr. David George, from Sierra Leone in Africa, Given by Himself in a Conversation with Brother Rippon in London and Brother Pearce in Birmingham," *Annual Baptist Register* 1 (1793): 480–82.

Gilroy, Marion, comp. *Loyalists and Land Settlements in Nova Scotia.* Halifax: Public Archives of Nova Scotia, 1980.

Helsley, Alexia Jones. *South Carolinians in the War of American Independence.* Columbia: South Carolina Department of Archives and History, 2000.

Holcomb, Brent H., comp. *Petitions for Land from the South Carolina Council Journals.* Vol. 5, 1757–1765. Columbia: South Carolina Magazine of Ancestral Research, 1993.

——, comp. *South Carolina Deed Abstracts, 1770–1783.* Columbia: South Carolina Magazine of Ancestral Research, 1993.

——, comp. *South Carolina Marriages, 1688–1799.* Baltimore: Genealogical Publishing, 1983.

——, comp. *South Carolina's Royal Grants.* Vol. 2, *Grant Books 10 through 17, 1760–1768.* Columbia: South Carolina Magazine of Ancestral Research, 2007.

House Documents. 15th Cong., 2nd sess., 4, no. 84.

House Reports. 17th Cong., 1st sess., 4, no. 92.

Jeffery, Reginald W., ed. *Dyott's Diary, 1781–1845.* Vol. 1. London: Constable, 1907.

Jones, Jack Moreland, and Mary B. Warren, comps. *South Carolina Immigrants, 1760 to 1770.* Danielsville, Ga.: Heritage Papers, 1988.

Journal of the South Carolina Court of General Sessions, 1769–1776. South Carolina Department of Archives and History, n.d. Microform, 1986.

Kennedy, Lionel H., and Thomas Parker. *An Official Report of the Trials of Sundry Negroes, Charged with an Attempt to Raise an Insurrection in the State of South Carolina.* Charleston: Schenck, 1822.

King, Boston. "Memoirs of the Life of Boston King." *Methodist Magazine* (London), March, April, May 1798, 105–10, 157–61, 209–13, 263–65.

Knight, Helen C. *The New Republic.* 2nd ed. Boston: Massachusetts Sabbath School Society, 1851.

Leonard, Peter. *Records of a Voyage to the Western Coast of Africa in His Majesty's Ship Dryad and of the Service in That Station for the Suppression of the Slave Trade in the Years 1830, 1831, and 1832.* London, 1833.

"Letters from John Lewis Gervais to Henry Laurens, 1777–1778," *South Carolina Historical Magazine* 66 (January 1965):15–37.

Lloyd's Registry. London: Society of Merchants, Ship-owners, and Underwriters, 1812.

Macaulay, Zachary. *A Letter to His Royal Highness the Duke of Gloucester, President of the African Institution.* London: Ellerton & Henderson, 1815.

Matthews, John. *A Voyage to the River Sierra Leone, on the Coast of Africa: Containing an Account of the Trade and Productions of the Country.* London: White, 1788.

Montefiore, Joshua. *An Authentic Account of the Late Expedition to Bulam, on the Coast of Africa: With a Description of the Present Settlement of Sierra Leone.* London, 1794.

Moore, Carolina T., comp. and ed. *Abstracts of the Wills of the State of South Carolina, 1760–1784.* Vol. 3. Columbia, S.C.: Bryan, 1969.

Moss, Bobby Gilmer, ed. *Journal of Capt. Alexander Chesney, Adjutant to Major Patrick Ferguson*. Blacksburg, S.C.: Scotia-Hibernia, 1998.

282 ——, ed. *Roster of Loyalists in the Battle of Kings Mountain*. Blacksburg, S.C.: Scotia-Hibernia, 1998.

——, ed. *Roster of South Carolina Patriots in the American Revolution*. Baltimore: Genealogical Publishing, 1983.

Moss, Bobby Gilmer, and Michael C. Scoggins, eds. *African-American Loyalists in the Southern Campaign of the American Revolution*. Blacksburg, S.C.: Scotia-Hibernia, 1998.

——, eds. *African-American Patriots in the Southern Campaign of the American Revolution*. Blacksburg, S.C.: Scotia-Hibernia, 2004.

Motes, Jesse Hogan, III, and Margaret Peckham Motes. *South Carolina Memorials: Abstracts of Land Titles 1774–1776*. Vol. 1. Greenville, S.C.: Southern Historical Press, 1996.

Moultrie, William. *Memoirs of the American Revolution, So Far as It Related to the States of North and South Carolina*. Vol. 2. New York: Arno, 1968.

Newton, John. *Thoughts upon the African Slave Trade*. London: Buckland & Johnson, 1788.

Owen, Nicholas. *Journal of a Slave-Dealer, A View of Some Remarkable Axcedents in the Life of Nics. Owen on the Coast of Africa from the Year 1746 to the Year 1757*. London: Routledge, 1930.

Quincy, Josiah, Jr. "Journal of Josiah Quincy, Junior, 1773," *Massachusetts Historical Society Proceedings* 49 (June 1916): 424–81.

Ramsay, David. *The History of the American Revolution*. Vols. 1 and 2. Philadelphia: Aitken, 1789.

Revill, Jamie, comp. *A Compilation of the Original Lists of Protestant Immigrants to South Carolina, 1763–1773*. Columbia, S.C.: State, 1939.

Seeber, Edward D., ed. and trans. *On the Threshold of Liberty: Journal of a Frenchman's Tour of the American Colonies in 1777*. Bloomington: Indiana University Press, 1959.

Sierra Leone Company Report. London, 1808.

Showman, Richard K., ed. *The Papers of Nathanael Greene*. Vol. 6. Chapel Hill: University of North Carolina Press, 1991.

Stedman, Charles. *The History of Origin, Progress and Termination of the American War*. Vol. 2. London, 1794.

Tarter, Brent, ed. *The Order Book and Related Papers of the Common Hall of the Borough of Norfolk, Virginia, 1756–1798*. Richmond: Virginia State Library, 1979.

Thorpe, Robert. *A Letter to William Wilberforce, Esq. Etc by R. Thorpe, Esq. Etc*. London, 1815.

——. *A Reply "Point by Point" to the Special Report of the Directors of the African Institution*. London: Rivington, 1815.

Tustin, Joseph P., ed. and trans. *Diary of the American War: A Hessian Journal by Capt. Johann Ewald*. New Haven: Yale University Press, 1979.

Uhlendorf, Bernhard A., ed. and trans. *The Siege of Charleston*. Ann Arbor: University of Michigan Press, 1938.

Wadstrom, C. B. *Essay on Colonization*. London: Printed for the author by Darton and Harvey, 1794.

Watson, Winslow C., ed. *Men and Times of the Revolution; or, Memoirs of Elkanah Watson, Including His Journals of Travels in Europe and America, from the Year 1777 to 1842, and His Correspondence with Public Men, and Reminiscences and Incidents of the American Revolution*. 2nd ed. New York, 1856.

Wigfall, Edward T. *The First Accurate Account of One of the American Colonists Who Has Returned to the United States of America.* N.p., 1821.

Wiggins, Rosalind Cobb. *Captain Paul Cuffe's Logs and Letters, 1807–1817.* Washington, D.C.: Howard University Press, 1996.   **283**

Willcox, William B., ed. *The American Revolution.* New Haven: Yale University Press, 1954.

Newspapers

Charleston (S.C.) Courier

National Intelligencer (Washington, D.C.)

New Bedford (Mass.) Mercury

New York Evening Post

Niles' Weekly Register (Baltimore)

Nova-Scotia Packet: And General Advertiser

Pendleton (S.C.) Messenger

Royal Gazette (Charleston)

Royal American Gazette (Shelburne, Nova Scotia)

Royal Gazette and Sierra Leone Advertiser

Sierra Leone Gazette

South Carolina Gazette

South Carolina Gazette and Country Journal

Secondary Sources

Abraham, Arthur. *An Introduction to the Pre-Colonial History of the Mende of Sierra Leone.* Lewiston, N.Y.: Mellen, 2003.

Acker, Sarah, and Lewis Jackson. *Historic Shelburne, 1870–1950.* Halifax: Nimbus, 2001.

Ackerson, Wayne. *The African Institution (1807–1827) and the Antislavery Movement in Great Britain.* Lewiston, N.Y.: Mellen, 2005.

Adler, Mortimer J., and Charles Van Doren, eds. *The Negro in American History, Volume III, Slaves and Masters, 1567–1854.* Chicago: Encyclopedia Britannica Educational Corporation, 1969.

An Aging Database for Nova Scotian Black Cultural History in Runaway Slave Ads in South Carolina for the 18th Century. Halifax: Nova Scotia Museum, n.d.

Andreano, Ralph Louis, and Herbert D. Warner. "Charleston Loyalists: A Statistical Note," *South Carolina Historical Magazine* 60 (1959): 164–68.

Anstey, Roger. "A Re-interpretation of the Abolition of the British Slave Trade, 1806–1807," *English Historical Review* 87 (1972): 304–32.

Aptheker, Herbert. *"One Continual Cry": David Walker's Appeal to the Colored Citizens of the World.* New York: Humanities Press, 1965.

Archibald, Mary. *The Militia of Shelburne County, 1783–1868.* Shelburne, Nova Scotia: Shelburne Historical Society, 1991.

Ashmun, Jehudi. *Memoir of the Life and Character of the Rev. Samuel Bacon.* Washington, D.C.: Gideon, 1822.

Barnwell, Joseph W. "The Evacuation of Charleston by the British in 1782," *South Carolina Historical Magazine* 11 (January 1910): 1–26.

Bass, Robert D. *Ninety Six, The Struggle for the South Carolina Back Country.* Lexington, S.C.: Sandlapper Store, 1978.

Bibliography

Bell, A. N. "The Debt to Africa—The Hope of Liberia," *American Church Review*, July 1881.

Bell, Michael E. "The Anomaly of Charleston, South Carolina's Antebellum German-America." Ph.D. diss., University of South Carolina, 1996.

Bergner, Daniel. *In the Land of Magic Soldiers: A Story of White and Black in West Africa*. New York: Farrar, Straus & Giroux, 2003.

Berkeley, Edmund, and Dorothy Smith Berkeley. *Dr. Alexander Garden of Charles Town*. Chapel Hill: University of North Carolina Press, 1969.

Berlin, Ira. "Time, Space, and the Evolution of Afro-American Society on British Mainland North America." In *The Slavery Reader*, edited by Gad Heuman and James Walvin, 122–53. London: Routledge, 2003.

Berlin, Ira, and Ronald Hoffman, eds. *Slavery and Freedom in the Age of the American Revolution*. Charlottesville: University of Virginia, 1983.

Bogger, Tommy L. "The Slave and Free Black Community in Norfolk, 1775–1865." Ph.D. diss., University of Virginia, 1976.

Bolster, W. Jeffrey. *Black Jacks: African American Seamen in the Age of Sail*. Cambridge, Mass.: Harvard University Press, 1997.

Boone, Sylvia Ardyn. *Radiance from the Waters: Ideals of Feminine Beauty in Mende Art*. New Haven, Conn.: Yale University Press, 1986.

Borick, Carl P. *A Gallant Defense: The Siege of Charleston, 1780*. Columbia: University of South Carolina Press, 2003.

Bridenbaugh, Carl. *Cities in Revolt: Urban Life in America, 1743–1776*. New York: Oxford University Press, 1971.

Brooks, George E., Jr. *Landlords and Strangers: Ecology, Society and Trade in Western Africa, 1000–1630*. Boulder, Colo.: Westview, 1993.

——— . "A View of Sierra Leone ca 1815," *Sierra Leone Studies*, n.s., no. 13 (June 1960): 24–31.

——— . *Yankee Traders, Old Coasters and African Middlemen*. Boston: Boston University Press, 1970.

Brooks, Joanna. *John Marrant's Journal: Providence and Prophecy in the Eighteenth Century Atlantic*. Austin: University of Texas Press, 1999.

Brown, Isaac V. *Biography of the Rev. Robert Finley*. 2nd ed. Philadelphia: Moore, 1857.

Cahill, Barry. "The Black Loyalist Myth in Atlantic Canada," *Acadiensis* 29 (Autumn 1999): 76–87.

Campbell, Mavis C. *Back to Africa, George Ross and the Maroons, from Nova Scotia to Sierra Leone*. Trenton, N.J.: Africa World, 1993.

Carney, Judith A. *Black Rice: The African Origins of Rice Cultivation in the Americas*. Cambridge, Mass.: Harvard University Press, 2001.

Carretta, Vincent. *Equiano the African*. Athens: University of Georgia Press, 2005.

——— , ed. *Unchained Voices: An Anthology of Black Authors in the English-Speaking World of the Eighteenth Century*. Lexington: University of Kentucky Press, 1996.

Clark, Murtie June. *Loyalists in the Southern Campaign of the Revolutionary War*. Vols. 1 and 2. Baltimore: Genealogical Publishing, 1981.

Clarkson, Thomas. *History of the Rise, Progress, and Accomplishment of the Abolition of the African Slave Trade by the British Parliament*. London: Parker, 1839.

Coclanis, Peter A. *The Shadow of a Dream: Economic Life and Death in the South Carolina Low Country, 1670–1920*. New York: Oxford University Press, 1989.

————, ed. *The Atlantic Economy during the Seventeenth and Eighteenth Centuries: Organization, Operation, Practice, and Personnel.* Columbia: University of South Carolina Press, 2005.

Collections of the South-Carolina Historical Society. Vol. 3. Charleston, 1859.

Collier, George R., and Charles MacCarthy. *West African Sketches.* London: Seeley, 1824.

Corey, Mary. "Daniel Coker: Between an Oppressive Culture and a Liberating God." Ph.D. diss., University of California at Los Angeles, 1988.

Cross, J. Russell. *Historic Ramblin's through Berkeley.* Columbia, S.C.: Bryan, 1985.

Crow, Jeffrey J., and Larry E. Tise, eds. *The Southern Experience in the American Revolution.* Chapel Hill: University of North Carolina Press, 1978.

Curtin, Philip D. *The Image of Africa, British Ideas and Action, 1780–1850.* Vol. 1. Madison: University of Wisconsin Press, 1964.

Dameron, J. David. *King's Mountain: The Defeat of the Loyalists, October 7, 1780.* Cambridge, Mass.: Da Capo, 2003.

Dangerfield, George. *The Era of Good Feeling.* New York: Harcourt, Brace, 1952.

Davis, David Brion. *The Problem of Slavery in the Age of Revolution, 1770–1823.* Ithaca, N.Y.: Cornell University Press, 1975.

Day, Lynda Rose. "Afro-British Integration on the Sherbro Coast: 1665–1795," *Africana Research Bulletin* 12 (1983): 82–107.

————. "Historical Patterns in a Stateless Society, Sherbro Land, 1750–1898." Master's thesis, University of Wisconsin, 1980.

Dennis, Clara. *Down in Nova Scotia, My Own Native Land.* Toronto: Ryerson, 1934.

DePeyster, J. Watts. "The Affair at Kings Mountain," *Magazine of American History* 5 (December 1880): 401–23.

Dillard, J. L. *Black English.* New York: Vintage, 1973.

Donnan, Elizabeth. "The Slave Trade into South Carolina before the Revolution," *American Historical Review* 33 (July 1928): 804–28.

Douty, Esther M. *Forten, the Sailmaker.* New York: Rand McNally, 1968.

Dow, George Francis. *Slave Ships and Slaving.* Salem, Mass.: Marine Research Society, 1927.

Draper, Lyman L. *King's Mountain and Its Heroes.* Cincinnati: Thomson, 1881.

DuBois, W. E. B. *The Souls of Black Folk.* 1903. New York: Gramercy, 1994.

————. *The Suppression of the African Slave Trade.* 1896. Baton Rouge: Louisiana State University Press, 1969.

Dunkerly, Robert M. *The Battle of King's Mountain: Eyewitness Accounts.* Charleston, S.C.: History Press, 2007.

Edelson, S. Max. *Plantation Enterprise in Colonial South Carolina.* Cambridge, Mass.: Harvard University Press, 2006.

Eltis, David. "Labour and Coercion in the English Atlantic World from the Seventeenth to the Early Twentieth Century." In *The Slavery Reader,* edited by Gad Heuman and James Walvin, 58–73. London: Routledge, 2003.

Eltis, David, and David Richardson. "West Africa and the Trans-Atlantic Slave Trade, New Evidence of Long-Term Trends." In *The Slavery Reader,* edited by Gad Heuman and James Walvin, 42–57. London: Routledge, 2003.

Fenn, Elizabeth A. *Pox Americana: The Great Smallpox Epidemic of 1775–82.* New York: Hill & Wang, 2001.

Bibliography

Fergusson, Charles Bruce, ed. *Clarkson's Mission to America, 1791–1792*. Halifax: Public Archives of Nova Scotia, 1971.

Foote, Andrew H. *Africa and the American Flag*. New York: Appleton, 1854.

Frey, Sylvia R. *Water from the Rock: Black Resistance in a Revolutionary Age*. Princeton, N.J.: Princeton University Press, 1991.

Frey, Sylvia R., and Betty Wood. "The Survival of African Religions." In *The Slavery Reader*, edited by Gad Heuman and James Walvin, 384–404. London: Routledge, 2003.

Fyfe, Christopher. *A History of Sierra Leone*. London: Oxford University Press, 1962.

———. *Sierra Leone Inheritance*. London: Oxford University Press, 1964.

———. "Thomas Peters: History and Legend," *Sierra Leone Studies*, n.s., 1 (1953): 4–13.

Gerzina, Gretchen Holbrook. *Black London*. New Brunswick, N.J.: Rutgers University Press, 1995.

Gibson, Gail. "Costume and Fashion in Charleston 1769–1782," *South Carolina Historical Magazine* 82 (July 1981): 225–47.

Gilchrist, M. M. *Patrick Ferguson: "A Man of Some Genius."* Edinburgh: NMS Enterprises, 2003.

Gongaware, George J. *The History of the German Friendly Society of Charleston, 1766–1916*. Spartanburg, S.C.: Reprint Company, 1999.

Grace, John J. "Slavery and Emancipation among the Mende in Sierra Leone, 1896–1928." In *Slavery in Africa: Historical and Anthropological Perspectives*, edited by Suzanne Miers and Igor Kopytoff, 415–31. Madison: University of Wisconsin Press, 1977.

Graves, William T. *James Williams: An American Patriot in the Carolina Backcountry*. Lincoln, Neb.: Writers Club Press, 2002.

Greene, Harlan, and Harry S. Hutchins Jr. *Slave Badges and the Slave-Hire System in Charleston, South Carolina, 1783–1865*. Jefferson, N.C.: McFarland, 2004.

Greene, Lorenzo J. "Some Observations on the Black Regiment of Rhode Island," *Journal of Negro History* 37 (April 1952): 142–72.

Greene, Robert Ewell. *Black Courage, 1775–1783: Documentation of Black Participation in the American Revolution*. Washington, D.C.: National Society of the Daughters of the American Revolution, 1984.

Gregoire, Henri. *An Enquiry Concerning the Intellectual and Moral Faculties and Literature of Negroes*. Brooklyn, N.Y.: Kirk, 1810.

Hall, Henry Usher. *The Sherbro of Sierra Leone*. Philadelphia: University Museum of the University of Pennsylvania, 1938.

Hamilton, James. *Negro Plot: An Account of the Late Intended Insurrection among a Portion of the Blacks of the City of Charleston, South Carolina*. Boston: Ingraham, 1822.

Harris, Sheldon H. *Paul Cuffe: Black America and the African Return*. New York: Simon & Schuster, 1972.

Heinegg, Paul. *Free African-Americans of North Carolina, Virginia and South Carolina from the Colonial Period to About 1820*. 4th ed. Vol. 2. Baltimore: Clearfield, 2002.

Heuman, Gad, and James Walvin, eds. *The Slavery Reader*. London: Routledge, 2003.

Heywood, Linda M., and John K. Thornton. *Central Africans, Atlantic Creoles, and the Foundation of the Americas, 1585–1660*. New York: Cambridge University Press, 2007.

Higgins, W. Robert. "Charleston: Terminus and Entrepot of the Colonial Slave Trade." In *The African Diaspora*, edited by Martin L. Kilson and Robert I. Rotberg, 114–31. Cambridge, Mass.: Harvard University Press, 1976.

Bibliography

——. "The Geographical Origins of Negro Slaves in Colonial South Carolina," *South Atlantic Quarterly* 70 (Winter 1971): 34–47.

Hoare, Prince. *Memoirs of Granville Sharp Esquire.* 2nd ed. Vol. 2. London: Colburn, 1828.

Hodges, Graham Russell. *The Black Loyalist Directory: African Americans in Exile after the Revolution.* New York: Garland, 1996.

Holsoe, Svend E. "Slavery and Economic Response among the Vai." In *Slavery in Africa: Historical and Anthropological Perspectives,* edited by Suzanne Miers and Igor Kopytoff, 287–303. Madison: University of Wisconsin Press, 1977.

Huberich, Charles Henry. *The Political and Legislative History of Liberia.* New York: Central Book, 1947.

Hunt, Gaillard. *Life in America One Hundred Years Ago.* New York: Harper, 1914.

Johnson, L. G. *General T. Perronet Thompson, 1783–1869: His Military, Literary and Political Campaigns.* London: Allen & Unwin, 1957.

Jones, Adam. *From Slaves to Palm Kernels: A History of the Galinhas Country (West Africa), 1730–1890.* Weisbaden: Steiner, 1983.

Jones, George Fenwick. "The Black Hessians in South Carolina and Other Colonies," *South Carolina Historical Magazine* 83 (October 1982): 287–302.

——. "The 1780 Siege of Charleston as Experienced by a Hessian Officer, Part Two," *South Carolina Historical Magazine* 88 (April 1987): 63–75.

Jordan, Winthrop D. *White over Black: American Attitudes toward the Negro, 1550–1812.* Baltimore: Penguin, 1969.

Kaplan, Sidney. *The Black Presence in the Era of the American Revolution, 1770–1800.* Washington, D.C.: Smithsonian University Press, 1973.

Kilson, Martin L., and Robert I. Rotberg, eds. *The African Diaspora,* Cambridge, Mass.: Harvard University Press, 1976.

Klingberg, Frank J. *An Appraisal of the Negro in South Carolina.* Washington, D.C.: Associated Publishers, 1941.

Koger, Larry. *Black Slaveowners: Free Black Slave Masters in South Carolina, 1790–1860.* Columbia: University of South Carolina Press, 1985.

Kup, A. P. *A History of Sierra Leone, 1400–1787.* Cambridge: Cambridge University Press, 1961.

Lambert, Robert Stansbury. *South Carolina Loyalists in the American Revolution.* Columbia: University of South Carolina Press, 1987.

Landers, Jane G., ed. *Against the Odds: Free Blacks in the Slave Societies of the Americas.* London & Portland, Ore.: Frank Cass, 1996.

Little, Kenneth L. *The Mende of Sierra Leone: A West African People in Transition.* Rev. ed. New York: Humanities Press, 1967.

Littlefield, Daniel C. "Charleston and Internal Slave Redistribution," *South Carolina Historical Magazine* 87 (April 1986): 93–105.

——. *Rice and Slaves, Ethnicity and the Slave Trade in Colonial South Carolina.* Urbana: University of Illinois Press, 1991.

Lofton, John. *Insurrection in South Carolina: The Turbulent World of Denmark Vesey.* Yellow Springs, Ohio: Antioch, 1964.

Logan, John H. *A History of the Upper Country of South Carolina from the Earliest Periods to the Close of the War of Independence.* Vol. 2. Easley, S.C.: Southern Historical, 1980.

Louise, E. *Elizabeth Clevland Hardcastle, 1741–1808: A Lady of Color in the South Carolina Lowcountry.* Columbia, S.C.: Phoenix, 2001.

Bibliography

MacCormack, Carol P. "Slaves, Slave Owners, and Slave Dealers: Sherbro Coast and Hinterland." In *Women and Slavery in Africa*, edited by Claire C. Robertson and Martin A. Klein. Portsmouth, N.H.: Heinemann, 1997.

——. "Wono: Institutionalized Dependency in Sherbro Descent Groups." In *Slavery in Africa: Historical and Anthropological Perspectives*, edited by Suzanne Miers and Igor Kopytoff, 181–203. Madison: University of Wisconsin Press, 1977.

Manning, Patrick. *Slavery and African Life*. Cambridge: Cambridge University Press, 2000.

Massey, Gregory D. *John Laurens and the American Revolution*. Columbia: University of South Carolina Press, 2000.

Mbiti, John S. *African Religions and Philosophy*. Garden City, N.Y.: Doubleday, 1970.

McCowen, George Smith, Jr. *The British Occupation of Charleston, 1780–82*. Columbia: University of South Carolina Press, 1972.

Merrens, H. Roy. "A View of Coastal South Carolina in 1778: The Journal of Ebenezer Hazard," *South Carolina Historical Magazine* 73 (October 1972): 177–93.

Miers, Suzanne, and Igor Kopytoff, eds. *Slavery in Africa: Historical and Anthropological Perspectives*. Madison: University of Wisconsin Press, 1977.

Migliazzo, Arlin C. *To Make This Land Our Own: Community, Identity and Cultural Adaptation in Purrysburg Township, 1732–1865*. Columbia: University of South Carolina Press, 2007.

Miller, Floyd J. *The Search for a Black Nationality: Black Emigration and Colonization, 1787–1863*. Urbana: University of Illinois Press, 1976.

Moore, Frank. *Diary of the American Revolution*. Vol. 2. New York: Scribner, 1860.

Moore, Glover. *The Missouri Compromise, 1819–1821*. Gloucester, Mass.: Smith, 1967.

Morgan, Philip D. "Black Life in Eighteenth-Century Charleston," *Perspectives in American History*, n.s., 1 (1984): 187–232.

——. "Black Society in the Lowcountry, 1760–1810." In *Slavery and Freedom in the Age of the American Revolution*, 83–142. Charlottesville: University of Virginia, 1983.

——. *Slave Counterpoint: Black Culture in the Eighteenth-Century Chesapeake and Lowcountry*. Chapel Hill: University of North Carolina Press, 1998.

——. "Work and Culture: The Task System and the World of Lowcountry Blacks, 1700 to 1800." In *The Slavery Reader*, edited by Gad Heuman and James Walvin, 194–223. London: Routledge, 2003.

Nash, Gary B. "Thomas Peters: Millwright and Deliverer." In *Struggle and Survival in Colonial America*, edited by Gary B. Nash and David G. Sweet, 69–85. Berkeley: University of California Press, 1981.

Nash, Gary B., and David G. Sweet, eds. *Struggle and Survival in Colonial America*. Berkeley: University of California Press, 1981.

Nicol, Davidson, "The Jones Family of Charleston, London and Africa." In *Sierra Leone Studies at Birmingham, 1988*, edited by Adam Jones, Peter K. Mitchell, and Margaret Peil, 88–89. Birmingham: University of Birmingham, 1990.

Niven, Laird. *Birchtown Archaeological Survey (1993)* Lockport, Nova Scotia: Roseway, 1994.

Olwell, Robert. "Becoming Free: Manumission and the Genesis of a Free Black Community in South Carolina, 1740–90," *Slavery and Abolition* 17 (April 1996): 1–19.

——. *Masters, Slaves and Subjects: The Culture of Power in the South Carolina Low Country, 1740–1790*. Ithaca, N.Y.: Cornell University Press, 1998.

Bibliography

Orvin, Maxwell Clayton. *Historic Berkeley County, South Carolina, 1671–1900*. Charleston, S.C., 1973.

Ottley, Roi, and William Weatherby, eds. *The Negro in New York*. New York: New York Public Library, 1967. 289

Palmer, Gregory. *Biographical Sketches of Loyalists of the American Revolution*. Westport, Conn.: Meckler, 1984.

Parramore, Thomas C. *Norfolk, the First Four Centuries*. Charlottesville: University of Virginia Press, 1994.

Pearson, Edward A. *Designs against Charleston*. Chapel Hill: University of North Carolina Press, 1999.

Perkins, Bradford. *Prologue to War: England and the United States, 1805–1812*. Berkeley: University of California Press, 1974.

Peterson, John. *Province of Freedom: A History of Sierra Leone, 1787–1870*. London: Faber, 1969.

Piecuch, Jim. *Three Peoples, One King*. Columbia: University of South Carolina Press, 2008.

Piersen, William D. *Black Yankees, The Development of an Afro-American Subculture in Eighteenth-Century New England*. Amherst: University of Massachusetts Press, 1988.

Porter, Arthur T. *Creoledom: A Study of the Development of Freetown Society*. London: Oxford University Press, 1963.

Porter, Kenneth Wiggins. *The Jacksons and the Lees*. Vol. 2. Cambridge, Mass.: Harvard University Press, 1937.

Pulis, John W., ed. *Moving On: Black Loyalists in the Afro-Atlantic World*. New York: Garland, 1999.

Pybus, Cassandra. *Epic Journeys of Freedom*. Boston: Beacon, 2006.

Quarles, Benjamin. *The Negro in the American Revolution*. Chapel Hill: University of North Carolina Press, 1961.

Raymond, W. O. "Benjamin Marston of Marblehead, Loyalist, His Trials and Tribulations during the American Revolution," *Collections of the New Brunswick Historical Society* 3 (1907–1914): 204–77.

———. "The Founding of Shelburne," *Collections of the New Brunswick Historical Society* 3 (1907–14):204–77.

"Records of the Regiments of the South Carolina Line, Continental Establishment," *South Carolina Historical and Genealogical Magazine* 7 (January 1906): 20–26.

Rediker, Marcus. *The Slave Ship: A Human History*. New York: Viking, 2007.

Reinert, Gertha, trans. *The First Consistory Book of the German Evangelical Lutheran Church of St. John's the Baptist*. Charleston, S.C., 1981.

Richardson, David. "Shipboard Revolts, African Authority, and the Atlantic Slave Trade." *William and Mary Quarterly*, 3rd ser., 58 (January 2001): 69–92.

Riley, Helene. "Michael Kalteisen and the Founding of the German Friendly Society," *South Carolina Historical Magazine* 100 (January 1999): 49–70.

Robertson, Claire C., and Martin A. Klein, eds. *Women and Slavery in Africa*. Portsmouth, N.H.: Heinemann, 1997.

Robertson, Marion. *King's Bounty: A History of Early Shelburne Nova Scotia*. Halifax: Nova Scotia Museum, 1983.

Robinson, Donald L. *Slavery in the Structure of American Politics, 1765–1820*. New York: Harcourt Brace Jovanovich, 1971.

Rodney, Walter. *A History of the Upper Guinea Coast, 1545 to 1800*. London: Oxford University Press, 1970.

290 Roeber, A. G. *Palatines, Liberty, and Property: German Lutherans in Colonial British America*. Baltimore: Johns Hopkins University Press, 1993.

Rogers, George C., Jr. *Charleston in the Age of the Pinckneys*. Columbia: University of South Carolina Press, 1980.

Ruchames, Louis, ed. *Racial Thought in America*. Vol. 1. Amherst: University of Massachusetts Press, 1969.

Rucker, Walter C. "The River Floweth On: The African Social and Cultural Origins of Slave Resistance in North America, 1712–1831." Ph.D. diss, University of California at Riverside, 1999.

Ryan, William R. *The World of Thomas Jeremiah*. New York: Oxford University Press, 2010.

Sabine, Lorenzo. *Biographical Sketches of Loyalists of the American Revolution*. Vol. 2. Baltimore: Genealogical Publishing, 1979.

Salley, A. S. Jr., ed. *Documents Relating to the History of South Carolina during the Revolutionary War*. Columbia: Historical Commission of South Carolina, 1908.

Schama, Simon. *Rough Crossings: Britain, the Slaves and the American Revolution*. New York: HarperCollins, 2006.

Scoggins, Michael C. *The Day It Rained Militia*. Charleston, S.C.: History Press, 2005.

Scotland, Douglas W. "Notes on the Banana Islands A.D. 1462–1846," *Sierra Leone Studies*, n.s., 11 (December 1958): 149–60.

Sellers, Leila. *Charleston Business on the Eve of the American Revolution*. Chapel Hill: University of North Carolina Press, 1934.

Shaw, Rosalind. *Memories of the Slave Trade: Ritual and the Historical Imagination in Sierra Leone*. Chicago: University of Chicago Press, 2002.

Sidbury, James. *Becoming African in America: Race and Nation in the Early Black Atlantic*. New York: Oxford University Press, 2009.

Smith, David. *Biography of Rev. David Smith of the A.M.E. Church*. Xenia, Ohio, 1881.

Smith, Page. *A New Age Now Begins: A People's History of the American Revolution*. 2 vols. New York: McGraw-Hill, 1976.

Somé, Malidoma Patrice. *Of Water and the Spirit*. New York: Penguin, 1994.

Spray, W. A. *The Blacks in New Brunswick*. Fredericton, N.B.: Human Relations Study Centre, St. Thomas University, n.d.

Spring, Gardiner. *Memoirs of the Rev. Samuel J. Mills*. London: Westley, 1820.

Staudenraus, P. J. *The African Colonization Movement, 1816–1875*. New York: Columbia University Press, 1961.

———. "Victims of the African Slave Trade," *Journal of Negro History* 41 (April 1956): 148–51.

Stephenson, Jean. *Scotch-Irish Migration to South Carolina*. Washington, D.C., 1971.

Stevens, Michael E. "'To Get as Many Slaves as You Can': An 1807 Slaving Voyage," *South Carolina Historical Magazine* 87 (July 1986): 187–92.

Thomas, Lamont D. *Paul Cuffe: Black Entrepreneur and Pan Africanist*. Urbana: University of Illinois Press, 1988.

Thompson, Robert Farris. *Flash of the Spirit*. New York: Vintage, 1984.

Tucker, Peter L. *The Tuckers of Sierra Leone, 1665–1914*. London, 1997.

Turner, Michael J. "'Setting the Captive Free': Thomas Perronet Thompson, British Radicalism and the West Indies, 1820s–1860s," *Slavery and Abolition* 26 (April 2005): 115–32.

Walker, James W. St. G. *The Black Loyalists*. London: Longman & Dalhousie University Press, 1976.

———. "Blacks as American Loyalists: The Slaves' War for Independence," *Historical Reflexions/ Reflexions Historique* 2 (Summer 1975): 51–67.

———. "The Establishment of a Free Black Community in Nova Scotia." In *The African Diaspora*, edited by Martin L. Kilson and Robert I. Rotberg, 205–36. Cambridge, Mass.: Harvard University Press, 1976.

———. "Myth, History and Revisionism: The Black Loyalists Revisited," *Acadiensis* 29 (Autumn 1999): 88–105.

Walsh, Richard. *Charleston's Sons of Liberty, A Study of the Artisans, 1763–1789*. Columbia: University of South Carolina Press, 1959.

Ward, W. E. F. *The Royal Navy and the Slavers*. London: Allen & Unwin, 1969.

Wesley, Charles H. *Richard Allen: Apostle of Freedom*. Washington, D.C.: Associated Publishers, 1969.

Wiencek, Henry. *An Imperfect God: George Washington, His Slaves and the Creation of America*. New York: Farrar, Straus & Giroux, 2003.

Wilberforce, Daniel F. *Sherbro and the Sherbros; A Native African's Account of His Country and People*. Dayton, Ohio: United Brethren Publishing House, 1886.

Wilson, David K. *The Southern Strategy: Britain's Conquest of South Carolina and Georgia, 1775–1780*. Columbia: University of South Carolina Press, 2005.

Wilson, Ellen Gibson. *John Clarkson and the African Adventure*. London: Macmillan, 1980.

———. *The Loyal Blacks*. New York: Capricorn, 1976.

———. *Thomas Clarkson: A Biography*. New York: St. Martin's, 1990.

Wilson, Joseph T. *The Black Phalanx: A History of the Negro Soldiers of the United States in the Wars of 1775–1812, 1861–1865*. New York: Arno, 1968.

Winch, Julie. *A Gentleman of Color, The Life of James Forten*. New York: Oxford University Press, 2002.

Wood, Peter H. *Black Majority: Negroes in Colonial South Carolina*. New York: Knopf, 1974.

———. "'Taking Care of Business' in Revolutionary South Carolina: Republicanism and the Slave Society." In *The Southern Experience in the American Revolution*, edited by Jeffrey J. Crow and Larry E. Tise, 68–93. Chapel Hill: University of North Carolina Press, 1978.

Woodson, Carter G. *Negro Orators and Their Orations*. Washington, D.C.: Associated Publishers, 1925.

Woodson, Hortense. *The Palatines of Londonborough*. Edgefield, S.C.: Old Edgefield District Genealogy Society, 2005.

Zornow, David M. "A Troublesome Community: Blacks in Revolutionary Charles Town, 1765–1775." Master's thesis, Harvard University, 1976.

INDEX

ABOUT THE AUTHOR

A graduate of Dartmouth College, KEVIN G. LOWTHER served as a Peace Corps teacher in Sierra Leone from 1963 to 1965. In 1971 he helped found Africare, a humanitarian organization supporting development and relief programs throughout Africa. He later managed Africare's work in southern Africa for nearly thirty years. A former newspaper editor, Lowther has written on African issues for the *Washington Post*, *Christian Science Monitor*, and other publications. Coauthor of *Keeping Kennedy's Promise: The Peace Corps' Moment of Truth*, Lowther lives in Springfield, Virginia.